THE POETRY OF

Ted Hughes

THE POETRY OF

Ted Hughes

Form and Imagination

LEONARD M. SCIGAJ

University of Iowa Press

Iowa City

Library of Congress Cataloging-in-Publication Data

Scigaj, Leonard M.
  The poetry of Ted Hughes.

  Bibliography: p.
  Includes index.
  1. Hughes, Ted, 1930–   —Criticism and interpretation.   I. Title.
PR6058.U37S884   1986   821'.914   85-28924
ISBN 0-87745-141-9

University of Iowa Press, Iowa City 52242

Copyright © 1986 by the University of Iowa

Printed in the United States of America

First edition, 1986

Jacket and book design by Richard Hendel

Typesetting by G&S Typesetters, Inc., Austin, Texas

Printing and binding by Kingsport Press, Kingsport, Tennessee

For Jamie,
who had the love
and the patience

Every writer if he develops at all develops either outwards into society and history, using wider and more material of that sort, or he develops inwards into imagination and beyond that into spirit, using perhaps no more external material than before and maybe even less but deepening it and making it operate in the many different inner dimensions until it opens up perhaps the religious or holy basis of the whole thing. Or he can develop both ways simultaneously. Developing inwardly, of course, means organizing the inner world or at least searching out the patterns there and that is a mythology. It may be an original mythology. Or you may uncover the Cross—as Eliot did. The ideal aspect of Yeats' development is that he managed to develop his poetry both outwardly into history and the common imagery of everyday life at the same time as he developed it inwardly in a sort of close parallel . . . so that he could speak of both simultaneously. His mythology is history, pretty well, and his history is as he said 'the story of a soul.'

—Hughes,
1971 Faas interview

CONTENTS

Acknowledgments / xi

Preface / xiii

1. A Two-Way Journey toward Reality
   (Introduction) / 1

Part I   **The Formalist Fifties**

2. A Craftsman Calm
   (*The Hawk in the Rain*, 1957) / 31

3. Mouths Clamped Well onto the World
   (*Lupercal*, 1960) / 55

Part II   **The Surreal Sixties**

4. Goodbye to the Cenotaphs
   (*Wodwo*, 1967) / 85

5. Nothing Escaped Him
   (*Crow*, 1970–1971) / 122

Part III   **Suffering and Serenity in the Seventies,
and the Enlightened Eighties**

6. Flying Astride the Earth
   (*Gaudete*, 1977) / 165

7. Taking Each Other to the Sun
   (*Cave Birds*, 1978) / 205

8. From Emptiness to Brighter Emptiness
   (*Remains of Elmet*, 1979) / 234

9. No Wing to Tread Emptiness
   (*Moortown*, 1979) / 257

10. Sanctus Sanctus
   (*River*, 1983) / 287

Notes / 317

Bibliography / 341

Index / 353

ACKNOWLEDGMENTS

Most of chapter 4 of this study originally appeared in *The Achievement of Ted Hughes* (1983), as "Oriental Mythology in *Wodwo*." Half of chapter 2 originally appeared in *Modern Poetry Studies*, 12 (1985), as "Ransoming the World's Body: The Influence of the New Criticism upon the Early Poetry of Ted Hughes." The publisher and I are grateful to Manchester University Press, and to the University of Georgia Press, for reprint permission for the former essay, and to *Modern Poetry Studies*, for reprint permission for the latter essay. We are grateful to the University of Kentucky Press for permission to reprint content in chapter 5 of this work from my "Genetic Memory and the Three Traditions of *Crow*," *Perspectives on Contemporary Literature*, 9 (1983), 83–91.

The publisher and I are also grateful to Ted Hughes, and to the British Broadcasting Corporation, for permission to quote unpublished BBC radio scripts written and broadcast by him.

For permission to quote extensively from the copyrighted poetry of Ted Hughes, we are especially grateful to the following: Faber and Faber, Ltd., for quotation from Hughes volumes published by them—*The Hawk in the Rain*, © Ted Hughes 1957, *Lupercal*, © Ted Hughes 1960, *Wodwo*, © Ted Hughes 1967, *Crow*, © Ted Hughes 1970, 1972, *Season Songs,* © Ted Hughes 1976, *Gaudete*, © Ted Hughes 1977, *Cave Birds*, © Ted Hughes 1978, *Remains of Elmet*, © Ted Hughes 1979, *Moortown,* © Ted Hughes 1979, *River*, © Ted Hughes 1983, *What Is the Truth?*, © Ted Hughes 1984; Harper and Row Publishers, Inc., for quotation from Hughes volumes published by them—*The Hawk in the Rain*, © Ted Hughes 1957, *Lupercal*, © Ted Hughes 1960, *Wodwo*, © Ted Hughes 1967, *Crow*, © Ted Hughes 1971, *Gaudete*, © Ted Hughes 1977, *Remains of Elmet*, © Ted Hughes 1979, *Moortown*, © Ted Hughes 1980, *River*, © Ted Hughes 1983, *What Is the Truth?*, © Ted Hughes 1984; Olwyn Hughes, for quotation from Ted Hughes poems published by the Rainbow Press—*Poems: Ruth Fainlight, Ted Hughes, Alan Sillitoe*, © Ted Hughes 1971, *Prometheus on His Crag*, © Ted Hughes 1973—and for quotation from poems published in other private presses, and those not yet collected in book form; *Poetry*, for the Hughes poem "After Lorca," © Ted Hughes 1963; Viking Penguin, Inc., for quotation from Hughes volumes published by them—*Season Songs*, © Ted Hughes 1975, *Cave Birds*, © Ted Hughes 1978.

The publisher and I are also grateful to the following for permission to quote lines from the copyrighted verse of other poets: George Braziller, Inc., for the Wen Fong translations of the Tao-chi poems "Plum Blossoms and Bamboo" and "Orchids," © Wen Fong 1976; Doubleday & Co., Inc., for the William Blake poems *The Four Zoas* and *Jerusalem*, edited by David V. Erdman, © David V. Erdman and Harold Bloom 1965; Paragon Book Gallery, Ltd., for the Shigeyoshi Obata translations of the Li Po poems "On Seeing Off Meng Hao-Jan," "Parting at Ching-Men," and "An Exhortation," © Shigeyoshi Obata 1935, Paragon Book Gallery 1965; Persea Books, Inc., for the János Pilinszky poem "World Grown Cold," © János Pilinszky 1977, © Ted Hughes (translation) 1977; Random House, Inc., and Alfred A. Knopf, Inc., for the John Crowe Ransom poems "Winter Remembered" and "Janet Waking," © John Crowe Ransom 1955; Viking Penguin, Inc., for the A. K. Ramanujan translation of the Dasimayya poem "To the utterly at-one with Śiva," © A. K. Ramanujan 1973.

PREFACE

Critical reception of the poetry of Ted Hughes in the United States has been lethargic for years. The *MLA Bibliography* typically lists a few short articles on individual poems or elementary reviews of recent volumes. Hughes remains undiscovered country to most American readers, largely because we often find his poetry difficult, if not forbidding, and because his changes in style and subject matter leave us wondering if his interests are very eccentric. Stuart Hirschberg, the only American critic to publish a volume-length study of Hughes to date, placed it at Wolfhound Press, Dublin. The first volume of critical essays on Hughes's poetry, *The Achievement of Ted Hughes*, co-published at the University of Georgia Press (1983), went unreviewed by the *New York Times*, the *New York Review of Books*, and every American scholarly journal for nearly three years. A large sector of the American reading public did not become acquainted with Hughes's recent work, for Harper and Row did not issue paperbacks. Throughout the seventies *Crow* was the only inexpensive Hughes paperback one could order for American college courses. Recently Harper and Row has issued paperbacks of *Moortown*, *River*, and *New Selected Poems*.

Now that Hughes has received the accolade of Poet Laureate, one expects the critical lethargy to cease. But no one can predict what directions the American critical reception of Hughes will take. Early studies will be very influential in establishing these directions. Let us hope that they will proceed as boldly and originally as Hughes's poetry, that they absorb the best criticism available from past assessments, and that they do not simply parrot the responses of many reviewers from past decades.

Hughes's North Country heritage naturally accents his vision with bleakness and tough-mindedness, and he therefore refuses to ignore the violence within nature. Also behind the struggle for survival in his poetry lies our postholocaust world of arms races and nuclear scares. Yet some of Hughes's critics regularly take exception to his poems that treat violence. Often these critics—especially those who prefer the anti-Romantic rationalism and empiricism of the group of postwar British poets and critics known as the Movement—adopt a special pleading focus that isolates only instances of violent action and diction in Hughes. Then they generalize with *ad hominem* attacks, inferring adolescent preoccupations with violence or nihilism. This facile use of psychological projection begs the question, especially when these critics make no effort to consider a complex of style, structure, and motif—in other words, modernist form. Modernist form does not provide the reader with everyday landscapes and the empirically observed action of mimetic realism. Doting upon surface action and the projective fallacy would create reductive, useless accounts of any modernist work—*Ulysses*, *Four Quartets*, *The Cantos*, and so forth.

The Poetry of Ted Hughes: Form and Imagination proceeds from the axiom that Hughes is a modernist poet whose work supports the New Critical tenet that form and content are inseparable. Hughes is a modernist for two reasons: his poetry reveals a penchant for nonmimetic spatial arrangements of motifs rather than an emphasis upon empirical observation in realistic settings, and it attempts to revitalize tradition by addressing the postwar contributions of anthropologists, folklorists, and specialists of comparative religion. Because of the breadth encompassed by Hughes's adult poetry—over five hundred and fifty published poems to date—the incorporation of the drama, the children's work, and *Season Songs* (originally a sequence of songs for children's voices) became impossible.

This study reveals Hughes's poetry as richer, more well-disciplined, substantive, and rewarding, than the *ad hominem* attackers would have us believe. Hughes completed a Cambridge degree in anthropology and archeology and absorbed the most difficult school of American formalism, the New Criticism, *before* he attempted his first volume. Throughout his long career his work has evolved with a great deal of attentiveness to form and organization. In his adult poetry, form and imagination contain important clues to theme and meaning, at the same time curbing occasional excesses of diction.

In this study I treat the nine major volumes of Hughes's adult poetry, 1957 through 1983 (*Season Songs* is excepted as a minor work), as an organically evolving whole, articulating three stages in a maturation process: an early New Critical formalism (*The Hawk in the Rain*; *Lupercal*); a sixties mythic surrealism (*Wodwo*; *Crow*); and an often mystic landscape poetry from the mid-seventies to the present (*Remains of Elmet*; *Moortown*; *River*). Not in substance or in depth but in terms of Hughes's emerging vision, *Gaudete* and *Cave Birds* represent a transitional stage between the second and third periods, for both contain elements of the earlier mythic surrealism, but with third-period resolutions where the suffering soul enlists the imagination to transmute experience into a heightened awareness. The beginning of each of these three stages coincides with a pivotal event in Hughes's life: his reading of the poetry and criticism of John Crowe Ransom in 1955; a meeting with Chou Wen-chung at Yaddo in the fall of 1959,

and Hughes's subsequent work on an unpublished libretto of the surrealistic *Tibetan Book of the Dead*; and Hughes's portrayal of the suffering
soul in his *Orghast* drama, performed by Peter Brook's international troupe
of actors in Iran in 1971.

Each chapter treats a single volume, with careful attention to modernist
form within the poem and the volume, supplemented by Hughes's own
insightful comments from essays and unpublished BBC radio scripts written near the publication date of each volume. This format reveals purposeful changes in Hughes's conception of the creative imagination that parallel
the three stages of his development: from a New Critical focus upon the
artist as a highly self-conscious craftsman, welding meaning to nature's
concrete particularity, to a more social-psychological conception of the
imagination as therapeutic in the sixties surrealism, and a Blakean/Taoist
emphasis upon the artist as visionary seer in the most recent work. In the
process this study integrates Hughes's predominantly Western approach to
experience with his continuing interest in Oriental studies.

Hughes's considerable British reputation evolved from the power and
presence of his verse, the strength of his imagination, the vividness and
accuracy of his imagery, and the richness of his metaphors, not from his
Oriental studies or his interest in mythology. His literary projects often
develop from festival commissions, events in his private life such as pur-
chasing a farm, or his creative responses to the work of artists from other
fields—the music of Chou Wen-chung, the drawings of Leonard Baskin,
and the photography of Fay Godwin and Peter Keen. Hughes is hardly a
cloistered, bookish figure interested only in recondite knowledge and cultural arcana. Yet he does hold a degree in anthropology and archeology,
and his essays and reviews regularly manifest a strong interest in cultural
history. His rich knowledge of global mythology, folklore, and comparative
religion naturally enters his creative activities. Hughes's knowledge in these
areas has led to a habit of thinking that penetrates to the cultural roots of
our attempts to comprehend ourselves, our society, and our befores and
afters. Often Hughes's deep psyche and creative unconscious will use
themes and structures from his reading to organize and guide his thinking,
without any deliberate attempt to rely upon sources other than his own
wits. This study exists to offer the more discerning reader satisfaction for
the intuition that a profundity of thinking and a coherent development also
exist in Hughes's poetry.

Given the large corpus, and the charges of indulging in violence, sadism,
and nihilism that critics have leveled at him, an approach dedicated to presenting Hughes as an intellectually sound, rigorous craftsman ought to

proceed with clarity and strong documentation. Finding clear lines of development in Hughes means locating figures in his evolving carpet; and if one finds figures in carpets where no one before has found them, one ought to make enough threads visible to convince. One must also limit the number of figures one finds, due to Hughes's prolific output and publication constraints.

Because I treat nine volumes of poetry, and maintain a specialized focus upon form and imagination, it is inevitable that I do not treat individual poems fulsomely and that I make no attempt to evaluate and rank the poems. Mine is the first study to consider Hughes's work as an organically evolving whole and to show how modernist *paideumae* in the organization of the volumes add to the thematic richness of each poem. So I must consider a sufficient number of poems per volume to substantiate the figures I see, first mapping the territory from a middle distance before separating individual tall trees from their surrounding thickets. One cannot begin the process of ranking the poems in ignorance of themes and levels of meaning that become visible only when meditating upon groups of poems within the fabric of each volume.

Length restrictions and the specialized focus have also made it impossible to discuss certain obvious influences. The absence of Lawrence in my treatment of *The Hawk in the Rain* is a case in point. Of course Lawrence is an important influence for Hughes's early animal poems and for his early attitude toward nature. But my focus restricts itself to identifying those sources that have proved major influences upon form and imagination. Hughes himself identified Ransom as his major formal influence in *The Hawk in the Rain*, and the polished New Critical formalist is evident in most of the poems in this first volume. Alvarez in *The Shaping Spirit* argues very persuasively that fidelity to feeling, and to the intimacy of the mind's flow in the moment of awareness, constitutes the main formal element in Lawrence's poetry.

The schematic organization of this study derives from my attempt to follow as clearly and carefully as possible the complex development of Hughes's vision, as reflected in his poetry and essays. I found I could not articulate this development comprehensively without discussing the profound relevance of Hughes's continuing interest in Oriental literature. Because some in the critical establishment find schematic studies repugnant or retain deep-seated biases against Oriental studies, I have proceeded with ample, concrete documentation. I aspire toward elucidating patterns that are significant and that *do exist* in an *oeuvre* so complex and tangled that Alan Brownjohn has called it a "bibliographer's nightmare." One should not confuse an attempt to elucidate patterns that do exist in a complex corpus with the deleterious process of descending upon the *oeuvre* with a complicated, ready-made, Procrustean apparatus. I also know that I am mining only a few select veins branching out from a very rich mother lode. Nothing would please me more than to have this study generate hundreds of new ideas among readers and critics, ideas that take Hughes research into areas untouched by this study or that initiate a process of refining particular areas further than the scope of this study allows.

I would like to thank the American Council of Learned Societies for a 1980 Recent Recipients of the Ph.D. Fellowship that gave me released time from teaching to research and write a portion of the manuscript; and the National Endowment for the Humanities, for a 1979 Summer Stipend that allowed me to travel to London and Reading to research unpublished Hughes radio scripts. I reserve special thanks for Ted Hughes, for meeting with me on three occasions in the summer of 1979 to discuss his work, for his comments and support in letters, and for his responses to the final manuscript. Sincere thanks also to Keith Sagar, for his support and invaluable critique of the manuscript. I appreciate Monica Lera's help with the geography and landmarks in the Mytholmroyd/Heptonstall area of Yorkshire and Olwyn Hughes's gracious assistance in matters of permissions. Thanks also to Challice Reed and her staff at the BBC Script Library, Portland Place, London, and to Jacqueline Kavanaugh and her staff at the BBC Written Archives, Reading, for their cheerful and expert aid.

This manuscript would not have reached fruition without the strong support of many of my colleagues and the staff of the Virginia Tech English Department. Warm thanks to Head Arthur Eastman for his support, especially for his stern wit, and to Associate Head Hilbert Campbell for his steady, humane, generous advice, and his willingness to respond to portions of the manuscript. Professor Dennis Welch's advice on Blake never failed, nor did the unswerving support of other colleagues, especially Professors Tony Colaianne, Ruth Salvaggio, Alison Sulloway, and Herb West. Thanks also to Ann Eastman for her assistance with computer disks and to Kim Cooper and, especially, Vanessa Williams for their expert word processing.

Special thanks go to Earl Brown of the Radford University English Department and to Maggie Brown, recently of the Concord College English Department, for their genuine support, encouragement, and understanding over many years.

Finally, brief thanks to a few mentors in my past, who saw a faint glimmer of light in the rough student: to the late Professor Leslie C. Warren of Canisius College; to Professor John T. Shawcross, currently at the University of Kentucky; and to Professors Walter B. Rideout, Annis Pratt, and the late Paul L. Wiley of the University of Wisconsin–Madison Graduate English Department.

THE POETRY OF

Ted Hughes

CHAPTER 1

A Two-Way
Journey
toward
Reality

Introduction

*Our common dream, as archetypal as any, of the
two-way journey toward Reality—toward the objectless radiance of the Self, where the world is a
composition of benign Holy Powers, and toward the
objective reality of the world, where man is a virtuoso bacteria—goes in the aspect of a tramp, rejecting ego and possessions, claiming equality with
all life. . . . For the good citizen, tramps live in the
region of a dream. Even after he's thoroughly inves-
tigated the lives those men lead, and knows what
emptied wretches they mostly are, his dream persists in finding in them the symbol of the Holy Pilgrim, the Incorruptible Soul, the all-sufferer, the
stone the builders reject again and again.*
—Hughes, 1963[1]

Dividing a major poet's career into periods is
a commonplace of twentieth-century criticism. Thematic and stylistic
changes in a poet's craft, and changing influences from reading, private
life, and the larger social and cultural context, necessitate clear divisions.
Through the efforts of literary critics one can readily distinguish the early
Laforguean symbolism of Eliot; his *Waste Land* "mythical method" period
that commenced when he read chapters of *Ulysses*; and the later devotional
poetry, beginning shortly after his 1927 conversion to Anglicanism, that
flowered in the incomparable *Four Quartets*. One can better appreciate the
poetry of Dylan Thomas by dividing it first into the early womb/tomb fears
of death (his father's cancer and his own worm beneath his nail); then the
less introverted, less self-centered representative man of *The Map of Love*
who can reconcile love and death; and finally the heron-priested celebrant
of sacramental nature in the late poetry and the "Author's Prologue" to the
Collected Poems.

The careers of other major twentieth-century poets more readily divide
into four periods. In Auden one can readily discern the early Freudian di-
agnoses of a sick society; then the socialist involvement and disenchantment of the thirties; later the existential Christianity from *New Year Letter*
into the forties, heavily influenced by Kierkegaard and Charles Williams;
and finally the Christian resignation and acceptance of human physicality,
from the end of World War II through *About the House*. Yeats of course
began his career with a *fin de siècle* dreamy estheticism, a poetry of longing

and complaint filled with Rosicrucian and other occult symbolism. When Maud Gonne married in 1903, Yeats shifted his attention to public service and began to write poetry more directly concerned with objective reality. After he spent three winters with Ezra Pound (1913–1916), and liberated his imagination through his new wife's automatic writing a year later, Yeats entered his major phase, writing poetry of insight and knowledge and filtering social and political events through an elaborate artifice. Late in his life Yeats demolished his system to inspect the heart's rag and bone shop and to let gaiety transfigure the dread of death.

A poet's talents and reading, private life, and events in the social and cultural context in reality exist in dynamically changing relationships that begin before and continue throughout the quarter to half century of a career. No computer could ever catalogue these changing influences and relationships with comprehensiveness or finality. When the critic artificially arrests them into periods, it is in order to elucidate the literature with sufficient clarity to enhance the reader's appreciation and to map the literary territory accurately and insightfully enough to encourage more detailed scholarship in known areas and new scholarship in hitherto unknown areas. At the same time the critic endeavors to specify important influences that were insufficiently understood. Ideally, by dividing into periods one hopes in the end to unify—to penetrate to the core of the literature in order to reveal a series of developmental stages that are purposeful and organic. One also hopes to avoid being reductive or slanted, to highlight the work in a way that heightens our esthetic appreciation of subtle or sudden changes in the arc of the poet's development, and in the end to discover some of the poet's unique contributions.

At this writing Ted Hughes, now in his mid-fifties, is too young to have entered a final period. Yet his output has been prodigious enough and sustained over a sufficient period of time—a quarter century—to warrant a careful division into periods. Through 1984 Hughes has published nine major and three minor volumes of adult poetry, ten stories, ten volumes of children's poetry and stories, and at least three dozen reviews. He has broadcast, published, or produced eighteen plays and broadcast two dozen or so self-scripted BBC talks, some of which have been collected in *Poetry in the Making* (*Poetry Is*). Hughes has written numerous essays and introductions, dozens of limited edition chapbooks, and scores of poster poems and uncollected poems. He has also assisted in numerous translations of European poetry and read and recorded his own poetry many times. If one counts each section in the main narrative of *Gaudete* as a separate prose poem, Hughes has published to date over five hundred and fifty poems in the nine major volumes of adult poetry alone.[2]

Though the sheer size of Hughes's output makes writing comprehensively about his poetry difficult, his stylistic changes and varied reading interests—which range from North American Indian folklore and the mythology of primitive cultures to Sufi fables, Tamil *vacanas*, and Indian and Chinese mysticism—complicate the attempt exponentially. Hughes has received acclaim from such prominent critics as Alfred Alvarez, M. L. Rosenthal, Keith Sagar, and Ekbert Faas, among others. But new volumes often stymie reviewers and academic critics into glossing over the content with glib catchwords, restricting commentary to superficial points of language and taste, or admitting outright bafflement. Because Hughes incorporates into his poetry influences that are even more extensive and varied than his publishing career, the critic of necessity must limit the focus to specifying only a few of the most significant patterns in a very richly woven carpet.

The critical volumes available on Hughes's poetry offer important contributions from a variety of approaches. Yet three appeared too early to include the very clear movement away from surrealism in the most recent Hughes volumes. Terry Gifford and Neil Roberts discuss *Moortown* and *Remains of Elmet*, but since they believe that Hughes's major work begins with *Crow*, they discuss only a few poems from the first three volumes in summary chapters dealing with finding a voice and with the themes of nature and death. Their main purpose is to reevaluate critical charges against Hughes's diction and to judge individual poems according to basically Leavisite canons of taste, rank, and the clarity and aptness of language and poetic devices.[3] Only Keith Sagar offers a full chapter on each major volume, with the promise of periodic updates. His second edition, however, ends with *Gaudete* and *Cave Birds*. In flexible and concise prose Sagar synthesizes a wealth of significant biography and sources. Sagar understands Hughes's main influences to be the major twentieth-century British poets in the early poetry; Blake, Kafka, and East European poets such as Vasco Popa assist Hughes in the sixties and early seventies; and folklore, myth, religion, the Greeks, Shakespeare, and Milton, in his latest work. To Sagar these changing sets of influences help Hughes to map ground where humans can negotiate with nature, but they do not of themselves reveal any deeply motivated direction.[4] Sagar and Stephen Tabor have recently produced an impeccable and much-needed bibliography of Hughes's publications and broadcasts through 1980.[5]

Stuart Hirschberg and Ekbert Faas organize their respective studies according to central thematic motifs derived from mythology and folklore.[6] Hirschberg develops the mythic figures of shaman, trickster, and scapegoat that appear primarily in the poetry written in the sixties. Yet these figures do not apply to *The Hawk in the Rain*, and apply only marginally to *Lupercal*; nor do they assist us in understanding the recent volumes *Remains of Elmet*, *Moortown*, and *River*. After excellent opening chapters on Hughes's poetics and his place in a new polyhistoric global tradition, Ekbert Faas concentrates upon the hero's descent to the underworld to save his desecrated bride in *Crow* and *Gaudete*. Faas considers the core of Hughes's poetic energy to reside in this theme, the origins of which derive from private life tragedies—the suicide of Sylvia Plath (11 February 1963) and the deaths of his companion Assia and her daughter Shura in March of 1969. But no underworld exists in *Remains of Elmet*, *Moortown*, and *River*. Faas considers Hughes's Oriental influences primarily as they apply to his introductory statements on poetics; Sagar offers a few specific Oriental sources for individual poems.

The time is ripe for a study of the major adult poetry of Ted Hughes as an organically evolving whole, in a way that divides the poetry into three distinct phases: the New Critical formalism of the fifties, the mythic surrealism of the sixties, and the mystic landscape poetry of the late seventies and early eighties. Hughes is a modernist poet who regularly reveals meaning through the formal organization of each volume and its relationship to a central architectonic. This study also shows that Hughes's Oriental influences are substantive and deep—that they comprise a major portion of the central meaning and organizational plan of the poetry. In the process this study reveals important shifts in Hughes's conception of the creative imagination: from a New Critical emphasis upon the craft of poetry in the fifties, to a more sociological emphasis upon the necessity of nurturing the reader's imaginative life in the sixties, and to a more purely visionary conception of the artist as seer in the poetry of the late seventies and early eighties. This study also integrates substantive comments from Hughes's essays and reviews, as well as neglected comments from his published and unpublished BBC talks, to guide or confirm interpretation. Important points of style are discussed insofar as they contribute to revealing the content and the formal organization.

The twin foci and three-period division substantiate a central evolutionary architectonic at the heart of the poetry that Hughes himself hinted at more than two decades ago. In a little-known 1963 book review, Hughes actually offered a prophetic announcement of the direction his prodigious corpus would take—an insight that, with some interpolation, applies to all of his work. "Our common dream, as archetypal as any," writes Hughes, is that of a "two-way journey toward Reality—toward the objectless radiance of the Self, where the world is a composition of benign Holy Powers, and toward the objective reality of the world, where man is a virtuoso bacteria."[7] We can achieve an assured sense of selfhood, Hughes reasons, either through the "objectless" asceticism of Oriental thought (the *ātman* of the Upanishads or the *samādhi* of yoga, for instance), where one perceives nature as a "benign" extension of the self's interior serenity, or through the Western quest for an ideal, involving psychological rounds of nature's cycle of struggle, death, and rebirth—the world of the "virtuoso bacteria." Both journeys reveal a spiritual element in nature, confirmed by centuries of primitive and modern literature, that promotes a growth toward enlightenment and an enlargement of consciousness.

Though Oriental philosophies and religious systems do not value Western notions of the individual's uniqueness or of impassioned engagement with temporal experience in the interests of realizing one's own self-responsible destiny, the goals of the self-absorbed Oriental ascetic and the action-oriented Western quest hero are ultimately the same. According to Joseph Campbell, both inner and outer journeys end ideally in exalted states of spiritual illumination—in a consciousness of the oneness of being, with the awakened self as creator of reality.[8] These states of spiritual enlargement, interfusions of self and other in moments of heightened awareness or mystical vision, comprise what Hughes calls "Reality," the goal of the all-suffering pilgrim's two-way journey. These exalted moments occur for Hughes only after painful but necessary struggles for psychic reclamation and reintegration. The poetry demonstrates that one liberates the creative intuition needed to achieve the exalted vision only after struggling with temporal obstacles and with one's repressed instinctual life, or after renouncing temptations to indulge overmuch in egocentric behavior and a rational, utilitarian analysis of the objective world.

Hughes reiterated his inward/outward distinction in 1970, when he observed that some writers—Yeats is his example—are uniquely able to develop simultaneously "outwards into society and history" and "inwards into imagination . . . and spirit."[9] Hughes's poetry does develop simultaneously in both inner and outer directions, but in each decade of his publishing career the relationship between the Occidental and Oriental approaches to experience differs in significant ways. The fifties poetry is thoroughly Western. Hughes arrives with the exuberance of the great lord of the castle riding home from hunting ("A Modest Proposal"); he is confident of his craft and comfortable in his received cultural orientation toward experience. The personae either struggle to liberate instinctual energies from the culturally enforced rationalism and repression that inhibit psychological integration or are satirized for failing to do so. The Oriental element exists only as a theoretical possibility, in whatever knowledge Hughes retained from his anthropology studies at Cambridge.[10] The only Oriental reference in the entirety of *The Hawk in the Rain* and *Lupercal* is a use of the Buddha's poised self-absorption as an alternative to the neurotically Christian subjugation of the flesh in "The Perfect Forms." Even the source is Western: the Buddha's "one thought" that "fills immensity" in the poem is a quotation from plate 8 of Blake's *Marriage of Heaven and Hell*. Hughes completed the poems of *Lupercal* before the fall of 1959, when he met Chou Wen-chung at Yaddo and began working on his *Bardo Thödol* libretto, a central pre-Buddhist text that had an immense effect upon his imagination.[11]

The sixties poetry typically presents Occidental and Oriental modes of experience as opposites, with the Occidental path of the two-way journey blocked by a mood of revulsion against Western culture. The sixties poetry and comments in Hughes's prose writings that relate to this period indicate that the revulsion results from a searing realization of the carnage and chronic reappearance of war in Western culture and from Hughes's analysis of what he believed to be its causes. On the one hand, Hughes believed that the regularity of war in modern Western culture proved Freud's analysis of genetically inherited aggression. On the other hand, Hughes argued that modern Western culture perpetuates these chronic eruptions of aggression: the overreliance of modern science upon the purely factual and rational, coupled with the repression of the instincts in Protestantism, leads to a demonization of instinctual energies followed by periodic explosions of mass rage.[12] The great lord has encountered more than wodwos on his quest. The Oriental path of asceticism and the abandonment of the ego is strongly developed in the sixties poetry; it exists as an ironic commentary upon Crow's hyperkinetic urge to manipulate the environment or it moderates the inordinate phallicism of Lumb's Double in the "Epilogue" of *Gaudete*, originally a 1964 screenplay. Or it offers the persona of part III of *Wodwo* a therapeutic refuge, a mantralike state of determined concentration upon the simple and the natural, a battening down of the hatches in an otherwise surreal gale of deathly Western aggression. Paradoxically, the center of poetic power in the sixties poetry resides in scathingly analytic indictments of modern Western culture, in poems such as "Gog," "Out,"

"Scapegoats and Rabies," "Crow's Account of the Battle," "Crow's Account of St. George," and "Crow Tries the Media."

The poetry written in the seventies and early eighties reveals significant growth. The verse indicates that Hughes now believes the journey outward and the journey inward to be one and the same in most respects, that the real journey is a matter of transmuting within the self the suffering and pain of existence into the kind of wisdom that liberates the creative intuition and leads to psychological wholeness and visionary states of perception. One can achieve this transformation either through an Occidental journey in temporal experience or through an Oriental ascetic discipline and abnegation of the analytic ego. Prometheus attains his transformation by absorbing the daily pain that attends purposive temporal action in *Prometheus on His Crag*. The persona of the *Gaudete* "Epilogue" endures the anguish of wrestling with his mortality before he can perceive the visionary oak "flying / Astride the earth." To accomplish this he must undergo the shamanistic death of the self: he must scrape "the flesh from the flesh" and then "Soak it all / In the crushed-out oil of the life." In *Remains of Elmet* and *River* Hughes advocates more Oriental ascetic disciplines, a divesting of one's egocentric objectivity. A more Oriental tree "Lets what happens to it happen" in *Remains of Elmet*. In *River* the persona of "Go Fishing" instructs us to "Join water," to wade into the river in order to "Lose words / Cease" and to "Let brain mist into moist earth" and be "Dissolved in earthwave." The mortality inscribed in salmon egg and human egg, a major theme in *River*, becomes an opportunity for a Taoist immersion in the concrete and the immediate, a reconciliation with natural processes that yields visionary moments. Like Eschenbach's Parzival or the Bodhisattva of the *Panchatantra*, the great lord achieves Reality, the goal of his quest, by enduring suffering, transmuting the pain into vision, and imbuing his daily life with love and compassion for all created beings.

Hughes's reading of Carl Jung may have prompted the creative insight that led to the "two-way journey toward Reality" statement. Hughes wrote in a 1977 letter to Faas that he had read "all the translated volumes" of Jung early in his career.[13] If Hughes did not read Jung during his Cambridge anthropology studies, he certainly must have become familiar with central Jungian tenets during his *Bardo Thödol* work in 1959–1960: Jung's "Psychological Commentary" to the *Bardo* has prefaced the standard Evans-Wentz translation in every reprinting since the 1955 third edition. Hughes alludes to Jung often in his reviews and essays during the years 1964–1967; he twice recounts a specific incident in Jung's 1961 autobiography.[14]

Jung, who developed many of his central insights from Oriental literature and philosophy, often criticized what he believed to be Western over-reliance upon rationalism and objectivity. Passages from *Psychology and Alchemy*, for instance, are very close not only to the language of Hughes's "two-way journey toward Reality" statement, but also to the central nerve of his sixties poetry, the first Faas interview, and the two "Myth and Education" essays.[15] According to Jung,

> The demand made by the *imitatio Christi*—that we should follow the ideal and seek to become like it—ought logically to have the result of developing and exalting the inner man. In actual fact, however, the ideal has been turned by superficial and formalistically-minded believers into an external object of worship, and it is precisely this veneration for the object that prevents it from reaching down into the depths of the psyche and giving the latter a wholeness in keeping with the ideal. Accordingly the divine mediator stands outside as an image, while man remains fragmentary and untouched in the deepest part of him. . . .
>
> The mistaken idea of a merely outward *imitatio Christi* is further exacerbated by a typically European prejudice which distinguishes the Western attitude from the Eastern. Western man is held in thrall by the "ten thousand things"; he sees only particulars, he is ego-bound and thing-bound, and unaware of the deep root of all being. Eastern man, on the other hand, experiences the world of particulars, and even his own ego, like a dream; he is rooted essentially in the "Ground," which attracts him so powerfully that his relations with the world are relativized to a degree that is often incomprehensible to us. The Western attitude, with its emphasis on the object, tends to fix the ideal—Christ—in its outward aspect and thus to rob it of its mysterious relation to the inner man. . . .
>
> If the supreme value (Christ) and the supreme negation (sin) are outside, then the soul is a void: its highest and lowest are missing. The Eastern attitude (more particularly the Indian) is the other way about: everything, highest and lowest, is in the (transcendental) Subject. Accordingly the significance of the Atman, the Self, is heightened beyond all bounds. But with Western man the value of the self sinks to zero. Hence the universal depreciation of the soul in the West.[16]

The emphasis upon the necessity for inner growth, the admiration for Oriental systems that affirm the inner self as the generator of experience, and the deliberate contrast of Oriental subjectivity to Western objectivity are patterns so similar in Jung's work and in Hughes's sixties poetry that they should not pass unnoticed. Hughes's two-way journey statement about attaining the "objectless radiance of the Self, where the world is a composition of benign Holy Powers" definitely alludes to the *ātman* of the Upanishads, the concept that Jung discusses in one of the above quotations. One attains the *ātman*, a transcendent union of the subjective soul and cosmic world-space, through acquiring self-mastery in the ascetic disciplines of yoga.[17] Another of the above-quoted passages from *Psychology and Alchemy* provides a helpful gloss upon a statement Hughes made in the first Faas interview about shifting the primary locus of values to within the self. Though Hughes appeared to be speaking about Vasco Popa at one point in the interview, the "new Holy Ground" he believed one must locate in the collapse of Western civilization is an interior, Oriental state—the same metaphysical "Ground" Jung describes in another of the quoted passages.[18]

Hughes's comment about the Holy Pilgrim (see the epigraph to this chapter) that followed the two-way journey statement in the 1963 review derives from a central motif in *Psychology and Alchemy*. Hughes asserts that in the West the self survives in dream visions of "the Holy Pilgrim, the Incorruptible Soul, the all-sufferer, the stone the builders reject again and again." Three times in *Psychology and Alchemy* Jung alludes to the jewel in Carl Spitteler's *Prometheus and Epimetheus* as the alchemical *lapis*, a Christ symbol and a symbol of the self. The materialists in Spitteler's work do not perceive the common stone to be valuable and toss it into the street as worthless. At one point Jung describes the *lapis* by translating a line from Spitteler: the *lapis* or self is "the stone which the builders rejected."[19] Finding that *lapis* or self through Oriental or Occidental means is the penultimate goal of Hughes's story of a soul, his two-way journey. Without the wholeness of the integrated self, exalted visions of Reality are simply not possible.

Hughes doubtless recognized that Jung provides such a wealth of psychoanalytic commentary on literature, the occult tradition, and dreams that he reveals constants about how the human mind has organized experience throughout the ages—constants that could enrich a poet's scope immeasurably. Hughes does not himself avow any particular Oriental or Occidental orthodoxy, but his poetry written in the sixties and essays referring to that period indicate that he does agree with Jung's belief that Westerners since the Industrial Revolution have been so exclusively concerned with objective fact and exploiting the material environment that they are in danger of losing contact with the soul—the foremost entity that, properly nurtured, could restore a sense of balance, sanity, and wholeness to life. Jung's polarization of Eastern and Western cultures, a deliberate strategy for criticizing Western repression of instinctual life and deification of scientific objectivity, is precisely the formal tactic Hughes adopts in *Wodwo*, *Crow*, and *Gaudete*. Whether the similarity is due to deliberate borrowing or happened subliminally, the result of a natural affinity in philosophical orientation, is really a moot point.

This polarization of Oriental and Occidental cultures in the sixties poetry, though somewhat reductive of post–Industrial Revolution Western culture, has its purpose. However extreme, the device functions as simply another modernist formal technique, an ironic juxtaposition of cultures similar to Eliot's mythical method, that defines a current problem and provides an answer from the reservoirs of tradition. The one significant difference is that, with research from contemporary social anthropologists and scholars of comparative religion—our Lévi-Strausses, Suzukis, and Eliades—this tradition is rapidly acquiring a global character. Library resources in these areas now provide what Donald Davie has described as an "imaginary museum," an immense storehouse testifying to the fact that "the artistic past of the human race is far richer and more various" than we had believed and that our literary tradition comprises "innumerable orders," not just the Greco-Roman-Christian.[20] It is only natural for a poet trained in social anthropology to offer advice about how to enrich one's life from other significant cultures in the history of *Homo sapiens*. Through his eclectic but very careful use of Indian, North American Indian, African, Eskimo, Chinese, Japanese, and Mesopotamian cultural influences, Hughes both fills what he perceives to be a void in modern Western culture and continues one of the central aims of the modernist enterprise: what M. L. Rosenthal considers the modernist poet's willingness to reinvigorate tradition with "widened, fresher meanings" and unwillingness to let "vital continuities" lapse in a cultural suicide caused by "submitting to organization, institutionalization, and mechanization for their own sake."[21]

Hughes's extensive reading of Jung in the early sixties is important not only as a source for the formal opposition of Oriental and Occidental approaches to experience in the sixties poetry, but also because many of Jung's central tenets inform the structural patterns of individual volumes from *Wodwo* through *Cave Birds*. Actually, every volume of Hughes's poetry since the 1963 two-way journey statement contains a journey at its center, though in *Crow* (until Hughes chooses to revise it) the journey toward reunion with nature as bride is incomplete. In the recent volumes *Remains of*

Elmet, Moortown, and *River*, the journey outward into concrete nature is simultaneously a journey inward, a reintegration of intuition into an analytically dominated psyche, with a sudden liberation of creative energy. For Jung the individuation process, the central psychological experience for the adult, is a goal-directed unfolding and reorganization of innate tendencies, a reformulation of the self through contact with the demonic and the creative in the personal unconscious, to achieve a new synthesis of conscious and unconscious opposites. During this process the voyager integrates the four functions of thinking, feeling, sensation, and intuition and brings to consciousness new energies from the unconscious in a way that afterwards allows the conscious portion of the self actively to shape one's future.[22]

To achieve this Jungian personality integration one undergoes a journey that commences with a sloughing off of the unsuitable present self-image, followed by a descent into a *nekyia* or underworld—the negative, devouring mother aspect of one's unconscious self. Here one receives aid from the genetic residue of prior human encounters with adversity—the archetypes of the collective unconscious as purely formal categories that one impregnates with one's own instinctual energies and then interprets in dream visions according to events and needs in one's personal life.[23] The new knowledge won from this struggle becomes a boon or healing elixir for the self and for all humankind. Hughes doubtless read Jung's first and most comprehensive exposition of this journey paradigm in *Psychological Types*. If not, he certainly did not miss Joseph Campbell's very Jungian investigation of the hero myth in *The Hero with a Thousand Faces*: the enigmatical "Author's Note" that prefaces *Wodwo*, Hughes's first two-way journey volume, speaks of a "single adventure" at the heart of the poetry, a phrase that echoes Campbell's "adventure of the hero," his label for the Jungian individuation journey.[24]

Other Jungian tenets inform the structure and content of the sixties poetry and of *Gaudete* and *Cave Birds*, two volumes that are transitional not in substance or depth but only in terms of Hughes's emerging vision. Hughes's use of North American Indian trickster material in *Crow* is well known, but his comment about Crow being a "shadow man" is not.[25] The phrase recollects Jung's analysis of the trickster as a collective Shadow figure, an archetype of a person's or a culture's darker, inferior traits. Paul Radin includes Jung's "On the Psychology of the Trickster Figure" in *The Trickster*, and Hughes alludes to Radin's trickster work in a 1966 review of two volumes of trickster folklore.[26] The structure of *Crow* contains an application of Jung's use of Heraclitian *enantiodromia*, a psychological law of conversion to the opposite whenever an excessively one-sided attitude threatens to damage the psyche. Hughes used it in *Crow* for the same purpose that Jung used it in his writings: to provide a social-psychological explanation of war as a violent reflex of instincts repressed by a culturally enforced religious taboo against eros and by a deification of analytic reason. *Enantiodromia*, the Shadow, and Jung's belief in the compensatory nature of dreams combine in the surreal descent to the underworld and the dreamscape atmosphere of *Gaudete*. And of course Jung's three volumes on alchemy, a pseudoscience that Jung believes provides evidence of the individuation process, inform the structure of *Cave Birds*, subtitled "An Alchemical Cave Drama." Though Jung is hardly the only major influence upon Hughes's sixties poetry, his perspectives permeate both the form and the content of the sixties works, and the transitional *Cave Birds*, and provide the surest guide to interpretation.

As the depth psychology and social analysis of Jung dominate the sixties poetry, so the formal esthetics of John Crowe Ransom and the New Criticism dominate the fifties volumes *The Hawk in the Rain* and *Lupercal*. The poetry reveals that Hughes learned from Ransom to prize the ability to weld one's intended meaning directly to images from the world's body of concrete experience as the central task of the creative imagination. This fusion of the poet's intended meaning, however provisional, and the external image redolent with nature's concrete particularity is a cornerstone of the New Criticism, a benchmark of the well-crafted, fully realized poem. Allen Tate calls this fusion of the intensional verbal world with the extensional world of nature a "tension" in poetry, and Ransom calls it his "concrete universal"; Cleanth Brooks simply calls it "metaphor."[27] Both Ransom and Brooks discuss similarities to the fusing power of Coleridge's secondary imagination. Hughes has often spoken of an early Ransom influence; chapter 2 specifies the biographical origin of the Ransom influence, examines how New Critical craftsmanship dominates the formal esthetics of composition in *The Hawk in the Rain*, and reveals how the formalist esthetics dovetails with Hughes's early preference for a Western journey in time and historical experience.

The literary tradition of reconciling opposites into new unities through imaginative perception is a rich one. One thinks of Blake's proverbs in *The Marriage of Heaven and Hell*, Boehme's mysticism, Plotinus's One and the Many, and the *Fragments* of Heraclitus. But the technical emphasis in New Criticism upon fusing the opposites of mind and sensuous image in the poetic icon represents a flowering of the Imagist tradition. Eliot affirms that the sensibility of the true poet can be characterized as one wherein thought and sensuous experience unify, producing new wholes. Western culture since the rise of science in the seventeenth century supposedly dissociated this sensibility, producing Victorian poets like Tennyson and Browning—poets who can alternately think and feel, but who do not, according to Eliot, "feel their thought as immediately as the odour of a rose." The great poet for Eliot is one in whom disparate experiences are always "forming new wholes."[28] Many of the poems in *The Hawk in the Rain* and *Lupercal* contain the high level of imaginative power, dexterity of formal craft, and sensuous immediacy that meet the exacting standards of Eliot and Ransom.

The immediacy of thought and sensuous apprehension that Eliot advocates underscores an important characteristic of the Imagist tradition that one actually finds throughout all three phases of Hughes's career. As the Imagists rebelled against the rhetorical posturing and attitudinizing of late Victorian and Georgian poets, they came to value poetry that eliminated the distance between the original experience, the poet's analysis and evaluation of that experience, and the formal craft that produced the final poem. Pound, of course, defined the image as "that which presents an intellectual and emotional complex in an instant of time."[29] Charles Olson, heir like Hughes to this Imagist emphasis upon immediacy, perhaps best expresses Pound's "instant of time" when he asserts that the poet ought to strive for a language that conveys experience directly, as the "act of the instant," not "the act of thought about the instant."[30] Hughes often achieves this directness through carefully crafted metaphors that control the substance and movement of the entire poem.

After Hughes ended his April 1958 Harvard reading with "Acrobats" (*Lupercal*), Sylvia Plath wrote in her journals that the poem described "a perfect metaphor, really, for himself as a poetic acrobat-genius."[31] Fresh metaphors extended with ease throughout the fabric of the poem, metaphors that sustain a fusion of thought and sensuous image, constitute Hughes's poetic signature. One finds this fully realized metaphoric fusion and extension in every volume; a list of superlative New Critical poems from Hughes's major volumes would certainly include "A Modest Proposal," "Acrobats," "Skylarks," "Magical Dangers," the final poem of *Prometheus on His Crag*, the penultimate poem of the *Gaudete* "Epilogue," "Bride and groom lie hidden for three days," "Bridestones" or "Heptonstall Cemetery," and "Go Fishing." One can readily see how an esthetics that emphasized the welding of outer and inner worlds in the instant of experience could prepare Hughes for the seemingly improbable leap, in the sixties poetry, from the New Criticism to Jungian concepts of the self as a tension of conscious and unconscious opposites, and for the development of an outward/inward two-way journey architectonic.

The New Critical fusion of thought and sensual experience that collapses temporal distance into the living moment of the poem is a feat of craft, a technique that in some ways approximates the vividness and intensity one experiences when viewing the reformulated reality of an analytical cubist painting—where the essence of an object is rendered through an all-at-once presentation of partial insights combined from differing angles of vision.[32] The vividness and immediacy Hughes achieved through mastering this New Critical technique in his early poetry functioned as a perfect method for highlighting his early belief in the efficacy of an outward Western journey in temporal experience. Form and content intersect.

The language of metaphor, and the immediacy and directness of presentation prized by the New Criticism, refashions experience into what Brooks calls a "simulacrum": it reconstructs reality in a way that *approximates* the complexity and the contradictions of one's actual daily experience, while at the same time it "triumphs" over these contradictions "by unifying them into a new pattern."[33] In "Acrobats" the poetic somersaulting "Bodily out in space" occurs as the result of the "prayer of long attempting," the deliberate effort of craft that "flashed / Above the earth's ancient inertia." This is not mimesis, but an artful reconstruction of experience through tensions built from carefully developed ambiguities, ironies, metaphors, contrasts, and patterns of imagery. From the poetry and criticism of Ransom, Hughes learned the New Critical axiom of the inseparability of form and content—how, in the words of Wimsatt and Brooks, "'form' in fact embraces and penetrates 'message' in a way that constitutes a deeper and more substantial meaning than either abstract message or separable ornament."[34] Form for Hughes is not a matter of separable structure, style, and techniques such as meter, metaphor, and symbolism. The definition of form best suited to Hughes is the New Critical definition devised by Wellek and Warren in *Theory of Literature*. Here the word "form"

> names the aesthetic structure of a literary work—that which makes it literature. Instead of dichotomizing 'form-content', we should think of matter and then of 'form', that which aesthetically organizes its 'matter'. In a successful work of art, the materials are completely assimilated into the form: what was 'world' has become 'language'. The 'materials' of a literary work of art are, on one level, words, on another level, human behavior experience, and on another, human ideas and attitudes. All of these, including language, exist outside the work of

art, in other modes; but in a successful poem or novel they are pulled into polyphonic relations by the dynamics of aesthetic purpose.[35]

Though Hughes after *The Hawk in the Rain* outgrew the New Critical style of cramming individual poems with elaborate ironies, ambiguities, and contrasts that occasionally risk losing the reader ("Incompatibilities" in *Hawk* is one such dizzying experience), every volume from *Lupercal* forward contains a central controlling purpose, an intersection of form and content that reveals significance as it subsumes choices of style and technique. The Roman Lupercalia; the shamanistic quest of *Wodwo*; Crow's trickster inversion of this quest in a satiric "mishmash of scripture and physics"; attempts to transcend the sodden earth of procreation, decay, and limited awareness in *Gaudete* and *Moortown*; the alchemical journey to psychic wholeness in *Cave Birds*; the significance of the Calder Valley moors in *Remains of Elmet*, and of the river of temporal experience in *River*—these organizational foci introduce readers to form/content amalgams, crafted to artistic purpose by a skilled hand, that reveal significance and guide interpretation of individual poems. All contain outward and/or inward journeys toward psychic reclamation and (except for *Crow*) toward a restoration of equilibrium with the environment after exorcising demons within the self and in the cultural context. The reintegrated self then evinces new powers in a final ascent to a vision of Reality. Hughes remains a New Critical poet throughout his career in one respect: the central architectonic of each volume reveals meaning, and at the same time the organization of individual poems, as subsequent chapters exhibit, comprises more than separable structure.

Hughes retains his gift for metaphor, ambiguity, irony, and contrast throughout the seventies and early eighties, but after *Hawk* he uses them for ends other than the New Critical "simulacrum" that triumphs over daily living by forging a transcendent esthetic unity. In the sixties poetry Hughes combines uses of metaphor, irony, satire, and ambiguity with elements of surrealism and primitive myth, to reveal the *disunity* of experience and the impossibility of continuing the outward, Western portion of his two-way journey. Here the persona is thrust back upon his own inner resources, and the landscape of nature either becomes internalized, metaphoric of psychic maladjustment ("Reeds, nude and tufted, shiver as they wade" in *Wodwo*), or is externalized in a reductive, satiric way to reveal our culture's "mishmash of scripture and physics" (*Crow*). In *Gaudete* metaphor reveals Lumb's Double's inability to transcend appetites that root him in nature's hothouse of sexual urgency, generation, and decay. His anxious dreams of personal freedom only reveal impersonal metaphors of sexual enchainment, daydream scenarios "Each with a bed at the centre. A name. A pair of shoes. And a door." Metaphor in the sixties poetry regularly reveals a profound disequilibrium, a discontinuity between the demands of the psyche and the values offered by the commonly accepted myths of contemporary Western culture.

The use of metaphor in the New Critical reformulated reality of the fifties poetry, and in the surreal and mythic contexts of the sixties poetry, raises a question that demands a precise answer. Just what is the extent of Hughes's modernism? In a provocative review Donald Davie writes that the real focus of the violence in *Wodwo* is not animal or human psychology, but national psychology, with Hughes questioning whether anything is left of the English cultural tradition after Gallipoli except chronic violence. Davie avers that Hughes is therefore not a modernist, because "he has not broken free from the English cultural tradition, with which he grapples constantly."[36] In other words, since two well-known characteristics of modernists are their despair over contemporary culture and their conviction that history is bereft of purpose, is Hughes in fact a modernist, given his preoccupation with violence in the history of Western culture? Does the typical subject matter of Hughes's metaphors place him within the tradition of realism, even though his attitude toward this tradition appears otherwise in the content of the poem?

Certainly *Wodwo*, in specifying the violence in modern Western culture, emphasizes the historical recurrence of that violence. But *Wodwo* is no more mimetic of temporal sequence than is any other Hughes volume. Joseph Frank reasons very persuasively that a central facet of modernism is the desire to transcend a chaotic temporality through form—to juxtapose fragments of past and present history in an organization determined by spatial arrangement, in order to promote a simultaneity, as the reader apprehends the work, that facilitates a transcendent moment of awareness in that reader. Frank alludes to Wilhelm Worringer's *Abstraction and Empathy* to argue that mimesis and realism flourish in ages when the artist feels secure, engaged in an ordered, harmonious equilibrium with nature and culture. The nonnaturalistic, nonmimetic visual and spatial forms of modernism, however, derive from the artist's attempt to create his or her own order in a time of disequilibrium, when the temporal flux of events seems chaotic and purposeless.[37]

Davie should ponder the hint in the "Author's Note" to *Wodwo* of an organizational relationship between the volume as a whole and the journey motifs in Jung, Campbell, and Eliade's *Shamanism*. The arrangement of the poems in *Wodwo*, and in every other Hughes volume, manifests a formal unity developed through a sustained artistic purpose that does not depend upon mimesis and realism. The great moderns Yeats, Eliot, Joyce, and Pound regularly juxtapose fragments of history in formal methodologies that reveal purpose and meaning, without rigid adherence to the conventions of realism. Because Hughes's poetry evinces an acceptance of the New Critical axiom of the inseparability of form and content, and because within each volume Hughes emphasizes formal arrangement rather than verisimilitude or temporal sequence, his poetry is modernist.

Further clarification of Hughes's status as a modernist also sheds new light upon the problematic reception of his poetry among one group within the British critical establishment. A very perceptive analysis of modernism by David Lodge provides the requisite insights. Recently Lodge has stated that the modern period actually contains at least three kinds of writing, "only one of which is modern*ist*" (italics mine). The contemporary *postmodern* writer (Barthelme, Pynchon, Ashbery, et al.) broods over what he or she perceives to be the absence of answers and continuity by emphasizing randomness, discontinuity, and by blurring the distinction between author and fictional character—all of which raises questions about the actual process of fabricating literary fictions. The *antimodern* writer (Wells, Bennett, Snow, Hardy, Larkin, Davie, Amis, the Georgian and other Movement poets) adopts a metonymic mode that emphasizes contiguous space-time; historicity; mimetic cause/effect and temporal sequence; an aversion to formal experiment; a prosaic, conversational language; and content discovered in the "real" world. The *modernist* writer (Joyce, Woolf, Yeats, Eliot, Pound) adopts a metaphoric mode to locate meaningful similarities in apparently disparate experience and dissimilar objects, using symbol, motif, myth, metaphor, ambiguity, paradox, and elaborate devices of formal organization developed from these techniques, for the purpose of forging a new unity that redeems a purposeless history.[38]

Lodge observes that these three modes operate "according to different and identifiable formal principles, and . . . it is therefore pointless to judge one kind of writing by criteria derived from another."[39] Yet a number of British critics whose essays and reviews indicate that they espouse the antimodernist realism of the Movement poets inveighed against Hughes throughout the sixties and seventies by focusing only upon matters of diction and taste and by contending that instances of violence and primitive myth do not help us to solve the problems we face in our daily lives. Hughes soon wore out the patience of these critics by regularly preferring formal dislocation over comfortably realistic settings for his poems. Yet these critics, instead of surveying the whole, regarding the writer's end, avoiding extremes, and knowing how far their reach and learning go—as Pope once counseled critics—voiced sweeping complaints against myth kitties and obscurity, along with *ad hominem* attacks against what they perceived to be adolescent poetry preoccupied with violence and voyeurism. Calvin Bedient, David Holbrook, and Ian Hamilton found *Crow* especially exasperating, though it contains, as chapter 5 specifies, a finely wrought and very purposive formal organization.[40] In their impatience with form and excessive concern with diction and a narrow referentiality, these critics fail to reach the heart of Hughes's poetry. They are, metaphorically speaking, attempting to evaluate the school of John Donne with critical precepts derived from the school of Ben Jonson. The results are too often severely limited or irrelevant.

Hughes's poetry fits the modernist mode especially because its elaborate formal organization and metaphors *are* educational. When Pound in "Canto LIII" directs poets to "MAKE IT NEW," he speaks as a quintessential modernist and as an educator. Pound demands of poetry the creation of a new *paideuma*, a new cultural construct forged in the literary text, to compensate for the absence of a discernible culture in the outside world. Artistic compression and formal dexterity forge this new cultural construct; *paideuma* for Pound entails both a "complex of the inrooted ideas of any period" and "a very complicated structure of knowledge and perception, the paradise of the human mind under enlightenment."[41] Pound further associates *paideuma* with the words "culture" and "education,"[42] for in creating a new culture in the literary work the modernist writer helps the reader to organize fragmentary experience, in part by specifying what is lacking in the purblind present through the formal techniques of historical and metaphoric juxtaposition. Through formal organization Hughes creates a new *paideuma* in every volume of his poetry. His own mythical method in *Hawk*, his use of the Lupercalia ritual in *Lupercal* and the "single adventure" of the hero in *Wodwo*, his satiric contrasts and surrealistic exaggerations in *Crow* and *Gaudete*, and organizational motifs derived from primitive myth, the occult, and Oriental philosophy—these formal devices serve to make us aware of excesses and defects in Western habits of perception and action. Like Pound, Hughes shares what Lodge perceives to be a central tenet among modernists: the belief that "we compose the reality we perceive by mental structures that are cultural, not natural in origin, and . . . it is art which is most likely to change and renew those structures when they become inadequate or unsatisfying."[43]

Furthermore, what Hughes said of his children's stories works equally well for his adult poetry. Motifs, characters, and bits of narrative action also function on the psychological level as spatially arranged metaphors for portions of our psychic life. The formal organization of these metaphoric parts into the completed volume provides what Hughes calls an "imaginative blueprint" for healing the psychic life of the reader. Precisely because the story or volume of poetry is freed of pretensions to verisimilitude, "completely free of any realistic points to pin it down and hold it," each reader is free to "make metaphorical applications of it"—to apply it to his or her own life.[44] Crow and "Egghead" caution us to curb our egotism and whatever traces of utilitarian conduct reside within us. "Second Glance at a Jaguar," "Ghost Crabs," and "Scapegoats and Rabies" remind us to control our aggressive impulses. "Lovesong" reminds us of the brutality of possessive love, "Bride and groom lie hidden for three days" of the beauty of mutual sharing in love, and "Song" and "September" of the holiness of romantic love. Readers who acknowledge their own demons and desires while participating in the imaginative life of the poetry have a much better chance of integrating their conscious lives with their buried selves, and thus achieving peace. Because they will not be filled with unresolved tension, such readers will more likely be vigilant and discerning voters and be less vulnerable to warmongering demagoguery and calculated appeals to patriotism. The chapters of this study support the assertion that at both the rational and the affective/psychological levels Hughes delights us with his metaphors and formal dexterity as he teaches us how to understand our culture and achieve personal wholeness: the twin imperatives of Horace survive.

Hughes also educates through his adaptation of Oriental and occult sources. In Hughes's very able hands these sources serve to convince us that we are not passive *tabulae rasae* moved by empirical forces that determine our fortunes, but generators of our own perceptions and potentially in full control of what values we choose to posit on external phenomena. All of the Oriental and occult sources Hughes brings to bear upon his poetry—Zen Buddhism, the Hindu Upanishads, Chinese Taoism, the Tibetan *Bardo Thödol*, the disciplines of yoga, cabbalistic doctrine and alchemical lore, South Indian *vacanas*, and Sufi and Japanese fables—have in common an emphasis upon the subjective self as an active component in determining what is real for that self.

In the sixties poetry the Oriental and occult sources function primarily as an antidote to the defects of Western science and religion. Hughes has stated in essays, reviews, and interviews that Western culture from the Protestant Reformation forward—through the New Science, the Industrial

Revolution, and the age of nuclear energy and the triumph of technology—has promoted a dangerous alienation of the subjective self. Einstein happily opines that scientists developed the empirical attitude to free "ideas from the taboo attached to them, and thus to achieve greater freedom in the formation of ideas or concepts." Hence he observes that "the physicist seeks to reduce colours and tones to vibrations, the physiologist thought and pain to nerve processes, in such a way that the psychical element as such is eliminated from the causal nexus of existence. . . ."[45] Hughes responds by questioning what this freedom has wrought. The divorce between inner and outer worlds in Hughes's sixties poetry simply reflects a schizoid Western culture: especially in Crow's escapades and in the fate of Lumb's Double Hughes shows us what ensues when scientists "reduce" and eliminate "the psychical element" as a "causal nexus of existence." In a 1970 review Hughes states his argument against modern Western culture very succinctly:

> The fundamental guiding ideas of our Western Civilization. . . . derive from Reformed Christianity and from Old Testament Puritanism. . . . They are based on the assumption that the earth is a heap of raw materials given to man by God for his exclusive profit and use. . . . The subtly apotheosized misogyny of Reformed Christianity is proportionate to the fanatic rejection of Nature, and the result has been to exile man from Mother Nature—from both inner and outer nature. The story of the mind exiled from Nature is the story of Western Man. It is the story of his progressively more desperate search for mechanical and rational and symbolic securities, which will substitute for the spirit-confidence of the Nature he has lost.[46]

In the sixties poetry the Oriental inward journey appears to be the one way to survive the nuclear glare wrought by Western empiricism. Reiser recounts an incident in his biography where Einstein, annoyed by a questionnaire about his interest in Bach, responds with the advice "In reference to Bach's life and work; listen, play, love, revere, and—keep your mouth shut!" In *Wodwo* Hughes questions this apparent divorce of the subjective pleasure from the objective work; in part III of "Wings" he presents Einstein playing Bach in a futile attempt to blot out the empirical reality he inadvertently created. Though Einstein did not participate in the Manhattan Project, he did write the letter to Roosevelt (2 August 1939) that ushered in the atomic age: in it he advised exploiting nuclear chain reactions in the production of bombs, for Germany had become interested in uranium from recently captured Czechoslovakian mines. Hughes presents Einstein playing Bach as if to distract himself, through esthetic (subjective, ironically) concentration, from the consequences of his scientific research. The flies of existentialist freedom and conscience that haunt Orestes in Sartre's *Les Mouches* (Sartre is the subject of part I of "Wings") mix with mushroom clouds from atomic blasts to haunt the noble scientist.[47]

In the sixties poetry Hughes articulates his case against the myths of contemporary Western society, and his proposals for transcending these defective myths, not only in individual poems such as "Wings," "Gog," and "Out," but also through essentially nonmimetic formal patterns, spatial arrangements, motifs and metaphors that operate throughout the individual volume. The volumes of poetry written in the sixties do not supply what Erich Auerbach considers a mimetic context—an imitation of an objective historical/cultural background motivating and dominating the fictional event.[48] Yet Hughes superimposes the shamanic journey upon forty poems on various subjects in *Wodwo*, with the five stories and the radio play at the center of the volume dividing the poems in half. This complex formal arrangement in *Wodwo* appears arbitrary until one ponders the important clue in the "Author's Note" that "the stories and the play are . . . chapters of a single adventure to which the poems are commentary and amplification." Crow's adventures at first remind us of the episodic satire of the picaresque tradition, until we recognize that the landscape is not that of realism, but of folklore surrealism—a function of Crow's culturally trained perceptions, a *self-created* antagonist. And the main narrative of *Gaudete* at first appears to be a satire on a shopworn theme, the secret sexual escapades of the country parson, with an incongruous "Epilogue" added as an afterthought, until we understand that the seemingly endless sexual escapades of Lumb's Double are far too improbable to be realistic and that they take place in a surrealistic dreamscape within the personal unconscious of the real Reverend Lumb, with the "Epilogue" containing the superior commentary of the newly healed prelate. The very sophisticated use of form, as the following chapters specify, largely clears the poetry of the charge of an adolescent indulgence in purposeless violence, at the same time offering a clear focus for determining theme and meaning in the individual poem.

Formal design also dominates the transitional volume *Cave Birds*. The birds of *Cave Birds* are states of consciousness within the mind of a single persona undergoing an alchemical individuation process. There is no historical context beyond the persona's reverie save the content of the formal paradigm, yet that paradigm encompasses centuries of Western cultural experience. What Auerbach says of Proust, Joyce, and Woolf also applies to

Hughes: that modernists prefer a synthetic mode of presentation where formal organization replaces the "chronological representation of a total exterior continuum" of history and culture that influences action apart from the designs of the protagonists. As modernists emancipate characters or personae from the hegemony of external circumstance, they offer in its place the omnitemporality of the perceiving consciousness searching for new unities.[49]

As the fifties poetry is modernist rather than realist because the New Critical form refashions reality into new unities in individual poems, so the complex surrealistic and mythic formal amalgams of poetry, prose narrative, and drama also place the sixties volumes in the modernist mode. The landscape poetry of the late seventies and early eighties may at first appear to be realistic, but in actuality it is equally nonrealistic. After completing *Crow* Hughes said to Faas that the poet may, after many years of toil and meditation, finally penetrate to the core of his poetic impulse and open up "the religious or holy basis of the whole thing."[50] From the *Gaudete* "Epilogue" forward the stern critic of Western culture becomes the seer engaged in lifting matter to the realm of spirit. Both the Western and the Oriental paths of the two-way journey toward Reality open for the poet. Here the emphasis resides in the perceiving consciousness of the persona, but a persona equipped with far more than the neutral or even omniscient camera eye of realism. Nor does Hughes limit the reality perceived to the everyday "objective" world.

In his third period Hughes discovers that one of the central themes of his poetry has been the attempt to escape the limitations of unenlightened natural humans—whose life is determined by cellular biology, appetites, material constraints, and the passive endurance of natural cycles that inevitably lead to death. In the title poem of his very first volume Hughes articulates his concern about the "clay that clutches my each step to the ankle / With the habit of the dogged grave." This preoccupation continues throughout the poetry—from the mud-bespattered faces of Ripley (*The Wound*) and the soldier of "Scapegoats and Rabies"; to Crow's head spraddled in beach-garbage ("Crow and the Birds"); Lumb's Double's daydream of being buried chin-deep in mud among his parishioners in *Gaudete*; the farmer's stubborn burrowing of boundary post holes "In the knee-deep mud of the copse ditch" ("A Monument"); and Adam's realization of being "Two little lifted from mud" in *Moortown*. The major organizational movement of all of the late seventies and early eighties volumes is liberation from these constrictions with the wings of visionary perception—the vision of the flying oak tree at the conclusion of the *Gaudete* "Epilogue";

the winged vision of departed family spirits in "Heptonstall Cemetery" (*Remains of Elmet*); the phoenix flight of visionary utterance, dripping transformational flames, in the penultimate poem of *Moortown*; and the hierophany of nature's creative liturgy, illuminated by heavenly light, at the conclusion of *River*. In all these cases the perceiving consciousness of the persona is active, informed with the creative imagination. It has the capacity to seize instantaneously upon the spiritual significance behind appearances. Similarly, the reality seen is an imperfect symbol of a transcendent Reality capable of being perceived by a psyche that is neither a purely passive register of impressions nor safe in an assumed and impossible omniscience.

The process of liberating the imaginative faculty and enlarging the spiritual world within an awakened self becomes the central formal movement of Hughes's third period. The onset of this third period has a biographical pivot point as precise as Hughes's contact with the *Bardo Thödol* in the fall of 1959, which begins his second period. In the summer of 1971 Hughes joined Peter Brook and an international troupe of actors in Iran to produce the as yet unpublished *Orghast* drama at the Fifth Annual Festival of the Arts near Teheran. Through conflating numerous Persian and Western sources, especially the *Prometheus Bound* of Aeschylus, Hughes reaffirms his early faith in the Western mythic mode of gaining knowledge and wisdom through suffering and temporal experience. Hughes conceived the story of *Orghast* to be enacted within the body of Prometheus as he is chained to the rock in his daily agony. One of the central themes of the drama, stated in the program note, is the "search for liberation through knowledge." In *Orghast* life becomes destructive because Krogon, a tyrant whom Hughes compared to the Holdfast of Cretan myth, persists in murdering his progeny rather than yielding his power. Sogis ultimately succeeds in deposing Krogon because *orghast*, a word from Hughes's invented language for the drama meaning "spiritfire" or "the fire of being," is repeated *within* Sogis, so that he can reconcile within his spirit conflicts and dilemmas that neither the immortal Pramanath (a Prometheus figure) nor the all too mortal Agoluz (a Hercules figure from Seneca's *Hercules Furens*) can reconcile in the purely transcendent or purely earthly realms. In Hughes's own outline of the *Orghast* mythology, "Sogis is able to resolve in spirit what Agoluz can never resolve in flesh, and what Pramanath can never resolve in eternity."[51]

Though Hughes does not mention Blake in the program note for *Orghast*, he has admired Blake since the mid-fifties,[52] and Blakean parallels are numerous and significant here. The struggle between Sogis and Krogon is very like the agons between the creative imagination (Los) and authoritarian reason (the Spectre) in *Jerusalem*. In Blake's late work and in Hughes's third period the formal organization reveals a Jungian individuation paradigm, a struggle to reconcile reason and the creative imagination (intuition) with emotion and sensation. The events of the poems primarily serve to figure forth this interior drama. In Hughes's third period the landscape and events in the natural world are edited and meditated upon by an enlightened persona with a well-developed Blakean sensibility, to promote this psychic event, not to imitate the interplay of consciousness with a concrete, present-day historical/cultural context. That context, if it operates at all in Hughes's third period (as it does in the "Earth-numb" section of *Moortown*), typically inhibits or permanently maims psychic growth. Like Blake, Hughes believes the personae of his poems to be capable of achieving the organized innocence of wisdom that Blake wrote in his marginal note to Night VIIb of *The Four Zoas*. When Milton joins Adam in Urthona in Blake's *Milton*, he becomes regenerated through his indwelling imagination, a power that Blake elsewhere describes as "the Divine Body in Every Man."[53] Hughes's task in his third phase mirrors that stated by Blake at the opening of *Jerusalem*:

> To open the Eternal Worlds, to open the immortal Eyes
> Of Man inwards into the Worlds of Thought: into Eternity
> Ever expanding in the Bosom of God. the Human Imagination
> O Saviour pour upon me thy Spirit of meekness & love:
> Annihilate the Selfhood in me, be thou all my life![54]

One further Western parallel that aids in comprehending Hughes's third period is Coleridge's distinction between primary and secondary imagination. Like that of Blake and Hughes, Coleridge's thinking is to a large extent motivated by an antipathy to mechanistic philosophy and science. In the *Transcendental Idealism* of Schelling, Coleridge finds support for a conception of the imagination that can synthesize objective nature with the perceiving subject. In the famous close of chapter XIII of the *Biographia Literaria*, Coleridge distinguishes a secondary imagination that is a symbol-making power, the product of conscious effort, from the primary imagination, a symbol-perceiving power that "brings the whole soul of man into activity" (XIV) in experiencing the oneness of matter and spirit, thus revealing the Reality behind the immanent object or event.[55] Hughes's fifties formalism and the complex organization of his sixties works most closely resemble the operation of Coleridge's secondary imagination, while the mystic vision of nature in the later works corresponds to Coleridge's primary imagination.

Occult and Oriental sources offer even more important aids in characterizing Hughes's recent work. In the Cabbala one ascends the Tree of Life through achieving states of heightened meditative awareness that begin with Malkuth, the most material and earth-bound state, and end with mystic visions of the Unmanifest in the realm of Kether. The Baskin snake on the dust jacket and paperback cover of *Moortown* is a stylized version of the Serpent of Wisdom whose three and one-half coils climb the Tree of Life in the Cabbala to reveal the path toward the spiritual. The serpent points the way for the fallen Adam—the farmer in the opening elegies—to become Adam Kadmon, the cabbalistic figure whose visionary imagination contains the entire edenic world—the Adam of the closing "Adam and the Sacred Nine."[56]

The strongest influence in the landscape poetry of *Remains of Elmet* and *River* derives from Taoism. According to Chang Chung-yuan, the essence of Taoism consists of the ontological experience of the interpenetration of subject and object.[57] Unlike Western orientations, disciples of Taoism must divest themselves of personal ego, ordinary rational thinking, and striving for goals in the temporal world, in order to cultivate the spirit and achieve a serenity and compassion for all creation. Through developing the inner world of spirit adepts can penetrate the phenomenal world of changing *yin/yang* opposites to glimpse the supreme Tao, the unvarying source of all temporal flux, often symbolized as a heavenly Light.[58] Oriental disciplines such as Taoism occasionally dovetail with Blakean and other Western sources in Hughes's third period, inasmuch as all inform the organizational movement toward opening up the inner world through liberating the creative imagination. The fiery furnaces of Blake's Los conflate with a Taoist Light that signifies the transphenomenal unity of being, for example, in "Open to Huge Light," from *Remains of Elmet.*

A few closing remarks, before launching into individual poems, to answer charges of inaccessibility and obscurity occasionally leveled at Hughes. Among modernists Hughes is unique because his power of metaphor, richness of texture and observation, and skillful combination of traditional narrative with spatial form have won him a large audience. Early Hughes volumes have undergone numerous reprintings, and more recent volumes will no doubt follow the same path. The Sagar and Tabor bibliography lists in England alone, as of 1980, a total of ten printings and 46,500 hardbound or paperback copies of *The Hawk in the Rain*, ten printings and 37,250 copies of *Lupercal*, five printings and 19,500 copies of *Wodwo*, and nine printings and 68,000 copies of *Crow*. Many of Hughes's children's volumes have also undergone reprintings, with *The Iron Man* outdistancing all with over 175,000 copies printed as of 1980. Reading Hughes is a satisfying experience at many levels; he has not alienated his audience with invective, moral hectoring, impassable layers of allusions, or arcana cluttering the surfaces of his poems.

Similarly, Hughes's use of primitive mythology is very careful, considered, and worth reflection. Like Jung, Hughes searches for important constants in the history of *Homo sapiens*, though contemporary research in social anthropology and comparative religion has allowed him to extend his reach beyond that of Jung in some respects. The biased perception of primitives as uncouth aboriginals lingers, but one need only read Lévi-Strauss to realize that primitive humans actually displayed much intelligence in language, rituals, social customs, and taboos. Hughes is especially interested in those elements of myth and religious practice that allowed primitives to establish and maintain psychic wholeness and peace without resorting to the levels of abstract organization and the iron application of will and power that produce huge armies and large-scale holocaust. Of course primitive people were by no means innocent of wholesale slaughter, but Hughes no doubt agrees with Konrad Lorenz's observation that moderns are the worst violators of the delicate balance between aggression and social inhibitions among members of the same species, by the capacity to produce the quick annihilation of millions through mechanical and nuclear weapons that remove the aggressor completely from having to experience the immediate consequences—viewing the actual death of the individual victim.[59]

Hughes's use of the shamanic journey, the *Lupercalia*, and other primitive rituals and symbols as organizational forms in his sixties poetry, reminds one of how constantly people have needed to mythicize their environment and to construct rituals that control or transmute the drives toward aggression and erotic abandon. Those who prefer to ignore these drives, and argue that moderns live by reason and common sense alone, should consult the mortality statistics for cult disasters like Jonestown, or for any one major battle in the world wars of the twentieth century. The fourteen-hour Allied firebombing of Dresden, for instance, killed twice as many as at Hiroshima—135,000, according to one estimate—less than three months before Germany surrendered.[60] One might also ponder an observation by Alvin Toffler: that if the last 50,000 years of human existence were portioned into lifetimes of 62 years, the record would show that 650 of the resulting 800 lifetimes were spent in caves, and only in the last 6 did humans see the printed word.[61] Hughes's use of primitive sources compels us to confront rather than repress our nonrational inheritance and to recognize that, until the Industrial Revolution, Western civilization survived by converting the power and energy of these drives into social cohesion and personality development through myth and religion. Poetry for Hughes is "the record of just how the forces of the Universe try to redress some balance disturbed by human error."[62] Hughes also believes that, when humans attempt to enlist the larger energies of the universe for their purposes, including the promotion of important cultural ideas and values, the wise help to contain and control the effects of such energies on human drives with "rituals, the machinery of religion. The old method is the only one."[63] The world wars of the twentieth century prove for Hughes that these drives cannot be palliated with consumer goods and a narrow myth of scientific rationalism.

Charges of obscurity in Hughes's use of Oriental sources are not tenable either, for Hughes does not bewilder his reader with numerous specific references to Oriental sources that must be specified to gain an elementary comprehension of a poem, as Pound often does. A rigid refusal to consider the use of Oriental sources in Western literature may betray a deep-seated cultural bias that books like Edward Said's *Orientalism* have helped to uncover. Communicating the achievement of a personal serenity and the experience of the self as an active generator of values through the use of Oriental sources is a legitimate literary response from a poet, trained in anthropology, who spent his early teens enduring the deprivations, tensions, and aftermath of World War II in England.

Furthermore, we can no longer afford to remain as culturally insular as when Philip Larkin complained about myth kitties in the fifties. Competition, dwindling energy reserves and other natural resources, and the proliferation of nuclear capabilities have necessitated cooperation and joint economic ventures among Western and non-Western nations. The survival of humankind will increasingly depend upon sufficient knowledge and appreciation of the cultures and religions of non-Western nations—and not just among negotiators and career diplomats, for demagogues often enlist mass ignorance, fears, and stereotypes to mask ignoble foreign policy decisions. Oriental disciplines can strengthen the personality and make us less susceptible to political chicanery. Einstein, a lifelong pacifist, once wrote that "perhaps someday, solitude will come to be properly recognized and appreciated as the teacher of personality. The Orientals have long known this. The individual who has experienced solitude will not easily become a victim of mass suggestion."[64]

Hughes, thoroughly a modernist, uses Oriental sources purposefully and educationally. In the sixties poetry he uses them to underscore by contrast an atrophied Western psyche that prefers possessions and statistical pabulum to the process of coping with the eros and the thanatos within the self. In the seventies Hughes uses Oriental sources to offer a compensatory vision—a positive ethic of enlightenment and reverence for nature, gained through suffering and self-abnegation, to counteract the bloodstained record of Western culture that he analyzed a decade earlier.

But the Oriental approach is not the only path of the two-way journey toward Reality open for Hughes in the volumes written after *Orghast*. By studying modernist form and changes in the operation of Hughes's artistic imagination in subsequent chapters, we can gain a deeper appreciation of how this extremely gifted and perceptive poet turns his highly agile, syncretic mind and inexhaustible curiosity and energy to the service of humanity in the creation of new *paideumae*.

PART I
The Formalist
Fifties

my poems . . . are attempts to prove the realness of the world, and of myself in this world, by establishing the realness of my relation to it.

—Hughes, 1957[1]

CHAPTER 2

A Craftsman Calm

The Hawk in the Rain

1957

Publication of *The Hawk in the Rain* in America in 1957 caught many in the British literary establishment by surprise. Auden, Spender, and Marianne Moore selected *Hawk*, over 286 other entries, for immediate publication at Harper, as the first prize in a competition sponsored by the Poetry Center of the Young Men's and Young Women's Hebrew Association of New York City. Though Faber immediately accepted *Hawk* and the volume soon became a choice of the Poetry Book Society, its contents raised eyebrows among many British critics. Robert Conquest, for instance, felt sufficiently uneasy to observe that many of the previously published poems of *Hawk* had appeared in American magazines. Before he addressed the poems he felt compelled to admit that "whole sectors" of modern American poetry "are quite extraordinarily alien" to contemporary Britons.[2]

Conquest was the perfect man to admit bafflement with *Hawk*: his *New Lines* anthology, printed just a year earlier, launched the Movement—the poetry of Philip Larkin, Donald Davie, John Wain, Kingsley Amis, Elizabeth Jennings, John Holloway, and others. As Conquest notes in his "Introduction," Movement poets reject the id, metaphor as a principle of organization, and the excesses of diction and feeling of neo-Romantic forties poets like Graves and Dylan Thomas. Movement poets prefer light satire and irony, a witty and sceptical urbanity, and demand what Conquest calls a "rational structure and comprehensible language," with a background of everyday realism. Hughes's verbal energy, his vivid metaphors, his willingness to involve himself in the depths and heights of human experience, his serious treatment of the main themes of poetry—love, death, time, nature, transcendence, and God—and his deft use of complex formal designs disturb those who prefer the pleasantries and restraint of Movement poetry. Though Conquest considered *Hawk* a "very promising" effort, his reservation about American editors who accept experimental verse foreshadowed the later discontent of most Movement-oriented British critics with Hughes's poetry. Other British critics were struck by the muscular verbiage; the vivid, compelling imagery; and the highly dramatic nature of Hughes's poems, but also failed to provide penetrating comments—because they too could not identify the formal principles operating beneath the surface of the poems.

A few British reviewers, however, did partially succeed in making substantive comments about *Hawk*. Their observations direct us toward identifying the formal principles involved. Graham Hough and an anonymous *Times Literary Supplement* reviewer both applaud Hughes's ability to circumvent the excesses of neo-Romantic introspection by basing his poems upon public images and events that remain rooted in the real world.[3] This is basically true, and a source of strength in Hughes's early Western orientation toward experience, but the realism of *Hawk* is a realism with a difference, as we shall soon see. W. I. Carr notes that the highly dramatic nature of these poems derives in large part from "a consciously erected persona," a "willed dramatic figure who takes Mr. Hughes's place at the centre of events, and both feels and comments for him."[4] Hough offers the most astute observation. While he admits that he does "not always understand the formal organization" of *Hawk*, he offers a revealing cause for Hughes's vivid imagery, and he carefully separates Hughes's form from the popular Movement model of description plus summary evaluation propagated by Yvor Winters and others:

The first impression [on reading *Hawk*] is one of great verbal vitality, not always under control; but the second is pure poetic intelligence. The phrase poetic intelligence really does mean something; it means not the kind of intelligence that condenses a few clever critical observations into verse, but the kind that can penetrate and transform a fragment of experience, without thinking at all about making a pronouncement, and at the same time say something memorable about the world, almost as it were by accident. "Fallgrief's Girl-Friends" and "The Man Seeking Experience Enquires His Way of a Drop of Water" are, I believe, profound poems. They are very unlike the current philosophic-epigrammatic mode with its anxiety to make a point—a two-line point after the statutory ration of descriptive imagery. What these poems have to "say" runs all through them; partly because they are written dramatically or objectively, and the imaginative effort needed to compass an outer object keeps up a high tension throughout the poem, does not leave it all to be screwed up by a neat twist at the end.[5]

Hough but glimpsed Hughes's very perceptive application of the main tenets of the American New Criticism. The charge of "imaginative effort" that "runs all through" the poem and avoids the anxious summations of Movement poems is a feat of poetic craft—New Critical acrobatics. *Hawk* contains poems where the reformulated reality of New Critical design replaces historical context, to affect the reader more powerfully and vividly than through discursive statement.

Though they never met to share their ideas or poetry in person, Ted Hughes met John Crowe Ransom in print in the fifties, when the New Criticism was at its apogee of literary influence. Keith Sagar, the leading Hughes critic, reports that Hughes, during and immediately after his Cambridge years (1951–1954), admired Ransom's work "unreservedly."[6] Hughes's close friend at Cambridge, with whom he roomed at St. Botolph's Priory, was E. Lucas Myers, a hopeful poet and cousin of Allen Tate.[7] After Hughes met Sylvia Plath (1956), they shared their admiration for Ransom's poetry, and Plath supplied him with Ransom's principal critical essays, brought over from America.[8] As late as in a 1977 interview, one finds Hughes quoting the first line of Ransom's "Antique Harvesters" as an example of a carefully "planned" poem that Hughes believes conveys "an extreme density where every movement and every word in the line is physically connected to the way it's being spoken."[9] When Hughes recounted his formative influences in a 1970 interview, he stated that "up to the age of twenty-five I read no contemporary poetry whatsoever except Eliot, Thomas and some Auden. Then I read a Penguin of American poets that came out in about 1955 and that started me writing. After writing nothing for about six years. The poems that set me off were odd pieces by Shapiro, Lowell, Merwin, Wilbur and Crowe Ransom. Crowe Ransom was the one who gave me a model I felt I could use. He helped me get my words into focus. That put me into production."[10]

Hughes is actually referring to Geoffrey Moore's 1954 selection, entitled *The Penguin Book of Modern American Verse*. It contains the Ransom poems "Dead Boy," "Here Lies a Lady," "Antique Harvesters," "Dog," and "Painted Head." These standard anthology selections, though not Ransom's best efforts, were enough to pique Hughes's curiosity. In what sense was Ransom a "model" for Hughes? How exactly are Ransom's poems "planned," with an "extreme density"? Could the cross-cultural fertilization, so characteristic of modern verse, concern Ransom's ontological preference for the density of the "world's body" of concrete experience—the way that the poetic icon, in Ransom's theory, is superior to the scientific abstraction?[11] Is

Hughes championing the power of metaphor, which Ransom, Allen Tate, and Cleanth Brooks all stress?[12] Or do the apt diction, the carefully crafted ironies, and the sonorous rhetoric of a strong persona, in Ransom's poetry, constitute the main features of the "model" that Hughes emulated?[13]

For Hughes's early work, especially for *The Hawk in the Rain*, the answer is *all of the above*. The first of Hughes's very infrequent statements on poetics, appearing in 1957, echoes with relish the main principle of Ransom's critical theory—the preference, derived from Kant and the Imagist poets, for the kind of poem that communicates not through vague emotions or bald statement, but through fusing the poet's thoughts into images and metaphors that incorporate the "thick *dinglich* substance" of the "world's body" of concrete experience.[14] Here Hughes writes that his poems "are attempts to prove the realness of the world, and of myself in this world, by establishing the realness of my relation to it. Another way of saying this might be—the poems celebrate the pure solidity of my illusion of the world."[15] *The Hawk in the Rain* celebrates a young writer's faith in the Western mode of self-development through headlong encounters with experience. These encounters with the "world's body" of immediate experience occur either through confrontations with salutary or menacing forces in the environment or between ordinary psychic life and the deeper instinctual and goal-directed energies that periodically arise from the unconscious. At every turn in *Hawk* Hughes affirms the "solidity" of "real" experience, but through the polyphonic relations of complex formal designs that subsume ontological preference, imagery, and metaphor into consciously crafted esthetic purpose.

Hughes especially follows the preference of both Ransom and Tate for the concrete metaphor that houses the poet's intended metaphysic without overt moralizing, sentimentalizing, or transferring feelings evoked from one object to another in the poem. As Ransom admires Yeats's swan metaphor in "Nineteen Hundred and Nineteen" and Eliot's etherized patient, so Tate admires the closing metaphor of the sea girls in "Prufrock," the opening quatrain of Shakespeare's "Sonnet 73," and the metaphor concerning the ductility of gold in Donne's "A Valediction: Forbidding Mourning." The poet's metaphysic or kernel of intended meaning *inheres* in the concrete image in these instances. Ransom often chooses concrete metaphors for his poems that fuse the sensuous world of experience with his intended metaphysic. In "Winter Remembered," for instance, the persona presents his bereavement at the loss of a loved one by fusing his anguish with the "furious winter blowing." He decides it is "Better to walk forth in the frozen air / And wash my wound in the snows." Ransom then fuses the tactile, psychological, and metaphysical levels of loss in the final image of inert, uprooted life suspended in the winter's cold:

> Dear love, these fingers that had known your touch,
> And tied our separate forces first together,
> Were ten poor idiot fingers not worth much,
> Ten frozen parsnips hanging in the weather.[16]

Tate contrasts the coherence and organic unity of meaning and metaphor in such poetry, which produces richness and clarity, with poetry that articulates a confused affective state (his example is James Thomson's "The Vine"), or that lapses into bald denotative statement (he cites Cowley's "Hymn to Light").[17]

Of particular relevance to Hughes, as we shall see, is Ransom's ability to extend his use of concrete metaphors so that they control the form of the entire poem. One need only remember the severed tree limb as a central metaphor for the tragedy of "Dead Boy"; the tempest destruction as character revelation in "Miriam Tazewell"; the extended metaphor of the "Good Ships" at Mrs. Grundy's Tuesday teas; the central metaphor of the chivalrous knight in battle as revelatory of the Calvinist qualms of the would-be seducer in "Spectral Lovers"; or the setting of neurotic after-dinner preoccupations, in "Prelude to an Evening," as a concrete manifestation of a refusal to confront wartime realities. Tate calls such fusions of the poet's intensional meaning and the concrete extensional image a purposeful "tension" in poetry; Ransom calls them "concrete universals."[18]

As the above examples indicate, Ransom in his poetry typically takes an ironic stance toward the possibility of controlling invasions of the world's body of immediate experience. One can readily assent to Robert Penn Warren's observation that "the method of irony, in Ransom's poetry . . . may be called psychological. Factors in the make-up of his heroes which might work for strength actually work for weakness."[19] But Hughes is not constrained by academic qualms about abandoning oneself to experience, or by Protestant prohibitions against sex. Hughes's early zest for living partakes of the fifties spirit of the Angries, and of the feisty bravado and impatience of a young writer stalking experience in a more passive, technologically deadened contemporary society. Yet Hughes's early adventures on the Western path of his two-way journey toward Reality very definitely affirm the worth of Ransom's preference for metaphors and formal designs that convey a sense of the world's body of concrete experience. Occasionally Hughes even presents successful encounters with such experience.

One of the clearest instances in *The Hawk in the Rain* both of a successful encounter with "real" experience and of modernist form controlling the content of a poem occurs in "The Dove-Breeder." Here Hughes presents the psychic conflict caused by the forceful entry of love into the self-conscious propriety of an unnamed, "mild-mannered" individual, through extending an initial simile of a hawk's raid into a dovecote. The simile beginning in line 2 initiates a dramatic action, Homeric in length, that runs the length of the poem at the same time that it figures forth the meaning—the process of accommodating within the self this newly awakened emotional life:

> Love struck into his life
> Like a hawk into a dovecote.
> What a cry went up!
> Every gentle pedigree dove
> Blindly clattered and beat,
> And the mild-mannered dove-breeder
> Shrieked at that raider.[20]

But after the dove breeder's first lament at the loss of prim appearances ("He will win no more prizes / With fantails or pouters"), the reader is given to believe, solely through the development of the barnyard vehicle, that the individual has matured by wrestling with this forceful invasion of eros and taming it to his service. The poem ends with the lines "Now he rides the morning mist / With a big-eyed hawk on his fist." The extended simile becomes a formal device that controls the energies of the poem at the same time that it conveys meaning more directly than through discursive summary. We learn infinitely more about the psychological impact of love upon the male through the graphic diction and the dramatic action of the extended simile than any collection of representational details could possibly convey.

Hughes's poetry is therefore more presentational, the product of painstakingly self-conscious formal craft, than the representational poetry of Movement writers. The latter mimetically reproduce the interplay of poetic consciousness with a present-day historical/cultural context. The church entered in Larkin's early poem "Church Going" (*The Less Deceived*), for instance, confronts him with an actual tradition. The persona removes his cycle clips "in awkward reverence" and enters. Limiting his interaction to the observations of an intelligent tourist, he soon concludes "there's nothing going on" within. Larkin then offers us a transcription of the persona's airy remarks about a tradition that no longer speaks to him. He admits to being bored and uninformed and to having "no idea / What this accoutered frowsty barn is worth." The persona expresses his uneasiness through guarded responses to particular objects within the church. Metonymy and synecdoche, the principal devices of realism, predominate. Through these devices Larkin exposes the limitations of the persona, and this happens because the church—and the "real" historical/cultural tradition it metonymically represents—dominates the poem. The summary offered in the final stanza deflates; the persona registers a gentlemanly propriety and generalizes that people confronted with such edifices will typically surprise themselves by realizing a "hunger" to be "more serious"—if only because "so many dead lie round." Whereas Larkin and Movement poets interact matter-of-factly with a received historical/cultural context and respond to situations through editing and coloring particular observations—Larkin's "sprawlings of flowers" and "tense, musty unignorable silence" within the church, for instance—Hughes considers Western culture to be dead and usually interferes with the realistic illusion by intensifying his foreground action and by heightening his diction and extending formal devices such as metaphor and myth in a self-consciously visible way, to heighten the immediacy of impact.

Hughes's capacity to weld meaning and concrete metaphor in "The Dove-Breeder," to mesh tenor with vehicle, is what Hough observes when he acknowledges an "imaginative effort" that can "compass an outer object," "penetrate and transform" it, and maintain "a high tension throughout the poem" so that the meaning "runs all through" it. This imaginative effort that translates into formal craft is the *sine qua non* of the New Critical poem. Edwin Muir, in his review of *Hawk*, mistakenly asserts that Hughes "seems to be quite outside of the currents of his time," but Muir also notes this capacity to fuse disparate experience under imaginative pressure: "[Hughes's] distinguishing power is sensuous, verbal and imaginative; at his best the three are fused together."[21] In *The New Criticism* Ransom, discussing Richards's *Coleridge on Imagination*, interprets that synthetic, "esemplastic" power of the *Biographia* as the imaginative ability to penetrate beneath the surfaces of objects and events in order to interanimate tenor and vehicle, thus reconciling the opposed parts of a metaphor into a new unity.[22] In Hughes's early work this fusing power operates through consciously crafted design—Coleridge's secondary imagination. This power cannot really be learned; at best Ransom's poetry and New Critical theory performed a maieutic function, helping Hughes to become conscious of an ability that remains indigenously his own.

"The Thought Fox," one of the most memorable poems in *Hawk*, also exemplifies Hughes's imaginative capacity to weld metaphor and meaning and to sustain the fusion throughout the poem through formal design. Here Hughes explores the "realness" of psychological experience and poetic intuition. He sustains an analogical identity throughout the poem between the creative process and the forest movement of a fox into its lair. Outer and inner worlds ultimately cohere in the modernist timeless moment of creative perception. All becomes unified in the creative instant, the imagined "midnight moment's forest." "The page is printed" while a passive observer would record only a starless window and a ticking clock. Hughes personifies the exercise of creative intuition as a stealthy fox returning home. He presents the entry of imaginative insight into the ordinary mind of the writer with the concrete immediacy and sensuality of an animal's "sudden sharp hot stink"; as the animal enters its forest hole an energy arises from the poet's unconscious into his conscious life. Hughes believes that the poetic experience for both writer and reader is one of connecting the "deepest and most alien seeming powers of [one's] own mind, which are the correspondents of the outermost demon powers of space" in the poem; hence the fox entering his forest lair is also entering "the hole in the head."[23]

In the pursuit of the Western goal of his two-way journey toward Reality Hughes, like Ransom, frequently employs the imagery of husbandry and the landscapes of farming. But Hughes's purposes differ from those of the southern agrarian. The personae of Ransom's poems often receive from nature an adequate mirror of their private grief, or a soothing consolation. Occasionally, in poems such as "Vaunting Oak," nature's mutability reproves human yearnings for perfection. Or, as in "Persistent Explorer," nature's unspeakable presence ironically resists human attempts at conceptualization or visionary grandeur. Ransom's Methodist heritage and his essentially conservative outlook typically cause him to reveal human frailties and pretensions by undercutting or even dwarfing his central characters with the presence of a nature that embodies the strictures of traditional religious and philosophic truths. Hence Miller Williams writes that in Ransom's poetry the central analogies and contrasts most often "domesticate the erotic and render mundane the noble."[24]

Hughes in his early poetry, however, insists upon the human liberating capacity for self-development. Nature functions primarily on a psychological plane, as providing a libidinal imperative for growth. Landscape offers analogies and a necessary testing ground for the human capacity to accept experience and to manage it successfully. Whenever individuals evade or repress invasions of the world's body of concrete experience in Hughes's early work, the retreat into domesticity or mundaneness is presented with a disapproving, biting satire. In "Macaw and Little Miss," for instance, the daytime fondling of the caged macaw by the adolescent girl is symptomatic of a prissiness that conceals a neurotic syndrome of repressed eros. In the daytime she pokes fun at the caged bird, but at night has dreams of a warrior who comes "Smashing and burning and rending towards her loin." The macaw's fiery eyes become a "torturer's iron instrument" for drawing out the girl's unfulfilled dreams of loin-rendings. Her daytime cooings and cage-rockings amount to a childish regression, a refusal to recognize the birth of erotic desire within the self. The eruption of enraged energy in the macaw at the conclusion of the poem foretells the consequences of such repression in the girl's future:

> She caresses, whispers kisses. The blue lids stay shut.
> She strikes the cage in a tantrum and swirls out:
>> Instantly beak, wings, talons crash
>> The bars in conflagration and frenzy,
>>> And his shriek shakes the house.

Ransom's focus in a similar situation is quite different. "Janet Waking," a Ransom poem that may have formed a partial structural model for Hughes's "Macaw and Little Miss," introduces a young girl who sleeps "beautifully," but who awakens to the knowledge that her favorite hen has died. Poison from a bee sting has taken the life of her "dainty-feathered hen." But Ransom ends his poem with a sympathetically drawn portrait of an immature girl facing the incomprehensible facticity of death, one of nature's central truths:

> So there was Janet
> Kneeling on the wet grass, crying her brown hen
> (Translated far beyond the daughters of men)
> To rise and walk upon it.
>
> And weeping fast as she had breath
> Janet implored us, "Wake her from her sleep!"
> And would not be instructed in how deep
> Was the forgetful kingdom of death.

Ransom uses dramatic irony to place the reader in the more mature, privileged position of resignation to a truth that the innocent, "beautifully" sleeping girl has yet to learn, whereas Hughes's more explosive conclusion makes us apprehensive for the consequences of the girl's neurosis. Hughes takes the gentle irony of Ransom's sleep/waking contrast and invests it with purposeful psychology. The animal in the Hughes poem is also more directly integrated into the main theme of the poem: the writhings of the caged macaw become a concrete visual symbol of the girl's buried erotic life. Ransom's catharsis evokes pity for another; Hughes's evokes a fear that the girl's mismanaged psychic life—her repressed, caged eros—may lead to her own future undoing. Satire always works to ridicule refusals of concrete experience in *The Hawk in the Rain*; "Secretary," "Egghead," "Famous Poet," "Two Wise Generals," and "The Hag" are other prominent examples.

Hughes's penchant for underscoring decisive action with muscular diction occasionally results in crowded imagery or strained verbal or syntactical effects. But the meaning-bearing structural oppositions, extended metaphors, and dramatic interest typically moderate and contain the imperfections. The line "By the bang of blood in the brain deaf the ear" in "The Jaguar" is certainly overdone: the syntax is contorted and the consonance labored. In the poem's context, however, the effect is purposeful, for it aptly describes a rage so compelling that it mesmerizes the attention of the normally apathetic onlookers at the zoo. This points the reader toward the poem's center, where the jaguar embodies the positive cultural value that the poet places upon energy over indolence.

When individual lines are taken out of context, even as polished a craftsman as Ransom can be guilty of contorted syntax or a wooden, awkwardly latinate or germanic diction: consider "Deep in the belly of a lugubrious wight" ("Necrological"), or "Grey doves from the officious tower illsped" ("The Equilibrists"). In context, of course, we do not dwell on such lines, for the musical effects of Ransom's diction and the fresh surprises of his rhymes subsume the occasional weak line into the overall structure and tone of the poem. In Hughes's case the strength of the extended metaphors and his power of imaginative conception absorb the reader's interest and moderate the effects of the occasional weak line. In his review of *Hawk* Alan Brownjohn decries what he considers to be Hughes's excess of diction. Others have followed suit over the years, especially in the wake of *Crow*. The judgment is occasionally valid in the specific instance, but too often these critics jump from the specific instance to generalizations about a retreat to an emulation of nihilistic violence.[25] But this is special pleading, for these critics systematically fail to consider the esthetic and philosophical purposes behind Hughes's choices of form, technique, and structure.

Hughes does become carried away with a musclebound rhetoric in a few isolated passages in *The Hawk in the Rain*. In the title poem of the volume he contrasts the hawk's effortlessness with the arduous effort of the persona to rise from the mud of temporal meaninglessness. The development of this structural contrast is careful and balanced, but overly adorned with insistently muscular verbiage and strings of consonants dominated by harsh gutturals and plosives. Here deliberate neo-Romantic effects such as "Bloodily grabbed dazed last-moment-counting / Morsel in the earth's mouth" simply do not age well. In "Phaetons" Hughes conveys a sense of how difficult it is for the young poet to manage his emotions in verse, but since nowhere else in Hughes's work does one find such neo-Romantic exaggerations, one concludes that Hughes was simply experimenting with the idioms of several of the poets he admired at the time. Concerning the above-quoted line, one cannot forget that Dylan Thomas—with his gnarled assonance, tortuous syntax, and mitotic image progression—was lionized in his last American tour less than half a decade before the publication of *Hawk*. The New Critics rehabilitated Donne and metaphysical poetry in the forties and early fifties; the metaphysical conceits—another idiom that Hughes dropped after *Hawk*—of "Incompatibilities," "Egghead," and "Fair Choice" could derive from the poet's passionate love of Shakespeare, enriched by the rejuvenation of critical interest in metaphysical poetry that the New Critics effected. The periodic rhythm and heated rhetorical admonishment at the end of "Egghead," for instance, sound very much like Hamlet's reproach of his mother in the closet scene (especially III:iii:193–97).

In the poems where he consciously adopts figures and archaic language from past historical periods, Hughes structures a deliberate mythic method formal counterpoint throughout *Hawk* to reinforce his Western quest for vitality through historical experience. The hunting prowess of the medieval lord ("A Modest Proposal"), the tragicomic sobriety of the Renaissance humanist ("Fallgrief's Girl-Friends"), the splenetic ("Fair Choice," "Complaint") or misanthropic Jacobean ("Soliloquy of a Misanthrope"), and the amoral Romantic isolato ("Invitation to the Dance")—all these character types cry out their passionate engagement in the moment of lived experience. In contrast, the contemporary urbanites in *Hawk* ("Secretary," "Famous Poet," "The Hag," "Vampire," "Egghead," "Macaw and Little Miss," and to some extent "Parlour-Piece") live in a spiritless present and are satirized for their defense mechanisms and the sophistries of reason that wall out involvement in the moment. Through this structural juxtaposition Hughes makes a frontal assault on the contemporary English sensibility, by subtly parading before the eyes of his readers concentrated scenes from the literary history of England, to warn his compatriots against a loss of nerve that threatens to deaden its cultural roots and cripple its character.

Hughes's ability to balance oppositions within complex structural designs typically moderates the occasional rhetorical excess. He achieves this harmony by adhering to a central facet of the New Criticism articulated by Brooks and Ransom. The gist of Ransom's pronouncement, borrowed from Coleridge, that the poem ought to achieve a "balance or reconciliation of opposite or discordant qualities" appears in Hughes's first statement on poetics.[26] Mixing war and musical metaphors, Hughes writes that he creates an "inner figure of stresses" by sending musical champions from the body, heart, and mind, onto the battleground of the poem. Then he affirms that he "brings to peace all the feelings and energies" by "resolv[ing] the whole uproar into as formal and balanced a figure of melody and rhythm as [he] can. When all the words are hearing each other clearly, and every stress is feeling every other stress, and all are contented—the poem is finished."[27] Hughes's comment about creating an "inner figure of stresses" and his musical metaphor paraphrase rather closely Cleanth Brooks's central definition of the structure of a poem, in *The Well Wrought Urn*: "The essential structure of a poem . . . resembles that of architecture or painting: it is a pattern of resolved stresses. Or, to move closer still to poetry by considering the temporal arts, the structure of a poem resembles that of a ballet or musical composition. It is a pattern of resolutions and balances and harmonizations, developed through a temporal scheme."[28]

In their criticism the New Critics emphasize structural reconciliations of disparate forces in the poem to some extent as a reaction to the emerging scientific myth of twentieth-century culture. Poems can be understood, the New Critics believe, without recourse to impressionistic exegesis or purely biographical reference; the poem-as-poem can be analyzed through the application of clear rules and a carefully defined methodology. Though poetry as a discipline is not as exact as laboratory science, it incorporates more of the concrete welter of actual experience (Ransom's "thick *dinglich* substance" of the world's body) in its images and metaphoric vehicles and then resolves such experience in ways that maintain a sense of the integrity and complexity of daily living. Poetry therefore is truer to life *as it is lived* than the abstract laws of science, which operate in the unreality of ideal laboratory conditions and usually do not enlighten us about how to manage our daily lives. Brooks believes that the complex structural patterns of New Critical poems are more true to life than scientific abstractions because the poet's attentiveness to concrete images and structural pressures (through irony, contrast, paradox, ambiguity, and formal design) acknowledges and survives "the complexities and contradictions of experience." Brooks avers that in this way poetry "preserves the unity of experience": its richness and resistance to univocal formulas "triumphs over the apparently contradictory and conflicting elements of experience by unifying them into a new pattern."[29]

Many poems in *The Hawk in the Rain* reveal a New Critical influence through sustaining a tautly balanced but unresolved opposition throughout the poem, as in the counterpoint of honor and desire in Ransom's "The Equilibrists." Or the surprise of a final paradox partially resolves a tension of opposites. In such cases the unresolved or partially resolved tension schools the psyche with an adult lesson in "real" living. One of the best examples of an unresolved tension of opposites that Hughes unifies through formal dexterity in *The Hawk in the Rain* is "Parlour-Piece." As the setting of a languid summer evening on the front porch in Ransom's "Piazza Piece" reveals the southern belle's fragile romanticism, so the afternoon tea in "Parlour-Piece" represents an undercurrent of inhibited resignation to convention. The lovers' silence, in preferring not to engage in small talk, is an indication of their mutual regard, but diction and modifying phrases qualify the experience with counterpoint. "Pale cool tea" chaperones an afternoon where the lovers strain toward the fire of experience, but refuse its expression. The small talk could be "strawy small talk"—tinder for their passion. Is their refusal to speak a mature recognition of the limitations of the situation or an awkward submission to the conventions of the afternoon tea? Artfully juxtaposed diction stretches both inferences to a taut ambiguity, as the lovers hypnotize themselves into a stillness "Where fire and flood strained." The reader feels both the ardor of their passion and the social restraint that douses it—the "Pale cool tea" and teatime proprieties. The formal counterpoint directs us to the hidden conflicts—the "proprieties" Hughes encountered when he courted Sylvia Plath, the Fulbright poet, under the matronly protection of Newnham College, Cambridge, and the social pressures that caused weeks of anxiety over expulsion should Plath announce their engagement before her graduation.

A resolution of the struggle between evolution and regression informs the structure and content of another typical *Hawk* poem. In "Childbirth" Hughes presents the woman's ordeal both as an elemental confrontation with the world's body of concrete experience, as an "instant of struggling and blood," and as an example of a power in nature that can defeat the forces of genetic regression, forces that Freud believed are potentially operative in every generation.[30] Hence childbirth for Hughes is a confrontation between nature's evolutionary forces and the aggressive urge to-ward deterioration in the species that Freud recognized in his concept of the primal horde:

> Through that miracle-breached bed
> All the dead could have got back;
> With a shriek and heave and spout of blood

> The huge-eyed looming horde from
> Under the floor of the heart, that run
> To the madman's eye-corner came
> Deafening towards light

Paradox, reinforced by more subdued diction, finally resolves the tension; the child at birth, at its most helpless moment, yet possesses all of nature's evolutionary power to replace chaos with cosmos:

> whereon

> A child whimpered upon the bed,
> Frowning ten-toed, ten-fingered birth
> Put the skull back about the head
> Righted the stagger of the earth.

"The commonplace became so strange," another line from the poem, could serve as a subtitle for the entire volume. Only in confronting the unex-pected in the concrete, physical moment is life lived purposefully, accord-ing to Hughes.

The most elaborate and successful example of a partially resolved ten-sion of opposites in *The Hawk in the Rain* occurs in "The Martyrdom of Bishop Farrar." Paradox and reversal function both as tools of intelligible New Critical structure in this poem and as an affirmation of Ransom's pref-erence for the incorporation of the world's body of concrete experience. Hughes presents a vivid, believable historical portrait of frail townsfolk struggling to comprehend the extraordinary faith of Farrar amid the reli-gious and political power struggle of the late Renaissance. Bloody Mary and Farrar attempt to impress opposing interpretations of this burning at the stake upon the townspeople, who initially stand, like the reader of the poem, in an uncomfortably ambiguous position. The paradoxical reversal begun in stanza IV, however, at least partially resolves the ambiguity, for it asserts that the key to the hearts and minds of the townsfolk lies not in Bloody Mary's conceptualization of the event as a moral example, but in the sensuous immediacy of undergoing the physical ordeal—a device Farrar is so certain of that he is willing to trade his life for its effect. The "black oozing twist of stuff bubbles" from the steaming wood and the prelate's silent endurance of his agony burn his wordless beliefs to heaven, to be tongued with Pentecostal fire. Experience becomes the best proselytizer; its argument persuades better than any sermon and is pocketed hot by the townsfolk.

Yet, after the empathy and the final catharsis, the reader still retains an undercurrent of fear—a fear of the extremity of Farrar's situation and of the radical nature of his response—so that the tension is only partly relaxed. Hughes resolves his "inner figure of stresses" in a way that leaves the reader with a sense of the ambiguous aftertaste of "real" experience, for the heroism that enriches Farrar's public worth also impoverishes his private agony:

> Gave all he had, and yet the bargain struck
> To a merest farthing his whole agony,
> His body's cold-kept miserdom of shrieks
> He gave uncounted, while out of his eyes,
> Out of his mouth, fire like a glory broke,
> And smoke burned his sermons into the skies.

Farrar, in establishing ownership of his flock through an "ignorant" or wordless means, undercuts all his years of pastoral work: the physical ordeal burns his sermons to smoke. Hughes's facility with ambiguity also allows him to accentuate the unnaturalness of Farrar's refusal to express his pain.

Besting Bloody Mary in the actual historical context is not, however, the central point of the poem, for the modernist poet is more concerned with evaluating a potentially usable past than interacting with it. Here Hughes isolates both the heat of pre-Industrial Revolution Protestant conviction and the chilling "cold-kept miserdom" of its idealism. Hughes, a Farrar on his mother's side (*née* Edith Farrar), is identifying both a personal and a national inheritance. As in "Two Wise Generals," a past historical context serves only to introduce a foregrounded dramatic action that is the product of a free-flowing, omnitemporal modernist imagination. Even in the war poems of *Hawk*, vitality and survival in the present moment, or ironic variations thereof, command the focus of the poem. The context functions as nature's testing ground for this Western urge toward vitality in the moment of lived experience. In the "mythical method" formal contrast of the entire volume, we note that pre–twentieth century personae or untainted rural types are more successful at this test than contemporary urbanites.

John L. Stewart writes that "balancing opposing forces within a harmonious and unified order is the fundamental principle of Ransom's style and the communication of his unique vision of man."[31] What Hughes especially shares with the southern agrarian is the knowledge of life that motivates these formal balancing acts, the understanding of the man of the soil that the poem distills into esthetic form—especially the recognition that reality resists the visions of the Romantic idealist. An ironic vision often precipitates from partial resolutions of real-life stresses. In essays from *The Fugitive* such as "Thoughts on the Poetic Discontent" (June 1925), Ransom speaks of the ironic mode as the twentieth-century poet's acknowledgment of the failure of science to allow human domination of the environment through abstractions. This recognition of the inadequacy of reason as the sole guide derives as much from the counsel of the land, the weather, and the elements as from Ransom's southern Calvinist heritage. Studying Ransom's work may have caused Hughes to realize the potential of the rural Yorkshire portion of his roots for his art.

In poems such as "Meeting," "Two Wise Generals," and "Six Young Men," Hughes develops ironic confrontations to qualify human faith in the power to control experience through the exercise of reason. In "Meeting" the central character, who initially sees in the mirror a man confidently in control of his abilities, progresses toward a deeper self-scrutiny in a recollection of personal vulnerability, a confrontation with a black goat on a mountain slope. The "square-pupilled" and "yellow-eyed" look of the goat develops naturally from the central situation of self-scrutiny at the mirror; the extensional animal becomes a concrete metaphor for the character's buried psychological life. Initial confidence in one's public persona or "role" (line 3) may, upon further scrutiny, lead to a confrontation with previously unrecognized, darker forces within the personality—what Jung has called the encounter with the Shadow. Curiously enough, Jung once wrote that gazing into a mirror can precipitate such a confrontation: "Whoever goes to himself risks confrontation with himself. The mirror does not flatter, it faithfully shows whatever looks into it; namely, the face we never show to the world because we cover it with the persona, the mask of the actor. But the mirror lies behind the mask and shows the true face."[32] The mirror-gazer initially feels confident enough to "outloom life like Faustus," but deeper probing reveals repressed uncertainty. Hughes's imaginative grasp penetrates beneath the surface memory to confront the "yellow-eyed" chthonic energies, lodged at the bottom of the psyche, that loom "like a living hanging hemisphere." The ironic ending readjusts the initial overconfidence to a healthier, more realistic norm.

The ironic contrast that informs the subject matter of "Two Wise Generals" involves a comparison of the efforts of Black Douglas, the Scottish nobleman who died in 1330 en route to Palestine, where he expected to bury the heart of his dead king Robert II, with the cynicism and effete rationalism of the "wise" generals. Diction reinforces the contrast. The decisive, action-oriented Black Douglas "hacked for the casked heart" and advanced "breakneck with blood." This sinewy consonance appears preferable to the pedestrian command to divide the spoils, or the thin, hollow "twinkled their armies." The generals appear to be wise in acknowledging their age, safety, and creature comforts, and their sophisticated awareness of how civilization has sadly advanced beyond the time when individual deeds of valor won the day. But they are blind in their unrealistic belief that outbursts of violence in war can be palliated by a reasonable dividing of lands amid the parading of status and medals. This static retreat from experience, in a setting complete with bottle and "lit" tent, proves inadequate; subordinates have taken the matter into their own hands with night raids that cancel out both armies. Black Douglas, killed fighting the Moors in Spain en route to the burial of his dead king's heart, emerges as the preferable man of decisive action, while the last line of the poem reveals the "wise" generals as victims of their own rationalizations.

Hughes builds a complex ironic vision from the paradoxical nature of a photograph in "Six Young Men." Irony and paradox reveal the complex feelings of the persona, which the structure resolves into a balanced figure of inner stresses. The World War I historical context enters the poem only obliquely. In the photo the setting and postures of the men appear unremarkable, as predictably ordinary as in most holiday photos. The awkward posturings and then-fashionable clothing of these men are also as familiar to the persona as those of any group on a "Sunday jaunt." Their casual demeanor recollects endearing memories of their quintessentially human worth as representative, ordinary men. Yet the stasis of the photo also brings an insidious reminder of the group's fate, for to a man they died in World War I. The intrusion of a bullet's split second, like a camera's flash, has permanently quelled their "smoking blood." The irony quickly becomes compounded. As the static photo comes to life for the persona, recollections of their several moments of death intrude. Furthermore, though landmarks in the photo endure in the landscape, the bodies of the men do not, and nature appears indifferent to their absence: "And still that valley has not changed its sound / Though their faces are four decades under the ground." The resolution of these multiple ironies at the conclusion of the poem, in the simple statement of the persona's grief, also reconciles the conflicting feelings that the poem arouses—sympathy, regret, and a sorrow that contains a genuine element of pathos. The poem rings true to the complex emotions often elicited by poignant experiences of loss; Hughes weighs and reconciles these emotions with sophistication and tact.

For Brooks the devices of irony and paradox serve to dramatize an experience, which is preferable to direct statement. Irony and paradox also unify antithetical aspects of experience, and so provide a "simulacrum" of the unity we perceive in our involvement in life, in a way that transcends the conventional.[33] As in "Childbirth," Hughes employs paradox in "The Jaguar" to dramatize a compelling intrusion of vitality into the humdrum of daily living. The poem opens with a static situation of an ordinary hot summer day at the zoo, where indolent animals lie still as fossils, and "The apes yawn and adore their fleas in the sun." Stanza III, however, introduces the frenzy of the jaguar into the foregound of this vapid contemporary context. The jaguar's eye is "satisfied to be blind in fire," but his continual striding across the cage floor reveals a highly unsatisfied vital energy that seems inexhaustible. Though more confined, the jaguar has infinitely more vitality than the crowd and therefore always mesmerizes it. A second paradox follows: the caged animal also exercises more freedom in his deliberate expenditure of energy than the physically unconfined audience. The jaguar scorns the bars of his cage, preferring to stalk the wilderness of an inner world:

> there's no cage to him

> More than to the visionary his cell:
> His stride is wildernesses of freedom:
> The world rolls under the long thrust of his heel.
> Over the cage floor the horizons come.

Each of the last three lines convinces not by straightforward summary statement, but by synecdoches ("stride," "heel") meshed with imagery that suggests the expansiveness of the jaguar's inner freedom.

The jaguar's activity reinforces the premium Hughes places upon vitality in his fifties Western journey toward Reality. The squeamish "Secretary" and defensive "Egghead" are satirized for their lack of it, but it intrudes in quaint old ladies' parlors ("Macaw and Little Miss"), and even in farmers' fields ("The Casualty") and the purlieus of ministers ("The Conversion of the Reverend Skinner"). The real cultural context behind many of the poems of *Hawk* is that of the Angries' revolt against inertia: the accusations, often hurled by artists with working-class roots, about intellectual and social stagnation in the middle class and aristocracy in postwar England. The virile impatience of Osborne's Jimmy Porter in *Look Back in Anger* (also 1957) is of a piece with many *Hawk* poems, though Jimmy's irony is more blunt and abrasive:

Why do I spend ninepence on the damned paper every week? Nobody reads it except me. Nobody can be bothered. No one can raise themselves out of their delicious sloth. . . . Oh heavens, how I long for a little ordinary human enthusiasm. Just enthusiasm—that's all. I want to hear a warm, thrilling voice cry out Hallelujah! (*He bangs his breast theatrically.*) Hallelujah! I'm alive! I've an idea. Why don't we have a little game? Let's pretend that we're human beings, and that we're actually alive. Just for awhile. What do you say? Let's pretend we're human.[34]

Occasionally, when New Critical devices are absent, the rhetoric in a *Hawk* poem generates too much unchecked heat. Dramatic monologues overly adorned with metaphysical conceits and periphrasis, as in "Fair Choice," "Complaint," and "Incompatibilities," can become bewildering. "Egghead," a satire on the defense mechanisms of the Freudian ego, depends too entirely upon direct, declamatory statement to achieve its effect. The persona dances like Jimmy Porter at the edge of his irritability, and his rhetoric is left unqualified by irony, paradox, structural oppositions, or a concrete dramatic setting, to moderate or contain its energies. Diction becomes too insistent and exaggerated in phrases like "circumventing sleights / Of stupefaction, juggleries of benumbing. . . ."

Normally, however, the New Critical formal devices, the dramatic effects, and the strongly developed personae moderate the rhetoric and distance the subject matter of the poems so to enlist, not hypnotize, the reader's critical faculties. In the title poem of the volume, for instance, the hawk's controlled muscular effort, which allows him to dominate the landscape so effortlessly, is the ideal residing at the center of a spatial contrast. A paradox, and the dramatic setting from which it arises, moderates the poem's rhetorical energies. The effortless dominance of the hawk is the central point of orientation for the persona's struggles, a polestar to a drowning seaman. The polestar and fulcrum images lead us toward the eye of the tornado, away from the turbulence of temporality, to the moment of "weightless quiet," that center of self-control where "the hawk hangs still." The artifice controls the reader's vision of the dramatic scene and just manages to balance the poem's rhetorical effects. Structure and content interpenetrate in New Critical form: a central theme of the poem concerns the persona's desire to organize his turbulent emotional life and to develop his esthetic gifts through effort and willpower. As he does so, he also raises nature to the level of culture and resolves the tensions into formal balance. The alternately kinetic and restful diction underscores this contrast: the hawk controls the "banging wind" and the "drumming ploughland" in a "weightless quiet, / Steady as a hallucination in the streaming air."

Actually, though agreements in craft and theory are central portions of the "model" that Ransom provides Hughes, what initially attracted Hughes to Ransom was the richness of character and strength of speaking voice in the personae of his poems.[35] Ransom's personae are typically engaged in sifting and evaluating experience in the course of the poem and exhibit an eccentric playfulness of wit; a vernacular speech heightened and occasionally spiced with elliptical syntax, erudition, and archaisms; and a warm, engagingly personal tone. His unique blend of homespun, culture, and craft invited Hughes to tap his knowledge of rural Yorkshire and his university reading in Elizabethan and Jacobean drama. Through his poems Ransom suggested to Hughes ways of utilizing *dramatis personae*, and ways of condensing, telescoping, and sharpening the focus of dramatic encounters. But the attitude toward experience in Hughes is much more positive, and the energy and vitality of his poetic line couples with his native English roots to create fresh, unique poetry.

The more one reads *The Hawk in the Rain*, the more one recognizes how Hughes's adoption of New Critical theory and techniques facilitated the articulation of a fine maturity in the variety of poems dealing with allotropic states of love and passion. Hughes understands the paradoxes of freedom in the love bond, and isolation in forced conquest ("Two Phases"). He explores the destructive anxiety behind possessive love ("Incompatibilities") and grudgingly recognizes the restrictions of courting conventions ("Parlour-Piece"). He fears the consequences of repressed love ("Macaw and Little Miss") and understands the gnawing pains of severance ("The Decay of Vanity"), the honesty of one who loves from existential need ("Billet-Doux"), the pressures of competition between lovers ("A Modest Proposal"), and the turbulence of the onset of love in the male ("The Dove-

Breeder"). He even probes the probable physical reality beneath the religious sublimation of love ("Complaint"). "Song" and "September," two more straightforwardly lyrical love poems, articulate a visionary transcendence of time in the mutuality of the love embrace. Absorption in the fully experienced concrete moment of the world's body allows one to transcend the limits of isolated selfhood. In such fleeting moments Hughes's imaginative power interanimates self, other, and world, to create in "September" a moment of mystic calm and oneness, a unitive reconciliation of all experience where the intensity of the foregrounded dramatic situation all but obliterates the actual historical context:

> We sit late, watching the dark slowly unfold:
> No clock counts this.
> When kisses are repeated and the arms hold
> There is no telling where time is.

> It is midsummer: the leaves hang big and still:
> Behind the eye a star,
> Under the silk of the wrist a sea, tell
> Time is nowhere.

Conversely, "A Modest Proposal" presents love degenerating into divisive competition. Instead of making the "two-line point after the statutory ration of descriptive imagery" that Hough finds in Movement poetry, Hughes portrays the irascibility and the anxiety beneath competition through an extended metaphor of two wolves skirmishing for dominance over each other and for possession of the entire forest. Beneath the irascibility lies an egotism so omnivorous that neither is able to sleep or hunt until "the other's body and the whole wood is its own." Alternately each attacks the other with taunts and insults and then retreats to thickets of introversion to lick psychological wounds that fester into hatred. Both become obsessed with some "mad final satisfaction." As in "The Dove-Breeder," Hughes's use of the extended metaphor to fuse meaning with content in a dramatic encounter conveys the experience more vividly and adequately than a realistic presentation of lover-poets engaged in the stresses of achieving public recognition. The opening of "A Modest Proposal" recollects the speech on order by Ulysses in *Troilus and Cressida* (I : iii), where concord degenerating into oppugnancy appears in its last stage as the omnivorous "universal wolf" of appetite.

A purposeful formal contrast balances these negative stresses at the conclusion of the poem. Suddenly the wolves perceive the great lord riding by, in unity with his greyhounds in the stable social role of hunting in medieval society, a role that channels aggressive impulses into socially approved activity. The peering wolves recognize the concord and the sanguine relationship with nature in this medieval pageantry, but will never attain it themselves. The last six lines evoke the ebullience and prowess of Bertilak and his hounds bringing down the hind in part III of *Sir Gawain and the Green Knight*. As the title allusion to the Swift satire implies, the wolves will doubtless revert to maiming each other. Eyes that shine "brighter than is natural" reveal egocentric cravings that promote a chronic maladaptation to the outer world.

As previously discussed, the New Critical fusing of the poet's intensional meaning with the extensional substance of the world's body of concrete experience originates in a basically Coleridgean concept of the imagination. In his second "Myth and Education" essay Hughes writes that "outer world and inner world are interdependent at every moment," that imagination "embraces both worlds simultaneously," and that tales and myths are "blueprints" for organizing the inner world and managing the give and take between our ordinary objective life and our deepest psychic energies. In one central passage Hughes describes the larger spiritual and social consequences of fusing the inner and outer worlds:

> This really is imagination. This is the faculty we mean when we talk about the imagination of the great artists. The character of great works is exactly this: that in them the full presence of the inner world combines with and is reconciled to the full presence of the outer world. And in them we see that the laws of these two worlds are not contradictory at all; they are one all-inclusive system. . . . We recognize these works because we are all struggling to find those laws, as a man on a tightrope struggling for balance, because they are the formula that reconciles everything, and balances every imbalance. . . . The inner world, separated from the outer world, is a place of demons. The outer world, separated from the inner world, is a place of meaningless objects and machines. The faculty that makes the human being out of these two worlds is called divine. That is only a way of saying that it is the faculty without which humanity cannot really exist. It can be called religious or visionary. More essentially, it is imagination which embraces both outer and inner worlds in a creative spirit.[36]

The power of the imagination to "reconcile" (Hughes uses the word twice in the above passage) the inner and outer worlds comes from Coleridge through Ransom: it is Coleridge's secondary imagination, a power that, in Coleridge's words, "reveals itself in the balance or reconciliation of opposite or discordant qualities."[37] For the poet this is a matter of inspired but very conscious craft. In this 1976 essay Hughes also alludes to the intuitive, visionary seizure of reality in the instant of perception—Coleridge's primary imagination—but this power does not reveal itself in Hughes's own poetry until the *Gaudete* "Epilogue" of the mid-seventies.

Of course *The Hawk in the Rain* contains poems that are not influenced by Ransom or New Critical techniques. "Roarers in a Ring" derives from the medieval ballad tradition, "Song" from Romantic prayers for inspiration like Keats's "When I Have Fears," and poems such as "The Horses," "October Dawn," "Invitation to the Dance," and "The Ancient Heroes and the Bomber Pilot" depend primarily upon a rightness of mood and tone rather than the pyrotechnics of New Critical metaphor and structure. Many of the war poems convey an Audenesque disenchantment and understatement. But the majority of the poems in *Hawk* are deeply imbued with a New Critical emphasis upon concrete and extended metaphors; the fusion of tenor and vehicle or intensional and extensional worlds; the copious use of ambiguity, irony, and paradox; and structural balances empowered by a Coleridgean imagination.

The foregoing discussion of New Critical influences in *The Hawk in the Rain* indicates that the often astonishing virtuosity that we have periodically come to expect from Hughes actually arrived full-blown in his very first volume. In *Hawk* he mastered the theory and techniques of one of the most difficult and demanding schools of poetry ever developed, one not native to current English poetry trends, and accomplished it while that school was still coming into its own in popularity. The extent of Hughes's absorption of the New Critical influence also reveals how deeply and seriously he imbued his first work with a well-organized, coherent, and consistent philosophical and esthetic rationale. This attitude toward experience changes rather immediately in *Lupercal*, but *Hawk* does indicate that we can expect a dexterity of formal organization—in both poem and volume—and a richly coherent and consistent attitude toward experience to be the earmarks of a Hughes volume.

The portrait Hughes conveys in *The Hawk in the Rain* is that of a very aloof, dexterous craftsman, a writer very assured of his technical powers, who confidently reconciles the conflicts and agonies of inner and outer experience or directs satiric barbs at those who fail to do so. Fully convinced of the validity of the Western lure to concrete action in time and cultural history, Hughes appears on the literary scene having mastered much of the best in the modern British tradition and the current American scene in his very first volume. He mounts the horse of his poetic craft with the ease and *sprezzatura* of the Renaissance horseman, his boots never touching the stirrups. He is as confident in *Hawk* as the folktale hero going out to seek his fortune and is almost as unaware as that hero of the cultural ogres and ordeals that await him in the woods. Like the persona in "Griefs for Dead Soldiers," Hughes has no difficulty conveying either the public significance of tragedy (stanza I), or the private sorrow (stanza II). The skilled, aloof craftsman reconciles the claims of each by locating, in the concrete ordeal of interment itself, an adequate metaphor for the poetic process of balancing and reconciling contraries. The grief becomes enshrined in an esthetic object for our contemplation, as the poet fuses the outer and inner worlds into a new unity, the poem itself:

> Cursing the sun that makes their work long
> Or the black lively flies that bite their wrists,
> The burial party works with a craftsman calm.
> Weighing their grief by the ounce, and burying it.

CHAPTER 3

Mouths
Clamped
Well onto
the World

Lupercal

1960

Usually, in a poem that seems to be about a bird, animal or fish, it is evident that the poet is in fact writing about some element of human nature in the guise of a creature. . . . Some of the very best [poems] . . . record the most subjective of all occasions—the visitation of an angel.

We all know this angel . . . it seems like a reminiscence of paradise, because . . . it redeems, momentarily, time and death. . . . Perhaps the paradise from which this angel comes is simply the condition of our animal selves. By this account, which some poets seem to believe, the birds, beasts and fish are still in paradise. . . . Indeed, some poets have found themselves able to embody their experience of the angel most purely and directly in the form of a creature. . . .

—Hughes, 1960[1]

Near the center of *Lupercal* rests "To Paint a Water Lily," a poem whose persona self-consciously reconciles the claims of the meat-eating dragonfly above a pond and the "Jaws for heads" below, as he paints the lily—the poem itself. The esthetic lily links both worlds, while the formal artifice balances and controls the menaces of each. The complex structure of "To Paint a Water Lily" makes it a fine New Critical poem. Yet, except for "Acrobats," it is the only New Critical poem in *Lupercal*.

The New Criticism provided Hughes with a perfect apprenticeship in structure and technique, but its limitations soon became apparent in a poet whose devotion to his art has never allowed him to repeat successes. Hughes admitted that he "felt very constricted" in writing "To Paint a Water Lily," as if he were "writing through a long winding tube" or "squeezing language out at the end of this long, remote process."[2] Following a New Critical regimen had become an encumbrance that distanced him too far from direct experience. The artifice of packing poems with oppositions and antithetical undercurrents then felt labored, and the final expected reconciliation, a transmutation of the experience onto the plane of esthetic stasis, seemed remote from the original events that prompted the poem. Resolving tensions into new unities places the poet in the position of a highly self-conscious craftsman who seldom makes direct claims upon the reader's sensibilities. To achieve the pleasure of high artifice the poet sacrifices immediacy of impact; one might even say that he predigests experience into formal design rather than communicating it afresh. Seen from this perspective, the devices employed by the New Critical craftsman conspire to limit the experience. Irony deflates rather than inspires, and paradox almost dismisses, with its illogical logic, unresolved private and public experiences that stubbornly remain in one's daily life.

Hughes's departure from the New Criticism after *The Hawk in the Rain* paralleled that of many contemporary poets in the late fifties, notably Sylvia Plath, Robert Lowell, and Charles Olson. All tired of the aloof craftsman status, because the complex artifice inhibited the expression of the poet's real feelings and the urgency of pressing situations, or because the formal structuring preinterpreted experience for the reader, or because the machinery of the craft largely excluded treatments of chronic public menaces and pressures—the Cold War and early nuclear scares, the threat of monolithic bureaucracies, and the impact of international crises like Suez, Hungary, and later Viet Nam and Czechoslovakia. When Lowell began writing "Skunk Hour" in the summer of 1957, he parted with New Critical formalism because he felt that his early style seemed "distant, symbol-ridden and willfully difficult" and because his "old poems hid what they were really about."[3] Hughes simply reminisced that his earlier approach "excluded too much of what [he] wanted to say."[4]

After "To Paint a Water Lily" Hughes wrote "View of a Pig," to attempt a more "simple concrete language," one more "authentic" and "still" than the comparatively more artificial, kinetic language of *Hawk*. After this he wrote "Pike," where the subject, setting, and straightforward treatment unlocked his past, so that the "poem became charged with particular memories and a specific obsession."[5] Like "The Hawk in the Rain," "Pike" is also a poem about writing poetry, but an entirely different kind of poetry—one more meditative, passionately involved, and closer to normal speech. In a BBC radio talk entitled "The Gentle Art" (24 February 1961), some of which later appeared in the "Capturing Animals" and "Learning to Think" chapters of *Poetry in the Making*,[6] Hughes talks about relaxing himself into a deeply meditative state while staring at his fishing float, in order to divest himself of all the arithmetic, Latin, and science that his schoolmasters banged into his head, and to activate a process of capturing real knowledge already stored in the unconscious. The pike-poem arrives, states Hughes, in a trancelike meditative state once the distractions of everyday life dissolve. Here you enter one of the orders of bliss. Your whole being rests lightly on your float, but not drowsily: very alert, so that the least twitch of the float arrives like an electric shock. And you're not only watching the float. You are aware, in a horizonless and slightly mesmerized way, like listening to the double bass in orchestral music, of the fish below there in the dark. At every moment your imagination is alarming itself with the size of the thing slowly leaving the weeds and approaching your bait. Or with the world of beauties down there, suspended in total ignorance of you. And the whole purpose of this concentrated patient excitement, in this area of apprehension and unforeseeable events, is to bring up some lovely solid thing like living metal from a world where nothing exists but those inevitable facts which raise life out of nothing and return it to nothing. It's easy enough to see how this can set the pattern for a whole style of meditation, as it did with me.[7]

From this passage we can see that the imagination in Hughes is gaining greater power and responsibility. It still thrusts its energies into the outer world, to fuse with the concrete particulars of nature, but it is *also* responsible for actually *discovering* the poet's intended meaning, as it raids the poet's personal unconscious for the innate knowledge, childhood memories, and genetic residue that reside there. Earlier in the BBC talk Hughes writes a passage, most of which later appears in the "Learning to Think" chapter of *Poetry in the Making*, that indicates that he is shifting his New Critical inner/outer balance in favor of the superiority of the inner life:

My schoolteachers evidently assumed, as most people do, that thinking is a natural activity, like your blood circulation. . . . and when a child can't answer questions in school everybody, including the child often enough, supposes he was born too dumb. The mistake here is in confusing the inner life, which is the world of final reality, the world of memory, emotion, imagination, intelligence, and natural common sense and which does go on all the time, consciously or unconsciously, like the heart beat, with the process by which we break into that inner life and capture answers and evidence to support the answers, out of it. That process of raid, or persuasion, or ambush, or dogged hunting, or surrender, is the kind of thinking we have to learn. . . .

In another BBC radio program ("Creatures of the Air": 26 June 1962), Hughes discusses the genesis of "Hawk Roosting" in broadly New Critical terms: "So every poem, not only poems about birds, is an armed truce between the life of energy inside men and the facts of the world outside, after severe fighting and heavy losses on both sides. Every poem is both a violation of the facts it uses and a violation of what we feel about the facts."[8] This may appear to be very much like Ransom's idea of the struggle between the author's intended or determinate meaning and meter and indeterminacy—the metrical, linguistic, and referential demands that cause modifications of the poet's original intentions in the process of writing the poem.[9] But the phrase "life of energy inside men" and the passage about imaginative raids upon the unconscious are very un-Ransomlike. A larger edifice is being erected upon the New Critical foundation.

Whenever Hughes speaks of the imagination in the early sixties BBC talks, he speaks of becoming passionately involved in living the experience with one's whole being. "See it and live it," says Hughes; "grip hold of it with your imagination, and never let it go till you had studied every grain of it"—even if you need to tear bedspreads to pieces with your teeth to imagine a character's anguish, as Balzac once did.[10] In the epigraph to this chapter, a quotation from a BBC radio program ("Creatures": 5 May 1960) broadcast just two months after the publication of *Lupercal*, Hughes writes of *embodying* a numinous subjective experience in the form of a creature. In that same talk he speaks admiringly of Marianne Moore's "The Frigate Pelican," for Moore, according to Hughes, "fuses the detail of her subject and her delight in it, in a way that becomes very pure and selfless celebration of the bird." Poetry for Hughes now becomes the embodiment of one's whole inner being in a meditative, imaginative grasp of an external object or event. The Coleridgean/New Critical fruit is aging into Yeatsian wine.

The passionate involvement of the entire personality *living* the experience in the moment, delighting in it, and fusing with the object or event in the full rush of the poet's total attention is exactly Yeats in his major phase. Hughes, who admitted to being "spellbound" by Yeats's poetry, folklore, and magic "for about six years," and who claimed to know "the whole of Yeats's *Collected Poems*, including the longer ones, off by heart,"[11] began "The Gentle Art" with an allusion to Yeats as his mentor for learning how to think imaginatively. Late in his life Yeats wrote that he strove to develop a poetry of "impersonal meditation" conveyed in the language of "passionate, normal speech" that "comes most naturally when we soliloquise."[12] With this voice the poet can articulate meditations and feelings more directly to the reader, without an elaborate, distancing apparatus. He can also convey his own passionate engagement with knots of obsessions that can lead him, if he is capable, to moments similar to those marvelously sudden shifts in worlds of reference, and sudden enlargements of vision, in "Among School Children" and "The Second Coming." The famous statement by Yeats, "Man can embody truth but he cannot know it,"[13] receives a gloss from the Yeats scholar Thomas Parkinson that suits Hughes's *Lupercal* phase equally well: "Objective knowledge and personal expression become identified so that the man disappears into his total apprehension of reality: expression is a part of study, study is the process of experience, poetry is that stabilized (embodied) process, truth."[14]

"Pike," the poem that reviewers of *Lupercal* consistently singled out for their highest praise, not only conveys vividly realized images of these "killers from the egg," but a complete capture of their essence through an imaginative grasp that rivets itself to both the surface action and the depth significance of the animal. Throughout Hughes sustains a disquieting, eerie mood—exactly that of something coming out of the depths that we await with great apprehension because it somehow has a claim upon our souls. Though the language is simple and direct, it is not flaccid; we are never allowed to relax, shift our gaze from the threat that the pike pose, or set aside inklings that an affinity exists with forces within us that we normally refuse to inspect:

> In ponds, under the heat-struck lily pads—
> Gloom of their stillness:
> Logged on last year's black leaves, watching upwards.
> Or hung in an amber cavern of weeds
>
> The jaws' hooked clamp and fangs
> Not to be changed at this date;
> A life subdued to its instrument;
> The gills kneading quietly, and the pectorals.[15]

After these clear, hypnotically objective images come the terse and gruesome anecdotes of pike cannibalism. In the second, the persona discovers two six-pound pike, with "One jammed past its gills down the other's gullet: / The outside eye stared: as a vice locks"; this unforgettable image and perfectly suited simile present concrete, chilling reminders of the predatory in all animals.

"Pike" possesses the power to touch the reader's mind more deeply through an incremental process of imaginative insight than through the ornate artifice of *Hawk*. For without the slightest disturbance of a mood as deeply meditative as that moment of stillness between the second and third movements of Beethoven's *Fourth Piano Concerto*, the persona recognizes in an instantaneous moment of lucidity that he is fishing in a pond "as deep as England," one that contained "Pike too immense to stir." The reader suddenly remembers earlier phrases such as "the malevolent aged grin" with its "sag belly" and immediately recognizes that the poem's real subject is comprehending the genetic aggression in the history of a nation. This is a prime example of one of those sudden Yeatsian shifts in worlds of reference and enlargements of vision, arriving in this case with perfect naturalness and ease, without disturbing the mood of meditative calm, and without the need for emotional invocations or apostrophes (as in Yeats's "O Presences / That passion, piety or affection knows"). The ripples of meaning have spread out with perfect inevitability, and with the imagination progressing incrementally in its grasp of depth and significance, like the successive waves of discovery entering the consciousness of the persona in Pound's *periplum*. The final two stanzas of the poem slowly ease the accumulated tension, while the allusion "With the hair frozen on my head" provides us with the proper contextual frame—the ecstatic astonishment of a visitation of numinous Power, akin to those experienced in Old Testament prophetic works such as Job (4:14–15): "Fear came upon me, and trembling, which made all my bones to shake. Then a spirit passed before my face; the hair of my flesh stood up." The art of "Pike" appears artless, yet is a very subtle ordering of the reader's perceptions through a formal organization that simulates the moment of imaginative perception.

Some of the more penetrating reviewers caught the completeness of the imaginative seizures in the major poems of *Lupercal*, though without noticing the essentially Yeatsian craft. Stanley Kunitz wrote that *Lupercal* contained poetry "so steeped in the true element" that it transcended labeling into school or coterie; he admired how the poems "seem to be all process," but soon the reader discovers, "in a marvel of knowing, that they are completely things."[16] Alun Jones affirmed that Hughes "is fully engaged by the experience itself and completely immersed in the material of that experience," and John Holmes agreed that "the poet all but becomes what he observes."[17] E. Lucas Myers was equally perceptive: "Drawn from an uncommon endowment (of visual imagination and intelligence especially), which has undergone uncommon development, the elements of his poems fuse in the act of composition, and leave the finished work with an absolute immediacy, nothing to come between the object and the experience of it."[18]

If Hughes endows his inner world with greater imaginative powers in *Lupercal*, he also perceives more life and energy in his outer world, especially in his animals. The Cambridge anthropology studies become accessible to his poetic world in *Lupercal*. In the 1965 interview with John Horder, devoted entirely to *Lupercal*, Hughes states that he tried to present his animals as living "continually in a state of energy," which "arises from their complete unity with whatever divinity they have."[19] This "energy" and "divinity" mesh with Hughes's 1960 statements, reprinted in the epigraph to this chapter, about angelic, paradisal reminders of our animal selves. These comments indicate that the animal poems in *Lupercal* are to be understood within the context of primitive theriomorphism.

Anthropologists and students of comparative religion have long known that primitive people experienced revelations and intuitions of divinity in animal (theriomorphic) as well as human (anthropomorphic) forms. Joseph Campbell's discussion of the ritual behind the cave drawings of the bison in the crypt of Lascaux is one of numerous examples.[20] According to Mircea Eliade, "animals can reveal the secrets of the future because they are thought to be receptacles for the souls of the dead or epiphanies of the gods."[21] Eliade discusses the role of animals in shamanic trance, where they appear as protecting and helping spirits and, as the shaman mimics their sounds and movements, proof of converse and friendship with subhuman as well as superhuman realms.[22] This, to Eliade, was the case in *illo tempore*, the primordial, paradisal condition before the Fall, before the separation into superhuman, human, and subhuman realms.[23] Though the average Westerner's knowledge of myth stems from our anthropomorphic, Greco-Roman-Christian culture, Heinrich Zimmer, in his *Myths and Symbols in Indian Art and Civilization*, records the strong tendency of Indian myth to posit significance in the theriomorphic animal counterparts of Viṣṇu, Śiva, Gaṇeśa, and others in the Hindu pantheon. Theriomorphism also dominates primitive European cultures, Egyptian culture, the North American Indian, and most primitive cultures of the southern hemisphere, as the work of Campbell, Radin, Lévi-Strauss, and certain others amply proves.

In a BBC radio interview with Alfred Alvarez ("Poetry and Performance, IV": 2 August 1960), Hughes extends this idea of paradisal theriomorphic energy in animals to create an anthropological dissociation of sensibility in English history, a dissociation that becomes an important theme in many of his volumes. According to Hughes, the first part of "An Otter" presents the otter's nostalgia for an earlier paradisal existence; in the second the otter is a survivor who must expend a limitless amount of nervous energy to remain alive in the hunt of modern civilization. The point of cleavage for Paradise and Fall is the Roman Conquest:

While I was writing ["An Otter"] I was reading a great deal of old English history, in other words pre-Conquest history; and this notion of the life in England, and particularly of the life of the animals in England, carrying on from generation to generation, and through all the historical eruptions that were going over them, this life continues as a single life, as a single thread of life. So that, in fact, in the first part I speak about not generations of otters but one otter, as if the one otter were thousands of years old, and were a pre-historic animal surviving, and in a sense this is an image of this idea of which I speak. This life in fact never ceases, never dies, and the otter lives this hunted and fugitive existence, and this really is one of the main ideas running in the poem. And in the second part I make this more definite. Coming down from the succession of generations of otters, I come down to this particular otter—and this particular otter in a crisis when he's being hunted for his life. . . .

Historical and mythological motifs convey the nostalgia for a prelapsarian existence in the first part of "An Otter." This otter "Brings the legend of himself / From before wars or burials" and cries "to the old shape of the starlit land." His furtive melting alternately from land to sea and back again suggests a yearning for a reunion with "Some world lost when first he dived." Lines 15 through 17 present an otter version of the frog prince fairytale motif of imprisonment in a lower form of creation. The "three nights" of these lines conflate the motif of the moon, dark for three days only to be reborn again, with the Jonah motif of the night journey under the sea. These motifs express the desire for a form of regeneration that does not appear possible in modern history. Section II presents the otter's struggle for survival in modern history, in a withdrawn, degraded form, where he is only an object of sport, a trophy pelt. As in "Pike," Hughes's imaginative grasp suffuses every line of the poem, rendering the otter so completely that the reader recognizes an affinity with a basic drive that abstractions like eros and thanatos do not suffice to describe:

> Big trout muscle out of the dead cold;
> Blood is the belly of logic; he will lick
> The fishbone bare. And can take stolen hold
>
> On a bitch otter in a field full
> Of nervous horses, but linger nowhere.

Hughes controls his visitations of theriomorphic energy through the use of the Lupercalia ritual as a principle of formal organization for the entire volume. The early formalism remains in structuring the volume according to a final reconciliation of oppositions. In the Horder interview Hughes states: "A lot of my second book, *Lupercal*, is one extended poem about one or two sensations. There are at least a dozen or fifteen poems in that book which belong organically to one another." By first examining the Roman and primitive functions of the Lupercalia ritual, one can identify the "one or two sensations" and clarify Hughes's structural use of this ritual in *Lupercal*.

Until the triumph of Christianity, the ancient Romans on each February fifteenth chose two men of good family to meet at the Palatine, where the original Lupercal cave was believed to have been located, there to sacrifice a dog and some goats. Sections I and III of "Lupercalia" are, respectively, meditations on the theriomorphic power of the dog and goat in this sacrifice. The men were daubed with the blood and, naked save for loincloth, ran about striking everyone they met with strips of goat's hide. All who were struck were believed to be reinvigorated. Exactly where the Luperci ran and exactly what was the character of this reinvigoration has been the subject of some debate among classicists and anthropologists.

Most commentators, among them H. J. Rose and Karl Kerényi,[24] interpret the striking of the populace with strips of goat's hide as elements of a fertility ritual. Hughes emphasizes this function in sections II and IV of "Lupercalia," in the need to affix magically the "brute's quick" upon the woman's "surviving / Barrenness." The closing exhortation of section IV to "Touch this frozen one" continues this theme, with the implication widening to include poet, reader, and social fabric. But much evidence exists in *Lupercal* to indicate that Hughes was aware of the alternate interpretation of the Lupercalia as originally a propitiation of the dead in a pastoral society antedating the founding of Rome, with the striking of the Luperci as protection against the power of the dead manifesting themselves near the spring birthing of lambs in the form of predatory wolves.

Jane Harrison, for instance, discusses the Lupercalia and the Greek Anthesterion as both being exclusively concerned with purification of the dead and the placation of ghosts—for the purpose of acquiring "freedom from bad spirits and their maleficent influence" and thereby promoting spring fertility.[25] The most sophisticated explication of this position occurs in a 1953 article by the Bryn Mawr scholar of Roman antiquity A. K. Michels.[26] With thorough linguistic study and close scrutiny of over twenty ancient sources, Michels argues that no ancient source specifically indicates that the Luperci ran around the Palatine Hill, though there is evidence to indicate that instead they ran up and down the Sacra Via through the Forum Valley, which once contained the *sepulcretum* or burial place used by more primitive, pastoral communities living on the hills. Her evidence also affirms that the original Lupercalia took place on the third of the nine-day *dies parentales*, the period of propitiation of the dead, when spirits were believed to be wandering about at will and when marriages or orgiastic fertility rites were commonly forbidden. Michels concludes by noting that the name *Luperci*, an etymological stumbling block for all who have attempted interpretations of the Lupercalia (as there is no regular Latin derivation of *Lupercus* from *lupus*), derives from the common Roman practice, specifically noted by Varro, of attributing functional names to sects of Roman priests. Thus, before the abandonment of the *sepulcretum* and the change from pastoral to urban society, Michels hypothesizes a college of Luperci "composed of men who were believed to be naturally endowed with the gift for controlling wolves" and who practiced a forgotten ritual at the original lair entrance somewhere near the foot of the Palatine Hill.

The purificatory interpretation of the Lupercalia accounts for the preoccupation with the dead and with controlling inherited evil in a volume whose title, if following the conventional approach to the Lupercalia as a fertility ritual, would disallow such persistently somber meditations. In "Things Present," the opening poem of *Lupercal*, the reader learns of "Progenitors back to the sea-salt" who have "Honed their bodies away"; in "Mayday on Holderness" Mayday fertility brings nightmares of "Cordite oozings of Gallipoli"; in "February" the persona worries over the power of avenging wolves "lest they choose his head"; the reader hears of the "arrogance of blood and bone" in "Crow Hill" and of Thomas Browne's ability to "abash / The wretch of death that stands in his shoes" ("Urn Burial"); and the persona of "Historian" is preoccupied to distraction by the hectoring voices of the dead and their deeds. Only in the second section of "Lupercalia," the final poem of the volume, does Hughes dismiss the problematic influences of the dead:

> The dead are indifferent underground.
> Little the live may learn from them—
> A sort of hair and bone wisdom,
> A worn witchcraft accoutrement
>
> Of proverbs.

Love and aggression, or fertility and genetically inherited evil, constitute the "one or two sensations" that Hughes transmutes into the heart of the formal organization of *Lupercal*.

Hughes emphasizes both the fertility and purificatory aspects of theriomorphic animal power in the three poems other than "Lupercalia" that extend the ritual wolf symbolism: "February," "The Retired Colonel," and "Crag Jack's Apostasy." All three focus upon the clear visual motif of the wolf's head. Primitive people, according to Frazer, regarded the animal head as particularly sacred, as the residence of the guardian spirit of a tribal member who protects and guides them.[27] Eliade notes that "the shaman also enjoys the protection of a 'spirit of the head,' which defends him during his ecstatic journeys."[28] In "February" a bodiless and headless daydream apparition searches for the teeth and "quick eyes" of its vanished godhead intuition of divinity, while disdaining confinement in a prosaic contemporary world. The final three lines of the poem present both the reempowering energy and the purificatory symbolism of the wolf's head, as protection against evil:

> Now, lest they choose his head,
> Under severe moons he sits making
> Wolf-masks, mouths clamped well onto the world.

The poem becomes wolf mask as Hughes enlists the theriomorphic power of the animal, while at the same time learning, like the Luperci, to control that power through confronting his emotions and organizing his perceptions. As in "The Dove-Breeder" and other poems in *Hawk*, Hughes affirms the primacy of self-control and successful management of one's own psychic life. The meditative imagination and personal struggles of the personae in *Lupercal* replace the need for the dramatic plots of *Hawk*, in the process achieving a significant gain in directness.

The "they" whom the persona of "February" needs to control in line 22 of the poem are the potentially destructive powers of theriomorphic wolf energy, presented in part in the first stanza in stories of avenging Nibelung wolves (from the Eddic lays *Atlakviða* and *Atlamál*), and in malicious fairytale figures such as the wolf in *Little Red Riding Hood*, whose belly is "stitched full of big pebbles" after death. Primitive people erected stuffed effigies of slain animals to honor the indestructibility and continued influence of the god; they also believed that the honorific head contained a portion of the god's divine life.[29] Theriomorphic energy may be divine in its power, but it antedates notions of morality that our Western culture normally ascribes to divinities. Hughes apparently believes that primitive people were more honest in recognizing potential complicity with the destructive powers of nature and less inhibited about attempting to control that energy through ritual. Wolves in Norse mythology (such as Fenrir, Loki's avenging wolf of Ragnarok doom, and Odin's wolves Geri and Freki) and in other cultures often embodied the most cruel demons of death and destruction;[30] they desecrated battlefield corpses, attacked the vulnerable progeny of flocks, and howled loudest during their exceptionally early February mating season (cf. the title of the Hughes poem), to remind guilt-ridden primitives of unappeased ancestral evil loosed from the underworld in the prespring cold.

The "dream cries 'Wolf!'" in "February" because all wolf energy in contemporary civilization is either "caged, or storied, or pictured," represented in photograph, painting, fairytale, or ancient myth—but not experienced, wrestled with, worked through. In the first Faas interview Hughes states that contemporary civilization is dreaming a nightmare dream of violence because our inert, rationalist outlook keeps our chthonic and supernormal energies dormant and undeveloped, repressed, locked in the realm of dream only, and replayed continually in the violence of pulp fiction and television, which the passive viewer peers at in "anaesthetized unconcern." So too the persona of "February" is possessed by visions of demonic wolf energy that remain locked in the realm of dream only, to "pursue, siege all thought." Psychologically speaking, to articulate this energy is a first step toward learning to manage it. The poem becomes a therapeutic blueprint for psychic health.

"Fourth of July" and "Nicholas Ferrer" articulate what Hughes has called the "oppressive deadness" and "spiritless materialism" of our contemporary civilization.[31] The persona of "Fourth of July" speaks not of independence, but of claustral confinement on an earth bereft of mysterious adventures to whet the imagination, a world too completely *known*. "The right maps have no monsters" because the materialistic urge behind the "huckstering breath" of Columbus and late Renaissance economic expansion produced an alienating world where instinctual and supernormal energies, "the mind's wandering elementals," atrophy as they "Wait dully at the traffic crossing, / Or lean over headlines, taking nothing in."

Similarly, in "Nicholas Ferrer" the fire of the Protestant Reformation dwindles to the "blue calm" of the inner light as the leveling fervor of Cromwell seems, echoing Weber and Tawney, to work hand in hand with a decay in spiritual resolve and commitment symbolized in the decayed manor farm of Little Gidding. Though Ferrer's housekeeping of the faith of martyrs indicates a diminished status, his resolve was nevertheless actualized in a daily regimen of religious asceticism and good works in deliberate withdrawal from the getting and spending of London, and this is preferable to the "Burned down" tree of faith in the average Protestant "shut heart." The sun that now shines on Ferrer's retreat is an "estranged" sun; contemporary birds hover with "practical" moves, and the Eagle of biblical prophecy deteriorates to the status of a domestic ornament inside a landmark for tourists. Hughes's more personalistic style in *Lupercal* produces a meditative calm conducive to extending his historical reach: what at first appears to be description actually contains an implied judgment of how primitive human integration with psyche and soil through ritual has devolved through ages of materialism and religio-economic upheaval.

All that can be gleaned from post-Renaissance Britain is embodied in the stature, stamina, and courage of "The Retired Colonel," the second of the three wolf's head poems. The Colonel embodies, even in caricature, the dignity of an action-oriented individualism that fostered England's last heroic age, nineteenth-century imperialism. This neighbor of Hughes becomes a wolf's head guardian spirit in an ignoble age of timidity and urban pollution. At the end of the poem Hughes presents the Colonel's head "mounted, though only in rhymes," as a trophy, a remembrance of past grandeur. Hughes in "The Retired Colonel" conveys the strength of his meditative penetration without resorting to the rhetoric of *Hawk*; the run-on lines, where verbs, adjectives, and prepositions are separated from their objects, direct the reader's gaze more quickly to the next line, creating the effect of a single, concentrated movement of thought.

The persona of "Crag Jack's Apostasy," the last of the three wolf's head poems, prays for illumination from the god who comes to his "sleeping body through / The world under the world" of his unconscious. He hopes to find there more "than the memory / Of a wolf's head, of eagles' feet." Animals in dreams often mobilize libidinal resources as the unconscious attempts to heal the psyche. Once, when analyzing a dream about animals, Jung wrote that "Dreams are full of these theriomorphic representations of libido" and that "theriomorphic symbols always refer to unconscious manifestations of libido."[32] Crag Jack needs help from his unconscious, because the traditional vehicles of spiritual wisdom in his Christian culture have rigidified into layers of inert stone through the centuries. As he searches for the real power behind the "animal's dreamed head," he yearns for release from suffocating, antiquated religious systems.

Crag Jack's opposite is the hermit of "The Good Life," who insists upon living only within the confines of his consciously erected public persona, what Hughes calls the "constructed, spoilt part" of human life in the Horder interview. The hermit needs the reinforcement of a "square-shouldered self-respect" and the habiliments of the "plump, cuffed citizen" to provide the freedom and quietude needed to "hear God speak." Because he, unlike Crag Jack, refuses to search his unconscious, the only speech he hears, after his rationalizations, conformity, and creature comforts, is a steady diet of surface chatter that nervously camouflages a complete atrophy of spirit.

A similar weakness of spirit occurs in "A Dream of Horses," where Hughes compares contemporary men to stable grooms whose wealth is "horse dung and the combings of horses." Horses have often appeared in the history of myth and literature as symbols for libidinal energy;[33] in this poem they are fearsome and unapproachable, because the stable grooms refuse to allow instinctual energies into their conscious lives. Hence these energies reside deprived of development, locked in the realm of dream, to rip apart psyches that have lapsed to the impotency of custodians. This retreat from experience correspondingly magnifies the power of the horses, to the point where the grooms long fatalistically for death. Hughes accentuates the demonic power of the horses through the device of repetition, at the end of the second line in each three-line stanza, and at the end of every line in the last stanza.

"Crag Jack's Apostasy" and "A Dream of Horses" bring Hughes's inner/outer distinctions in *Lupercal* full circle, for the theriomorphic energy that Hughes posits in the outer world finds its cunning psychological parallel in our inner world. As in the extended metaphors and miniature dramatic plots in *Hawk*, and in the *Lupercal* theory of writing poetry as merging and controlling instinct and imagination, the emphasis for Hughes again rests upon the Jungian imperative to explore and wrestle with the unconscious and its darker energies, to achieve the still point of personality integration, the point where the "hawk hangs still." The outer energy actuates the inner drive toward personality development. In this direction one can answer the objections of Movement poets and critics (especially Philip Larkin) who complain about myth kitties, needless experimentalism, anthropological mumbo jumbo, and preoccupation with violence. Certainly Hughes does not expect the contemporary reader to believe in a Lupercalia ritual in the way that a primitive shepherd would. For Hughes the ritual functions primarily as metaphor—for the need to confront and accept our animal selves, and thus avoid mass explosions of violence.

Secondarily Hughes suggests that our behavior by habit and biological origin still bears the taints of our animal predecessors. We cannot simply deny the influence of the medulla and the cerebellum and operate as if only the cerebral cortex controls our actions. Hughes's poetry repeatedly asserts that a human being is a composite who asks for trouble by paying attention only to rational consciousness. As with "Lupercalia" and the three wolf's head poems, the purpose of the remaining animal poems in this volume is to liberate, through the poet's meditative power, the theriomorphic energy needed to reinvigorate the psychic life of both poet and reader.

Hughes's statement in the Horder interview that "'The Bull' is what the observer sees when he looks into his own head" is borne out in "The Bull Moses" by such lines as "a sudden shut-eyed look / Backward into the head" and "as onto the mind's eye." What awes the persona is the sure power and fertile strength of the bull, something "too deep in itself" to bother with the ordinary daylight world. This rapport with an inner strength, with "the locked black of his powers," gives the observer intimations of a supernormal, goal-directed energy—"some beheld future / Founding in his quiet." This Moses envisions a promised land and appears at times to represent an awesome genetic force, a power to be the progenitor of a chosen people, that lies far below the threshold of consciousness. Though the concrete pastoral setting does not invite mythological allusions, this bull's prodigious power of fertility is in the tradition of bulls as sacred fertility symbols in Sumerian and early Egyptian mythology.[34] Unlike "Egghead" or the hermit of "The Good Life," the persona of "The Bull Moses" has the courage to take a long, careful inspection of this fecund power; at the end of the poem the bolt is slid shut not out of fear, but to place this energy, after careful scrutiny, in safekeeping for future use. After over thirty lines of concentrated meditation upon the bull, the persona's lone concluding action follows a decision to store what he can of this power *within his own psyche*: "I kept the door wide, / Closed it after him and pushed the bolt."

The personae observe a careful distance as they evaluate the more predatory theriomorphic energy of the animals perceived in "Thrushes," "Pike," and "Hawk Roosting." This distance is evident in "Thrushes" and "Pike" in a tone of appalled fascination, and in the unflinching, unadorned accuracy of observation. In "Hawk Roosting" the complete subjectivity of presentation achieves a dramatic irony that impedes close identification. In each poem the persona's meditations expand beyond the individual predatory act, revealing the theriomorphic forces embodied and their relation to the human world. This sophistication of perspective argues against critical accusations of a Hitlerian fascination with violence or a desire to lapse into animal instinct.[35] Of course Hughes becomes absorbed with the question of violence in the sixties, but few notice that his masterful formal organization—including his control of imagery, tone, theme, and structure—tempers the violent language and subject matter. We can observe these craftsmanlike traits even before Hughes enters his sixties surrealism phase, in *Lupercal* poems that directly concern the predatory in nature and culture.

Of "Thrushes" Hughes states in the Horder interview that "the last stanza . . . shows how the life of the man at the desk has completely cut across any life of the senses, through which he might have reached fulfillment." The thrushes move the persona to fascinated speculation primarily because of the dichotomy between such instantaneous efficiency in the animal realm and the poet's difficulty in achieving any kindred meditative concentration in the agony of writing. Only a genius like Mozart is blessed with a plenitude of unwavering concentration. The poem contains no implicit or explicit wish to emulate the individual predatory acts of the thrushes; they are, as the first word of the poem indicates, "Terrifying." When the persona deepens his meditations he considers *why* the machinations of the thrushes are "Triggered to stirrings beyond sense." The shift in focus to human daydreams of heroism, devils of distraction, and the persona's inability to lose himself completely in his activity for any length of time suggests a nostalgia for nature's animal directness, for a unity with the animal's instinctive rightness of function, and its vital spontaneity of action, theriomorphic attributes of some note. For primitive people, according to Eliade,

> animals are charged with a symbolism and a mythology of great importance for the religious life; so that to communicate with animals, to speak their language and become their friend and master is to appropriate a spiritual life much richer than the merely human life of ordinary mortals. And, on the other hand, the prestige of animals in the eyes of the "primitive" is considerable; they know secrets of Life and Nature, they even know the secrets of longevity and immortality. By entering into the condition of the animals, the shaman shares their secrets and enjoys their plenitude of life.[36]

Especially in the last stanza of "Thrushes" one can readily see that Hughes stops short of the shamanic position of "entering into the condition of the animals"; here Hughes preserves the inquisitive but respectful distance of an evaluator. Hughes will develop the shamanic position thoroughly in the psychodrama of *Wodwo*. What is apparent in "Thrushes" is the envy of the desk-working poet for a more direct, concrete, intuitive absorption into the life process, without vacillation or qualms. "Thrushes" is a poem about the process of writing poetry; only the intensity of Hughes's description in the first stanza can lead one to mistake the poem for an emulation of violence. The rhetorical questions of stanza II and the applications to human creative aspirations in stanza III immediately distance persona and reader into a posture of contemplative scrutiny. Meanwhile, a Yeatsian meditative penetration yields another of those sudden, initially dislocating shifts of reference at the opening of stanza III that we admire once we understand the application of the thrushes to the desk-working poet.

The persona's observations in "Pike," a poem discussed earlier in this chapter, are objective, neutral; he adopts a tone of casual, matter-of-fact recitation of the more gruesome particulars of his encounters, as if he were pointing out the all-too-obvious. A very civilized, wry understatement attends the description: "The jaws' hooked clamp and fangs / Not to be changed at this date" or "And indeed they spare nobody." While the observation is harshly accurate and direct, the tone acts as a buffer against the sensationalism of the most memorable of the details. Only when the pike trigger memories of the genetic residue of aggression in self and species does the persona lose his composure—to admit fright, not emulation, over what "dream / Darkness beneath night's darkness had freed."

The hooked feet "locked upon the rough bark" in "Hawk Roosting" are metonymic of the hawk's belief that

> the one path of my flight is direct
> Through the bones of the living.
> No arguments assert my right.
>
> The sun is behind me.

What the hawk claims is direct, unthinking participation in the fiery energy at the root of created matter, without arguments or sophistry. In the first Faas interview Hughes mentions that he is attempting to portray a more feminine "Isis, mother of the gods" as "Nature thinking"—as if the ontological essence of Nature were conveyed through the aid of language.

Perhaps Hughes aims at presenting an insight similar to that of Jane Harrison, who observes that primitive thinking, not having yet differentiated the individual out of the group, typically expressed its wisdom in collective participation in strong or weak forms of *mana* power invading and exciting all levels of being, and residing particularly in birds. To the primitive, the theriomorphic *mana* power of the bird was thought of as more powerful and primary than its deified anthropomorphic counterpart; Isis herself was often thought of as the deified form of a holy bluebird.[37]

The power of Hughes's hawk is amoral, far from benevolent. But in "Hawk Roosting" Hughes does not intrude with a persona or with analogies to human enterprises; the poem is a dramatic monologue entirely from the subjective point of view of the hawk. Within the twenty-four lines of the poem, nineteen forms of either the pronoun "I" or the possessive "my" appear.[38] Hughes deliberately intends to have his readers recognize an aggressive, amoral impulse in the libido as having a divine counterpart, but without idealizing or moralizing it. Paradoxically, the predatory operations of certain animals, unchecked by sophistry or "Falsifying dream," indicate that the "distracting devils" ("Thrushes") of human cerebration often act as civilizing checks upon the will. But to deny the predatory in nature is to deny the simple truth of the natural biology of the food chain in favor of servicing the squeamish, something Hughes never does. The quixotic bravado of the hawk's last line, "I am going to keep things like this," calls into question the character of this predator, as in the best of Browning's dramatic monologues.

What relevance the aggressive impulses of animals have for an understanding of humans is more fundamentally the subject of the cat poems in *Lupercal*: "Esther's Tomcat," "Of Cats," "Cat and Mouse," and "Wilfred Owen's Photographs." Here the focus often rests upon the hereditary stain of aggression in both human and animal. As with Auden's meditations on the ambiguities of eros as a civilizing and destructive force, Hughes in "Esther's Tomcat" sees a veteran of "continual wars and wives" who is a representative specimen of nature's "unkillable" activity. In the medieval anecdote at the center of the poem, a cat kills an armored knight and leaves an indelible stain. Whether or not that particular cat survived the battle is beside the point; a Yeatsian leap to the generic level and an application to the human world occur here as the poet meditates upon catstains. "The tomcat still / Grallochs odd dogs on the quiet" is meant to be taken as a generic quality of aggressive behavior in cats; it does not mean that the cat that killed the knight at Barnborough actually survived the fight (it did not).[39] Humans inherit the same stain that all flesh is heir to; Hughes's point is that the best defensive armor, created by human intelligence for survival, is inadequate to this "unkillable" force. Hughes is meditating upon the same stain that Auden observes when "dwarf mutations" of aggression "are thrown out / From Eros' weaving centrosome" ("New Year Letter").

The cat of "Esther's Tomcat" is able to bring "His skin whole" through the centuries not through cerebration and self-defense, but through keeping "his mind on the moon" at night, in some Yeatsian instinctual rapport with the eternal erotic round of birth and death. As he encircles the human world with "his eyes and outcry," he circumscribes their culture with a cyclic round of fertility as old as the moon symbolism of the ancient Cretan and Sumerian civilizations.[40] The cats experience "owlish moons of bekittenings" as they participate in the erotic round of birth and death with an instinctive grasp of change. They represent a problematic oscillation of moods that humans share, but cannot completely control.

The progenitive powers of cats and humans are again the focus in "Of Cats." The close scrutiny of heredity in both continues in the first stanza. The prolific cat, often for Freud a sexual symbol in dreams, inherits its procreative power and its longevity from genetically transmitted elements within the species, even as the family nose, also a sexual symbol in dreams, derives its character in humans.[41] In the body of the poem Hughes conflates the sexual prowess of cats with their heightened affective life, seen especially in their undulations of songswell and dance. The heart's relationship to the moon is the locus of strength in the poem. The conjunction of the cats' nighttime wauling and the moonshine above becomes so intense as to lift the persona to a moment of Yeatsian rhapsodic vision. Here we experience an instant cognate with the primal moment of Uranus-Gaea creation, the Eliadian *illud tempus* moment of reunion with a primal creative energy, when darkness and light meet in the image of "a cat upon a cat." The poem affirms that harmony and ecstatic liberation derive from developing a largesse of heart and from paying attention to one's affective life. The poem's main images are striking, and the spirited tone and broad, dancelike rhythms are well-suited to the content. The final anecdote and concluding statement, however, fall too close to the level of flat prose statement to be placed in the same context with a "Cattic Bacchanal!" The diction of the last line ("utter mock") is incongruously artificial, a mannered echo of some of the archaic language of *Hawk*, and a stiff departure from the visionary moment at the center of the poem.

In "Cat and Mouse" a mouse is cornered by a cat, without cover or camouflage, on a sheep-cropped hill summit. Hughes ridicules the timid human need for covenants with deities, by analogizing the mouse's struggle to the human struggle with a god: "Whether to two / Feet or four, how are prayers contracted!" The mouse must face the cat's predatory instincts in the here and now. Prayers and covenants place power outside the self, whereas what is needed is a catlike quickness, courage, and native ingenuity in life's battles. But in the "Stupor of life" in "Time and a world / Too old to alter," prayers historically have dominated.

"Wilfred Owen's Photographs" continues the meditative focus upon the instinctual life of cats and humans. Here Parliament opposes an attempt to reform penal practices in the Royal Navy. The Parliamentarians demand the continued use of the cat-o-nine-tails, a nine-corded whip used for centuries to flog recalcitrant seamen. But when a "witty profound Irishman calls / For a 'cat' into the House" and introduces the actual torture implement into the proceedings, he exposes an aggressive taint beneath parliamentary bluster over tradition. This "cat" leaves "The gentry fingering its stained tails." What opposed the attempt of Parnell's Irish to abolish the whip was "of the species." Yet reminding Parliament of the concrete reality of aggression leads to the motion being passed without opposition.

The poem's title reveals the violent upshot of this repression. In two separate reviews of World War I poetry, Hughes refers to Wilfred Owen's photographs as propaganda intended to frighten Georgian England out of its complacent traditions, by presenting slices of life from the trenches, with all the vividness and horror he could muster.[42] If the body of "Wilfred Owen's Photographs" presents a parable of the complacency of tradition, the forms to be kept at all costs, then the title drives home the explosive results of the refusal—the violence of World War I, the product of a massive cultural repression.

Hughes's meditations on sex and aggression in the cat poems of *Lupercal* reaffirm the ambiguous legacy of love/death in historical time. These meditations repeat the old mythic intuition that love and war, the erotic and destructive portions of libidinal energy, are inseparably intertwined, as both the immortal (Pollux) and the beautiful (Helen) progeny of Leda are siblings with the mortal (Castor) and the death-bound (Clytemnestra), or as the sowing of the indestructible boneteeth of life produces both the city of Thebes and its *armed* Spartoi. The wisdom that comes from understanding the ambiguous legacy of instinctual energy in time is the message of "Crow Hill." The Cadmus-like energy that builds cities and humbles hills into farmland also raises "the arrogance of blood and bone." But in his cat poems Hughes offers a deeper level of social analysis. Developing only human conscious, rational powers exacerbates the aggressive taint in the species, especially when enshrined in accepted cultural myths. Though human passions raised to a fever pitch may result in personal conflicts and death (as in "Law in the Country of the Cats" in *Hawk*), only the total repression of libido, in the public realm of church and government, sends millions to their deaths in the global catastrophe of war.

Hughes voices an agreement with Owen's attempts to expose English warmongers and propagandists when he writes in a review that World War I was the "crime of fools who could not see because they *would not feel*" (italics mine).[43] The stained tails of instinctual life have their place. As a reminder of the unkillable theriomorphic powers and their counterparts in human psychic life, cats appear as tags or signatures in many other *Lupercal* poems and pass on their symbolic value to the incidental appearances of foxes, weasels, stoats, and other animals in many of the remaining poems in the volume.

The dual interpretation of the Lupercalia, as fertility ritual and as exorcism of ancestral evil, paralleled by the study of both the erotic and the aggressive impulses in the theriomorphic energy of animals, leads Hughes to contemplate the ambivalent effects of history and culture in *Lupercal* and to reaffirm his Jungian imperative to manage both the erotic and the aggressive impulses in order to achieve a whole, integrated personality. This psychic management can free one from "all sedentary belief." The effort or "prayer of long attempting" can lead to a balance, an integration of self and world where one can acquire the daring and grace to go somersaulting "Out onto nothing" ("Acrobats"). The formal organization of *Lupercal* balances the opposites of eros and thanatos, the imperative to develop one's libidinal energies and the inspection of the destructive forces in nature and culture. This New Critical formal technique continues in "Mayday on Holderness," "Fire-Eater," "Relic," and "The Voyage," where Hughes balances contrasting treatments of fire and water.

The life-consuming flames of inherited aggression, still smouldering in the heat of the earth's core, are the subject of "Mayday on Holderness." The persona meditates upon his English inheritance, transmitted to him from all facets of the environment: "Birth-soils, / The sea-salts, scoured me, cortex and intestine, / To receive these remains." From line 17 onward, the persona broods intensely upon heredity, only to receive nightmare visions of some of the most predatory of animal forebears: the lightning-quick eel, the carrion-eating vulture, the maniacal hyena (that attacks sleeping children, robs graves, and occasionally abandons what it kills), the bone-crushing "coils of the sleeping anaconda," and the "nightlong frenzy of shrews." The smouldering embers of Gallipoli arise in the poem's central visionary moment:

> The North Sea lies soundless. Beneath it
> Smoulder the wars: to heart-beats, bomb, bayonet.
> "Mother, Mother!" cries the pierced helmet.
> Cordite oozings of Gallipoli,

Mayday meditations unlock personal memories of aggression. In the Gallipoli campaign of World War I, the Turks and Allies lost a quarter of a million men each (eighty percent of the Allied casualties were British) in nine months of pointless beachhead warfare ending in an ignominious retreat.[44] A breast pocket paybook stopped shrapnel intended for Hughes's father, who was one of only seventeen survivors of an entire battalion of the Lancashire Fusiliers that went through its numbers three times at Gallipoli.[45]

An important mythological allusion and a slow but steadily increasing meditative pressure reinforce the surrealistic vision of the irrational and the predatory that "motherly summer" induces in the persona of "Mayday on Holderness." In the same chapter of *The Golden Bough* that provoked allusions in "The Green Wolf," a later *Wodwo* poem, Frazer states that the Beltane purgatorial fires of the Scottish Highlands took place on May Day. Here Frazer asserts that in antiquity midsummer fires functioned partly to stimulate by sympathetic magic the sun's generative rays in the cloudy northern climate, but principally to exorcise by purification all evil influences, especially demonic witchcraft. Witches as well as animals were tossed into the flames.[46] In line 13 the persona intimates a preconscious participation in the world of the sun's "incinerator," which recollects the earlier "furnace door" of the womb and the earth's core. The poem's ending presents a surrealistic nightmare, a revelation of complicity with all flesh-consuming energy, presented through carefully controlled imaginative leaps of reference and sinister sparks of visual imagery that smoulder to their kindling point.

Conversely, adjusting to the historical cycles of decay and regeneration within the self and in nature leads to survival in "Fire-Eater." The persona hopes to manage Orion and Sirius, the forces of cyclic renewal, in part by acknowledging the laws of energy transfer in all temporality. He comprehends, for instance, that the fuel that keeps the fiery stars aglow is the same compost (the "mouthful of earth") that powers the human and sub-human realms—hence the cryptic line "The death of a gnat is a star's mouth." The fiery skin of the star represents the suffering that attends all revelations of divinity on earth. Like the dolorous aftermath of Mary's conception of Christ under the stars at Bethlehem, or of Semele's death by lightning after lying with Zeus and conceiving Dionysus, all incarnations of divinity in a temporal world, both theriomorphic and anthropomorphic, are fraught with pain and danger. So the contemporary poet must learn, like the fire-eating circus performer, to swallow the often painful limitations of temporality and conform to "going where it is profitable."

At the conclusion of "Fire-Eater," the acceptance of suffering leads to a transfiguring vision of cosmic unity when the realm of starry permanence pierces the subhuman slug; and the Cosmic Tree, once a passageway to the gods for primitives, once again becomes "caught up in the constellations." This transcendent moment of unity appears with a Yeatsian concreteness and economy, and a proverblike obliquity:

> A star pierces the slug,

> The tree is caught up in the constellations.
> My skull burrows among antennae and fronds.

A similarly ambiguous diptych of erotic and destructive energy occurs when comparing "The Voyage" and "Relic," two poems in *Lupercal* where water imagery predominates. "The Voyage" indicates that survival sometimes requires a paradoxical risk taking. The sea of "The Voyage," like the sea of psychological experience, is filled with potential for self-development, as well as with mysterious and potentially sinister powers. The poet risks this sea in his love-impelled movement toward communication. Similarly, Hughes invites his readers to explore not the known self in reading the poems of *Lupercal*, but the unconscious within the self—to voyage into the ambivalent unknown, to allow these animal poems to coax unconscious energies to the surface. Self-development requires venturing onto the sea of the instincts and a working through the potentially destructive energies of this sea, where "other than men" devour the weak of heart.

In "Relic," however, the sea alone survives, because of its protean form-lessness and its power of tail-eating uroboros renewal: "Time in the sea eats its tail, thrives." All created matter is subject to jaws that "Eat and are finished and the jawbone comes to the beach"; the laws of created matter regularly lead to a universe of dissolution. Hence the poignancy of the final lines: "This curved jawbone did not laugh / But gripped, gripped and is now a cenotaph." As the grave devoured Yorick's laughless skull, so do all jaws ultimately devour each other, and Hughes parades no sophistry of reason to mask mutability. The "sea's achievement" is a continuing ebb and flow of flesh becoming flotsam.

Ironic contrast between a more heroic past and an ignoble present continues as a minor theme in *Lupercal*, in poems such as "Urn Burial," "Nicholas Ferrer," "The Retired Colonel," and "The Good Life." But as Hughes meditates upon erotic and aggressive instincts in the Lupercalia ritual, in theriomorphic energy, and in human psychology, he no longer offers that past categorically as a preferable stance toward experience. Instead he offers models of well-developed character, like "Nicholas Ferrer" and "The Retired Colonel"—individuals more reticently at home with principles and values put into practice in their daily lives. Character and conviction create peace within the psyche, a comfortable articulation of some of the best cultural values of their respective ages, and a stoic resignation toward death. The best representative of these models is Thomas Browne in "Urn Burial." The "improvement" upon the animal grip in "Urn Burial" is the strong character of Browne, a sanguine realist at home even with meditations upon Norfolk funeral urns. In graveyards Browne's quiet optimism remains undaunted, because it includes a sure knowledge of the real weight of death pressing daily upon his shoulders. Chapter 5 of *Urn Burial*, which Douglas Bush has called the "last great outcry . . . of the dying Renaissance against devouring Time,"[47] contains numerous cryptic statements attesting to Browne's mature grasp of the significance of death for the living:

> If we begin to die when we live, and long life be but a prolongation of death; our life is a sad composition; we live with death, and die not in a moment. . . . There is no antidote against the Opium of Time, which temporally considereth all things; Our fathers finde their graves in our short memories, and sadly tell us how we may be buried in our Survivors. . . . Oblivion is not to be hired: the greater part must be content to be as though they had not been, to be found in the register of God, not in the record of man.[48]

In his meditations Browne continually penetrates beneath the veneer of Christian rites, which he avers "have handsomely glossed the deformity of death,"[49] to study the reality of human decomposition. In "Urn Burial" Hughes pays tribute to the "word's strength" of Browne's unvarnished inquiry, and his quintessential articulation of the culture of the dying Renaissance. Browne can "abash / The wretch of death that stands in his side" by a sober and unflinching affirmation of its continual presence in human affairs. Hughes affirms his admiration for the mature tolerance in Browne that can integrate personal and cultural values with the beauty and the deformities of nature. By historicizing Yeats's dancer image, Hughes expresses Browne's rapport with nature's mutability and with the prevailing thought of his age: in Browne's life one finds no separation of personality from culture, "No foot wrong in the dance figure—."

One might affirm that Hughes in *Lupercal* agrees with Browne's affirmation that "Life is a pure flame, and we live by an invisible sun within us."[50] Tending this vital flame throughout life is more important than being preoccupied with inherited aggression in a universe of dissolution. Ferrer's hearth fire of faith, the energy of the Luperci "Hurrying the lit ghost of man / Age to age," and the combustible compost of "Fire-Eater" suggest that worthwhile action in the present is possible. The persona of "Historian" resolves to acquire "a live brain's / Envying to master and last" the cultural gains of the past. But the figure of the tramp—in "Things Present," "Crag Jack's Apostasy," and "November"—and the degenerate scene of idle suitors lacking a warrior-leader, in "Everyman's Odyssey," present a sobering portrait of the possibilities for cultural advancement in postwar England. One is reminded of Bernard Bergonzi's observation that postwar British writing is permeated with a sense of decline and readjustment from the status of the most powerful empire on earth to a power of the middle rank, nettled with chronic unemployment, cultural insularity, and a preoccupation with eccentricity that at times borders upon "the pathos and unreality of an Indian reservation."[51] The persona of "November" is struck by the tramp's "strong trust" in nature, by his pride, his patience, and his dogged endurance, but he is also aware, as the tramp is not, of the cross of self and culture that they bear—that ominous keeper's gibbet with its dried-out animal skins. This sense of cultural loss recollects the persona's comparison in "Things Present" between ancestors who filled "stout shoes" and the intuitions of the "tramp in the sodden ditch" that the progeny of these ancestors have lost their vitality—have "Honed their bodies away."

In *Lupercal* Hughes carefully examines the destructive portion of libidinal energy in humans and nature—the amoral sun of "Hawk Roosting" and the smouldering fires of Gallipoli in "Mayday on Holderness." In "The

Perfect Forms" he suggests a cultural cause for some of this aggression, a cause that he will develop with great richness and dexterity in *Wodwo* and *Crow*. The Greeks used rational inquiry to comprehend the laws of nature, so Socrates can smile. The Buddha aspired toward a monistic oneness of nature for the perceiver, so he fills immensity with his one thought. But Christianity *separates* humans from nature, thus relegating the instincts to "ages of Godforsaken darkness." Christianity will forever be preoccupied with trying to manage the "difficult child" of the flesh it has disowned. Earlier civilizations probed deeper into the mysteries of nature, and adjusted their culture to its laws rather than denying it a place. Cleopatra's power in "Cleopatra to the Asp," for instance, derives from her sympathetic participation in the theriomorphic fertility of the Sumerian-Egyptian moon-bull ("the moon-horned river") and in the fertility of the Nile waters issuing from her womb. When thwarted by the sexless efficiency of an Augustus and a rigid Roman imperialism more interested in acquisition and rule than in the mythological values it displaces, Cleopatra turns diabolical and predicts that the theriomorphic power of her asp will conquer Rome in the long coils of history. The Roman invaders only exhibit their obtuseness in neglecting natural forces that mythologies regularly remind us to acknowledge.

After the lengthy meditations upon the taint of aggression that stains all human enterprises, the renewed faith in historical and cultural efforts in "Lupercalia" convinces—because it is earned. The last section of "Lupercalia" expresses the confident power and strength of a poet who has used his wolf mask formal apparatus well; he has wrestled with his inner and outer demons to win a new sense of personality integration. His "appetite is good" ("Fire-Eater"), and his spirit renewed for mastering and adding to those past historical gains ("Historian"). The specters of jaws, talons, fangs, hooked heads and feet, vicelike locks and clamps—the main imagery cluster in the volume—have been met and improved upon, by raising them to the level of significance through the use of the poetic imagination. At the conclusion of *Lupercal* Hughes is still hungry and thirsty for further involvement in Western cultural activities in historical time. The "mouths" of his poems remain "clamped well onto the world" ("February"):

> Over sand that the sun's burned out
> Thudding feet of the powerful,
> Their oiled bodies brass-bright
> In a drift of dust. The earth's crammed full,

Its baked red bellying to the sky's
Electric blue. Their attitudes—
A theorem of flung effort, blades:
Nothing mortal falters their poise

Though wet with blood: the dog has blessed
Their fury. Fresh thongs of goat-skin
In their hands they go bounding past,
And deliberate welts have snatched her in

To the figure of racers. Maker of the world,
Hurrying the lit ghost of man
Age to age while the body hold,
Touch this frozen one.

The effort of the Luperci touches the reader's frozen affections with a directness and a meditative strength that appears artless. The language, pared down to a supple, lean muscularity, conveys the content more directly because the artistry does not call attention to itself. The run-on lines rush the reader along with the runners, and the concrete imagery adds a richness and a solidity that is neither mannered nor artificial—because it also calls attention to the subject and themes of the poem, not to itself. The reader is invited to share in the experience, to participate in the poet's meditative progress and in the reach and penetrating power of his poetic imagination.

Yet Hughes's new emphasis upon the imagination's power to capture and bring to the surface unconscious feelings and memories from his inner world soon cause him to take a completely opposite position on the question of Western cultural enterprises. The more he searches his inner world, the more he finds childhood memories and genetic residue of those "Cordite oozings of Gallipoli." The result is a rather abrupt plunge into his major mode of the sixties—surrealistic nightmare. Here New Critical formal balance defers to a "therapeutic torrent" of surrealistic energy.

PART II
The Surreal Sixties

CHAPTER 4

Goodbye to the
Cenotaphs

Wodwo

1967

*Everything we associate with a poem is its shadowy
tenant and part of its meaning, no matter how New
Critical purist we try to be. . . . [Dylan] Thomas's
life, letters, and legends belong to his poetry, in that
they make it mean more. . . . Then suddenly we
hear the voice that polished the voices, the demon
stylist, a cold, severe, even ruthless sort of person. . . . Clearly enough, an abandoned surrealistic
or therapeutic torrent was the last thing Thomas
allowed his reservoirs to become. . . . In his life, the
reflex of this vision was a complete openness toward
both inner and outer worlds, denying nothing, refusing nothing, suppressing nothing. . . . What he
was really waiting for, and coaxing with alcohol,
was the delicate cerebral disaster that demolishes
the old self for good, with all its crushing fortifications, and leaves the* atman *a clear field.*
—Hughes, 1966[1]

    Wodwo (1967) is a very complex, forbidding
book, possibly the most elusive and difficult book of poetry Hughes has
written to date. Its unique combination of surrealism, mythic psychodrama, and Oriental psychology distills a period of great productivity and
intellectual gain in Hughes's literary life and chronicles many complications in his private life. In the sixties Hughes's poetic psyche is thrown
back upon itself, to depend upon its own subconscious resources; initially
a divorce ensues between the inner and outer worlds of his art. The result
of the anguished withdrawal is no less than a loss of faith in the enterprises
of Western culture and human involvement in goal-seeking activity in historical time—a complete reversal from the formalism of the fifties. The
central persona of *Wodwo* recoils in surrealistic flight, like the Spectre of
Tharmas in Night VI of Blake's *Four Zoas*, from a Urizen-like destructive
universe of all-conquering science and webs of religious mystery that stunt
the development of emotional and imaginative life. But the poetic psyche is
not left helpless: through the agony of the ordeal, Hughes is able to locate
new powers within the self, powers deriving in part from surrealism itself,
from primitive folklore and the shaman's art, and from Oriental psychology. These new powers offer important survival strategies for moderns.

Between 1960 and 1967 Hughes published no less than thirty-seven book reviews, four introductions, four essays, and seven short stories. He also completed dozens of BBC scripts and broadcasts and thirteen dramatic works (some for children) and published four volumes of children's verse and stories. When one adds the thirty-two minor poems of *Recklings* (1966), the forty-one major poems of *Wodwo*, and the dozens of uncollected pieces published during these seven years, the total output becomes prodigious. The elliptical poems and the enigmatical tripartite structure of *Wodwo* reflect the enormous gains in knowledge and imaginative reach that the contents of Hughes's essays, broadcasts, and reviews of this period convey, gains that often caused reviewers to gloss lightly over the volume, or to admit that this "baffling" collection contained "impenetrable" poetry and a structure that appeared "hastily considered and arbitrary."[2]

As Hughes abandons formalism, the emotional content of his private experience surfaces more directly in his poetry. *Wodwo* expresses the many moods that a prolific writer trying to establish himself experiences under the joys, strains, and tragedies of a private life that included the birth of Frieda Rebecca Hughes (1 April 1960) to a pair of immensely talented but impecunious poets, the sharing of childrearing duties in a cramped London flat, the onerous difficulties of writing while refurbishing the rural Devon home that the family occupied late in 1961, the birth of Nicholas Farrar Hughes (17 January 1962), and finally the broken marriage and the trauma and aftershocks of Sylvia Plath's tragic suicide (11 February 1963). Hughes's private life seldom intrudes directly into his creative work—poems like "Full Moon and Little Frieda" and "Out" are exceptions—but one can locate oblique references and analogous moods in the torment of "Song of a Rat" and the painful self-examination of *Eat Crow* (originally composed in 1964) and identify in "Snow" an elaborate prose allegory of the desk poet struggling to concentrate his energies on his art amid emotional fluctuations and snowdrifts of domestic duties, deadlines, appointments, and piles of incoming mail.[3]

Under such pressures, the choice of surrealism as Hughes's major poetic mode in the sixties seems natural, a fitting outgrowth of his public and private circumstances. One may be tempted, given the above factors, to dwell on the biographical overtones of the definition of surrealism that Hughes supplied near the time he arranged the poems of *Wodwo*. In the "Vasco Popa" essay (1967), Hughes praises the Yugoslav poet's refusal to "surrender to the dream flow for its own sake" or to provide a "relaxation from the outer battle." Hughes considers Popa's form of surrealism to be similar to the surrealism of folklore, which is "always urgently connected with the business of trying to manage practical difficulties so great that they have forced the sufferer temporarily out of the dimension of coherent reality into that depth of imagination where understanding has its roots and stores its X-rays." He distinguishes this from literary surrealism, which he argues "is always connected with an extreme remove from the business of living under practical difficulties and successfully managing them."[4]

The vast majority of the poems of *Wodwo*, however, offer no direct biographical referents for these "practical difficulties." The poems, prose, and drama of parts I and II are filled with imagery and mythic allusions that adumbrate states of psychological withdrawal, and part III contains ecstatic moments of participation in nature. Personal biography in the surrealist works of the sixties exists only as an analogue, at a high level of generalization, that influences and parallels, but does not determine, the thought and content of the poems. Plath's suicide may have thrown the surrealistic mode into overdrive, after a two-year poetic silence, but "Snow," the most surrealistic story in *Wodwo*, was published before the move to Devon; "The Rescue," one of the most surrealistic poems in the volume, appeared in print before the marital breakdown; and *The Wound*, "Bowled Over," and "The Green Wolf" all antedate Plath's suicide.[5] Hughes's poetic intuition may have seen disaster coming in his private life, and he may well have opened the floodgates a few notches to allow his art access to feelings generated in his domestic life, but the sixties surrealism is more the direct, natural, and even inevitable outgrowth of the poet's obsession with the genetic inheritance of aggression in the individual and society and the testimony of his story of a soul, his imagination's relationship to the inner and outer worlds of his art.

Hughes's assessment of literary surrealism as being removed from the "outer battle" actually suits the cloudy reveries of symbolist poets such as Mallarmé and Verlaine, or the early Dadaist nihilism that spent itself by the time André Breton published his first surrealist manifesto in 1924. The original French surrealists were for the most part passionately concerned with embracing the outer world, *after recreating it*—after making it superreal by stripping it of the conventional descriptions of realism and people's naturalistic enchainment to their physical and social situation, and then *adding* the imaginative and psychological truths that free association, dreams, linguistic play, and automatic writing unlocked. Surrealism is one branch of modernist formal experiment; it recreates reality by adding the subjective dimension.

In their work the French surrealists principally responded to the social upheaval of the early twentieth century. Breton coupled Freudian therapy with his ministrations to the wounded as a neurological intern in Nantes during World War I to germinate many of the central tenets of surrealism that later found their way into his prose and poetry. Apollinaire's embrace of the concrete object as a celebration of the newness of life in *Calligrammes* (1918) was very much a survival tactic, a hopeful optimism in the wake of war. Paul Eluard, recognizing the necessity for social as well as artistic change, flirted with communism in the thirties, and Louis Aragon's early metaphysical anguish remained unchanged after three decorations in World War II. Save for a few short years of Dadaist revolt against logic and a dead culture, the original surrealists did not abandon the "outer battle." Pierre Reverdy, a cardiac patient most of his life, presents in "Sound of Bell" a striking image of depopulated Paris during World War I, as the world and his heartbeat stop at once. The alienation of feeling is very much like what one finds in poems such as "A Wind Flashes the Grass" in part I of *Wodwo*.[6]

Breton used Freudian therapy to awaken the subjective psyche; he obtained monologues from the wounded soldiers that were "unencumbered by the slightest inhibition" and "as closely as possible, akin to *spoken thought*."[7] This is very similar to the form Hughes's imagination takes in *Wodwo*. Hughes undergoes an "abandoned surrealistic or therapeutic torrent" that engages the imagination more immediately by circumventing the "demon of artistic or rather verbal self-consciousness, [the] super-ego stylist"—exactly what he believes Dylan Thomas failed to achieve late in his life, as quoted in part in the epigraph to this chapter.[8] By submitting to a surrealistic torrent, Hughes hopes to make his emotional life more directly and immediately accessible to his art and to uncover a more essential self than could be realized under the conscious control of his earlier formalism. This essential self appears in part III of *Wodwo*; it derives, as we shall see later, primarily from Oriental psychology, but only after a necessary surrealistic liberation of the subjective psyche.

Through alienated feeling and metaphysical thirst; suggestive miracles of language and macabre, absurdist humor; hallucination and contradiction; unusual juxtapositions of the concrete and the abstract, the human and the nonhuman; and farfetched similes and metaphors, the surrealists dislocated the outer world from its normal referential or realistic context, only to recover it transformed and enriched by the infinite perceptivity of the awakened imagination, augmented by subconscious resources.[9] One can see Hughes experimenting with surrealist techniques—especially the use of contradiction, the odd mixing of the human and the nonhuman, and the macabre humor—in "After Lorca," an uncollected 1963 poem that ends in a final terrifying release of godly song:

> The clock says "When will it be morning?"
> The sun says "Noon hurt me."
> The river cries with its mouthful of mud
> And the sea moves every way without moving.
>
> Out of my ear grew a reed
> Never touched by mouth.
> Paper yellows, even without flame,
> But in words carbon has already become diamond.
>
> A supple river of mirrors I run on
> Where great shadows rise to the glance,
> Flowing all forward and bringing
> The world through my reflection.
>
> A voice like a ghost that is not
> Rustle the dead in passage
> Leaving the living chilled,
> Wipe clear the pure glass of stone.
>
> Wipe clear the pure stone of flesh.
>
> A song tickling God's ear
> Till he laughs and catches it with his hand.
> A song with a man's face
> That God holds up in his fingers.[10]

Hughes uses some of these surrealist techniques in *Wodwo*, but most of the poems gravitate toward feelings of pained libidinal withdrawal from the landscape depicted, laced with oblique mythic allusions that delineate states of alienation and psychological dysfunction.

Though he certainly read Lorca and Kafka during this period, folklore and related primitive methods of solving "practical difficulties" provide the major sources for Hughes's surrealism in the sixties. Three influences converge here: his reviews of primitive folklore in the early sixties; his development of the concept of the poet as shaman, after a 1964 review of Eliade's *Shamanism*; and an unpublished libretto he wrote in 1960 on the

Bardo Thödol, the *Tibetan Book of the Dead*. In reviewing C. M. Bowra's *Primitive Song*, Hughes admires the primitive poets' total absorption in the moment, with the complete attentiveness of the whole psyche, not just the abstracting intellect. Bowra observes that this is a reflex of the close proximity of art and necessity in primitive living.[11] Hughes agrees: primitive poems function as "power-charms, tools and practical agents in the business of gaining desired ends, or deflecting the spirits of misfortune from planting their larvae in the psyche."[12] He refers his readers to Paul Radin's *African Folk Tales and Sculptures* in another review, and to B. H. Chamberlain's collection of Ainu tales, for weirdly engrossing stories that are as "inspired and astonishing" as Kafka's.[13]

The function of the shaman is central to Hughes's sixties surrealism. The shaman is a religious expert in the art of psychic healing—both for individual primitives and for society—who undergoes ecstatic psychic ascents to heaven and descents to hell, with all manner of related physiological pain, for the purpose of acquiring an elixir or healing power for patients. Eliade emphasizes several times in *Shamanism* that what is really central to the shamanic experience is undergoing the concrete psychological *process* of death, dismemberment, and resurrection. The process is similar to that of an initiation rite, except that the shaman experiences it repeatedly, whenever the psychic health of the individual or the society demands.[14] The first two stages are always replete with surrealistic experiences of alienation, maiming, and death—where the body is torn open and devoured by a ravenous animal, after the eyes, heart, bowels, and intestines are plucked out. This surrealistic process of deathly withdrawal, with the addition of mythic and Oriental elements, will become the formal paradigm for *Wodwo* and *Gaudete*, and Crow's inability to undergo this process will account for much of the satiric humor of *Crow*. Hughes describes the process and its purpose very clearly in his 1964 review of *Shamanism*:

Shamanism is not a religion, but a technique for moving in a state of ecstasy among the various spiritual realms, and for generally dealing with souls and spirits, in a practical way, in some practical crisis. It flourishes alongside and within the prevailing religion. . . . the most common form of election comes from the spirits themselves: they approach the man in a dream. . . . The central episode in this full-scale dream, just like the central episode in the rites where the transformation is effected forcibly by the tribe, is a magical death, then dismemberment, by a demon or equivalent powers, with all possible variants of boiling, devouring, burning, stripping to the bones. From this

nadir, the shaman is resurrected, with new insides, a new body created for him by the spirits. . . . His business is usually to guide some
soul to the underworld, or bring back a sick man's lost soul, or deliver
sacrifices to the dead, or ask the spirits the reason for an epidemic, or
the whereabouts of game or a man lost. . . . The results, when the
shaman returns to the living, are some display of healing power, or a
clairvoyant piece of information. The cathartic effect on the audience,
and the refreshing of their religious feeling, must be profound.[15]

Lévi-Strauss explains the therapeutic process involved by adopting the
psychoanalytic term "abreaction," the patient's intense reliving of the initial
trauma until it is overcome. In primitive cultures the shaman abreacts *for*
the patient, who empathizes with the intense, trancelike experience that
the shaman undergoes. Healing wisdom or a mythic kernel of knowledge,
imparted in the final resurrection stage, reorients the patient toward a
more useful and purposive relationship with society.[16]

Hughes broadens the scope of this shamanic process to encompass a
great deal of literature, in the process offering his readers a significant insight into the formal organization of *Wodwo*. In his *Shamanism* review,
Hughes conflates the shaman's psychic journey with "the basic experience
of the poetic temperament we call 'romantic'" and then asserts that this
journey is also "the outline, in fact, of the Heroic Quest." Joseph Campbell,
after detailed examination of the central myths of many primitive cultures,
also speaks of a "formula" for the "adventure of the hero," and in similar
terms: "a separation from the world, a penetration to some source of
power, and a life-enhancing return," or a "dying to the world" and a rebirth
"filled with creative power."[17] A three-stage surrealistic, heroic adventure,
toward a visionary achievement of a healing power, is the central formal
pattern underlying the structure of *Wodwo*. This pattern explains the enigmatical "Author's Note" that prefaces the volume: "The stories and the play
in this book may be read as notes, appendix, and unversified episodes
of the events behind the poems, or as chapters of a single adventure to
which the poems are commentary and amplification. Either way, the verse
and the prose are intended to be read together, as parts of a single work."[18]

Unlike the Coleridgean fusion of a vitalistic metaphysic with concrete
nature in *Hawk*, or the Yeatsian meditations upon concrete instances of
love and aggression in *Lupercal*, *Wodwo* begins with a complete divorce between the inner and outer worlds, the result of an anguished revulsion
from the landscape depicted. In parts I and II a single recurrent persona
undergoes states of neurotic and then psychotic withdrawal from the outer

world and finally experiences an imaginative death and dismemberment in *The Wound*. The *Bardo Thödol*, originally a shamanistic text, provides the Oriental psychology that informs many of the ecstatic moments of union with nature in part III. But rather than further postpone discussion of individual part I poems, we shall save consideration of the *Bardo Thödol* for a more appropriate moment, when elucidating part III.

Both the surrealism and the shamanism deepen Hughes's understanding of his inner world in *Wodwo*. The aggression that Hughes reconciled through New Critical formalism in *Lupercal* leaks its "Cordite oozings of Gallipoli" once again, but through surrealistic torrents that resolve themselves only in the shamanistic structural progression of the volume. The outer world causes of this aggression are specified in *Wodwo*, but left relatively undeveloped. "Boom" and "Public Bar TV" extend Hughes's meditations on the sterile materialism and scientific rationalism of modern Western culture that began in "Fourth of July" and the uncollected "A Fable." "Logos" (British *Wodwo* only) and part I of "Gog" deepen meditations on the denial of the instincts in Christianity that began in "The Perfect Forms."[19] Comprehending the causes of aggression is secondary to experiencing the inner suffering in *Wodwo*. Hughes will reverse this hierarchy in *Crow*.

Before *Wodwo* Hughes seems eager to applaud participation in temporal experience and cultural advancement. *The Hawk in the Rain* ends with a qualified approval of Bishop Farrar's martyrdom; *Lupercal* concludes with an expression of faith in the Luperci's ritual efforts to reempower man "age to age while the body hold." The personae of *Hawk* poems either wrestle with experience and their libidinal energies or are satirized for failing to do so. Hughes salutes Nicholas Farrar, Thomas Browne, and the Retired Colonel in *Lupercal* for articulating the best cultural values of their respective ages. In the early war poetry Hughes typically reconciles human aggressiveness in the tensions and artifice of New Critical or wolf mask formalism, while affirming the worth of the individual soldier's survival struggle. But in *Wodwo* this confidence in historical enterprises in Western culture vanishes completely. The personae (really one central persona) disdain cultural roots, for nightmarish obsessions with human destructiveness obtrude. In part I especially, imagery of fear, turmoil, blood, and death oscillates with imagery of emptiness, silence, sleep, and surrealistic fright at nature's cycles of birth, destruction, and renewal.

Oblique mythic allusions frequently compound the inner agony of part I of *Wodwo*, often to articulate a disaffection with modern Western culture. Joseph Campbell in *Creative Mythology* adopts the Old Germanic term wyrd to characterize the Western hero's central mythic adventure since the breakdown of medieval Catholicism. Wyrd signifies the process of winning a consciousness-enlarging transformation of eros within the self, after psychological rounds of love and death in time and historical experience.[20] Both Campbell in Creative Mythology and Graves in The White Goddess allude to the proliferation of animals as fertility symbols in primitive societies—pigs, boars, bulls—to underscore the pervasiveness of belief in this transformational round. The central persona of part I of Wodwo, however, openly fears this process. The persona of "A Vegetarian," as the title implies, refuses to partake of this carnal round; he sees only the destructive portion—the "snaring and rending"—and expects only death from his frightened stasis.

The central reason for the surrealistic disenchantment with Western culture in Wodwo is a more deeply and directly experienced consciousness of the effects of world war upon moderns. A bullet's "kiss of death" sends the persona reeling in "Bowled Over." Churches and farmland ("patched fields"), the products of human culture, spin in a disoriented loss of meaning and purpose, a convulsed "Desertion in the face of a bullet." "Unknown Soldier" and "Flanders," poems published early in the sixties and collected in Recklings, also attest to Hughes's preoccupation with war, as do reviews of the war poetry of Keith Douglas, Wilfred Owen, and others during this period,[21] and the Wodwo poems "Scapegoats and Rabies" (American edition of Wodwo only) and "Karma."

As Hughes's poetic consciousness is thrown back upon its own inner resources, childhood memories of World War I stories shared by his family surface. World War I affected him deeply because, in Hughes's own words, "my father fought in it, and brought home his share of scars and medals, and at the family gatherings everybody seemed to talk about nothing else but the war, who had been killed and how and so on."[22] World War I became a "fairy-story world" to him, because at an impressionable age his generation "got the experience secondhand but fairly whole. And as it occurred to the actual participants."[23] But in the surreal mood of Wodwo, this "fairy-story world" sours into a nightmarish indictment of Western civilization. Though placed in part III of Wodwo, "Out" provides a necessary thematic framework for the nightmarish visions of aggression in many part I poems. Here, in a tone of rueful indignation, Hughes considers his father's victimization and near death by Gallipoli shrapnel (section I), with an eye to the genetic consequences for himself as a more impoverished "luckless double" of the next generation, the product of an automatic regenerative power in nature (section II) that simply will not surrender.

Section III of "Out," however, presents a new insight into the mass warfare of the twentieth century. Here Hughes reasons that the stark anonymity of amassed millions, insulated from the enemy by machines, militates against even the ability of the psyche to place such slaughter within a larger humanistic retributive scheme. The function of the poppy, emblematic of a remembrance of the sleeping dead from antiquity to John McCrae's "In Flanders Fields" and contemporary Memorial Day customs, is rendered worthless; lost forever are the old ritual intuitions of the potential of the next generation to outlive historical animosities and to repay the debt owed the dead by following their ideals and conquering the foe. Hughes seems to ask McCrae how can we take up our countrymen's "quarrel with the foe" when the individual soldier's humane responses collapse as he stands in a no-man's land between astronomical body counts and inhuman but terribly efficient machine gun barrels. In a review of I. M. Parsons's anthology of World War I poets (*Listener*, 5 August 1965), Hughes writes that the four years of World War I were not enough to digest "the shock of machine guns, armies of millions, and the plunge into the new dimension, where suddenly and for the first time Adam's descendants found themselves meaningless."

This new dimension of meaninglessness in section III of "Out" replaces the persona's former faith in nature's cyclic ability (the "refreshing of ploughs / In the woe-dark under my mother's eye—") to imbue wartime death with value. The carnage of Gallipoli transforms the poppy, emblematic of the ideals and courage of the slain, into a "canvas-beauty puppet on a wire"—a worthless, "bloody-minded" flower. "Out" ends with the firm resolve to bid "Goodbye to the cenotaphs on my mother's breasts" and "Goodbye to the remaindered charms of my father's survival." Instead of the affirmation of the "old spark of the blood heat" in "Lupercalia," Hughes now affirms that he will no longer be constrained by genetic habit to participate unconsciously in repeat performances of the errors of Western cultural history. There is no stronger statement in *Wodwo* of a departure from Hughes's early faith in human potential in historical time.

On the subject of the involuntary transmission of aggressive tendencies Hughes writes, in a *Wodwo* period review (*New Statesman*, 2 October 1964), that "The possibilities of what a child might absorb from its lineage . . . are awful, which is what alarmed Freud." Freud treated violence in his late work as part of thanatos, the death instinct, which is usually fused with eros or libidinal energy in the ego, but can be directed outward in aggressive acts. More specifically, when Freud tried to explain the slaughter of World War I, one answer he developed was that of a repetition-compulsion biological urge, like cellular replacement, to regress to an earlier level of evolution. The other concept Freud developed was that of "archaic heritage" or "phylogenetic inheritance": inherited memory traces in the genes, innately present at birth, of the primordial crime—parricide, the son's first rebellious act against the cruel despotism and sexual covetousness of the patriarch in the primal horde.[24] In parts I and II of *Wodwo* Hughes treats aggression in ways similar to both Freudian theories—the compulsive repetitiousness that breeds hostility and the inherited phylogenetic predisposition toward violent behavior.

One can infer that the domestic antagonisms and their "blood weight of money" in "Her Husband" surface daily in that couple's life, and in the lives of millions of working-class families; the jaguar in "Second Glance at a Jaguar" exhibits a compulsive, inexhaustible power to "keep his rage brightening"; and in "Thistles" the warriors return to fight "over the same ground." The surreal "Ghost Crabs" symbolize both the aggressive traits and the repetition-compulsion urge present in the dissolution of the human personality during sleep:

> All night, around us or through us,
> They stalk each other, they fasten on to each other,
> They mount each other, they tear each other to pieces,
> They utterly exhaust each other.
> They are the powers of this world.
> We are their bacteria,
> Dying their lives and living their deaths.
> At dawn, they sidle back under the sea's edge.
> They are the turmoil of history, the convulsion
> In the roots of blood, in the cycles of concurrence.

In both "Ghost Crabs" and "Second Glance at a Jaguar" Hughes, like the shaman, *becomes* the animal; he experiences the animal's destructive power in a "surrealistic or therapeutic torrent" of intense, sustained, nightmarish energy.

Often in part I the mood of surrealistic revulsion is so great as to occasion a general libidinal withdrawal from the landscape depicted. The alternate shuddering and silence of the wind-blown trees and the vision of the shadow of the ploughman's bones in "A Wind Flashes the Grass" mirror the persona's own state of anxiety and fear at the prospect of mortality in the time-bound world of woe. In the last two lines of the poem, the conscious use of the pathetic fallacy reveals the persona's fear at the momentary nature of both humans and landscape. Similarly, the persona of "Sugar Loaf," in noticing the hill's time-bound vulnerability to erosion, becomes disconcerted by the hill's ignorance of the process. Unsettling images of naked susceptibility to pain mirror a torment within the psyche of the persona. Water becomes "wild as alcohol," and "nude and tufted" reeds shiver, mirroring the persona's vulnerability.

In certain part I poems the psychological torment occasioned by the private and the larger cultural tragedy is so great as to cause a complete displacement into the realm of surrealistic nightmare. In "Cadenza," "The Rescue," and "Stations" the central persona experiences more psychotic states of personality breakdown and libidinal withdrawal. In "Cadenza" and "The Rescue" the dissolution of the ego and the abandonment of a normal relationship with daily living is feared, but is taking place nevertheless. Noise is preferred in both cases as supportive reinforcement to the security needs of the ego. But in "Cadenza" the soloist's egocentric refusal to relinquish his dominance leads to an aggressive combat with the orchestra. Metaphors become mixed and metaphoric vehicles become purposely confused to present surreal images of disorientation. The soloist perceives himself as a "coffin attended by swallows," one that "will not be silent." But the attempt at an Osiris-like rebirth runs amuck. The sea "lifts swallow wings" and parts clouds that are "full of surgery and collisions." Then the sea-swallow becomes a sky that "dives shut like a burned land back to its spark—." Finally the soloist's frenetic playing takes its grim toll: "Blue with sweat, the violinist / Crashes into the orchestra, which explodes." Instead of the surreal humor that closes "Logos" and "Ghost Crabs," the psychotic frenzy of "Cadenza" leads to a complete annihilation of ego and will. The soloist's refusal to accept the dissolution of his former self-image (the coffin) causes a rather complete disintegration of the psyche.

In "The Rescue" the persona learns that the reality of his psychological state is one of silence, a dying away from the temporal world. The "five," perhaps the five senses, are too fragile for noises from the world of the living. What the psyche wants to see—"The flash of wet oars slashing their eyes back alive" and the rescue by "the long white liner anchoring the world"—is "wrong." In reality the five "just stood sucked empty / As grasses by this island's silence." Hughes conveys a mood of deathly surrealistic estrangement from normality through nightmare images of "sailors white / As maggots" and "mummies with their bandages lifted off," followed by the soundless "pouring faces" from the ship's "dazzling side."

The meditations of "Stations" present a more complete abandonment of the conscious analytic ego, prized by our empirical culture as the prime locus of thinking and experiencing. In section III the persona is "complacent" in his inability to ratiocinate, to make even "one comparison," and feels completely estranged even from his former artistic labor. Only an "Absence" remains to weep "its respite through [his] accomplished music." In section IV the abandonment of language is presented surrealistically as a severing of the head by the trainwheels of time, in an unfamiliar landscape, a dream image of alienation:

> Whether you say it, think it, know it
> Or not, it happens, it happens, as
> Over rails over
> The neck the wheels leave
> The head with its vocabulary useless,
> Among the flogged plantains.

The mythic psychodrama in part I of *Wodwo* leads toward a total dissolution of the ego-oriented personality. The "abandoned surrealistic or therapeutic torrent" is therapeutic to the extent that the central persona gradually acknowledges his suffering and his preference for emptiness, withdrawal, and absence, over participation in goal-directed activity in Western culture. The persona learns to submit, to suffer his fate or "*dree his weird*," as the Scots say, and repudiate the Western *wyrd* of Campbell's monomyth.

"Scapegoats and Rabies" is perhaps the quintessential part I *Wodwo* poem. Though it appeared only in the American edition, its first publication in early 1967 (*New Statesman*, 13 January 1967) indicates that it was probably written in mid or late 1966, at the time Hughes was organizing *Wodwo*. In "Scapegoats and Rabies" one recognizes a complete surrealistic dislocation into nightmare, the most straightforward analysis of war in terms similar to the Freudian repetition-compulsion biological urge, the extreme moral anguish and sensitivity of the poet to human suffering, and a clear expression of an Oriental way out of this impasse.

Nightmarish images of anonymous dead soldiers obtrude in a garish montage in the first section of "Scapegoats and Rabies." Both heredity and the nurture provided by Western culture combine as causes: stares from old women, trembling chins from old men, bow-legs from toddlers, facelessness from "the mouldering / Of letters and citations / On rubbish dumps." The funeral parade is endless, for the repetition-compulsion "drumming / Of their boots" is "concentrating / Toward a repeat performance" in future generations. The sardonic, almost misanthropic mood of the poem leads to surrealistic images of loathing, disgust, and putrefaction, as the persona perceives the soldiers getting

> their hopelessness
> From the millions of the future
> Marching in their boots, blindfold and riddled,
> Rotten heads on their singing shoulders,
> The blown-off right hand swinging to the stride
> Of the stump-scorched and blown-off legs
> Helpless in the terrible engine of the boots.

Sections II and III present the poet as General undergoing the psychic shock of having his head torn apart by each memory-trace of the events of war, by a searing, agonized consciousness of human aggression through the ages, presented as a paranoid sensitivity to every bullet, every shell-burst. The General's face is a lantern of light in the darkness of war, its flame blown out and relit in response to the explosive staccato outside.

Sections IV and V continue the sardonic mood with an allegory of a sol-dier's outfitting for battle, his near-death and resuscitation in the mud of historical time. Since the poet-General, like Diogenes searching with his lantern for an honest man, cannot locate a receptive culture, the only alter-native is to exorcise that culture's aggressiveness for the self's sanity. As Christ once exorcised a demon into the Gaderene swine (Mark, 5), so Hughes creates a faceless stereotype as collective cultural scapegoat. This soldier's battledress is woven by some of the most reprehensible elements of contemporary civilization—its materiality and smug conspicuous con-sumption, niggard of self-comprehension (IV: stanza I), its petty small-mindedness and selfishness (IV: stanza II), and the poverty and scurrility of its cultural, political, and economic products (IV: stanzas IIIff.). After being shot while traversing no man's land "In a shouting flight / From his own stink," the soldier in section V embraces London and the mud of time and human history in a state too hopelessly maimed to muster any resis-tance. More so than any other passage in *Wodwo*, sections IV and V of "Scapegoats and Rabies" present an indictment of the enterprises of con-temporary Western civilization, though the specific images are geographi-cally British in reference.

The way out of the impasse presented in "Scapegoats and Rabies" is through the abandonment of the Western analytic ego—a machine that passively ingests information from the outside and functions as a security-

seeking defense mechanism against the outside world—and a retrench-
ment to a sense of self as the generator of one's own perceptions of reality,
in a way that *unifies* the perceiving consciousness with external reality.
Hughes's imagination, initially employed in *Wodwo* in coaxing to consciousness a torrent of surreal images from the depths of his inner world
and identifying with shamanic animal energy, once again is able to unify
the inner and outer worlds of his art—from the locus of an Oriental subjective monism.

The poet as General in section II of "Scapegoats and Rabies" transcends
the subject/object dualism of his Western culture by opting for an excarnation of the fleshy body and its automatic responses to the environment and
adopting an Oriental subjective monism, a realization of the self as the creator of reality-for-the-self, of its own unitive relationship with nature:

> Knives, forks, spoons divide his brains.
> The supporting earth, and the night around him,
>
> Smoulder like the slow, curing fire
> Of a Javanese head-shrinker.
>
> Nothing remains of the *tête d'armée* but the skin—
> A dangling parchment lantern
>
> Slowly revolving to right, revolving to left,
>
> Trembling a little with the
>   incessant pounding,
>
> Over the map, empty in the ring of light.

III

Wit's End

> The General commits his emptiness to God.

To leave the fleshy body's instinctual and emotional dependencies upon a
comforting external environment, and to abandon the analytic ego and dualistic thinking, is to experience the Buddhist state of *śūnyatā*, a state of
complete personality dissolution and a realization of emptiness, of the full-

ness of nothingness, where "nothing" is understood as a nondualistic involvement in the plenitude of *all* of reality (i.e., no one thing).[25] What is accomplished in the process is a fresh, direct, precognitive perception of reality in its suchness, before the conscious mind labels with Aristotelian classes and categories, semantic descriptions, and their underlying cultural assumptions. After achieving the *śūnyatā* state, the initiate can progress to a state of perception where the self-as-creator fuses with the activities of nature, in any of a number of ways: a recognition of the *ātman* or self-soul of the Upanishads as the generator of all that is perceived;[26] or the yogic *īshwara pranidhāna*, the God within the self as the creator and ground of all being;[27] or the *satori* sense of ecstatic participatory involvement in the isness of all reality, in Zen.[28] Section III of "Scapegoats and Rabies" begins with a resurrection of the self as creator of reality; the line "The General commits his emptiness to God" indicates a movement from *śūnyatā* to yogic *īshwara pranidhāna*. By the end of the section the General has realized a new sense of power as the generator of reality-for-the-self, as his hand sweeps the battlefield "flat as a sheet of foolscap" and he affirms a sympathetic commitment to his brethren:

> I AM A LANTERN
> IN THE HAND
> OF A BLIND PEOPLE

In sections II and III of "Scapegoats and Rabies" Hughes may also have been meditating upon passages in the Śvetāśvatara Upanishad (1:14; 2:11–16), wherein the macrocosmic all-space fuses with the soul within the subjective self to create the *ātman* of Oriental monism. In this passage the two concepts fuse into the *ātman* through imagery of fire, God, crystal, and inwardly illuminated lantern, similar to that of sections II and III of "Scapegoats and Rabies." Both the fire of yogic meditation and the purgative fire at the end of section II of "Scapegoats and Rabies," the "slow, curing fire / Of a Javanese head-shrinker," lead to a death of the old conscious ego and the attainment of an inner personal godliness. The motif of the willed, self-devouring of the carnal self leading to an excarnation of the flesh, and of the presence of God in all fiery, world-destroying cataclysms, leaving only the "Face of Glory" mask, is a prominent motif of Vedic Śivaite mythology. This fiery, self-destructive aspect of Śiva particularly delighted the aboriginal Javanese long after their conversion to Hinduism.[29]

One must be careful to realize that Hughes does not subscribe to a simplistic either/or, Western versus Eastern, position; nor is he an ardent devotee of a particular branch of Oriental orthodoxy. Hughes is entirely eclectic, mainly interested in the survival of the spirit and the integrated psyche, and will use, as he has told Ekbert Faas, whatever serves: "You choose a subject because it serves, because you need it."[30] Like Jung, Campbell, and Lévi-Strauss, Hughes is particularly interested in conflating the folklore, myth, and ritual patterns of primitive and non-Western cultures in order to comprehend the psychological and spiritual common denominators operative, and to discover what survival potential these kernels may hold for contemporary people.

One who is capable of the perceptual and psychological revolution of recognizing the *ātman* as generator of all that the self perceives is freed from bondage to instinctual cravings and attachments, from dualistic thinking and preoccupation with temporality, and becomes the world-all, as in the Bṛihad-Āraṇyaka Upanishad (4.4.12–13):

> If a person knew the Soul [Atman],
> With the thought "I am he!"
> With what desire, for love of what
> Would he cling unto the body?
>
> He who has found and has awakened to the Soul
> That has entered this conglomerate abode—
> He is the maker of everything, for he is the creator of all;
> The world is his: indeed he is the world itself.[31]

The *ātman* of the Upanishads was very much on Hughes's mind as he organized the poems of *Wodwo*; one need only repeat the last epigraph quote to this chapter, from Hughes's review of Dylan Thomas's *Selected Letters* (*New Statesman*, 25 November 1966): "What he [Thomas] was really waiting for, and coaxing with alcohol, was the delicate cerebral disaster that demolishes the old self for good, with all its crushing fortifications, and leaves the *atman* a clear field."

The *ātman* union of inner and outer worlds exemplifies the "that art thou" doctrine of the Chāndogya Upanishad (6:8–16), where the "that" is the totality of the perceived environment as it exists for the perceiving consciousness, and the "thou" is the God, the creator-originator of all that is perceived. In yogic meditation the adept can achieve a state of *samādhi*, of agreement or unity with the whole of reality; this union can be achieved either by focusing upon an object of consciousness ("with seed"; *sampraj-ñāta*) or without consciousness of an object ("without seed"; *asampraj-*

ñāta).[32] In Chinese and Japanese Zen the experience of *satori* or totalistic unity with the infinite is also cognate, though it dawns upon the initiate in an instantaneous and ecstatic epiphanic moment.[33] Through such meditative practices one can obliterate the mental baggage acquired from an overly rational and overly aggressive culture and experience reality afresh, direct, without labeling.

Certain poems in part I of *Wodwo* assist in liberating the *ātman* by achieving the *śūnyatā* state of emptiness, of death to the analytic ego, in order to experience the fullness of nothingness, the fullness of *all* creation. In section III of "Root, Stem, Leaf" (American edition only) the persona imagines himself to be utterly anonymous, as forgotten as a discarded heirloom spoon "blackening / Among roots in a thorn-hedge." This leads to a knowledge of the plenitude of all existence at the end of the section, wherein "Everything is inheriting everything." Of the part I poems in *Wodwo*, section III of "Stations" relates the most completely realized state of *śūnyatā* emptiness; here the persona experiences a queer state of complete dissolution and absence, of estrangement even from his own act of writing:

> You are a wild look—out of an egg
> Laid by your absence.
>
> In the great Emptiness you sit complacent,
> Blackbird in wet snow.
>
> If you could make only one comparison—
> Your condition is miserable, you would give up.
>
> But you, from the start, surrender to total Emptiness,
> Then leave everything to it.
>
> Absence. It is your own
> Absence
>
> Weeps its respite through your accomplished music,
> Wraps its cloak dark about your feeding.

"The Green Wolf" and "The Bear," the concluding poems (except for "Scapegoats and Rabies" in the American edition) of part I of *Wodwo*, further assist in demolishing the old egocentric self, as prelude to recognizing the sleeping *ātman* within. In "The Green Wolf" the title allusion to the scapegoat victim of the purgatorial Beltane Fires of Normandy combines with imagery of a cerebral hemorrhage or stroke (the "dark bloodclot" of line 9) to reinforce a state of deathly neurotic withdrawal.[34] In this state of self-negating passivity, forces in the external environment assist in a destructive process: hawthorn blossom and beanflower symbolize, respectively, powers of erotic seduction and destruction.[35] The "deathly perfume" of the hawthorn blossom, and the tiger stripes of the beanflower, "unmake and remake" the persona in a surrealistic vision of death:

> One smouldering annihilation
> Of old brains, old bowels, old bodies
> In the scarves of dew, the wet hair of nightfall.

"The Green Wolf" was originally published as "Dark Women" (*Observer*, 6 January 1963), with only minor differences from the *Wodwo* version. The original poem title contains a cryptic allusion concerning the sundering of the old conscious ego. In cabbalistic lore Ama is the destructive aspect of Binah or Understanding, the third Sephirah in the cabbalistic Tree of Life. Ama attests to the arduous labor needed to achieve any goal and the necessity of disrupting and destroying the old self-image to create fertile ground for personality growth. She is usually known as the "Dark Mother," carries a disciplinary bar of wood in her left hand, and is depicted as a gigantic Mother Superior completely shrouded in black.[36]

In "The Bear," the final poem in the part I psychodrama of withdrawal and personality dissolution, the bear represents the "gleam in the pupil" of a transcendent self, which can be revealed through opening the *prajñā-cakṣu*, the Buddhist third eye of transphenomenal wisdom.[37] The bear's "price is everything"—a resignation to the death of the conscious ego. In return he grants a largesse of comprehension of self-and-world, gluing beginning and end, offering knowledge deeper than a well, wider than the universe. He is a "ferryman / To dead land," but not as a functionary like Charon, for in primitive cultures he symbolizes a godly regeneration-through-death. In shamanic initiations the bear is often a theriomorphic vehicle of dismemberment toward the attaining of new life and mystical powers.[38] The bear's abode is "In the huge, wide-open sleeping eye of the mountain," the principal residence of the gods to primitives.[39] The Ainus of northern Japan practiced the earliest form of the "animal master" ritual known, with a bear as its focus; its purpose was to affirm that the process of destruction was only a stage in a recurring cosmic drama of rebirth and regeneration. Hence the young bear, sacrificed with elaborate ritual, was *joyously* sent home to its cosmic abode.[40]

The stories of part II repeat the mythic psychodrama of surrealistic withdrawal and dissolution of the personality. The central characters exhibit varying stages of neurotic and psychotic behavior caused by the repression of instinct and withdrawal from other-directed libido. Grooby's inability to withstand three hours of harvest heat in "The Harvesting" leads to an anguished preoccupation with mortality. As aging victim of the temporal round of birth/death, but without the capacity to transcend his situation, he himself becomes the hare hunted by the "big, white bony greyhound," as in the epigraph chant from the seventeenth-century Allansford witch coven.[41] In "Sunday" what at first appears to be a sexual initiation for Michael results in neurotic flight. The girl is inaccessible, presided over by an "expert" male companion, and instead of a knowing lure to sexual initiation she offers only "mesmerized incredulity." The girl is too much a product of the "harmless, church-going slopes" to be of aid in Michael's sexual quandary. The only initiation into the birth/death sexual round offered in the story is the sham, degraded showmanship of Billy Red's rat catching. Neither the girl nor Billy Red's grotesquery appeals to Michael, who flees in speechless revulsion at the entire ordeal.

The more severe estrangement from object-directed libido in "The Suitor" and "The Rain Horse" leads to more pronounced neurotic behavior. In "The Suitor" the estrangement from eros is presented symbolically and in a surrealistic landscape—in the continuing darkness and blocked bedroom window of the girl's house, the pummeling received by the man in the trilby (the repressed instinctual component of the suitor's ego), and the final surrealistic tableau of alienated instinct when the suitor faces away from the flute-playing man in the trilby. Here the flute notes of Pan work their way up the house wall in complete dissociation from the suitor, though he has walked five miles in never-used dancing shoes in the hope of an encounter based entirely upon the girl's chance smile in the school corridors. In "The Rain Horse" the alienation of instinctual life is so total that an eruption of demonized eros ensues when the young adult businessman returns home after a twelve-year absence. The environment of his nurture elicits only boredom and impatience, and the impatience soon turns to anger at the discomforts of mud and rain. The horse appears exactly at this point and becomes malevolent *only* when the man resolves not to deal with the animal's watchful presence—when he decides to repress his emotions and banish the horse from consciousness. Thus the horse symbolizes the repressed libidinal energies in the man's own psyche, a favorite technique of German expressionist drama.[42] Of course whatever is banished from consciousness will return to confront the agent of the repression as a demonized force that appears to be outside the agent. So the horse that originally "was watching him intently" soon returns as a destructive agent in a surrealistic guise:

> He took control of himself and turned back deliberately, determined not to give the horse one more thought. If it wanted to stare at him, let it. He was nestling firmly into these resolutions when the ground shook and he heard the crash of a heavy body coming down the wood. Like lightning his legs bounded him upright and about face. The horse was almost on top of him, its head stretching forwards, ears flattened and lips lifted back from the long yellow teeth. He got one snapshot glimpse of the red-veined eyeball as he flung himself backwards around the tree. Then he was away up the slope, whipped by oak twigs as he leapt the brambles and brushwood, twisting between the close trees till he tripped and sprawled.

After a final truce the persona feels lobotomized, but fails to recognize that the cause of this feeling is his having shirked the burden of the experience, of having refused the chance for psychological reclamation.

"Snow" is at once the most psychotic of the short stories and the one that most foreshadows the Oriental conclusion of part III. Here the normal rational thinking process is equated with the blinding, lifeless snow, the strangling snowdrifts of conscious rationality. In "Snow" a partly amnesiac survivor of a plane crash in the Arctic wilderness must concentrate and discipline his survival energies and distrust his tendency to lapse into a muddleheaded optimism. The key to successful endurance provided by the story is to withdraw one's awe, fears, and attachments to the temporal world and learn to awaken a deeper, more essential self at the root of one's inner being. The survivor learns that "My mind is not my friend" and that "It's my mind that has this contemptible awe for the probably true, and my mind, I know . . . is not me and is by no means sworn to help me." The central character of "Snow" appears to heed the warning of Patanjali, at the outset of his *Yoga Sutras* (no. 2), that one must control the mind's habitual flow of ideas and conventional choice making, through concentration and meditation.[43] The Hindu chant invoked by the survivor, "O Jewel of the Lotus," is the mantra of Chenrazee, *Om Mani Padme Hum*, used like all mantras as a power charm to focus one's willpower and meditative energies and to invoke supernormal powers for practical or religious reasons. The survivor remains alive at the conclusion of the story because he trusts his inner powers and disciplines his need for reassurances from conventional rationalizations, or even from his chair, his one anchor to the phenomenal world. As he develops this meditative control he is even tempted to "go deep into the blizzard" and leave the chair altogether.

The radio play *The Wound* presents the second stage of the shamanic/heroic "single adventure" of *Wodwo*, the shaman's experience of dismemberment, or the hero's visit to the underworld. In an interview with Anthony Thwaite, broadcast on BBC radio ("New Comment": 29 January 1963), Hughes states that the action of *The Wound* occurs entirely inside Ripley's wounded head in the space of two seconds after he is shot in battle. The play illustrates certain psycho-physiological realities that Ripley must confront as he decides whether to live or to die. "The hero," Hughes remarks to Thwaite, "is just the personality absolutely collapsed back into a world which is the body—this body of mud and decomposing things." Like the Eskimo shaman who must confront a mystical vision of his own skeleton during his initiation,[44] Ripley must confront the reality of his dying self—take an instantaneous psycho-biological inventory, recognize his potential collapse into the decomposition of animal instinct and death, and decide whether to submit to the blood-drinking ogresses (Persephone's minions) at the white chateau. If he cannot muster the necessary vital forces to survive, then he should exchange his soldier's uniform for the more rigorous formal attire of the dead and dance with them at their ball later in the play.

Ripley actually confronts his skeleton twice in *The Wound*. Early on he gazes incredulously at his prone body, cataloguing each part serially, as if dismembered, but not recognizing it as his own. The vital signs are weak; only a single finger flicks at the stars. The central confrontation with his wounded self occurs later, when he gazes at Massey's dead body in the adjacent armory-museum. Hughes has told Thwaite that at this point "Massey is the projection of the thing that's wrong with Ripley." Here Ripley comprehends the import of his projection and resolves to live, to terminate what Hughes characterizes as the "traditional visit to the House of the Dead." As he gathers his energies in his inner world, Ripley survives a nine-mile walk for help in the "real" world in a state of unconscious automatism.

Ripley survives because he is able to reunite with his anima, the feminine principle that Jung perceived as the "leaping and twinkling of the soul" that brings man out of his idleness and ensnares him into life.[45] To Thwaite, Hughes characterizes the Girl of the drama as "the gift itself," the "little bit of life that brings him through all this ordeal and enables him to come back into life and the real world." The reclamation process is not easy, for Ripley has very definite inhibitions and fears, a "bitch-proof" misogyny exacerbated by battle stress. The Girl gives Ripley his first conscious inkling that he is indeed shot in the head, in her second visit. She accentuates with romantic irony the ambivalence of life and death in our aggressive Western culture in her third visit: she tells Ripley that the noise he hears is both "your life, working at the hole in your head," and "the war, working at all the undead." In her fourth and last visit she supplies needed support to return Ripley to the world of the living. The Girl is a power mobilized from Ripley's unconscious, as was the insight that Massey is his potentially dead self: the armory-museum is illuminated by a rotten phosphorescent fish, a surrealistic version of the archetypal Christian symbol of sustenance won from the unconscious.[46]

Much textual evidence exists in *The Wound* to indicate that Hughes attaches a great deal of ambivalence to Ripley's survival. The action takes place on midsummer's eve, "when all the disasters occur"—when, according to Frazer, scapegoat victims were traditionally immolated in fires in primitive Western societies.[47] Surrealistic images of horror, devouring, even of cannibalism, abound in *The Wound*, and there is deep irony in Ripley's muttered offer of marriage to his vision of femininity when he is finally rescued. The two soldiers who rescue his bleeding body, encased in the mud of war, accentuate the irony: "what's he smiling at? Look at this, grinning away as if he'd been crowned."

The mythic superstructure of *The Wound* is entirely Western, but the fruit of the quest is not spiritual enlargement. The dominant images of this radio play are entirely negative, and Ripley's mantra is the unreflective "Keep going!" Massey hammers this inane command into Ripley at the outset of the play. If Massey is, in Hughes's own words, a "projection of the thing that's wrong with Ripley," then his problem is the malaise of modern Western culture. For what *The Wound* reveals of this culture is its hyperkinetic adventure urge, an obsession so poisoned by its repetition-compulsion aggressiveness that it is incapable of striving for any humanistic goals. Like the soldiers "helpless in the terrible engine of the boots" in "Scapegoats and Rabies," Ripley is more the victim of destructive energies than a successful quest hero. Ripley barely survives this initiation into the destructive horrors at the bottom of the self and contemporary Western civilization; he returns to the wartime world of "Bleeding mud" in a state of utter helplessness. As soldiers carry Ripley's limp body to camp, the voyage to the underworld ends. The *Wodwo* leitmotif of the dissolution of the conscious Western ego also ends here, allowing the leitmotif of the development of the *ātman* within the self to flower in part III.

Though Hughes became acquainted with Oriental mythology during his undergraduate work in anthropology at Cambridge, his work on the *Bardo Thödol* libretto immediately after *Lupercal* was crucial in deepening this interest. While at Yaddo in September 1959, Hughes met the Chinese composer Chou Wen-chung, who persuaded him to write the libretto for a large orchestral composition based upon the *Tibetan Book of the Dead*. According to Hughes, the work involved a "Gigantic orchestra, massed choirs, projected illuminated mandalas, soul-dancers and the rest." Though the project ultimately died for lack of expected funding, Hughes worked and reworked the libretto a great deal after his return to England that autumn, at least through November 1960, later admitting that he "got to know the *Bardo Thödol* pretty well" during that period.[48] More than deathbed prayers and instructions to the dying, the *Bardo Thödol* is to be used throughout adult life as a meditative guide to the Buddhist art of dying to the phenomenal world.[49] As Carl Jung writes in his "Psychological Commentary" to the *Bardo*, the purpose of the meditation is deliberately to induce a psychological state "transcendent over all assertion and predication," where the initiate realizes that "the 'giver' of all 'given' things dwells within us" and that "even the gods are the radiance and reflection of our own souls."[50]

As the deceased passes from the *Chikhai Bardo* state of the first four days after death into the *Chönyid Bardo* state of the fifth to fourteenth days, the possibility of experiencing the liberating *nirvana* of the Void, the *Dharma-Kāya* of Clear Light, lessens markedly, for karmic illusions appear, urging the soul back to participation in the phenomenal world. Here the text constantly exhorts the deceased not to fear or desire such illusions, to abandon egotism and recognize that all thought-forms are "the radiance of thine own intellectual faculties come to shine. They have not come from any other place. Be not attracted towards them; be not weak; be not terrified; but abide in the mood of non-thought formation. In that state all forms and radiances will merge into thyself, and Buddhahood will be obtained."[51] For those unable to abandon egotism, the devices of intellect, and fears or attachments to objects in the phenomenal world, the final *Sidpa Bardo* state of involvement with animal instinct dawns on the fifteenth day after death; here the deceased are whirled about by karmic winds and the play of instinct until reincarnation at the womb door results forty-nine days after death.

The central persona of part I fails to recognize that fears of participation in temporal experience in Western culture are self-created. The persona of "A Vegetarian," for instance, is tripped on "Eternity's stone threshold," by his fear of sundering his automatic instinctual dependency upon the environment. Both "A Wind Flashes the Grass" and "Sugar Loaf" contain imagery of wind-driven environments similar to that of the *Sidpa Bardo*, and for similar reasons: in each case the persona fails to recognize that his own winds of instinctual dependency cause the macabre, fearful gusts. The *Bardo*, originally an animistic, shamanistic text of the pre-Buddhist Bön-pos, contains numerous surrealistic passages with constant reminders that the causes of the surreal visions are entirely within the self, in cravings and instinctual attachments to the environment that manifest themselves in what we in the West know as the Seven Deadly Sins. The *Bardo* counsels the need for a higher level of self-possession that can free one from such automatic emotional responses. The real beauty of the *Bardo*, however, is that it also reveals how one's emotional state influences one's perceptions, or how a surrealistic vision is a self-caused refusal to achieve the lucidity of the *Dharma-Kāya*. Consider the following passages from the *Sidpa Bardo*:

> O nobly-born, at about that time, the fierce wind of *karma*, terrific and hard to endure, will drive thee [onwards], from behind, in dreadful gusts. Fear it not. That is thine own illusion. . . . Apparitional illusions, too, of being pursued by various terrible beasts of prey will dawn. Snow, rain, darkness, fierce blasts [of wind], and hallucinations of being pursued by many people likewise will come; [and] sounds as of mountains crumbling down, and of angry overflowing seas, and of the roaring of fire, and of fierce winds springing up.
>
> When these sounds come one, being terrified by them, will flee before them in every direction, not caring whither one fleeth. But the way will be obstructed by three awful precipices—white, and black, and red. They will be terror-inspiring and deep, and one will feel as if one were about to fall down them. O nobly-born, they are not really precipices; they are Anger, Lust, and Stupidity. . . .
>
> Then [one of the Executive Furies of] the Lord of Death . . . will cut off thy head, extract thy heart, pull out thy intestines, lick up thy brain, drink thy blood, eat thy flesh, and gnaw thy bones; but thou wilt be incapable of dying. Although thy body be hacked to pieces, it will revive again. . . .
>
> Thy body being a mental body is incapable of dying even though beheaded and quartered. In reality, thy body is of the nature of voidness; thou needst not be afraid. The Lords of Death are thine own hallucinations.[52]

Imagery of the demonic and disorienting in nature and animals always precedes a counsel directed toward achieving a knowledge of the self as generator of values, a counsel similar in some respects to the *ātman* of the Upanishads. The last two passages present a Bön-po version of the shamanistic stages in the heroic adventure, especially the surrealism of the first stage.

The goal of Hughes's use of Oriental psychology is not, however, to attain the self-absorbed, world-annihilating state of yogic *samādhi* or the *nirvana* of the Clear Light in *Bardo* thought, but to return to the world cleansed of overdependence upon a rational analytic ego that leads to aggression, fortified with the awakened *ātman* within the self as the generative center of experience and capable of merging with a nature newly perceived as benign. This is closest to the practices of modern Zen. The psychic process in Zen begins with the *Mahāyāna* principle of emptiness, *śūnyatā*, when all impediments of consciousness are annihilated, and the mind rests in a passive state of personality dissolution, devoid of thoughts, experiencing the fullness of nothingness. The process ends in *satori* as a psychological upheaval occurs wherein the intellect as the primary seat of knowledge is displaced by an intuitive grasp of the totality of Being, a grasp that is periodically realized *within* the world of mundane tasks.[53]

The personae of part III of *Wodwo* look upon life from a newly won position of self-assurance and self-control, with a calm exercise of judgment. Moods of Oriental serenity (*śānti*) and a Buddha-like compassion and pity for those who cannot transcend the temporal world predominate in part III. The personae are often able, especially in the final poems of the volume, to fuse with the landscape, to view nature with a new beatitude of spirit, and thus to envision a universe of plenitude, of "benign holy powers." Poems such as "Mountains," "Gnat-Psalm," "Skylarks," "Full Moon and Little Frieda," and "Wodwo" present nature as benevolent, transfigured by a newly won sense of freedom wherein the psyche of the persona is not subject to an emotional dependency or ego dependency upon either the environment or cultural givens, but is rather a bemused spectator who can view nature as a soothing companion because of an already achieved calmness of mind. The persona of part III, like the adept of Japanese Zen, views nature "as a friendly, well-meaning agent whose inner being is thoroughly like our own, always ready to work in accord with our legitimate aspirations," in the words of D. T. Suzuki.[54] This is the result of what Thomas Merton has called Zen's "ontological awareness of pure being beyond subject and object, [its] immediate grasp of being in its 'suchness' and 'thusness.'"[55] In *Wodwo* Hughes finds the serenity of Zen preferable to a culture where repressed libido periodically erupts into mass violence, and a necessary healing balm for a distressed psyche.

"Skylarks" and "Gnat-Psalm" in part III of *Wodwo* are similar in the ability of the central persona to revel in a sense of identity with the animal or insect viewed. In a totally absorbed state of mind, the persona participates in the activities of the perceived object. In Zen this is the contemplation of the object in its *sono-mama* state, in the broadest and deepest aspects of the "situation as it finds itself," in the words of Suzuki; it is an experience of an "underlying sense of identity" with the perceived object most often found in haiku artists such as the eighteenth-century Zen poet Bashō.[56] In section IV of "Skylarks," for instance, the persona's visionary gaze parallels the upward flight of the lark and its downward exhaustion in a sense of communality with the lark's energetic aspirations:

> Dithering in ether
> Its song whirls faster and faster
> And the sun whirls
> The lark is evaporating
> Till my eye's gossamer snaps
>   and my hearing floats back widely to earth
>
> After which the sky lies blank open
> Without wings, and the earth is a folded clod.

At the conclusion of the poem the persona attains such a state of sympathy and harmony with the larks' escapades that he recognizes in the arc of their efforts a metaphor for the entire joyous agony of life, a paying back with their labor the life-principle that gave them the breath of existence.

Similarly, in "Gnat-Psalm," the persona's absorption in the frenetic, untiring activities of the gnats inspires him to create a metaphor for the totality of life as an unceasing expenditure of energy:

> O little Hasids
> Ridden to death by your own bodies
> Riding your bodies to death
> You are the angels of the only heaven!
> And God is an Almighty Gnat!
> You are the greatest of all the galaxies!

> My hands fly in the air, they are follies
> My tongue hangs up in the leaves
> My thoughts have crept into crannies

When one's thoughts have "crept into crannies" one experiences a fusion of psyche and landscape, a sense of *ātman* self-identity with the environment. Hughes may have been meditating upon an often repeated passage of Suzuki's where he contrasts Bashō's ability to make his ecstatically absorbed contemplation of a flower a *sono-mama* unitive experience of the entirety of the situation in which the flower is found with the analytic Tennyson ("Flower in the Crannied Wall"), who must pluck his flower from its cranny and surround it with abstractions.[57]

In "Gnat-Psalm" the gnats, environment, and persona also fuse with the poet's moment-to-moment activity of writing the poem. All are at work "Scrambling their crazy lexicon" in an expenditure of joyous suffering; insistent relative clause repetitions reinforce a frenetic tone wherein everybody is "everybody else's yoyo." The persona discovers that the gnats "are their own sun / Their own brimming over / At large in the nothing." The solar fire motif heightens the import of the self-consuming energy of the gnats by fusing it with the self-consuming energy of nature in the poem. The gnats in their sacrificial energy are "giving their bodies to be burned"; their wings are "blurring the blaze" even as the fiery energy of the sun "blasts their song." This is similar to the vision of the world as a sacrificial fire of energy in the Chāndogya Upanishad (5 : 4 – 8); Hughes himself once alluded to the "Heraclitean/Buddhist notion that the entire Universe is basically made of fire."[58]

"Gnat-Psalm" is an apt illustration of what the ninth-century Chinese Zen master Rinzai called "sincerity," a placing of one's whole being into action in the moment, holding nothing in reserve. The final image of the gnat's dizzying fury as rolling the persona's skull into outer space approximates Rinzai's "true man of no-title" who pervades the entire world of time and space.[59] In utter sympathy with the tarantellalike joyous suffering of the gnats, the persona achieves an *ātman* identity with the created universe, a perception so fully and ecstatically experienced as to indicate a state of *satori*.

Both "Skylarks" and "Gnat-Psalm" employ the casuistical tendency of Zen to express the transcendence of dualistic thinking through expressions of negations. In section IV of "Skylarks" the persona views the upward flight of the lark as "Scrambling / In a nightmare difficulty / Up through the nothing." The psalmody in "Gnat-Psalm" is "of all the suns," of a unitive experience possible because initially the gnats are "their own sun / Their own brimming over / At large in the nothing." Their bearded faces weave and bob "on the nothing." The monism behind this overspill of the subjective onto the objective is what negates the objective universe into "no matter" and creates a sea of "nothing." The casuistical reasoning employed in these uses of negations parallels that used by Nāgārjuna in his doctrine of the "Eight No's," which Suzuki compares to seeing things in their *sono-mama* "suchness" or "allness." [60] According to Suzuki, what is accomplished by such negating is a transcendent, godly affirmation of life, for whereas temporality is always becoming, changing or negating itself moment by moment, "The eternal must be an absolute affirmation which our limited understanding defines in negative terms." [61] The complete negation is thus "no one time" or "no one thing"—an unchanging, all-encompassing fullness, an allness of benign nature in an absolute present. Through the use of Zen casuistry, the exuberant tone, and the fusion of persona and landscape with the activities of the gnats, Hughes successfully conveys the most fully realized experience of *satori* in *Wodwo*.

Unlike the worried persona of "Sugar Loaf" in part I, the persona of "Mountains" admires the mountains' detachment from the world of human emotions and nature's cycle of birth and death and responds warmly to their peace and contentment. Both mountains and persona are oblivious to all striving or anxious yearning for temporal rewards; they are at home in an essential selfhood that cannot be disturbed by the flux of the phenomenal world. Mountains, often in the history of literature a symbol for the integrated self, here represent an integration of self and cosmos. A fresh ambiguity in the first lines of the poem reinforces this integration. It is impossible for the reader to tell if the configuration of stones, which becomes a pointing finger, leads the persona's gaze up the mountain's shoulder to the sleeping divinity believed by primitives to be residing in the center or up the persona's shoulder to his own eye. A both/and congruence of perceiver and object is intended.

Both "Full Moon and Little Frieda" and "Wodwo," the closing poems of *Wodwo*, present affirmative experiences of congruence with a benign nature. The persona of "Full Moon and Little Frieda" views the child as a "mirror," a brimming pail of offering, who gazes at the moon, the largest reflecting object in the cosmos available to the naked eye. The resulting astonishment at the recognition of an identity of mirroring artworks is very striking and describes another experience of *satori*, of the undifferentiated original essence of the cosmos, at times called by Buddhist poets the "full moon of suchness." [62] When little Frieda speaks the word "moon," one of the first words she ever articulated as a toddler, subject and object, self and environment merge in ecstatic recognition of self-in-other, in the clarity of spotless, mutually reflecting mirrors. The cows that loop the hedges "with their warm wreaths of breath" earlier in the poem convey an almost nativity-scene sense of the purity and supportiveness of a benign nature in attendance. The cows, sacred in Oriental symbology as representations of the plenitude of creation, are an apt background for Frieda's offering of self as a brimming pail of youthful purity to an equally pure moonlight.

Hughes has stated that his objective in writing "Wodwo," the final and title poem of the volume, was to catch this "half-man half-animal spirit of the forests," originally from *Sir Gawain and the Green Knight*, in a moment of self-discovery, and with a sense of bewilderment as to just what *is* to be its relationship to the world it is in the process of discovering.[63] In the poem the Wodwo discovers itself *as* it discovers the world; both experiences, identical when the *ātman* is awakened in the "exact centre" of existence, lead to the Wodwo's discovery that it "can go anywhere" and that it seems "to have been given the freedom of this place." As "exact centre" of existence-for-the-self, the Wodwo is the generator, the creator of its own universe, moment by moment. This frees it to inspect, rather than accept unthinkingly, the assumptions and beliefs of different cultures—and frees it especially from acquiescing to a Western goal-oriented adventure mythos tainted by aggression. With such freedom the Wodwo becomes, like Hughes himself, the peripatetic, eclectic anthropologist.

Though poems placed earlier in the ordering of part III of *Wodwo* do not relate instances of *satori* fusion with the landscape, they usually articulate positions of self-assurance and self-control from personae exercising calm judgment. Only in "Gog," "New Moon in January," and "Karma" do personae express moods of agitation, and in each case the disquiet is resolved, unlike part I, in the individual poems themselves. Many of the more baffling poems are influenced by Oriental concepts.

In "Karma" the poet's meditation upon the sufferings and carnage created in a "hundred and fifty million years" of human civilization is the Buddhist retracing of time and karmic bondage to suffering (*pratiloman*) in order to absorb it and arrive at the timeless, the point before temporal duration where liberation is possible.[64] Then, by wiping away the dust of all earthly objects from the karmic mirror, as in the *Sidpa Bardo*,[65] one attains the objectless state. In "Karma" the persona experiences acutely the legacy of war; his suffering is so intense as to dislocate time and causality onto the plane of surrealistic nightmare, as in part I. But unlike part I, in "Karma" the persona solves his own problem in the poem itself. Unable to find a rationale or augury (the "poulterer's hare" knows nothing) to make this legacy of pain comprehensible, the persona finally achieves a quietude of spirit in a "seamless" state transcendent of the stitchings of time and causality. By absorbing the pain, instead of refusing the blame, the persona is finally able to stand firm in an assertion that the answer is "Not here," not available to analytic reasoning. At this point the persona's consciousness has achieved the objectless state of "the mirror's seamless sand." Wiping clean the dust of phenomenality from the karmic mirror is a favorite Zen simile for the process of attaining the objectless state of transcendence, as in the following verse by the Zen poet Yoka:

> The mind is an organ of thought and objects are set against it:
> The two are like marks on the surface of the mirror;
>> When the dirt is removed, the light begins to shine.
> Both mind and objects being forgotten, Ultimate Nature reveals
>> itself true.[66]

Section I of "Gog" is a meditation on the dragon of Revelations 12:4 who has been awakened by the Christian Logos-God's assumption of total power ("I am Alpha and Omega": Rev. 1:11; 21:6; 22:13) and his expulsion of the world and the flesh to the sphere of the devil. The world of created matter becomes a world of "motherly weeping" and uncontrolled action, for which the dragon suffers in the form of a consciousness of guilt and fear: "I do not look at the rocks and stones, I am frightened of what they see." But the persona of section II (British edition only) no longer suffers from this aversion to the phenomenal world: "The stones are as they were. And the creatures of earth / Are mere rainfall rivulets, in flood or empty paths." At this point the persona experiences a *śūnyatā* state of personality dissolution and a recognition of the fullness of all creation: "The atoms of saints' brains are swollen with the vast bubble of nothing." Apocalyptic writings of individual converts can no longer harm. In this state of dissolution the persona also recognizes that the dust of eros in the phenomenal world darkens the karmic mirror with "Death and death and death—." The "bright particles" of the dust that is "in power" produce the alluring "eyes and / Dance of wants" that ultimately lead to the dissolution of the grave.

Section III of "Gog" (also British edition only) is a prayer to the unborn child of Revelations 12:1–5, who is to "rule all nations with a rod of iron" and cast the dragon Gog from heaven. But the persona hopes that this quester will accomplish more than the Revelations prophecy of an aggressive conqueror; here he hopes that the child will be strong enough to penetrate beyond the illusory phenomenal world of love/death and its ultimately destructive energy. Because Christianity represses instinctual life, questing in a Western goal-oriented fashion in the temporal world will cause destructive outbursts of repressed libido: the quester's horse is "shod with vaginas of iron," the grail is "fanged," and it resides in an environment dominated by the "salt milk drug of the mothers." A better path would be to follow the *Bardo* exhortation to regard the phenomenal world as *māyā* or illusion and avoid entering the womb door into that world. By avoiding the womb door the initiate attains a supernormal birth into the world of the Clear Light, the *nirvana* release from rebirth.[67] In section III of "Gog" the persona advises the child to pierce the veil of phenomenality. Whereas Coriolanus relented from conquering Rome at his mother Volumnia's request, the child quester should be even more nonviolent; he should pierce with his awakened understanding through the temporal world of *māyā* and refrain from acting. He is exhorted rather to "follow his weapons toward the light," which in context is an alternative to octopus maw, cradle, and womb wall of *māyā*—perhaps the "*Dharma-Kāya* of Clear Light," the state of nirvanic illumination in the *Chikkai Bardo*. The ending of section III, however, indicates that the child is too blinded by his cultural givens to attain any liberation: his compass is his "lance-blade, the gunsight" and will only result in endlessly recurring cycles of destruction. The only "light" he follows is the one-sided rationalism of his religion and his Western culture. A soured attitude toward Christianity's banishment of the instincts predominates in the tone of "Gog," especially in section III, but in sections II and III the persona is in control of his subject matter, exercising firm judgment.

As with the three sections of "Gog," the progression of the three sections of "Song of a Rat" constitutes a penetration to a higher comprehension of reality based upon an Eastern model. The situation presented in section I is that of the trapped rats of the short story "Sunday." Yet the persona of section I, in contrast to the callow Michael, has compassion and pity for an animal too dependent upon its relationship with the physical environment to acquire an Oriental consciousness. "'This has no face, it must be God'" and "'No answer is also an answer'" are modernizations of ancient Zen *kōan* designed to destroy human dependence upon logic and objectivity en route to *satori*, as in Eno's *kōan* "Show me your original face before you were born," in response to Ming's request for instruction, or Shên-kuang's perfect silence in response to Bodhidharma's request to his pupils to exhibit their greatest insights, or the silent nonlectures on *satori* delivered by

Yakusan and Hayakujo.[68] *Kōan* are unanswerable, designed to reveal the limited contexts in which human reason operates, and to promote the realization that all authority, truth, and motivation must come entirely from within the self, not from external authority. By trying to escape its predicament the rat is merely pitiable, until it achieves a sudden moment of understanding, presented in section II, which differs markedly from the rat's resignation in "Sunday."

In "The Rat's Vision," section II of "Song of a Rat," a moment of insight into the meaninglessness of what is now perceived as a desolate, alienating landscape causes a withdrawal into a subjectively realized personal godliness or *ātman*, a "Forcing" of "the rat's head down into godhead." Paralleling this is a loss of the rat's sense of dependency upon the farmyard environment, due to a new perception of the futility of remaining in a futureless and fatalistic pastoral scene, now an illusory "wobbling like reflection on water."

The imagery and symbolism of section III, "The Rat's Flight," indicate that the rat has fled the temporal world. The rat supplants hell by casting its material body to the dogs while achieving a state "Never to be buried" as "the Shadow of the Rat / Cross[es] into power." This psychological process is attended by thunder and lightning imagery, standard procedure for instances of *ātman* illumination in the Upanishads and of *satori* in Zen.[69] The rat no longer screeches in his trap; he has attained a spiritual body and has freed himself by trusting to inner powers and self-reliance. In Hindu mythology the rat, because of its uncanny ability to overcome obstacles and find a route into the bolted granary, is the theriomorphic counterpart of Ganeśa, "The Lord and Master of Obstacles," son of Śiva and his consort.[70] If Hughes deliberately intends a reference to the Jungian archetype of the Shadow in section III, the reference is appropriate, for when the Shadow crosses into conscious life in Jungian psychology, the formerly unconscious abilities and energies become integrated into a higher state of consciousness, and with a new feeling of power.[71] The three parts of "Song of a Rat," one of the very few poems Hughes wrote soon after Plath's suicide,[72] recapitulate the structural organization of *Wodwo*.

As in sections II and III of "Song of a Rat," the persona of "You Drive in a Circle" recognizes the barrenness of temporality. As he careers through sheets of rain in a rural landscape, he realizes that roads offer a change of place not worth the taking, that the resistance of the elements is not worth the expense of energy, and that the scenery of sheep-filled moors contains for him only the futility of an unconscious obeisance to animal and vegetable function. This persona no longer fears landscape or animals, as in part I of *Wodwo*; with Buddha-like compassion and pity he addresses the sheep's enchainment to instinctual processes that go nowhere. A recognition of the yogic *īshwara pranidhāna*, the God within the self as the transphenomenal ground of all being, is the destination abandoned by the persona when he opened his automobile door. The fact that he does realize this during his journey indicates that he is beginning to acknowledge that inner self as the source of wisdom. The last line of the poem, "Your destination waits where you left it," echoes a line from *The Zenrin* on the inner location of wisdom: "If you do not get it from yourself, / Where will you go for it?"[73]

The persona of "You Drive in a Circle" also recognizes the necessity of merging subject and object within the self as he characterizes the low rainclouds as "the mist-gulfs of no-thinking." The word "no-thinking" is a precise term in Buddhist thought: both *munen* and *acintyā* mean literally "no-thinking" or "beyond thinking" and are aspects of the experience of Oriental Enlightenment dealing with the merging of rationality and irrationality, subject and object, when the spiritual self penetrates through the analytic thinking of consciousness and one achieves an intuitional state of self-identity with the universe.[74] The persona at the conclusion of "You Drive in a Circle" realizes that "Everything is already here"—within the subjective self's intuitional powers, which have no necessary "anchor" in the temporal world.

One final poem influenced by Oriental concepts is "Theology," the opening poem of part III of *Wodwo*. Unlike the serpent of "Reveille" in part I, the serpent of "Theology" ends rather than initiates a temporal process by digesting the Christian myth of the Fall and sloping off to another realm, a private "Paradise" unencumbered by the complaints of a peevish God. The serpent's power to isolate himself from the historical process and the collocation of his smiling with his private paradise suggest that the paradise alluded to is the Western Paradise of Amitabha, the realm away from historical time in the Pure Land School of Chinese Buddhism. In the "White Lotus Ode," a poem typical of the Pure Land School, whose title Hughes alluded to in an early poem,[75] the compassionate smile and transcendent abode of Amitabha is available to all those wandering in the depths of temporality who invoke his name. To those confined by "the body's oppressive sorrows" Amitabha offers "a spiritual body" in a paradise "brightened with gladness"; he "sends his smile out to the dwellings of the suffering" and "draws every burdened soul up from the depths / And lifts them into his peaceful abode."[76] The snake of "Theology," able to slough the skin of temporality, the "dark intestine" of Western cyclic renewal through temporal birth/death, is closest to Ananta or Śeśa, the Hindu cosmic snake, who resides in the supratemporal realm. Viśṇu dreams the lotus dream of the universe while reposing on Ananta. As Balarama, half brother of Kriśna, rests lost in thought beneath a tree on the ocean shore, the immortal serpent essence of Śeśa crawls out of his mouth and returns to the paradisal Abyss.[77]

The remaining part III poems, though not influenced by Oriental concepts, are similar in their recognition that goal-oriented striving in the temporal world of Western *wyrd* is folly. "Heptonstall," the town whose graveyard houses the remains of Sylvia Plath, is a "black village of gravestones" in which the only comfort and surety is the meaningless rain of mutability. Viking invaders in "The Warriors of the North" have tainted Western culture with the anal obstinacy, covetousness, and rapacity behind their urge for conquest. This taint affects the future: following Weber and Tawney, Hughes intimates that the intense worldly industriousness required by Calvinism and other Protestant sects as proof of Election differs very little from the avarice that attends the heroic urge for conquest. The wolves of "The Howling of Wolves" are pitiable; unlike the feared carriers of ancestral evil or reempowering wolf mask divinities of "February" in *Lupercal*, these wolves are uncomprehending creatures living by blind instinct. The landscape of "Pibroch" is destitute, worthwhile only as a veil of materiality to be pierced by the "staring angels" of one's visionary thoughts. Hughes finds the mind/spirit dichotomy of "Kreutzer Sonata" to be a laughable, self-castrating process of mutual cancellation, the product of the delusions of unenlightened, analytic reason. The three sections of "Wings" argue that the advancements of twentieth-century philosophy, literature, and science in the West attest to contemporary alienation from any form of ancestral wisdom, for each individual is now hopelessly isolated in existential agony (Sartre in section I) in a universe the teleology of which humans are incapable of understanding (Kafka in section II), but whose scientific advancements have blasted humans to star vapor (Einstein in section III).[78] The persona of "New Moon in January" utters the faint shriek of Shelley's "Epipsychidion" in the hope of transcending the temporal world of blood and death through inner powers. With the single exception of "New Moon in January," the personae of these part III poems articulate the folly of goal-oriented involvement in Western culture with self-control and calm judgment.

In *Wodwo* the central persona bids "Goodbye to the cenotaphs" as he disencumbers himself of failed cultural beliefs in the wake of world wars and relocates final authority within the strength of an awakened inner self.

Like the French surrealists, Hughes reverts to the dream world and subconscious energies to find a more direct, emotionally true mode of expressing the psyche's participation in external reality than could be had through the conventions of realism and naturalism. He supersedes the surrealists in constructing a complex formal design where shamanic journey and heroic quest meet in psychodrama, in the story of the soul's salvation. At the core of *Wodwo* resides a unique psychological and epistemologic movement from Western dualism to an Eastern subjective monism, as an antidote for an overly aggressive Western culture that has lost contact with the psyche's needs for wholeness and inward development. We comprehend this movement through the esthetics of the formal design, in recognizing how Hughes employs his imaginative resources in developing the changing relationship of persona to landscape. *Wodwo* contains no mimesis of "normal" reality, nor an imitation of life that incorporates any evaluation of conduct according to Western social mores. The more Hughes becomes the eclectic anthropologist, the more modernist form underlines and conveys meaning.

Hughes was not able in the sixties to sustain the serene vision of a benign nature that he achieved in part III of *Wodwo*. He completed an adaptation of the bloody psychodrama *Seneca's "Oedipus"* for Peter Brook in 1968, and then the deaths of his companion Assia and her child Shura in March of 1969 caused him to abandon the more positive ending that he had planned for his Crow sequence.[79] The *ātman*, the active organizer of perception within the self, is what Crow, imprisoned in his empirical eye, cannot attain. Hughes will once again use folklore surrealism, but in an entirely different way—to reveal Crow's inability to transcend his instinctual cravings and rational, dualistic thinking, and to specify the scientific and religious causes of aggression in Western culture. An extreme, almost Jainlike loathing of Western cultural enterprises will continue in *Crow* and in the main action of *Gaudete*, until *Orpheus* (1973) and the *Gaudete* "Epilogue" (written in 1975) revise this position. Achieving a state of serenity will be the goal of the highly syncretic poetry of the mid- and late seventies.

In *Wodwo* Hughes is not asking us to exchange our Bibles and pocket calculators for the loincloths of Oriental asceticism; he is clearing a fresh path for an important revolution in perception that can free the individual from unconscious habituation to failed values. He is also suggesting that we can acquire a self-control that can lead to a mastery of our instincts, emotions, and destinies. The Wodwo may be a pacifist given to reflection and meditation, but there is much quiet strength in the resolve to live through involved, moment-by-moment cognition rather than according to the usual unreflective acceptance of cultural givens. The Wodwo's opposite is Crow, who expects to achieve wonders through an uncritical, conventional involvement in the myths of his culture.

The poems of Wodwo indicate that the *Bardo Thödol* and the *ātman* of the Upanishads taught Hughes a wisdom similar to that of Blake's Los, who will not "Reason & Compare," for his "business is to create" (*Jerusalem*: plate 10). Perception in part III of *Wodwo*, as in late Blake, is an *active* process of seeing reality as an extension of the imagination's power to unify and transform, not a passive ingesting of empirical facts and concepts. This transformation of the outer world through an awakened imagination in part III of *Wodwo* prefigures the third phase of Hughes's story of a soul. But Hughes is not able to attain this enlightened mode of perception again until the mid-seventies, in the "Epilogue" of *Gaudete*. Before foregoing the surreal, kinetic energies of the sixties, Hughes delineates the outward scientific and religious causes of Western aggression in the mythic satire of *Crow* and in the sexual escapades of the changeling Reverend Lumb in *Gaudete*.

CHAPTER 5

Nothing Escaped Him

Crow

1970–1971

The fundamental guiding ideas of our Western Civilization . . . derive from Reformed Christianity and from Old Testament Puritanism. . . . They are based on the assumption that the earth is a heap of raw materials given to man by God for his exclusive profit and use. The subtly apotheosized misogyny of Reformed Christianity is proportionate to the fanatic rejection of Nature, and the result has been to exile man from Mother Nature—from both inner and outer nature. The story of the mind exiled from nature is the story of Western Man. It is the story of his progressively more desperate search for mechanical and rational and symbolic securities, which will substitute for the spirit-confidence of the Nature he has lost. . . . Christianity deposes Mother Nature and begets, on her prostrate body, Science, which proceeds to destroy Nature. . . .

—Hughes, 1970[1]

Crow (1970) extends the genetic analysis of violence in *Wodwo* with a broader, more pervasive social psychology that locates the causes of mass violence within Western society in post-Renaissance science and religion. Shamanistic psychodrama, the form of *Wodwo*, defers to a complex modernist myth that partakes of the magical world of fable and primitive trickster narrative. Hughes imbues the entire fabric of landscape and event in *Crow*, including departures from the known laws of physics, with a set of motifs that evaluate modern Western culture and also reveal how our culture perpetuates its problems by impoverishing the perceptual faculties and creative potential of each new generation. The inner and outer worlds in *Crow* are more than divorced. The outer world actively menaces and stunts the development of the inner world, because the inner world passively acculturates itself to what Hughes considers the inert objectivity of modern Western culture. Through the use of folklore surrealism and the trickster tradition, Hughes employs his imagination in creating a fantasy world, with its own internal consistency and physical laws, that chastens through ridicule Western unthinking, Crow-like credulousness toward science and religion and frequent addiction to acting only in ways that satisfy appetites for material goods and sensual pleasures.

Near the end of Crow's adventures, this ridicule undergoes a transformation into pathos and pity, a final sympathy for human Crow-like survival abilities and capacity to absorb pain, especially given the perceptual limitations derived from Western culture. As Crow peers into nature with the "COLD QUARANTINE" of a Western empirical, utilitarian eye ("Crow Hears Fate Knock on the Door"),[2] he alienates himself from any possibility of experiencing the "inner spiritual unity of nature" from the vantage point of the "essential human subjectivity" that Hughes believes is the human "center of gravity."[3] Just as semanticists understand that each language embodies metaphysical assumptions when defining terms such as "nature" and "reality,"[4] so each culture contains assumptions about nature and reality so deeply embedded that people can become blind to experiencing the external world in alternative ways. The more Crow becomes acculturated to the mythic fabric of Western culture, the more remote are his chances of comprehending nature *from the inside*—from his unitive *ātman* potential, where he can become the active generator of a community of humans-in-nature and participate in an organic, holistic process.

Crow is mythic in a typically modernist, formalist way, for it interprets the relevance of recent history in the West to the present moment, through a mythic construct that never existed in folk or oral culture and that juxtaposes values from alternative cultures rather than simply offering a mimesis of the social mores of our present culture. It educates readers to a perception of some of the best ideas in the living culture of the times, especially from anthropology and comparative religion, ideas that do not themselves inhere in our fragmented, alienating daily world of mass information and exploitation. *Crow* reinterprets the significance of Western culture since the Bible, but centers chiefly upon juxtaposing the inner apathy and outward violence of post–Industrial Revolution society, with the unitive serenity of Zen Buddhism. *Crow* is modernist not only because the cultural comparisons inhere in an innovative form, but because the very physical laws of this reconstructed universe operate according to a complex tangle of ideas (cf. Pound's *paideuma*) derived from current research in the living culture of the postwar present.[5] Though Hughes composed his Crow poems quickly, they are immeasurably enriched by a mind—as we have seen in *Hawk*, *Lupercal*, and *Wodwo*—that composes with a high degree of formal sophistication. Before discussing individual poems in the volume, one might usefully clarify the highly complex, presentational form of *Crow* and Hughes's very consistent use of mythic structure.

The world of *Crow* is the world of fantasy, not realism; it includes the

magical spells, shapechanging battles, anthropomorphized spirits and demons, emphasis on chance and luck, and regular abrogation of the laws of
the physical universe that one finds in fable, epic folktale, and the trickster
narratives of primitive cultures. Most of the fantasy elements of *Crow*, especially its departure from the accepted physical laws of nature, concern
violence. Crow crashes a rocket on the moon, only to find himself under
his mother's buttocks ("Crow and Mama"); tells a story about a St. George,
who changes into a psychotic killer ("Crow's Account of St. George"); observes a battle where geometry and mathematics become lethal weapons
("Crow's Account of the Battle"); develops hallucinations of violence ("In
Laughter"); is pulverized by his own thoughts ("Magical Dangers") or by
God ("Conjuring in Heaven"; "Crow's Song of Himself"); destroys whatever
he tries to create ("Crow Improvises"); and is killed in a shapechanging
battle ("Truth Kills Everybody"), only to be resurrected in the very next
poem ("Crow and Stone"). Ursula Le Guin, an expert fantasy writer, believes that fantasy is extremely difficult to write, for one exhausts one's
imagination first in developing an alternative world, then in remaining
consistent and purposeful in maintaining whatever departures one takes
from the recognized physical laws of the known cosmos.[6] Wherein, then,
lies the rationale for the surrealistic violence that impels the departures
from the laws of physics in *Crow*?

What at first appears to be an inconclusive series of escapades in a gra-
tuitously violent landscape gains purpose and meaning when one examines the consistent use of motifs in the mythic fabric of *Crow*. Action,
causality, and meaning in *Crow* derive from a series of six motifs that operate throughout the text; they inhere in the fantasy world form and, though
partly hidden beneath the episodic plot, motivate the action and determine
the meaning. 1. *Crow* contains a critique of Protestant Christianity as denying personality growth by repressing instinctual life, and of modern science as alienating humans both from nature and from inner life by valuing
only objective fact and quantifiable analysis. This is Hughes's mythic reinterpretation of the past three hundred years of Western cultural history.
2. These criticisms of Western science and religion operate in *Crow* in a
mythic landscape that presents reality *as Crow perceives it—according to his
passive acceptance of the values of his stunted culture.* The deity who epitomizes this spiritually atrophied scientific universe is a bored deistic watch-
maker who alternately teaches Crow through abstract concepts and inhibits his inner growth through violent opposition. 3. Hughes adapts Jung's
use of Heraclitus's *enantiodromia* as a physical law of the fantasy universe of
Crow to comprehend the pervasive violence of recent Western civilization.

The violence occurs in a cause-effect relationship, as a reflex of a culture whose religion and science repress human instincts to the point of bestialization. The more Crow educates himself to observe nature with the cold objectivity and utilitarian ethics of his received culture, the more he becomes acculturated to its violent underbelly and the more his own psychic health is undermined by a neurotic syndrome of repression and violence. 4. Hughes adopts the trickster figure of primitive cultures and colors his world with the blood and blackness of the *Sidpa Bardo* to underscore Crow's imperceptiveness of nature, to satirize human dependence upon satisfying instinctual cravings, and to question our tireless urge to manipulate the environment. 5. Hughes clarifies another modernist law of his *Crow* universe when, in a transcript note from a 1975 reading of *Crow* poems at Cambridge, he writes that "all history is happening simultaneously, so Crow is able to move freely from one era to another, from the beginning of the world to the end."[7] But the pervasive eye imagery in *Crow* indicates that Crow's freedom of movement in history leads nowhere, for he is inhibited at every turn by his habit of cold empirical analysis. Crow forever "peers" at, "looks" at, and "sees" nature, but he never feels secure *in* nature. 6. Throughout his escapades and ordeals, Crow never attains enough consciousness of self, enough spiritual enlargement or inwardness, to recognize his *ātman* potential as the generator of reality for the self, in a way that would create a satisfying, holistic bond of human-in-nature. Hughes underscores this failure throughout the adventures of Crow in ironic double entendres associated with Western and Zen Buddhist concepts of "nothing." As Crow acculturates himself to modern Western values, he perceives "nothing" only as the lack of discrete, quantifiable, empirical entities; "nothing" as Buddhist *śūnyatā*, the undifferentiated allness of nature that can be achieved when one abandons egotism, rational thinking, and philosophical dualism, always escapes Crow's blinkered vision.

Hughes summarizes the central arguments in his interpretation of the last three hundred years of Western religion and science in four works written at the conclusion of his *Crow* period: the first "Myth and Education" essay (1970), a review of Max Nicholson's *The Environmental Revolution* (1970), the first Faas interview (1971), and the "Introduction" to his selection of Shakespeare's verse (1971).[8] Hughes believes that Christianity suppresses imagination and natural life. The Protestant Reformation took this to extremes by denying Mary, Christianity's figure for the mythic goddess of creation, a prominent place in its worship. This led to the rational scepticism of the Puritan extremist, the father of modern science. Furthermore, the biblical tenet that made *only* man in God's image and gave him dominion over all of the natural world and its creatures (Genesis 1: 26–28) soon deteriorated, as the New Science gained in power and practical applications, to a utilitarian pragmatism wherein "the earth is a heap of raw materials given to man by God for his exclusive profit and use."

Modern science further alienates humans from any intuitions of unity with nature, according to Hughes, for the scientific attitude stresses an "inert objectivity" that leads to apathy and "mental paralysis." The scientist must be totally passive to record findings with factual accuracy, because "the slightest imaginative bias in his presentation of the facts invalidates his findings and reflects badly on his standing as a scientist." Hughes believes that this habit of "pure observation" may be "OK for scientists but disastrous for human beings in general," for it creates a neurotic paralysis of our inner world, the "mental space" where our imaginations, when enriched with literature, work therapeutically to heal us, to organize and balance our inner and outer lives, and to help us revise our self-concepts in order to attempt more with a reasonable surety of success. Thus Hughes contends that modern science and religion have created a "chronically sick society" for the past three hundred years; moderns are afflicted with mental paralysis and repressed instinctual energies, a sickness that is "the direct result of the prohibition of imagination, the breakdown of all negotiations between our scientific mental attitude and our inner life."[9]

On the Claddagh Records jacket of *Crow* (1973: CCT 9–10), Hughes writes that the God who accompanies Crow on many of his escapades is "the man-created, broken-down, corrupt despot of a ramshackle religion, who bears about the same relationship to the Creator as, say, ordinary English does to reality." This God, the creator of the mythic universe Crow wanders in, is a personification of the god created by our culture's three hundred years of Protestant Reformation and scientific empiricism. Hughes's "ordinary English" versus "reality" distinction reinforces the fact that the fabric of this mythic universe is not representational, but rather a formal reconstruction, like language itself, of *how our culture trains us to perceive reality*. This second modernist mythic motif of the *Crow* mythology begins when God has nightmares of a Voice and a Hand ridiculing his universe. God responds by claiming that his universe, built upon the values of the Protestant Reformation and scientific empiricism, is a complete success. After a message arrives stating that Man wants God to take back life, God challenges the invisible Voice/Hand to do better, and it promptly creates Crow. God then acculturates Crow to his universe through tests and ordeals.[10]

Mythologically speaking, the Voice and Hand are nature, reporting doubts to God during his dreams, when his Protestant repression syndrome relaxes. As in Hughes's characterization of Adonis's boar in Shakespeare's "Venus and Adonis," the nightmare Voice and Hand are "the forces of the Universe try[ing] to redress some balance disturbed by human error."[11] To redress the balance, a central problem of the adventures, Crow must become conscious of, and then develop, his inner life, in order to attain the "inner spiritual unity of nature" that the personae of part III of *Wodwo* experienced. Crow must recognize that his inner creative potential—his Jungian anima or Blakean imagination—is his true source of perception. Crow's difficulty derives in part from the fact that nothing exists in the received environment of his outer world, in the perceptual orientation to reality supplied by his God's culture, that would help him to recognize his inner world creative potential. On the Claddagh jacket Hughes writes that "Crow's whole quest aims to locate and release his own creator, God's nameless hidden prisoner, whom he encounters repeatedly but always in some unrecognizable form." This "nameless hidden prisoner" is nature itself in its creative aspect, both a power that God represses in his Protestant ethic/scientific universe and a faculty that, on the microcosmic, inner world level, is Crow's unawakened imagination. Crow fails to realize the "that art thou" doctrine of the Chāndogya Upanishad (6:8–16): that what he perceives originates within himself. If he could awaken his creative imagination he might achieve an *ātman* unity of self-and-world. But his cultural orientation only habituates him to defensively egocentric, utilitarian approaches to nature that often lead to violent behavior.

Crow therefore does not complete his quest in the trade editions of *Crow*. Hughes alludes to the incompleteness of Crow's quest in the aforementioned transcript note to his 1975 Cambridge reading of *Crow* poems: "During his adventures he begins to wonder who his own creator is and he encounters various female figures who are avatars of his creator, but he never recognizes her and always bungles the situation." Crow never awakens to a realization that his inner life is the true source of the values that he posits in the objective universe. Though he does attain an adolescent self-consciousness in the course of his adventures, his problem is a defensively egocentric method of inquiry that continues to alienate him from nature every time that he attempts to analyze it and reduce interaction *with it* to a series of operations *upon it*. Crow must renounce his egocentricity and find a less defensive and utilitarian approach to nature—as in many Oriental systems, where a holistic understanding of humans and nature as a single, ever-changing organism replaces egocentric dominance. Consider Hughes's remarks about egotism in the *Crow* poem "Truth Kills Everybody," in an October 1979 letter to Terry Gifford and Neil Roberts:

> What Crow is grappling with is not 'something dangerous' but what becomes—at the end of all his mistakes and errantry—his bride and his almost humanity. To every action, an equal but opposite reaction: in their alarming aspect, the transformation images are mirror-images of his method of interrogation. The hidden thing defends itself with these.
>
> The 'violence' of the poem, therefore, is limited to a purely psychological and even barely conscious event. It inheres in Crow's attitude to the hidden thing. And in the difference in electrical potential—in value potential—between his mentality and the nature of what he's trying to grasp—which is the difference between his ego-system and the spirit dimension of his inner link with his creator. The first cannot in any way cope with or know the second. For Crow to 'know' the second he will have to go through the annihilation of the first.[12]

The emphasis upon the increasing level of violence in "Truth Kills Everybody," a reinterpretation of the Homeric shapechanging battle with Proteus, is a reflex of Crow's stubbornly egocentric, possessive, and aggressive method of inquiry, a childishly anal retentive method that his culture has habituated him to use. The Western value system that Crow becomes acculturated to does not prize inwardness; on the contrary, in his Claddagh record jacket statement Hughes indicates that in *Crow* the God of our culture "accompanies Crow through the world in many guises, mis-teaching, deluding, opposing and at every point trying to discourage or destroy him."

God's mis-teaching begins soon after Crow's birth. In "Crow's First Lesson" God instructs Crow about love through rational means, substituting an abstract concept and a verbal command for the real-life experience. Crow's quest to find and release "his own creator, God's nameless hidden prisoner," and to experience the "inner spiritual unity of nature," already takes a wrong turn, for the lesson only creates a cleavage between Crow's inner and outer worlds. In the first two stanzas the overemphasis on the rational causes an alienation of Crow's instinctual life, revealed in his corresponding preoccupation with the violent and malicious in nature—sharks and disease-carrying insects:

God tried to teach Crow to talk.
"Love," said God. "Say, Love."
Crow gaped, and the white shark crashed into the sea
And went rolling downwards, discovering its own depth.

"No, no," said God, "Say Love. Now try it. LOVE."
Crow gaped, and a bluefly, a tsetse, a mosquito
Zoomed out and down
To their sundry flesh-pots.

Both surreal images of violence move downward, suggesting repression. The third and fourth stanzas parody primitive birth from the soil myths, validations of sacred spots of origin, and myths where a female creation goddess restores the male to life by reimplantation in the vagina, as in Hesiod and the Sumerian myth of Enki and Ninhursag.[13] Here Hughes widens cleavage to chasm by exposing a violent struggle, instead of a unity, between the sexual and the intellectual, body and spirit, female and male, as "woman's vulva dropped over man's neck and tightened. / The two struggled together on the grass."

Hughes writes in his first "Myth and Education" essay that the scientific attitude of detached objectivity leads to mental paralysis, a passive posture toward nature. God in *Crow* is typically bored and apathetic in the cultural construct he epitomizes. He either ponders himself asleep with problems ("A Childish Prank") or snores away, "exhausted with creation" ("Crow Communes"). Problems of the flesh incapacitate ("A Horrible Religious Error") or disgust him ("Crow Blacker Than Ever"). Crow endeavors to improvise on his own, but the God-created fabric of his cultural orientation quickly infects his perceptions and actions. Very early in his youth he begins to fear nature. "Crow and Mama" is a perfect illustration of Hughes's remarks in the Nicholson review about our religiously approved attitude of dominance over nature exiling the human to a "desperate search for mechanical and rational and symbolic securities, which will substitute for the spirit-confidence of the Nature he has lost."

In "Crow and Mama" Hughes utilizes his fantasy world freedom from the laws of physics to satirize the history of technological progress in the West, from the birth of the automobile to the moon landings, as an elaborate flight from nature. Crow's inability to accommodate himself to the pain involved in natural processes of growth leads him to fear and then flee his mother. He tries a car, a plane, and a rocket and feels secure only when he peers at creation from the great distance of his rocket porthole. But as he crashes on the moon he finds himself pinned "Under his mother's buttocks." Though his cultural values make him desirous of complete autonomy, Crow remains dependent upon nature, part of an organic whole that he forever fails to recognize. Crow's desire for independence remains equally strong and equally mistaken in "Crow and the Sea," though here his psyche does register doubt: when he turns his back on the sea, he begins to feel "crucified" to it. The agony he feels whenever he contemplates nature indicates a serious maladaptation to reality. The more he tries to comprehend nature through the visor slits of his narrow cultural orientation, the more defensively anxious and fearful he becomes. In "Oedipus Crow" the neurosis continues; this time Crow feels comforted in his flight from nature "by the watch on his wrist" and by the quantifiable "sound of his foot and its echo."

Crow's acculturation to inert objectivity results in the complete atrophy of his inner life. The defensive ego he develops to shield himself from nature leads him to treat all problems objectively, as conditions existing outside his own psychic life—in some Black Beast or outside irritant.[14] Like the modern consumer, his inner apathy becomes so great that he simply expects to be serviced. In "Crow's Courtship" Crow expects to solve the central problem of his adventures by demanding that God provide him with his bride.[15] But God is blind to the fact that the furnaces of his culture will never transform dead hags into brides and preoccupied with the technical perfection of his project: "'Silence,' shouted God, 'You are interrupting / The Great Work. Only get away and be patient.'" God is also maladapted to reality: at the conclusion of the poem he insinuates that Crow's impatience caused the project to fail, but it is not difficult to infer that the intrusion of reality into God's fantasy at any moment would qualify as "'The worst moment!'"

God's "Great Work," placed in capitals in "Crow's Courtship," is a parody of the alchemical Great Work and of the Great Work of the Sufi adept, the integration of microcosm and macrocosm, of inner and outer worlds, within the self through contemplation. Two neurotics at a furnace, one impatient and the other preoccupied, will never forge the "inner spiritual unity of nature" that would fulfill Crow's quest. The essence of the Sufic Great Work appears on the Emerald Tablet of Hermes the Threefold Sage; one can understand its substance from the opening statements, as translated by Idries Shah in his *The Sufis*, a volume that Hughes reviewed in 1964: "The truth, certainly, truest, without untruth. What is above is like what is below. What is below is like what is above. The miracle of unity is to be attained. Everything is formed from the contemplation of unity, and all things come about from unity, by means of adaptation." Shah considers the substance of the Emerald Tablet to be the equivalent of the Sufi dictum in the introduction to the *Perception of Jafir Sadiq*: "Man is the microcosm, creation the macrocosm—the unity. All comes from One. By the joining of the power of contemplation all can be attained. This essence must be separated from the body first, then combined with the body. This is the Work. Start with yourself, end with all. Before man, beyond man, transformation."[16] To achieve this unitive state, the Sufi adept must annihilate the ego and become lost in the allness of God (*faná*);[17] but in "Crow's Courtship" Crow and God can barely communicate because each is totally obsessed with self-serving desires.

The universe epitomized by the God of *Crow* contains no unity of self or transcendence of personal desire in a rich spiritual life. The Emerald Tablet lies broken in "Fragment of an Ancient Tablet." What is above is certainly not like what is below: the overemphasis on the rational and the suppression of the instincts in the universe of *Crow* causes fragmentation, a perpetual dichotomy between head and reproductive organs. What is available to consciousness (the rational portion) is certainly not the whole truth, or the Sufic Great Work; what is repressed (the creative energy of the instincts, as in Jung's Shadow) may lead to mass violence, "the ticking bomb of the future."

"Crow's Song About God,"[18] a portion of the narrative that antedates Crow's creation, reveals that the spiritual apathy of the universe of *Crow* derives from Western cultural values, and not from deficiencies unique to Crow himself. "Crow's Song About God" presents a static situation where Man sits exhausted and unconscious at the gatepost of heaven, having been beaten half to death by the violence and ecological waste that Western culture has visited upon nature. Like the soldier in sections IV and V of "Scapegoats and Rabies," Man's culture victimizes him: his eyes are as lifeless as an oak-stump "aground in the ooze of some putrid estuary," his solar plexus is a "plastic carnation / In a gutter puddle / Outside the registry office," and the shadows on his face are "like a village gutted with bombs." Yet he clings "to the tick of his watch." Man has developed no spiritual resources to support himself; his organic functions alone continue toward their last gasp in a body that his own culture has mutilated. Man waits at God's door apparently to ask him to take life back, but God, as usual, sees nothing of Man, being neurotically preoccupied with his own nightmare terrors, and himself awaiting the appearance of a savior. The poem concludes with God fondling his savior fantasy like a pet, and Man continuing in his mangled state, incapable of taking responsibility for his spiritual development.

When not bored, incapacitated, or preoccupied with private fantasies, the God of *Crow* preaches a suspect utilitarian gospel, precipitating the fall into self-consciousness with ego-inflating draughts of language and logic. In "Apple Tragedy" God awakens Adam and Eve to a thirst for intellectual and sexual knowledge by instructing them in how to manipulate nature. Here Hughes equates the birth of self-consciousness both with the desire to manipulate the environment and with a self-serving use of language.[19] One can produce the cider of self-consciousness from the apples of Eden, in the process severing the primal, unconscious unity with nature and converting language into a self-aggrandizing tool. The primal unity of the psyche splits into analytically differentiated compartments, into superego ("Adam drank and said: 'Be my god'"), id ("Eve drank and opened her legs"), and ego ("God ran and told Adam / Who in drunken rage tried to hang himself in the orchard"). Draughts of self-consciousness split even the serpent's syllable, hitherto unified "like the rustling of the spheres" ("A Horrible Religious Error"), into question marks and explanations. Fear and violence result from this severance. Eve fears the snake as a potential rapist, though it was universally revered by primitives as a symbol of the self-moving, divine creativity of nature,[20] and Adam smashes a chair on its head. God, objective and therefore removed from the human stress, is "well pleased" with accomplishing his designs, whereas all creation, especially awakened emotional life, "goes to hell."

Crow has already followed God's example of subverting nature to his will earlier in his adventures. The snake in *Crow*, given its symbolic value to primitives, functions as an avatar of the creative principle in nature, the recognition of which is the central objective in Crow's quest. But in "A Horrible Religious Error" Crow is uninterested in learning the source of the snake's power. While God writhes in a jealous grimace, and man and woman kneel in recognition of the serpent's power, Crow merely appropriates it as food, in an instant of aggressive action. He "Grabbed this creature by the slackskin nape, / Beat the hell out of it, and ate it." Crow also tries to manipulate nature to his purposes with the aid of language. Though Hughes presents words in "A Disaster" and "The Battle of Osfrontalis" as powerful tools for creating motives to kill, for poisoning nature with industrial waste, and impeding inner development with advertisements, laws, and contracts, Crow at first appears only detached and watchful, or myopically preoccupied with gratifying his appetites. But later in the volume the values of his culture infect him with ego-inflation and scheming.

Crow tries to manipulate nature with words in "Crow Goes Hunting." A shapechanging battle ensues, with nature proving infinitely more agile and potent than language. Crow naively violates the first principle of general semantics: that linguistic systems are abstract, conventional maps that should never be confused with the real territory they represent. Crow ironically is left wordless, "Speechless with admiration," but uncomprehending of the mistake he has made in preferring the thought over the thing. In "Magical Dangers" Crow's *thoughts* function as abstractions that alienate him from nature, in the process creating oppositions so powerful that he experiences surreal hallucinations of destruction:

> Crow thought of a palace—
> Its lintel crashed on him, his bones were found.
>
> Crow thought of a fast car—
> It plucked his spine out, and left him empty and armless.
>
> Crow thought of the wind's freedom—
> And his eyes evaporated, the wind whistled over the Turkish Saddle.
>
> Crow thought of a wage—
> And it choked him, it was cut unspoiled from his dead stomach.

Each abstraction Crow entertains cuts off his corresponding natural organ of apperception, sensation, or analogous microcosmic counterpart (palace structure/bones; fast car/spinal neurons, etc.), leaving him powerless. At best he can create clones of himself when his thought of "nature's stupor" mirrors the stupor of his spiritual life. Similar surreal energies are unleashed in "Crow Improvises," where haphazard attempts to join opposites in order to disguise, manipulate, or improve upon nature's temporal cycle of birth and death only cause counterproductive short circuits.

Violence in the *Crow* universe of modern science and the Protestant ethic is so pervasive, and Crow so often at the center of it, that it may come as a surprise to learn that in only seven of about a hundred published *Crow* poems does Crow initiate deliberately malicious, violent action. Otherwise the violence is unintentional ("Crow and Mama"), an appetitive reflex ("Crow Tyrannosaurus," "The Battle of Osfrontalis"), or the result of playful or well-intentioned attempts to understand or improve the human lot ("A Childish Prank," "Crow Communes," "Crowego," "Crow Improvises," "Crow Blacker Than Ever," "Truth Kills Everybody"). Crow's deliberately violent actions often derive from his acculturation—his inflated ego ("Crow's Fall") and utilitarian ethics ("A Horrible Religious Error")—or happen as an aggressive reflex of God's violent attacks upon him ("Crow's Song of Himself").

Crow maims *himself* in three of the seven poems where he initiates deliberately violent action ("Crow's Fall," "Crow Sickened," "Crow and Stone"). Crow's combat with the sun leaves him charred black in "Crow's Fall." Imperceptive in "Crow and Stone," he once again fails to recognize an avatar of the creative principle in nature and in himself when he battles Stone. North American Indian folklore associates the trickster figure with rock and sun as the oldest of natural elements. The Oglala Sioux consider Trickster as the firstborn son of Rock, who "named all things and made all languages."[21] Raven in the Tlingit trickster cycle is indestructible because he was born of a hot stone swallowed by Nas-caki-yel's sister.[22] Stone is also the alchemical *lapis*, symbol of the integrated self.[23] In one of the uncollected legends of Crow's birth that Hughes published, the stone, having slept beyond measurement, suddenly "opened its eye. / Crow blinked at the world."[24] The conclusion of "Crow and Stone" argues that Crow's aggressive perceptual orientation will ultimately wreak cosmic havoc—a destructive assault upon the ontological center of creation which is also a criminal act against the stability of the self. The cosmic dust created by Crow's failure to recognize the potential communality of spirit in nature and in himself leads directly to the nuclear age, where our Crow-like culture holds "the very globe in terror."

"Crow Sickened" follows "The Black Beast," the seventh poem where Crow initiates malicious violence, in providing the clearest instance of the formal paradigm of self-reflexivity that governs many of the more violent poems of *Crow*. Crow's problem in "The Black Beast" and "Crow Sickened" lies in his having accepted his culture's dualistic mode of perception and its bias against subjectivity. As Locke anchored the tradition of Western empiricism when he subordinated the subjective five senses to the objectively quantifiable solidity, extension, motion, and number, in *An Essay Concerning Human Understanding*, so Crow follows his logic centuries later by assuming that problem and resolution, need and satisfaction, lie outside himself, in some material acquisition or villain. When Crow in "The Black Beast" sits "in its chair, telling loud lies against the Black Beast," he is of course sitting in his own chair, and projecting his problems outside himself. He will never find the answer to the question "Where is the Black Beast" by splitting his enemy's skull or roasting the earth to a clinker. In "Crow Sickened" he

Decided to get death, but whatever
Walked into his ambush
Was always his own body.

Crow's sole response is fear when, "Unwinding the world like a ball of wool," he "Found the last end tied around his own finger." As a result he shuts his eyes and maims himself. "Crow Sickened" parodies plate 77 of Blake's *Jerusalem*, where Blake regains Paradise through an awakened imagination that unifies inner and outer worlds:

I give you the end of a golden string,
    Only wind it into a ball:
It will lead you in at Heaven's gate,
    Built in Jerusalem's wall.

Until Crow learns to develop his inner life, he will continue to mutilate himself with the perceptual orientation provided by his Protestant ethic/scientific empiricism culture and remain waiting at the gatepost of heaven, like Man in "Crow's Song About God," stubbornly refusing to take charge of his life. Crow's woolen ball of string in "Crow Sickened" carries an ironic allusion to the Sufis, whose name derives from the Arabic word for wool, *súf*, and relates to their coarse, ascetic garb. Self-denial, to promote the development of the inner life, is a garb Crow never considers wearing. What Crow needs is to learn the wisdom and humility of the transformed Reverend Lumb in the "Epilogue" of *Gaudete*. Lumb knows exactly where to locate the Black Beast—under his own coat.

In all seven poems where Crow initiates maliciously violent action, formal motifs operate to locate the causes of the violence in Crow's acculturation and his subsequent inability to develop his imaginative life. The self-reflexivity discussed above provides a clue to another formal motif that accounts for the violence pervading most of the remaining ninety-odd *Crow* poems—the violence that Hughes's deliberately graphic language so often calls attention to, and that many critics have mistakenly judged either gratuitous or adolescent.[25] In "The Black Beast," "Crow Sickened," and even "Magical Dangers" and "Crow Improvises," self-reflexivity occurs because the one-sidedly rational, abstractive, and manipulative attitude toward the outer world that alienates nature also demonizes it in the process. Consider once again Hughes's remarks in the first "Myth and Education" essay and the Nicholson review. When Christianity suppresses the devil, it "suppresses vital natural life," and the devil nevertheless "leaks out in every direction as a very evil, wicked and uncontrolled and unsuspected presence." Also, "The subtly apotheosized misogyny of Reformed Christianity is proportionate to the fanatic rejection of Nature. . . ." What Hughes describes in these reciprocal statements is the Jungian tenet of the compensatory nature of the psyche, which Jung based in part on Heraclitus's law of *enantiodromia* and proved in the pathology of severely neurotic and psychotic patients. *Enantiodromia* became an integral part of Jung's theory of the psyche, his dream therapy, mandala interpretation, and social analyses of contemporary civilization.[26] Textual evidence indicates that *enantiodromia* is the third modernist mythic motif that pervades the fantasy world of *Crow*.[27]

Enantiodromia simply means a "running counter to"—that any extremely one-sided attitude in time necessitates a reverse development toward its opposite. In the statements cited in the previous paragraph, both the "vital natural life" and the "misogyny" relate to the libidinal, instinctual energy that Hughes believes our one-sidedly rational culture represses. Decade after decade of Protestant ethic taboos and scientific objectivity reinforce the repression. In "On the Psychology of the Trickster Figure," an essay for Paul Radin's volume *The Trickster*, Jung writes that a society that satisfies only rational and material needs will mobilize the Shadow, the undifferentiated (i.e., neither morally good nor bad) instinctual energies (both inferior and superior, chthonic and spiritual) that lie dormant in the unconscious, whenever that society becomes troubled. But if the ego, the conscious self-concept of that individual or society, is based *entirely* upon a narrow rationalism that substitutes allegiance to what the laws allow for introspection and individual moral choice, it will spurn the Shadow and only permit its appearance in projection, as something demonic outside the self, to be feared because not known or understood. According to Jung, "as in its collective, mythological form, so also the individual shadow contains within it the seed of an *enantiodromia*, of a conversion to its opposite," in order to heal the psyche if the individual or culture can work its way through the dark archetype and bring to consciousness a new orientation. Otherwise, "increasing repression and neglect" will cause "a corresponding projection on other social groups and nations," with violent results.[28] In his "Trickster" essay Jung finds confirmation for his theory in the fanatical anti-Semitism of Nazi Germany, the psychological consequence of an apathy in the individual fostered by the rational absolutes of the totalitarian state. Thus the psychological maladaptation can cause more than misperceptions; it can promote fears and aggressive postures that lead to real-life violence, even genocide.

One year after the first British and American editions of *Crow*, Hughes combined his mythic interpretation of the last three hundred years of Western culture with Jung's *enantiodromia* in the provocative "Introduction" to his selection of Shakespeare's verse, *With Fairest Flowers While Summer Lasts*.[29] Here Hughes states that "every poet does no more than find metaphors for his own nature," and the best poet in doing so illuminates his whole age. As Shakespeare worked out his own sexual "knot of obsessions" in his plays, his poetic imagination also became a crucible for the forces that led to the Civil War and, by implication, the subsequent triumph of the Puritan ethos—rational scepticism—in modern science. Shakespeare, a Puritan sceptic himself according to Hughes, found in "Venus and Adonis" and "The Rape of Lucrece" metaphors for his and his culture's desire to repress the Virgin Mary and her predecessor, the Celtic goddess of sex and creativity, just as James I suppressed her in fact a decade later.

In Adonis's boar and Tarquin's destruction of Lucrece, Hughes sees "a sudden transformation, a frightening psychic event": an "occult crossover of Nature's maddened force—like a demon—into the brain that had rejected her." So "Shakespearean lust, this boar of blackness," emerges enantiodromically to haunt the lustful/misogynist Puritan heroes of subsequent plays, especially the tragedies. Richard III, Tarquin, Angelo, Hamlet, Othello, Macbeth, Lear, Antony, Coriolanus, Leontes, Posthumus—all are infected self-reflexively by their refusal to worship the goddess. In each case "this suppressed nature goddess erupts, possessing the man who denied her, and creating this king-killing man of chaos." In the late romances Shakespeare finally gave up the struggle, creating *deus ex machina* miraculous transformations to resolve conflicts. Finally, in *The Tempest*, Hughes finds Shakespeare guilty of creating grotesquely displaced masks for a stunted eros, as he replaces Venus with the hag Sycorax, Tarquin with the half-beast Caliban, and "within an impenetrable crucible of magic prohibitions, he married Lucrece (Miranda) to Adonis (Ferdinand). But what a wooden wedding! What proper little puritan puppets!" Hughes's interpretation of Shakespeare is intriguing, though only a partial account. His preoccupation with *enantiodromia* and projection in 1971, however, is important for comprehending the universe of *Crow*.

Violence in most of the remaining Crow poems derives from Adonis's enantiodromic "boar of blackness"—a demonized eros projected upon the environment by God and Crow, both of whom see nature through their culture's spectacles of rational scepticism. Neither God nor Crow can discern the *ātman* state of the Upanishads, the "inner spiritual unity of nature," or the Sufic Great Work of self-integration. Crow begins misperceiving reality early in his education; he sees sharks and disease-carrying insects when God tries to teach love through abstractions in "Crow's First Lesson." In "Crow's Account of the Battle" the "mishmash of scripture and physics" of contemporary Western culture promotes a well-planned war where orders, universal laws, and theorems obliterate both humans and landscape with horrifying ease, but without public outcry:

> The cartridges were banging off, as planned,
> The fingers were keeping things going
> According to excitement and orders.
> The unhurt eyes were full of deadliness.
> The bullets pursued their courses
> Through clods of stone, earth and skin,
> Through intestines, pocket-books, brains, hair, teeth
> According to Universal laws
> And mouths cried "Mama"
> From sudden traps of calculus,
> Theorems wrenched men in two,
>
> . . . .
>
> Reality was giving its lesson,
> Its mishmash of scripture and physics,
> With here, brains in hands, for example,
> And there, legs in a treetop.

The real horror of this scientific dissection of reality into unrelated parts is that we have become acculturated to viewing this with passive resignation, partly because we are happy when schedules and machines operate "as planned," and partly because the violence mirrors the mental chaos and suppressed rage of our daily lives that the surface happiness seldom touches:

> And when the smoke cleared it became clear
> This had happened too often before
> And was going to happen too often in future
> And happened too easily
>
> . . . .
>
> Blasting the whole world to bits
> Was too like slamming a door
> Too like dropping in a chair
> Exhausted with rage

Too like being blown to bits yourself
Which happened too easily
With too like no consequences.

Absorbing thousands of hours of television and other mass media has trivialized violence for most people and insulated them from its actual horrors, while our machine culture, as Konrad Lorenz observes, creates weapons that place such great distances between killer and victim that our psycho-biological inhibitions against intraspecies killing no longer function.[30] So eyes remain neutral and "unhurt" in "Crow's Account of the Battle," but "full of deadliness."

If rational scepticism can promote aggression as it distances us from nature, it can also produce enantiodromic fears that lead to psychotic violence. In "Crow's Account of St. George" the quintessential hero of the Protestant ethic pursues his belief that "everything in the Universe / Is a track of numbers racing towards an answer." As St. George "rides those racing tracks," he "refrigerates an emptiness" and dissects animals "With tweezers of number." But when he looks up from his frenzied research he sees a demon grinning at him. He tries to repress that apparition and continue his concentration, but a more horrible and aggressive demon replaces the first. Instinctual energies, denied a place in St. George's laboratory, have come bestialized and appear in projection as demonic aggressors. Psychosis and surrealistic violence follow:

He lifts a chair—fear lifts him—
He smashes the egg-shell object to a blood rag,
A limping sprawl, he tramples the bubbling mess.
The shark-face is screaming in the doorway
Opening its fangs. The chair again—
He splits that face and beats the chair to pieces
On the writhing unbreakably tough horror
Till it lies still. Now with a shriek
An object four times bigger than the others—
A belly-ball of hair, with crab-legs, eyeless,
Jabs its pincers into his face,
Its belly opens—a horrible oven of fangs,
The claws are clawing to drag him towards it—
He snatches from its mount on the wall a sword,
A ceremonial Japanese decapitator,
And as hacking a path through thicket he scatters

> The lopped segments, the opposition collapses.
> He stands trousered in blood and log-splits
> The lolling body, bifurcates it
> Top to bottom, kicks away the entrails—
> Steps out of the blood-wallow. Recovers—
>
> Drops the sword and runs dumb-faced from the house
> Where his wife and children lie in their blood.

In "Crow's Account of St. George" Hughes intends to reveal the consequences of the militant ethos; his source is a Japanese folktale about a Samurai whose pride and militancy rigidify into family-killing possession.[31] But enantiodromic violence in *Crow* is ubiquitous, not confined to family problems: it manifests itself as the "ticking bomb" of repressed eros ("Fragment of an Ancient Tablet") that our rationalist culture projects upon nature, that supercharges its voltage like a step-up transformer ("Magical Dangers," "Crow Improvises," "Truth Kills Everybody") and leaves civilization vulnerable to global catastrophe ("Crow and Stone") and nuclear holocaust ("That Moment," "Notes for a Little Play"). Violence in *Crow* even approaches interstellar proportions, where the instant of primal creation itself is attacked. In the uncollected "The Space-Egg Was Sailing,"[32] the second half of which became "Crow's Song of Himself," our universe (the cultural construct epitomized by the God of *Crow*) attacks the Brahmanic Cosmic Egg, the creation myth of the Chāndogya Upanishad (3:19:1–4), where a primal androgyne is split asunder to create silver and gold, earth and sky, and the rest of the world. In the Hughes poem the egg survives the attack of our universe, but soon life attacks it: a crow swallows and excretes it. Then "everything attacked." In the tumult Crow takes to his wings and sings "Crow's Song of Himself." An aggressive Western mythic construct has supplanted an ancient, nonviolent, and ecologically sound Oriental mythic construct. Crow merely imitates the violent scenario of his birth when he "stropped his beak and started in on the two thieves" at the end of the poem.

In such a violent universe Crow can only apprehend the pain of nature, not the creative principle that would spark his imagination into life and end his quest successfully. The God of this universe has tyrannically repressed that creative power. When Crow tries to listen to nature he hears "a cortege / Of mourning and lament" ("Crow Tyrannosaurus") or "the sea's ogreish outcry and convulsion" ("Crow on the Beach"). When Crow does have one of his infrequent glimmerings of thought and decides to sing to nature—an occupation that would certainly activate his imagination—the universe created by the God of his ramshackle religion and science rises against him. As in "Magical Dangers," when "Crow Tries the Media" his environment conspires against him to inhibit his organs of apperception. The Roman conquest, modern warfare, mass media fantasies, a stagnant capitalism, and ecological pollution—all the familiar features of a murderously efficient culture conspire to blot out Crow's voice, his eyes, his sense of touch, in surreal phantasmagoria:

> He wanted to sing very clear
>
> But this tank had been parked on his voice
> And his throttle was nipped between the Roman Emperor's
> > finger and thumb
>
> Like the neck of a linnet
> And King Kong in person
> Held the loop of his blood like a garotte
> While tycoons gambled with his glands in a fog of cigar smoke
>
> He shuddered out of himself he got so naked
> When he touched her breast it hurt him
>
> He wanted to sing to her soul simply
>
> But still Manhattan weighed on his eyelid
> He looked at the corner of her eye
> His tongue moved like a poisoned estuary
>
> He touched the smiling corner of her mouth
> His voice reverberated like the slow millstone of London
> Raising a filthy haze
> > her shape dimmed

"Crow's Undersong" is the closest Crow comes to an esthetic appreciation of nature. The personification of nature as a frightened, easily bruised lover who cannot manage much is the most his perceptual orientation allows him and an accurate depiction of her status in our culture. "She has come amorous" but "She cannot come all the way" when she has been exploited so much for so long. The ironical title allusion, however, supports her primacy as creatress: in Tlingit mythology "Old-Woman-Underneath" supports the world from below, like the Atlas of our male-oriented Western mythology.[33] Without the creative power of this anima figure there would be no city, civilization, or culture. But Crow's undeveloped esthetic sensibility cannot grasp this power.

Throughout the first "Myth and Education" essay Hughes stresses the importance of a richly developed imaginative life as the area where we "deal with both the outer world and our inner life." Imagination to Hughes is "the most essential piece of machinery we have if we are going to live the lives of human beings." "Without full operation of the various worlds and heavens and hells of imagination," declares Hughes, "men become sick, mechanical monsters." Crow fails to perceive the creative power of nature because he lacks a corresponding imaginative life where creativity is accorded a place, and because his cultural orientation systematically refuses to value creativity. The behavioral model God provides Crow contains equal parts of abstraction, apathy, and violence. In this constricting atmosphere love becomes a hurtfully possessive appropriation of the other to fill one's needs. "Lovesong" does not convey Hughes's characteristic attitude toward love ("Bride and groom lie hidden for three days" in *Cave Birds* provides the ideal), but one consistent with the possibilities available in the universe of *Crow*. Here giving and sharing in Christian *caritas* deteriorates to taking and hoarding, all to fill a yawning vacuum where an integrated self and a rich imaginative life should lie. When love in "Lovesong" is not selfish, it is an anesthetic used to obliterate any consciousness of self, or to escape the present moment. "Lovesong" demonstrates the folly of attempting to love another before achieving a wholeness within the self:

> He wanted to topple with his arms round her
> Off that moment's brink and into nothing
> Or everlasting or whatever there was
> Her embrace was an immense press
> To print him into her bones
> His smiles were the garrets of a fairy palace
> Where the real world would never come
> Her smiles were spider bites
> So he would lie still till she felt hungry
> His words were occupying armies
> Her laughs were an assassin's attempts

"A person can only do what he thinks he can do," argues Hughes in that first "Myth and Education" essay; and if one does not arouse one's own imagination, self-confidence, self-image, and future development will suffer, leaving "some tremendous inner fear" and society's notion of what is permitted. In other words, the self develops as one's imaginative life develops. Crow's development, in the sequence as presently ordered, is minimal. He gains just enough self-reflection to ask a few halfhearted questions that either puzzle or are superseded by cravings for food ("That Moment," "Crow Communes," "Crow Tyrannosaurus"); otherwise he rationalizes his limitations with egocentric bravado ("Crow's Theology," "Crow's Fall") or ponders a world of pain and guilt ("Crow on the Beach," "Crow's Nerve Fails") that his laughter often keeps at arm's length ("Crow's Battle Fury"). At other times he remains aloof ("The Battle of Osfrontalis," "A Disaster") or rearranges creation with expedients ("A Childish Prank," "Crow Blacker Than Ever"). The beauty and freedom of nature in its creative aspect does not register in Crow's narrow value system; a pause and a passing expression of ignorance is the typical response of Crow's apathetic brain ("Crow on the Beach"):

> His utmost gaping of brain in his tiny skull
> Was just enough to wonder, about the sea,
>
> What could be hurting so much?

Crow's behavior in "Crow Hears Fate Knock on the Door" illustrates Hughes's contention in the first "Myth and Education" essay that the prohibition of the imagination in our culture will lead to "a completely passive attitude of apathy in face of material facts." Crow articulates a promising prophecy in this poem but fails to act upon it. He believes he can own and be inside nature, instead of staring out at it, but he is already acculturated to the perceptual orientation of scientific rationalism. He perceives nature— even a little stream—in a Newtonian framework of mechanical analysis and feels utterly helpless:

> He looked in front of his feet at the little stream
> Chugging on like an auxiliary motor
> Fastened to this infinite engine.
>
> He imagined the whole engineering
> Of its assembly, repairs and maintenance—
> And felt helpless.

Crow's limited consciousness and wayward behavior parallel the trickster material Hughes used as background for the character and escapades of his hero *manqué*. The American engraver and artist Leonard Baskin visited Hughes three weeks after Sylvia Plath's death on 11 February 1963 and commissioned Hughes to write a poem entitled "The Anatomy of Crow," to be printed by Baskin at the Gehenna Press. Baskin, a member of the Smith College faculty and a friend since Plath's teaching year at Smith (1957–1958), hoped to drive Hughes "from despair into activity." But nothing came of the project until a letter arrived some five years later stating that the Crow idea had assumed epic proportions.[34] "A Disaster," the first *Crow* poem to reach print, appeared on 22 July 1967 in *Scotsman*. Intervening between the Baskin commission and the first *Crow* publication was Hughes's review of John Greenway's *Literature among the Primitives* and *The Primitive Reader* for the *New York Review of Books*, 9 December 1965, just eighteen months before "A Disaster" reached print. Each Greenway volume contains a chapter on the trickster figure; the title of Hughes's review, "Tricksters and Tarbabies," derives from a Greenway chapter principally about the trickster. Trickster folklore, the fourth modernist mythic motif of *Crow*, had at least as much to do with the inception of the volume as the Baskin Crow engravings that appeared after the commission. (*Eat Crow*, originally written in 1964, develops the crow only in a purely symbolic way, as an emblem of the indestructible will to live.) Crow and Trickster are closely related, but exactly how is open to question.

Trickster, probably the oldest protagonist in all of literature, appears to have had his debut in the embryonic stage of human culture, as an aimless amoral wanderer, at an infant stage of self-consciousness, who becomes caught up in the elemental incongruities of life. His personality, as handed down through oral tradition in thousands of differing tales among primitive tribes of worldwide distribution, chiefly manifests a rude cleverness and buffoonery, a voracious gluttony, and streaks of obstinacy, capriciousness, and occasional arrogance. Many, but not all, trickster cycles also contain an uninhibited venery. At root, Trickster expresses the indomitability and indestructibility of the will to live. Many trickster narratives, especially North American Indian, begin with Trickster appearing at the creation of the world, among the oldest elements of existence, and then creating or liberating, usually haphazardly or accidentally, most of the essentials of human culture: water, fire, food-gathering techniques, and so forth.[35] Most of Trickster's culture hero exploits, researchers agree, were later additions of priests at more highly developed cultural stages. Radin believes that Trickster embodies the great fund of instinctual drives at the base of all cultural development, especially because his escapades occur in an environment that embodies memories of a primordial past (an Eliadian *illud tempus*), before the separation of divine and nondivine.[36] For Jung, Trickster is an archetype of the Shadow, a fund of potentially positive instinctual energy for future personality development.[37] Reviewers of *Crow*, unaware of the trickster background, nevertheless hailed Crow's survival abilities as a positive response to our Cold War, post-Auschwitz cultural environment.[38]

In their books on Hughes's poetry, Sagar, Faas, Gifford and Roberts, and Hirschberg all note helpful resemblances between Crow and Trickster, and between Crow and primitive creation myths or appearances of crows in Western mythologies. All acknowledge, however, Hughes's comment that no consistent parallels exist between *Crow* and any particular trickster episodes or cycles. Though Hughes saturated himself for a time in trickster narratives, his purpose was to create, as he wrote to Sagar, "something autochthonous and complete in itself, as it might be invented after the holocaust and demolition of all libraries, where essential things spring again— if at all—only from their seeds in nature." So to Hughes "the comparative religion/mythology background was irrelevant to me, except as I could forget it. If I couldn't find it again in Crow, I wasn't interested to make a trophy of it."[39] The form of *Crow* does not derive from detailed structural parallels with trickster literature, but from the aforementioned six mythic motifs always in force in the self-enclosed fantasy universe of *Crow*. Thus far, three have been discussed: Hughes's reinterpretation of the past three hundred years of Western cultural history; his adaptation of this to a fantasy universe that, along with its God, acculturates Crow to reality as it is perceived and understood by the Protestant ethic and Western science; and the use of *enantiodromia*, as a meaning-bearing formal law of this fantasy universe, to specify a psychological cause for the violence of modern Western culture. By discussing the problem of Trickster's development, one can determine the essence of Hughes's use of Trickster, the fourth motif operating in the modernist formal universe of *Crow*.

Trickster's development in the primitive cycles is questionable, but the topic should be addressed because of its relevance to Crow's character. Radin and Jung affirm some degree of development; Kerényi and Greenway do not. Radin bases his developmental interpretation upon Jungian and Eliadian elements *added to* the narrative, whereas his very perceptive notes to the Winnebago cycle contained in *The Trickster* indicate without question that Trickster's obtuseness and stupidity continue to the end of the cycle. To Radin, the essence of trickster narratives concerns their relationship to "the vague memories of an archaic and primordial past, where there as yet existed no clear-cut differentiation between the divine and the non-divine" and the promise of differentiation within the trickster symbol itself.[40] For Jung, Trickster, as an archetype of personality development, must *per se* demonstrate developmental potential. The only evidence from Radin's Winnebago cycle that Jung finds to support his position is the statement that useful plants are created from Trickster's penis (but this appears in the same chapter where his gullibility results in Chipmunk devouring most of said penis) and the short episode about Trickster revenging himself upon coyote.[41]

Kerényi and Greenway, however, look more carefully at the trickster texts themselves and perceive no development. Kerényi sees Trickster as the original picaresque hero, the spirit of disorder and revolt who, released in the freedom of a literary work, demonstrates the power of the social order under ridicule.[42] Greenway surveys the main theories and indicates their weaknesses, especially in view of the storyteller's own changing recitation and the audience's inability to perceive any development in Trickster. Greenway contends that trickster narratives are cathartics to purge the audience of incest and avoidance restrictions and other stern regulations of conduct in primitive societies. The audience laughs at Trickster's ineptitude, all the while comprehending that such conduct in themselves would doubtless earn exile or death. The narratives release frustration while paradoxically reinforcing the social codes under ridicule.[43] In his review of the Greenway volumes Hughes commends Greenway's sensible approach, thorough investigation, and desire to advance "the literature itself, not some theory about it." He calls the volumes "a first-rate introduction to just what is to be looked for in primitive literature."

It appears that one can locate trickster narratives that advance either the developmental or the nondevelopmental theory. In the Tlingit version codified by Swanton, for instance, Trickster is definitely a culture hero who liberates light and the stars, rescues water from the hoarder Petrel, makes the rivers of British Columbia, and so forth. His every action results in some new implement or food-gathering technique. Coprophilia is never the focus of attention, Trickster usually outwits his competitors, and remnants of scatological humor are rendered into Latin by Swanton.[44] In Radin's Winnebago cycle the portrayal is reversed. Here the emphasis lies on broad, low humor; Trickster is the gull of every forest animal; and his stupidity extends even to a lack of awareness about his own bodily functions. But in neither cycle does Trickster actually develop *within* the episodes. One recognizes much priestly revision at a higher level of culture in the Tlingit account; the very opening tale of the child Trickster creating the natural elements while playing with bags and bundles indicates a degree of imaginative delicacy. The first sentence of Swanton's Tlingit cycle recorded at Sitka corroborates Greenway's point about the discretionary and creative latitude accorded the teller: "No one knows just how the story of Raven really begins, so each starts from the point where he does know it." Radin's Winnebago cycle is the only one Hughes specifically mentions as within his reading in the Greenway review; since Radin's work on African lore receives high praise from Hughes in this review, the Winnebago cycle reprinted in *The Trickster* may have been a main background source for *Crow*.

What Hughes no doubt saw in the Winnebago cycle, and probably applied to his *Crow* universe, was Trickster's incredible imperceptiveness about nature, a fit subject for primitive ridicule. Lévi-Strauss in *The Savage Mind* presents a convincing account of primitive people's intense absorption in nature and attention to detail, in language, botany, herbal lore, and domestic practices.[45] In *Primitive Song* C. M. Bowra explains the immediacy of passionate excitement, the concentration and clarity of primitive song, in terms of the singers' habit of keeping "their eyes and ears alert all the time," and their capacity for "seeing and feeling something very sharply and vividly for a short time."[46] Hughes similarly stresses primitive people's intense and perceptive absorption in nature, in his review of Bowra's book (*Listener*, 3 May 1962). In the Winnebago cycle, however, the laughter that Greenway finds essential to the trickster narratives results from Trickster's obtuseness concerning nature; this basic incongruity was certainly not lost on Hughes.

In Radin's Winnebago cycle, Trickster is hilariously inept in the natural world. In one typical episode (chapter XI), Trickster notices a figure dressed in black, on the opposite side of a lake, who appears to be pointing at him. When Trickster's queries receive no response, he obstinately decides to mimic: "I, too, can stand pointing just as long as he does." Only when his arm tires, and he takes a closer look at the opposite shore, does he realize that he has been pointing for hours at a tree stump with a protruding branch. Primitives would guffaw at this lack of instinctive knowledge of nature, for this knowledge is of utmost importance for survival—for their ability to feed, clothe, and protect themselves.

Radin's entire cycle is replete with such stumblejohn episodes. In another chapter (XXVI) Trickster tries to pick the plums he sees at the bottom of a pond. Only when puzzled and tired does he perceive that he has been trying to grab the reflection of plums in the water. Trickster falls into his own excrement in the laxative bulb episode (XXIII–XXIV); awakens to what he thinks is the chief's banner floating above him, only to find his own erection beneath his blanket (XV); punishes his anus for failing to keep watch over his roast duck by poking it with a red-hot stick (XVI); gets his head caught in the dead skull of an elk while trying to compete with flies for food (XXXII); catches a hawk by having it impale its beak in his rectum (XXXIV); and is forever outfoxed by other animals. The stupidity of inflicting pain upon himself, and the broad scatological humor of most of the episodes, certainly made Trickster the focus of much ridicule. Even at the end of the cycle, when he marries and settles down, Trickster remains incurably inept. He does not have enough savvy about nature to provide food for his wife; he must trick Muskrat, Snipe, Woodpecker, and Polecat into using their industry and favorite foraging techniques to provide for his family (XL–XLIV). One can imagine the ridicule a primitive would heap on an oaf who cannot bring home the bacon.

The purpose of Hughes's application of trickster material to his *Crow* universe now becomes clear. It does not concern character development. Crow's development in the 1970 ordering of the poems is minimal, principally because he fails to develop an imaginative life in his inner world and fails to perceive the creative principle in nature in the outer world. Nor do the background trickster narratives necessitate character development. Revision by a more advanced culture does not constitute character development *within* a trickster cycle, and this is really not possible, especially in the Winnebago cycle, given what is at root an essentially picaresque hero. What Hughes very sagaciously does note is Trickster's imperceptiveness of nature. Hughes easily penetrates to the imaginative center of trickster narratives, raises Trickster's lack of knowledge of nature to a theme of prime importance, and trades Trickster's occluded vision for modern people's equally occluded spectacles of rational scepticism. Both Trickster and Crow fail to perceive "God's nameless hidden prisoner," though they encounter her often. To this Hughes added an essentially naturalistic environment where Crow is the victim of his constricting post-Renaissance Western culture. As Crow remains chained to his appetites, his instinctual dependencies and cravings, he perceives only a world of birth, blood, fear, violence, and the blackness of decaying matter—the imagery and perspective of the *Sidpa Bardo*.

In the aforementioned 1975 Cambridge reading transcript note, Hughes writes that Crow's universe "is one in which all history is happening simultaneously, so Crow is able to move freely from one era to another, from the beginning of the world to the end." Poems like "Crowego" and "Truth Kills

Everybody" illustrate this modernist omnitemporality. This fifth mythic motif is complicated, however, by the fact that Crow's vision is restricted by his acculturation to the values of rational scepticism. Like Trickster mistaking a tree stump for a person, Crow's narrow cultural value system inhibits any growth in understanding nature throughout his omnitemporal travels. The persistent eye imagery of *Crow* develops Blake's maxim "As the Eye—Such the Object,"[47] as it reinforces the reader's understanding of Crow's blinkered vision. Crow throughout his escapades fails to awaken his inner world, so to reorganize his perceptions of the outer world. He needs to learn what Blake wrote Trusler about the imagination's role in perception: "to the Eyes of the Man of Imagination Nature is Imagination itself. As a man is So he Sees. As the Eye is formed such are its Powers."[48]

The "without eye," the one that views the objective world, perceives only decay and death in the first of "Two Legends." In "Lineage" the eye begets fear—the emotion that Hughes in his *Crow* period consistently associates with the psychological results of withdrawing from nature into abstractions and rational scepticism. Crow's eyes are "minimum-efficiency eyes" ("Examination at the Womb-Door") that shoot him blind ("A Kill"), that blind him to the creative principle in nature. With these blinded eyes Crow "peered out at creation" from the distance of his rocket porthole, in "Crow and Mama." Already Crow has become acculturated to the inert objectivity his culture prizes.

The womb door in the *Bardo Thödol* is the entrance to the *Sidpa Bardo* realm of birth, death, and sensual appetite. The initiate hoping to achieve self-command and self-mastery over the phenomenal world and personal desire must close the womb door.[49] But Crow passes through it and into the *Sidpa Bardo* in "Examination at the Womb-Door." He cannot master his instincts. Hughes in his essays affirms a cautious optimism about human educability; his position parallels Blake's belief that one can cleanse the doors of perception and see the infinite.[50] Crow, however, is content to focus his attention upon the *Sidpa Bardo* side of the "Black doorway: / The eye's pupil." Fearful projections of blood, blackness, and violence— the imagery of the *Sidpa Bardo*—will comprise his self-created vision. The source of the psychological projection that accompanies *enantiodromia* in *Crow* derives from Hughes's long acquaintance with the *Bardo Thödol*, the Bön-po sources of which antedate Heraclitus.

Crow in his escapades will "look," "see," "peer," "gape," "stare," and otherwise act violently against self-created menaces caused by the narrow vision provided him by his Western value system. When "Crow Alights" he sees only things existing in the objective world. His camera eye moves from telescopic and wide-angle lenses toward a final, unsettling close-up of his hand near his cup, while repetitions of the verb "saw" intensify the visual focus. But Crow's eye stops with the external, factual evidence. He sees nothing in his inner world. "The Black Beast" also must be something he can see as objectively as when he "peered into the brain of a dogfish." Interestingly enough, in the sixty-seven different poems that comprise the first British and American editions of *Crow*, Crow "imagines" only twice: once to feel helpless when he perceives the universe as a Newtonian mechanism (line 7 of "Crow Hears Fate Knock at the Door"), and again to calculate what he can gain from words (line 3 of "Crow Goes Hunting"). Crow's abstract "thought" of freedom evaporates his eyes, the organs that could liberate him, in "Magical Dangers." Crow's soul mate is St. George, who "sees everything in the Universe / Is a track of numbers racing towards an answer" ("Crow's Account of St. George"). "A Disaster" typifies Hughes's development of the sixth modernist mythic motif in *Crow*: here Crow only "saw," "peered," and then distanced himself. His objectivity produces no inwardness, offers him no capacity for self-reflection, and develops no mediate ground for the resolution of conflicts between self and world.

Crow condemns himself to acting upon automatic reflex in the satisfaction of ego and instinct. His "trapsprung" instinctual cravings in "Crow Tyrannosaurus" separate him from nature, producing the "eye's / roundness" and "the ear's / deafness." The images suggest a future of undeveloping cyclicity. After Crow has "peered" at the serpent in "A Horrible Religious Error," he subverts this creative principle of nature into food. When he avails himself of the opportunity to educate his perceptions from pre–Industrial Revolution Western culture ("Crowego"), he again fails to perceive nature in its creative aspect: "He strangled in error Dejanira." The error occurs because he preoccupies himself with self-serving motives for searching into the past: he "gazes" hungrily into the past "Like a leopard in a fat land."

The eye imagery in *Crow* underscores Crow's inability to develop beyond his acculturation. When Crow is finally on the brink of recognizing that he himself is the problem, and that the Blakean/Sufi ball of string leading to his inner world may be his salvation, "His eyes sealed up with shock, refusing to see" ("Crow Sickened"). Even a consciousness of death brings only physical pain to his eye in "Crow's Battle Fury." Like those of Trickster, Crow's responses seldom surpass the level of sensation. The longer he lacks an imaginative life, the more arrogant and misguided Crow's objective eye becomes. Near the end of *Crow*, as he battles Stone, an ontological first principle of being to primitives, he battles himself, with tricksterlike unconsciousness, and with "his mere eye-blink / Holding the very globe in terror" ("Crow and Stone"). Because Crow chooses to burn in the fires of desire and anger (cf. the Buddha's "Fire Sermon" at Benares), he forever fails to recognize that his perceptions can change, can become his source of salvation. As he persists in perceiving a world of sensual gratification and alienating fact, his potential for self-development dwindles to that of Custer at Little Big Horn. In "Crow's Last Stand" Crow's eye becomes the ego's defensive fort, continually scorched by the fires of need and desire.

Crow's eye is imperishable; it need not remain imprisoned in a fort. He could revise his perceptions to recognize that other cultures have perceived life as a divine energy that burns through all things, what Hughes has called the "Heraclitian/Buddhist notion that the entire universe is basically made of fire."[51] Transformation is possible if Crow could awaken his imagination long enough to abandon his defensive egotism and learn that he is the source of his perceptions in a holistic process of human-in-nature. With an awakened imagination he could end his quest, earn his bride, and continue toward the Blakean infinite or Sufic Great Work—the integration of inner and outer worlds, with the self as center of perception. The achievement of this integration becomes a major project for Hughes in the seventies.

Most of the reviewers who disliked *Crow* felt that the blood, blackness, and violence that pervaded the volume were too glib,[52] or nihilistically self-indulgent,[53] or they believed that the volume lacked viable alternatives.[54] The reverse is true. The mythic motifs that inform the self-contained fantasy universe of *Crow* are carefully considered, well motivated, unique and exceptionally creative vehicles for Hughes's analysis of contemporary Western culture. The fourth and fifth motifs just discussed—the sensual trickster hero *manqué* imprisoned in the *Sidpa Bardo* of his own instinctual cravings and the fantasy world freedom generated by a simultaneity of time—may provide the appearance of a lack of alternatives, but only to those who read with Crow's blinkered eyes. Crow's acculturation, narrow vision, and self-created projections fill the universe *he* perceives. He has passively adopted a mental construct that he is free to revise or disown. He could be as free as the birds of "Crow on the Beach" if he could revise his perceptions.

The diminutive robin of "Robin Song" sings unsullied by the Protestant ethic and scientific empiricism. He knows that he is the source of his own perceptions. The owl of "Owl's Song" takes a more positive view of nature;

after giving up his dualistic objectivity, he "sat still with fear," but a fear produced by a new interaction with nature. The stars bear his clawtrack, and the rock his wingbeat imprint, in a fusion of self-and-world:

> He sang
> How everything had nothing more to lose
>
> Then sat still with fear
>
> Seeing the clawtrack of star
> Hearing the wingbeat of rock
>
> And his own singing

Owl awakens to the realization that he is the creator of the values that he perceives as inhabiting nature. This happens after he loses his Western habit of perceiving nature as filled with separate, quantifiably distinct entities. The stars "dropped their pretence" to gain owl's "clawtrack"; the rock "surrendered its last hope" to gain his "wingbeat." If "everything had nothing more to lose," it has everything to gain, from owl's new vantage point—the *śūnyatā* state of the allness of nothingness that the persona of part III of *Wodwo* attained. One can achieve a comfortable assurance within nature by considering oneself an organic part of a holistic process.

Hughes offers Crow the very positive alternative of Buddhist *śūnyatā* through double entendres associated with the words "nothingness" and "emptiness." As Crow's fantasy universe contains the law of the simultaneity of time and space, Crow is free to absorb any new orientation toward nature he may desire from the museum of human culture. But as usual his passive acculturation blinds him. Ironic humor precipitates from intrusions of a superior authorial perspective. In "Crow Frowns" Crow tries to relieve his loneliness by searching for a directive from an undisclosed superior power. In Christian mysticism, this godhead's essence, the "something" Crow searches for, is "nothing"—unmoved substance beyond human comprehension. In Zen Buddhist terms, Crow wanders in illusion when he looks for "something" outside himself. He should return to his "original face" in the Zen *kōan*—nothing:

> He is the long waiting for something
> To use him for some everything
> Having so carefully made him
>
> Of nothing.

It is Crow's tragicomic fate to be in constant search for "something" outside himself.

As the giant Albion tore creation from himself, in a lapse of creative imagination, in Blake's *Jerusalem* (plate 27), so Crow's playmate gods tear themselves from him in "Crow's Playmates." Loneliness, a passive state, produces objectification and a loss of power; Crow's unawakened imagination cannot perceive the truth of Blake's doctrine that "all deities reside in the human breast":[55]

> God after god—and each tore from him
> Its lodging place and its power.
>
> Crow struggled, limply bedraggled his remnant.
> He was his own leftover, the spat-out scrag.
>
> He was what his brain could make nothing of.
>
> So the least, least-living object extant
> Wandered over his deathless greatness
>
> Lonelier than ever.

The loneliness Crow feels is the direct result of his viewing creation as something entirely apart from the self. Crow's brain cannot make rational sense of ("make nothing of") this process of objectification and loss. But an awakened imagination could (a positive "could") produce "nothing"—a *śūnyatā* undifferentiated identity with the created universe. Consider Suzuki's remarks:

> In Buddhist Emptiness there is no time, no becoming, no-thing-ness; it is what makes all these things possible; it is a zero full of infinite possibilities, it is a void of inexhaustible contents.
>
> Pure experience is the mind seeing itself as reflected in itself, it is an act of self-identification, a state of suchness. This is possible only when the mind is *śūnyatā* itself, that is, when the mind is devoid of all its possible contents except itself.[56]

The fantasy universe of *Crow* contains the possibility of annihilating the assumptions of the Protestant ethic and scientific empiricism and attaining a unitive participation in nature. *Śūnyatā* is a possibility that inheres in

Hughes's definition of reality, could Crow perceive it; emptiness exists beyond Crow's black rainbow in "Two Legends."

The most hilarious and at the same time most sorrowful double entendre occurs in "Crow Alights." When Crow's camera eye delineates the world according to rational scepticism, each object stands in its isolation, immovably and irrefutably alien, utterly silent. As long as he persists under the spell of this blinkered vision, he will never awaken his inner world imagination, never recognize what Jung understands as the central tenet of the *Bardo Thödol*, that "the 'giver' of all 'given' things dwells within us."[57] All empirical evidence in the outer world is available to Crow's objective vision, so nothing (no one empirical object) escapes him. But *śūnyatā* could and does escape him:

There was this coat, in the dark cupboard,
                              in the silent room, in the silent
                                                    house.
There was this face, smoking its cigarette between the dusk
                              window and the fire's embers.

Near the face, this hand, motionless.

Near the hand, this cup.

Crow blinked. He blinked. Nothing faded.

He stared at the evidence.

Nothing escaped him. (Nothing could escape.)

"Conjuring in Heaven," one of the funniest poems in *Crow*, ridicules the Western concept of nothing as an absence of matter or data. Every chink in nature is filled with something, as medievalists knew through their concept of plenitude. Though matter can change states, it is indestructible. Empirical operations that divide and quantify cannot negate the vitality in nature that Crow represents. Nature may deteriorate into cataleptic seizure under scientific scrutiny, but will not disappear. Similarly, the "Nothing" conceived by the God of rational scepticism in "Lineage" is the Western notion of absence or nonexistence, an unnatural idea that inhibits change with the obstinacy of the tyrant father's "Never" that follows. "Nothing" in this sense too easily becomes a refusal to see, a refusal to change.

The dramatic irony beneath the clash of Western and Oriental cultures, and intrusions of authorial irony, continues in other *Crow* poems. Crow peers into the karmic mirror of the *Sidpa Bardo* in "Crow's Vanity."[58] Ideally, the initiate wipes away the dust of phenomenality by absorbing past karmic pain and guilt. Crow wipes frenetically, but without any corresponding activity in his inner world, for the karmic obscurations continue their eerie parade. Crow's motive for wiping the mirror is impure—his egocentric vanity: "he peered / For a glimpse of the usual grinning face." When "Crow Communes" he tears off a mouthful of God's snoring carcass, and asks "Will this cipher divulge itself to digestion / Under hearing beyond understanding?" The question is an ironic allusion to the title of the *Bardo Thödol*. *Thödol* or *thos-grol* in Tibetan refers to "hearing" or comprehending on a transcendent (or "beyond") plane of understanding.[59] The omniscient narrator then intercedes with dramatic irony: "(That was the first jest.)" Crow's hearing is restricted to halfhearted listening; his digestion is restricted to the alimentary level.

The Elephant's peace in "Crow's Elephant Totem Song" that the hyenas cannot attain echoes chapter XXIII of *The Dhammapada* ("The Elephant").[60] The hyenas of the Hughes poem are like the gluttons, sluggards, and hogs of the *Dhammapada* chapter: they crave the Elephant's self-mastery, but their imprisonment in their sensuality breeds jealousy and malice. The Elephant's self-mastery is also far beyond Crow's abilities; Crow cannot rule his desires like the mahout rules the elephant with a hook of self-control. The Elephant in the *Dhammapada* chapter wins a freedom that Crow will never attain.

"Crow the Just," not collected in the trade editions of *Crow*, summarizes in Zen Buddhist terms the reality behind Crow's fears.[61] According to Buddhist belief, Crow's fears are self-caused projections of his inability to annihilate his dependence on ego, instinct, and rational thinking. To penetrate to a Zen consciousness of nature's oneness, Crow must experience what Hui-nêng, the Sixth Patriarch of Chinese Zen, called the Great Death of the intellect as the primary seat of knowledge and volition.[62] One experiences union with nature through liberating one's creative intuition (*prajñā-consciousness*), a faculty that Crow's culture does not value. Until Crow liberates himself he will remain in the blackened, decaying world of the *Sidpa Bardo*:

> Crow jeered at—only his own death.
> Crow spat at—only his own death.
> He spread rumors—only about his own death.

He robbed—only his own death.
He knocked down and kicked—only his own death.
He vowed revenge—only on his own death.
He tricked—only his own death.
He murdered—only his own death.
He ate—only his own death.

This is how he kept his conscience so pure
He was black

(Blacker

Than the eyepupils

Of the gunbarrels.)

Crow's eyepupils lead directly to the hardening lenses of Hagen's binoculars at the outset of *Gaudete*.

Hughes's original intention in composing *Crow* was to devise an epic folktale plot, with Crow achieving success at the end of his adventures through an encounter with an ogress at the bank of a river. The ogress informs Crow that she will not let him cross the river unless he carries her on his back. Once in the water, she forces upon him a series of seven dilemma questions about love. She demands instant answers and becomes heavier, with Crow sinking deeper into the water, with each wrong answer. Mythologically speaking, the ogress (or burden) that Crow carries on his back is his unacknowledged psychic life—his instincts and his creative intuition, distorted by repression—that his conscience (kept so pure in "Crow the Just" by willed refusal and arrogance) now forces him to recognize. The river (physical and psychological necessity), often in literature a boundary symbol for altered states of consciousness or for ontological barriers between heaven and earth, *forces* Crow into a situation of extremity where he *must* generate imaginative answers to heal his psyche. His near death should force him to awaken that atrophied inner world that God's ramshackle universe inhibited. In public readings Hughes identified "The Lovepet" (American edition only) as an answer to the ogress's query "Was it an animal? Was it a bird? Was it an insect? Was it a fish?" "Lovesong" became one of Crow's answers to the question "Who paid most, him or her?" And the lovely "Bride and groom lie hidden for three days," in *Cave*

Birds, was to be the right answer to the question "Who gives most, him or her?"[63]

The deaths of Hughes's companion Assia and her daughter Shura (*Crow* is dedicated to their memory) in March of 1969, however, brought the *Crow* poems to an abrupt halt.[64] The sequence as published in 1970 contains the subtitle "From the Life and Songs of the Crow," to indicate an unfinished sequence. Fully one-third of the published Crow poems lie scattered in limited edition, private press volumes, or in periodicals, but are not collected in the Faber and Faber or Harper and Row editions. What remains is the power of Hughes's indictment of the "ramshackle religion" and the "mishmash of scripture and physics" that impede Crow's development, and the dramatic irony, stemming from Crow's imperceptiveness about the workings of nature in his inner and outer worlds, whenever Zen Buddhist allusions enter the poems.

At the time of the original publication of *Crow*, Hughes expressed uncertainty about the degree of Crow's development. In a BBC broadcast of 24 June 1970, just three and a half months before the first Faber edition (12 October 1970), Hughes states that Crow is

the shadow of man. He's a man to correct man, but of course he's not a man, he's a crow, . . . he never does quite become a man. For most of the adventure, having been created he's put through various adventures, and disasters and trials and ordeals, and the effect of these is to alter him not at all, then alter him a great deal, completely transform him, tear him to bits, put him together again, and produce him a little bit changed. And maybe his ambition is to become a man, which he never quite manages.[65]

But in December of 1970, in prefatory remarks to a recording of "Crow's Nerve Fails" for a BBC broadcast, Hughes states that the effect of Crow's adventures is "to eventually make him a man."[66] Yet earlier that same year Hughes defines what he considered to be a human being, in the first "Myth and Education" essay: "imagination isn't merely a surplus mental department meant for entertainment, but the most essential piece of machinery we have if we are going to live the lives of human beings." Does Crow develop from trickster (and Jungian Shadow, in Hughes's own words above) to manhood, and how does this relate to Crow's progress in his quest to liberate the "hidden thing" and earn his bride?

The evidence in the originally published volume weighs against Crow having developed sufficient imaginative life to qualify as a man in Hughes's terms. The same deficiency causes his failure in his quest. In "Crow Tries the Media" and "Crow's Undersong" Crow attempts to develop his imaginative life and to perceive the creative principle in nature, but the tank of his acculturation is definitely parked on his imaginative voice. "Glimpse" may contain an Oriental flash vision of the self as creator of the perceived environment, but this one poem is too short, isolated, and undeveloped to assume such a pivotal importance. In "Glimpse" Crow, attempting a Whitmanesque communion with nature, becomes aware of its complete otherness. Then suddenly, before his usual defenses—his egotism and dualism— overtake him, he is able to glimpse nature as an extension of the self's perceptive powers. When Crow substitutes his own godhead for the otherness of nature, he glimpses with the Buddhist "eye of transcendental wisdom" that, in Suzuki's estimation, "has no particular reality as its object of sight; when it is said to see something, this something is not other than itself."[67] But this revelation comes too suddenly in the sequence. Poems do not exist nearby to indicate a gradual development in Crow's inner life: "Lovesong" and the equally predatory "The Lovepet" precede "Glimpse." Nor does Crow consolidate his gain in subsequent poems. "King of Carrion," the last poem to refer directly to Crow, places his kingdom in the world of death and decay, with a palace of skulls, a scaffold of bones. Though the final lines of the poem refer to an "empty" kingdom, the omniscient persona does not indicate that Crow *himself* comprehends *śūnyatā*; the lines seem to be authorial commentary from a higher plane of perception than Crow has realized—the same higher level that produces the ironic humor of the poems that develop opposite meanings of the words "nothing" and "emptiness."

"King of Carrion" exposes the one artistic problem in the 1970 ordering of *Crow* that makes any argument of development in Crow very difficult to sustain—the management of point of view. Often the disparity between Crow's trapsprung responses and the superior view of the omniscient persona, whether satiric or indulgent, is too great for the reader to note any development in the course of the adventures. Here Crow functions as the ever-present butt of ridicule for defects in modern Western culture. Hughes's command of surrealism, *enantiodromia*, and psychological projection is so sure and effective that the virtuosity of form and image impedes the reader from noticing any progress in Crow's perceptions. Poem titles often add to the difficulty. In poems entitled "Crow's Song of . . ." and "Crow's Account of . . ." one may infer that Crow himself is the author and comprehends the themes and content of these songs and accounts, or how else could he articulate them? But afterward Crow acts with his typical unconsciousness, and one concludes that no development has occurred. "Crow Sickened," "Apple Tragedy," "Crow's Last Stand," "Crow and the Sea," "Crow and Stone," "Fragment of an Ancient Tablet," "Lovesong," and "The Lovepet"—all of these very late poems in the sequence indicate that Crow's development is minimal in the 1970 ordering. If Crow continually fails to recognize the avatars of his creator, as Hughes writes in the 1975 Cambridge transcript note, then he cannot win his bride and end his quest successfully.

Hughes's 1979 letter about "Truth Kills Everybody" further complicates the question of Crow's development. Here Hughes affirms that Crow "advances" as his "culpable ego-machinery is exploded," with the components of each violent image changing accordingly. The explosion is really caused by Crow's "spiritfire," according to Hughes, his "inner link with his creator," which remains to continue his development after it annihilates his ego. Hughes affirms that "this is Crow's greatest step forward. But he regresses, and has to make it again and again, before his gain is finally consolidated in his union with his bride."[68] Apparently Hughes indicates that, as Crow persists, the enantiodromic projections and surrealistic imagery lessen in force, and this constitutes a development in his perceptions. But readers see so little of Crow's inner motives for his persistence, even in "Crow's Battle Fury," that they are uncertain whether Crow's drive is at all conscious or deliberate, or more tricksterish waywardness and indomitability, as in "Crow Blacker Than Ever." The intrusions from a superior persona too regularly appear ironic, and the Zen Buddhist tags call for a much deeper level of self-mastery than Crow's trapsprung appetitive consciousness can muster. Crow's objectivity murders to dissect early in the sequence, in "Crow's Nerve Fails," and the sense of guilt and complicity in a world of blackness and death that this creates in him merely deepens to a resignation to his palace of skulls and scaffold of bones at the end of the sequence, in "King of Carrion." "Crow and Stone," possibly the most terrifying poem in the volume, presents Crow unwittingly bent on the destruction of creation itself, yet the poem is placed near the end of the volume. Readers do not have enough linguistic cues in "Truth Kills Everybody" to comprehend that the explosion of Crow's ego is the focus of the shapechanging battle; and "Crow and Stone" immediately follows.

Hughes's comments about Crow's development refer more to the yet-to-be-completed epic folktale than they do to the 1970 ordering. One must separate the mood of the artist who abruptly terminated a project of at least two years' duration, and ordered the sequence in a mood of bereavement over the death of Assia and her daughter, from the mood of the artist who comments upon his original conception with nine years of distance, hindsight, public readings, and further meditations. The vivid and intense absorption in nature of *Remains of Elmet* (1979), the opening farm journal section of *Moortown* (1979), and *River* (1983) indicate that Hughes may soon be ready to cross that epic folktale river and complete Crow's adventures.

Changing Crow from trickster hero *manqué* to the hero of a poetic *Bildungsroman* will require a reordering of the poems in the sequence, and the addition of more poems that reveal Crow's inner development. The final volume will exist as a separate work with its own formal coherence and could offer readers a unique, much-needed paradigm for liberation from attachment to the almost exitless materialism and neurotic "go" of contemporary civilization. "Crow and Stone," and many other late poems, will need to be placed earlier in the sequence; "Crow Goes Hunting" and "Magical Dangers" will need to be placed before "A Disaster" and "The Battle of Osfrontalis" to indicate development in Crow's perception of the relationship of words to things, and more poems will be needed to develop the eye imagery in a positive direction, as in "Glimpse." "Crow Paints Himself into a Chinese Mural" should be dropped: its first-person point of view clashes with the episodic form of the rest of the volume, and the acute psychological torment and battlefield surrealism point back toward *Wodwo*. According to the logic of the first "Myth and Education" essay, literature offers the most promising vehicle to awaken Crow's atrophied imagination. Crow might gain enormously, no facetiousness intended, from reading a few of the escapades of Nanabozho, Raven, or other trickster heroes.

Hughes's hint that the surrealism dissipates as Crow develops also refers more to the yet-to-be-completed sequence than to the 1970 ordering; the late poems "Song for a Phallus," "Crow Paints Himself into a Chinese Mural," and "Truth Kills Everybody" all contain a great deal of surrealistic violence. A dissipation of *Sidpa Bardo* blackness should also parallel a dissipation in surrealistic charge; but the "solid ink" ("Crowego") of Crow's attachment to a world of decay and death continues to the skulls of "King of Carrion." No liberating *Dharma-Kāya* of Clear Light exists here to provide a foil, much less the humanistic Renaissance faith in the perpetuity of the self beyond the grave that one finds in the longevity of the art work—the black ink that shines so brightly in Shakespeare's "Sonnet 65."

The three latest Crow poems to be collected, in *The Achievement of Ted Hughes*,[69] present some of the development that Hughes describes for his final sequence. God continues his neurotic insecurity when he second-guesses his own creation in "Crow Fails": he has "second *thoughts*" (italics mine) about his universe and makes Crow promise not to spoil it. Crow continues to be the all-too-accepting pupil in this poem, with the *tabula rasa* empirical mind that Blake so fulminated against. Similarly, when God creates a clockwork universe in "Crow Compromises," Crow "happily chimed." But Crow finds God's second attempt, the existential "optical oscillation / Between Being and Nothing, Nothing and Being," too much to bear. When reality consists of the Sartrean dialectical relationship between a perceiving ("optional") consciousness whose essence is a void, a nothingness, and an *en soi* environment of unconscious, impenetrable, rocklike Being, Crow prefers a primitive alimentary vitalism as a compromise. The alternative he adopts, however, still leaves him with a dualistic, two-faced opposition between life and death, the altar of Druidic sacrifice and the "Serpent of Begetting." This is an impersonal ("Faceless") philosophy that predates individuation from the primitive group and grants no value to the development of personal consciousness. Nevertheless, Crow actively chooses his own alternative in "Crow Compromises" and chooses one that avoids the alienation from nature that existentialism produced.

"A Lucky Folly" describes Crow's creation of art by transforming the world dragon of primal chaos into the dragon of Schopenhauer's blind historical Will. Crow's choice of music is a *lucky* folly, for it opens his consciousness to resolutions in the imaginative world of art. The Schopenhauerian answer, however, is imperfect, for it calls for a never-ending sequence of momentary transmutations of this blind Will into an esthetic world, an exhausting process that also implies an initial dualism and assumes nature to be hostile. Yet more poems such as "Crow Compromises" and "A Lucky Folly" would move Crow further toward deliberate choice instead of passive acculturation and finally reorient his vision toward the liberating primacy of the imagination.

Minus this development, the main effect of the 1970 ordering is to expose Crow as "one of us," but in a decidedly postwar atmosphere that Conrad's Marlow could scarcely fit into his humanistic tradition. Many of the early reviewers commented that the decidedly male genitals in the Baskin dust jacket drawing mark Crow as a figure who bears some very obvious resemblances to a man. Poems such as "Crow and the Sea" and "King of Carrion," especially, evoke a final pity for limited human consciousness and egocentricity that the first of the "Two Eskimo Songs" further develops. Like Crow creating his playmates, Westerners have prospered by objectifying reality, by moving away from the primal song toward the inevitable gashes of pain that consciousness creates and the selfish use of reason. *Crow* reminds us how we crucify ourselves in the process. One could glibly say that, to an American audience, Crow conveys the indomitable smirk of Coyote in the Warner Brothers Road Runner cartoons (Coyote is the trickster hero of the Yokut Indians of California),[70] and the paradoxically ingratiating meanness and pluckishness of Garfield the Cat. But such observations miss the amazing originality of Hughes's conception, the power and almost throwaway richness of metaphor, and the beauty of his complex modernist formal design. In *Crow* Hughes is able to synthesize a very complex tangle of ideas into a lucid universe of motivated form that demonstrates how the invisible fabric of a culture affects individual perception in our post-Auschwitz present. As an imaginative feat of synthesizing complex ideas into the *paideuma* of modernist mythic form, *Crow* ranks with the best high modernist works—*Ulysses, The Waste Land,* and *The Cantos.*

PART III

Suffering and Serenity in the Seventies, and the Enlightened Eighties

CHAPTER 6

Flying Astride the Earth

Gaudete

1977

A child takes possession of a story as what might be called a unit of imagination. A story which engages, say, earth and the underworld is a unit correspondingly flexible. . . . In attending to the world of such a story there is the beginning of imaginative and mental control. There is the beginning of a form of contemplation. . . . Imagination which is both accurate and strong is . . . rare . . . outer world and inner world are interdependent at every moment. We are simply the locus of their collision. . . . So what we need . . . is a faculty that embraces both worlds simultaneously. A large, flexible grasp, an inner vision which holds wide open, like a great theatre, the arena of contention, and which pays equal respects to both sides. Which keeps faith, as Goethe says, with the world of things and the world of spirits equally.

This really is imagination. . . . [In great works] the full presence of the inner world combines with and is reconciled to the full presence of the outer world. And in them we see that the laws of these two worlds are not contradictory at all; they are one all-inclusive system. . . . So it comes about that once we recognize their terms, these works seem to heal us. . . .

—Hughes, 1976[1]

Hughes developed modernist formal *paideumae* in *Wodwo* and *Crow* to describe a disjunction between inner and outer worlds in Western culture and to identify the outer world causes of our contemporary malaise—the death wish of war as a reflex of the inadequacies of Western science and religion. In these sixties works Hughes offered the inner serenity of Zen Buddhism as an antidote for this cultural death wish and as a survival technique for the torn psyche. The volumes of poetry published in the late seventies and early eighties, however, reveal that Hughes's central project in his third phase is to reconcile inner and outer worlds in the mediatory realm of spirit. Oriental influences continue, but in the later poetry they work in consort with, not in opposition to, the Western round of birth, death, and transfiguration in the realm of spirit.

The goal of every volume in Hughes's third phase is the reconciliation of experience on the transcendent plane of spiritual illumination and understanding, a plane held together and kept intact by strong imaginative powers. One might say that the Coleridgean/New Critical fusing power of the secondary imagination becomes a general prescription for psychic health. After significant suffering a reborn Reverend Nicholas Lumb in the "Epilogue" of *Gaudete* generates a transcendent image of an oak tree "flying / Astride the earth" in the mediatory ground of his imagination.[2] This complex image synthesizes his plight and expresses the heroic beauty of his final resignation to his mortality. Later, in the landscape poetry of *Remains of Elmet* and *River*, Hughes develops the mystical, noetic powers of Coleridge's primary imagination to perceive a transphenomenal Reality behind the world of sense. In the late seventies and early eighties Hughes substantially deepens his "story of a soul" with a more comprehensive grasp of natural cycles in the outer world and a greater penetration into the imaginative basis of spiritual renewal and enlargement in the inner world. In his third period Hughes affirms the Blakean tenet that "to the Eyes of the Man of Imagination Nature is Imagination itself."[3]

Not in substance or in depth but solely in terms of Hughes's emerging vision, *Gaudete* occupies a transitional position between the sixties mythic surrealism and the suffering and spiritual liberation of the more recent work. Hughes originally wrote *Gaudete* as a screenplay in 1964, but never used it. The date and the mythic surrealism of the "Prologue" and the central narrative place *Gaudete* with the sixties works *Wodwo* and *Crow*. When Hughes revised *Gaudete* in 1971–1972, *after* the *Orghast* experience,[4] he transformed dialogue and camera directions into a very complex Jungian dreamworld form in the "Prologue" and central narrative; in 1975 he added the "Epilogue" poems, the first sustained example of the third phase spiritual enlargement through suffering in a major volume.

In the seventies the Western portion of the two-way journey toward Reality, the adventures of the virtuoso bacteria in historical time, reopens for Hughes. As mentioned in the introduction, in 1971 Hughes accompanied the British director Peter Brook and an international company of actors to Teheran, to write *Orghast*, the major dramatic undertaking of the Fifth Shiraz Festival of the Arts in Iran. In the festival program notes Hughes characterizes one of the major themes of *Orghast* as "the search for liberation through knowledge"; in the plot this refers primarily to the liberation of Sogis from the tyrant father Krogon through suffering and final enlightenment.[5] Similar themes appear in *Orpheus* and *Prometheus on His Crag*, both written in 1973. Orpheus learns that "every song has to be paid for"; his journey to the underworld ends with the realization that he can resurrect Eurydice only in the realm of spirit, through transforming his suffering into spiritual enlargement—his new "music of birth and death."[6] A resignation to suffering and a realization of its potential for growth and renewal lies at the center of the mystery of the vulture in *Prometheus on His Crag*, an offshoot of the *Orghast* work that Hughes later included in *Moortown*. After many poems describing the daily agony of having his liver eaten, Prometheus finally realizes that the vulture may indeed be "the Helper, / Coming again to pick at the crucial knot / Of all his bonds."[7] At the 1975 Ilkley Festival Hughes read poems from the *Gaudete* "Epilogue" and early versions of *Cave Birds* poems. In this latter work the central persona willingly undergoes acute psychological suffering in poems such as "The knight" to win the transfiguring experience of union in "Bride and groom lie hidden for three days."

To comprehend *Gaudete*, one must understand the complex formal relationship of "Prologue," central narrative, and "Epilogue" poems, and always keep clearly in mind the essential difference between the Reverend Nicholas Lumb and his loglike Double, the central character of the main narrative. The real Reverend Lumb appears *only* in the "Prologue" and in the three-page narrative interlude that opens the "Epilogue." The "Epilogue" poems written to the goddess of nature are composed by this real Reverend Lumb, after having achieved spiritual rebirth. The hallucinations that the real Lumb experiences in the "Prologue," however, introduce the dreamworld character of the entire central narrative. All of the central narrative takes place subliminally, in the personal unconscious of the real Lumb; here his psyche works to heal him through composing a complex Jungian individuation dream. In the "Prologue" archetypes of the anima (the wolf-skinned goddess Cerridwen) and the Shadow (Lumb's Double, a type of Hercules) appear, and the loglike Double then acts out a lengthy episode—the entire central narrative—that comprises the last day of his eccentric ministry. Hence the Lumb the reader becomes accustomed to through nearly one hundred and fifty pages of supercharged poetic narrative is not to be confused with the real Lumb; the Lumb of the central narrative is the infinitely more limited, loglike substitute, placed by the real Lumb's Jungian unconscious in a surrealistic dreamscape for the purpose of healing him.

The central narrative recounts the last day of the Double's ministry, when the male townsfolk finally realize that this ministry consists of Lumb fornicating with their wives to produce a savior. This dream narrative functions first to liberate the real Lumb's repressed eros, and then to show the real Lumb, ostensibly a half-aware spectator throughout the central narrative, the tragic limitations of purely instinctual gratification. The death of Lumb's Double at the hands of the enraged male townsfolk signals the end of the dreamwork.

The "Prologue" and central narrative of *Gaudete* rework familiar themes from the sixties poetry. The repression and enantiodromic violence paradigm readily surfaces. Lumb's spiritual torpor in the "Prologue" derives from the Protestant cleric's repression of eros, and in the central narrative Hagen, Estridge, Garten, and others are ripe for violence because they peer at life through eyes deadened by modern science and technology: through binoculars, telescopes, camera lenses, and gunsights. The explosion of repressed eros occurs in the men when they learn that Lumb's Double has cuckolded them all. But much more is happening in this surrealistic dreamscape, especially as it applies to the real Lumb, within whose mind the events of this central narrative take place, on the subliminal level. The "Epilogue" poems prove not only that the dream has healed Lumb, but that he has been able to raise its message to the level of significance and spiritual enlargement.

The form of the lengthy central narrative of *Gaudete* is that of a multifaceted Jungian individuation dream working to heal Lumb's fragmented psyche, first by releasing his instinctual life and then by detailing the tragic limitations of all erotic enticements that do not transcend the purely physical. Hughes composes his dream narrative through a complex interweaving of seven elements that weld form and content into one inseparable whole. In the dreamworld central narrative Hughes develops multiple viewpoints, all of which are distorted by abnormal reactions to eros; a surrealistically sound-deadened, claustral dream environment where obsessive images reign and minute details at times assume exaggerated importance; a dreamworld time that alternately stretches out and becomes foreshortened; the motif of music to signify repressed erotic desire; juxtapositions of silent images that reveal the state of the soul, as in a dream; character tableaux that depict portions of the real Lumb's psyche; and the extensive use of the loglike Lumb as a type of the Jungian Shadow, imprisoned in erotic desire and, like his trickster counterpart Crow, totally lacking in self-awareness. The central narrative dreamscape derives from a complex modernist *paideuma*, not a realistic mimesis of an objective cultural/historical context that interacts with characters in a "normal" setting.

In the "Epilogue" the real Lumb achieves what his Double fails to accomplish: he raises his suffering to an enlargement of self through imaginative energy and control and reconciles his inner and outer worlds—as

Hughes suggests in the epigraph to this chapter—by developing an awareness of suffering as inevitable and purposive. Mythology, that inner "realm of management between our ordinary minds and our deepest life,"[8] according to Hughes, can offer "blueprints" for organizing the inner life and for healing the division that Western culture creates between nature and our subjective selves.[9] The real Lumb's final reconciliation with the goddess of nature in the "Epilogue" poems often appears in mandalalike images of psychic integration, objects of contemplation on the liberated inner world plane of his spiritual understanding. Lumb sustains these visionary images through sheer imaginative power and control, as in the meditative art of the yogin. In the "Epilogue" Lumb transfigures his dreamworld experience, lifts it to the level of self-knowledge and self-mastery in the airy realm of an awakened imagination, the final resting perch of every major third-period volume. Here Lumb's humble self-abasement couples with an ethereal mood of tragic joy to create uniquely memorable, splendorous poetry. At the end of the "Epilogue" Lumb experiences enthrallment, a rapture of integrated thought and feeling, clearly captured in the flying oak tree image, a final vision of wholeness. This is a moment of impassioned yet contemplative enlightenment that most closely parallels the ecstasy of mystical illumination or the higher meditative states of Tantric yoga. Here the all-suffering pilgrim achieves Reality, the goal of the two-way journey.

The mass graves that Lumb hallucinates at the outset of *Gaudete* accurately portray a sterility of soul through a surreal projection of alienated instinct. Lumb, apparently a celibate, is spiritually dead. But his hallucinations in the "Prologue" serve to galvanize his unconscious in a healing action that continues until the end of the lengthy central narrative. Lumb is initially given the opportunity to minister to his soul by reviving a nearly dead Cerridwen, an ancient wolf goddess of nature,[10] an image of his anima. But as in *Parzifal*, alluded to in an opening epigraph to *Gaudete*, Lumb initially fails in self-awareness and compassion; he is completely alienated from his libidinal energies and proves as inadequate as was the would-be knight in his first encounter with Anfortas. Lumb's failure to minister to Cerridwen, like Parzival's failure to minister to Anfortas by inquiring about the cause of his malady, is a failure of *caritas*, of other-directed love:

> He declares he can do nothing
> He protests there is nothing he can do
> For this beautiful woman who seems to be alive and dead.
> He is not a doctor. He can only pray. (p. 15)

Yet Lumb's hallucinated visions of mass graves and of Cerridwen constitute the first stage of his psyche's attempt to heal him. The surreal dreamscape begins. Jung believes that dreams are not wish fulfillments of
repressed erotic desires, but spontaneous products of the unconscious, un-
governed by conscious attitudes, whose purpose is to reveal the actual
state of the soul, compensate for one-sided conscious attitudes, and initiate
healing processes that can reestablish psychic equilibrium.[11] To Jung, the
psyche "speaks in images" in dreams; it also "gives expression to instincts,
which derive from the most primitive levels of nature."[12] To interpret
dream phenomena, Jung believes, one should also insist upon locating
purpose instead of cause.[13] Until interpreted according to the situation of
the individual patient, the dream remains a silent complex of visual images. Purpose can only be ascertained by careful examination of dream
context, image juxtapositions, and recurring motifs.[14] Knowledge of mythology can assist in this process, for Jung asserts that "the ideas underlying all the motifs are visual representations of an archetypal character,
symbolic primordial images" that can often be elucidated with the aid of
world mythology, for both archetype and myth originate from the same
psychological core.[15]

Robert Graves, often a source for Hughes's mythological allusions, provides helpful mythological background for Lumb's "Prologue" hallucinations. Graves states that to earn one's credentials as a poet one must court
the primitive goddess Cerridwen, a type of the White Goddess in her
triple character as virgin, lover, and hag-devourer. The poet must dedicate
himself to wooing her truthfully, passionately, and with full knowledge
that, psychologically speaking, she will ultimately exact the poet's own
death.[16] Lumb will comprehend this mystery only in the "Epilogue" poetry, but his psyche, in tossing up the image of Cerridwen at the outset of
the "Prologue," is penetrating to the core of his culture's mythological
roots, for Cerridwen came to Britain circa 2500 B.C., during the New
Stone Age.[17]

In the oak tree crucifixion and flogging that follows Lumb's hallucination of mass graves, his unconscious suggests a therapeutic release of libidinal energy by prescribing the mythological paradigm of the dying and
reviving vegetation god, the male consort of the White Goddess. Graves
defines the pain and torment undergone in this love experience as the central test of the poet's oracular knowledge: "No poet can hope to understand
the nature of poetry unless he has had a vision of the Naked King crucified
to the lopped oak," with frenzied dancers shouting deathly cries.[18] Hercules' life and death, his exploits, oak tree crucifixion, dismemberment,

and sacramentally eaten flesh, define the poet's lot;[19] and this paradigm also contains the archaic residue of a healing process. The oak thus symbolizes both the privilege and the pain of mortality. Lumb actively and instinctively chooses this lot:

> He straightens from the pain and moves uphill and stops at the top, pointing to a young oak tree growing there. . . .
> Two men with axes fell the tree and trim the boughs, till the lopped trunk lies like a mutilated man, with two raised arms. Now Lumb is forced down, flat on his chest, and his arms are pulled above his head. Each of his wrists is tied to one of the two stumps. Because I am a priest, he is thinking, they will crucify me. The silent men arrange everything with great care. At last, Lumb and the tree lie, as if holding hands, their bodies stretched out opposite. . . .
> Lumb stares, uncomprehending, and tingling with the memory of that whip across his skull. Till a shock of real pain grips his back. His body clenches in spasm, like a fist. Hands lock round his ankles. Another whip is whistling in air, above him.
> So, stroke by stroke, he and the tree-bole are flogged, tied together, until Lumb chews earth and loses consciousness. (p. 16)

The main dreamwork occurs, according to Jung, in a "fugue-like sequence of images," a "pictorial flood" of "visual fantasies" that reveal compensatory obsessions.[20] One must interpret the motifs behind these images with careful consideration to the full context—both objective occurrences in the patient's daily life and representations of subjective components within the patient's psyche.[21] Since the reader has no knowledge of the real Lumb's past save for his religious calling, the subjective mode—relating the images and events of the central narrative to the state of the real Lumb's soul—becomes the primary concern when analyzing the hallucinations, dreamwork, and fantasies that occur in *Gaudete*.

In Lumb's bath in the white bull's blood, the last annunciatory hallucination before the main dream or central narrative, Hughes deepens his comparison of Lumb to the dying and reviving vegetation god by adopting an initiatory rite of the Phrygian god Attis. The devotee who bathed in the blood of a freshly sacrificed bull was cleansed of his sins and reborn into eternal life, according to Frazer.[22] Lumb's bath in the "Prologue" announces this rebirth as a possibility and introduces a bull symbolism into *Gaudete* that conflates the Hercules pattern with those of Dionysus and Osiris, two other dying and reviving vegetation gods who experience dismemberment and whose theriomorphic counterparts are bulls, agricultural fertility spirits.[23] Hagen breeds bulls through artificial insemination, and bulls attend both Mrs. Holroyd's sexually suggestive sunbathing and the loglike Double's death. As Lumb in the "Prologue" shoots the white bull in the head, he propels himself into the pattern of the dying and reviving vegetation spirit, consort and victim of the White Goddess.

Yet the figure who ministers sexually to the members of the Women's Institute in the central dream narrative of *Gaudete* is not the real Lumb, but his changeling Double, born of the oak tree flogging. "Elemental spirits" carry the real Lumb into the spirit world, as the opening "Argument" indicates (p. 9). When Lumb regains consciousness after the flogging, the figure being untied from the oak tree is another man in torn clerical garb. After "Lumb sees this other is himself," he realizes that his Double carries his scars, and that his own skin has mysteriously healed. Again Hughes announces the possibility of regeneration, with the transferring of scars indicating that Lumb's scapegoat substitute will experience the subsequent ordeals and become the primary vehicle of psychic reclamation. This substitute, the "Argument" reveals, is a "log," a "changeling" who will "interpret the job of ministering the Gospel of love in his own log-like way" in the central dream narrative.

The regeneration motifs announced in the "Prologue" and the introduction of a changeling substitute who closely resembles the real Lumb indicate that the "Prologue" functions as an induction, a framing preface to a dream—as in *The Taming of the Shrew*, but with a stronger emphasis in *Gaudete* upon purposive suffering than upon comedy/fantasy wish fulfillment. Evans-Wentz in his lengthy study of Irish folklore cites numerous instances of changeling substitution, from literary sources and from first-hand field research of scholars and preservers of the oral tradition. In all cases the changelings are subnormal: deformed misfits, shriveled old men, or sallow, sickly children who fail to mature past childhood.[24] In cases where the changeling substitution is only temporary, the cause may be demonic possession or a supernormal visit of the afflicted person to the underworld, experienced in trance or dream.[25] The subterrestrial fairy folk, originally the lordly Sidhe, may have derived from pre-Christian Celtic beliefs in rebirth doctrines, remnant examples of which Evans-Wentz found in the west of Ireland,[26] the location of the narrative interlude that introduces the "Epilogue" rebirth poems of *Gaudete*. Thus Hughes's use of the changeling motif in *Gaudete* reinforces both the dreamworld character of the work and the formal design of a visit to the underworld (the personal unconscious) to gain rebirth, wisdom, spiritual enlargement.

The deformities of the changeling also reinforce Lumb's Double's status as a representative of Jung's Shadow archetype—the epitome of the largely unconscious, negative character traits that therapeutic dreams mobilize for their reservoirs of libidinal energy. In *Gaudete* Hughes accentuates the log-like Double's archetypal character with Kafkaesque surrealistic details that often suggest distortions produced by sexual obsessions. Lumb's Double is described as a "goat-eyed vicar" (p. 75) with "powerful gymnast's shoulders" (p. 86), a "long, sallow skull" (p. 25), and a "long figure" (p. 36). The surrealistic details point toward the loglike Double's inner deformities—his absolutely compulsive libidinal fixations and his completely atrophied imagination. The Shadow carries a potentially positive charge of psychic energy, according to Jung, if the archetype is wrestled with and finally admitted to consciousness.[27] This will become part of the real Lumb's task in the "Epilogue" poems.

The surrealistic details that surround Lumb direct us toward important formal devices that operate throughout the central narrative to create a dreamworld atmosphere. The central narrative contains a narrator who moves in and out of the consciousnesses of the characters. As Hughes filters events through multiple consciousnesses (a standard modernist technique), he reveals how each character distorts reality according to how much of the instinctual and the erotic each allows to enter consciousness. This device of having the reader view events at a second remove—filtered through a narrator and double-filtered through the distorted perceptions of the characters—creates an insulating, buffering effect perfectly suited to the nearly silent dreamscape atmosphere of *Gaudete*.

For instance, when the sensual Jennifer tries to explain her sister's suicide as the misfortune of a love triangle, with Lumb having realized that he loves her instead of Janet, both Estridge and Westlake only partially hear her and distort—the former with defense mechanisms, the latter with an appetite for the erotic that literally tunes out his ears and bulges his eyes (p. 56). Estridge has already walled out the passion that surfaced in Jennifer's piano playing; he repaired to his Belvedere and his telescope to contemplate, with doddered Naval Commander's eyes, a distortedly pure image of the really very lusty Mrs. Holroyd. (Estridge laughably perceives her as an ideal, the "country love of his youth.") Hence much of Jennifer's frenetically feminine explanation of her sister's suicide fails to penetrate the bulwark of Estridge's ultra-Victorian conservatism:

> Old Estridge is trying vainly to reckon her words up,
> As if they were some gibberish formula of huge numerals

> Into which his whole family fortune is vanishing.
> Explosions from different directions have left him little
> more than mere outline. (p. 56)

Psychologically incisive similes and the use of "as if," devices that Hughes develops throughout the volume, usually place the action inside the heads of the characters and thus more in the realm of inference than reality.

Meanwhile, Westlake apprehends Jennifer's sensuality all too vividly. Westlake, a physician introduced to examine Janet's body, quickly becomes more concerned with examining Jennifer's hothouse beauty and disheveled condition. Her sensuality will soon lead him to the opposite extreme of Estridge. Westlake dotes upon impressions of her "loose, hot, tumbled softness, / Like freshly-killed game" (p. 72), and this obsesses him to the point of lunch hour drunkenness, broken spectacles, a bruised forehead, and the surety, despite all evidence to the contrary, that Lumb's Double is fornicating with his wife "through that hand on her ankle / In some devilish spiritual way" (p. 75). While Estridge represses, Westlake indulges in voyeurism; he

> follows what he can of her cascading explanations.
> Her creamy satin blouse, stretching and flexing like a skin,
>
> Her dark-haired ankles,
> Her sandals askew, her helpless uncontrol,
> Her giddy mathematics
> Which are constructing an abyss— (p. 56)

As Jennifer recites her tale we find Westlake losing her words in "the turbulence of her body and features"; he finds that he is completely caught up in the irrationality of her "religious mania" and singed by her emotional display:

> And immersing himself in her voice, which flows so full of
> thrilling touches
> And which sobs so nakedly in its narration,
> He is scorched by the hard fieriness,
> A jagged, opposite lightning
> Running along the edge of it
> Like an insane laughter— (p. 57)

The same event filtered and distorted in completely opposite ways, and in the same few seconds of Jennifer's recitation, creates a disorienting effect upon the reader. Meanwhile, Jennifer relates her explanation as if from a great distance. Her toneless, flat summary explanation echoes like soft reverberations in a huge, hermetically sealed tank. Interiorized distortions jostle against interludes of neutral summary to defamiliarize and jar the reader away from the conventions of realism. These techniques place the action in the central narrative in the realm of dream, the arena of juxtaposed, silent images, the domain where one relaxes control over instinctual life and where meaning-bearing distortions surface.

Often Hughes heightens the surrealistic atmosphere of his central narrative dreamscape through dissociating sound and sense or muffling both sound and sense. Estridge's incomprehension of Jennifer's riotous piano playing dulls the tumultuous sound; the shouts and laughter from Jennifer's Scherzo from Beethoven's Opus 110 simply bewilder him, for "He cannot interpret those atmospherics" (p. 43). Estridge next finds Jennifer "screaming something at him / As if in perfect silence" when she first tries to alert him to Janet's death (p. 48). Later, however, no one will hear Estridge's "restraining shouts about due process of law" at the Bridge Inn (p. 154), for irascible, violent emotions clamor too riotously in the men for logic to rule.

A dreamworld buffering that often approaches silence occurs throughout the central narrative. An angry Mrs. Westlake, having gouged the loglike Double's face, returns home in a fury of discord and begins "arguing at everything" in the empty rooms of her home (p. 38). Her inner turmoil leaks out surrealistically and soundlessly. Hagen's outrage with his wife at the opening of the central narrative "ignites the whole tree of his nerves" and causes an "avalanche" of thawed rhetoric from the ice of his Viking consciousness. The reader, however, receives this only through visual, cinematic images, without the rancorous dialogue of domestic argument. Pauline next watches Hagen kill their Labrador "as if it were all something behind the nearly unbreakable screen glass of a television / With the sound turned off." Hughes renders Hagen's "flash of malice" obliquely and visually, in the surreal image of the dog "spinning in a tight circle" with "foam at its jaws" (pp. 33–35). Even when Maud loses her dumbness and announces Lumb's perfidy at the climax of the central narrative, the reader receives a colorless summary, a packed sequence of relative clauses, but no quoted speech (p. 147). The only words uttered directly in the entire volume are Evans's "Bloody Hell!" in the chase scene (p. 161), an exclamation that recollects the Heraclitus epigraph about Hades and Dionysus being one and that offers a sardonically apt evaluation of this voyage to the underworld. The lack of dialogue and use of multiple consciousnesses serve to insulate the action so that it approximates a dream, the silent movie of the unconscious.

Also as in a dream, minor visual details jump out at the reader in the central narrative, with absurd and disproportionate emphasis. *Gaudete*, for instance, contains a running catalogue of specifically named automobiles, negligible details that our materialistic culture trains us to remember almost unconsciously, if only to rehearse in dreams. The catalogue includes Mrs. Westlake's white Ford Cortina, Lumb's blue Austin van, Westlake's gray Daimler, Dunworth's white Jaguar, Lumb's ill-fated old Bentley, and a landrover. Hughes handles the landrover with particularly surreal, dreamlike touches. It "keel[s] over," as if "capsized": the nautical metaphors create a slow-motion effect (p. 159). The rover subsequently "emits a shout" of purely visual recognition in Lumb's fevered psyche, when he realizes that he has come full circle in the chase scene (p. 160).

Hughes's development of the landrover exemplifies the frequent dreamlike stretching out and foreshortening of time in *Gaudete*. Walsall's Alsatian "Magnifies suddenly" when he leaps at Lumb at the beginning of the chase scene, and Lumb's hyperaware sense of entrapment causes him to apprehend this in slow-motion:

> Lumb
> Has a long second to marvel
> At the demented personal malignity
> Distorting the mask of this perfect stranger
> As it hangs in mid-leap, level with his face, in a halo of
> black bristles. (p. 153)

When Lumb stops momentarily in a hayloft during the chase, each moment is simultaneously accelerated in a whirr of mental reconnaissance and stretched out slowly in a deeply experienced moment of rest from physical fatigue (p. 158). Earlier in *Gaudete*, when Evans punches Garten after having seen the telltale photo of Lumb and Mrs. Evans making love, Hughes conveys the event in a quickened, expressionistic flash of jerking limbs and disappearing consciousness:

> Garten has no chance to move.
> His brain moves, but his body is too late to catch up.

Then his long hair lashes upward,
His jawbone jars sideways,
The amazed lose face-flesh jerks at its roots.
His limbs scatter, like a bundle of loose rods.
He falls into a pit. (pp. 114–15)

The effect is like that of a silent movie clip, complete with jaggedly quick-ened tempo. A similarly accelerated flash of sound-deadened visual imag-ery occurs when Evans tries to jab Lumb off a crumbling wall during the chase scene, but "sees too late / The stone block spinning in air in a shower of dust" above his head (p. 162).

Hughes created his amalgam of poetry and prose for *Gaudete* deliber-ately, for the effect of a "headlong narrative" that rushes one full speed through a narrow tunnel, "like a Kleist story." To achieve this he pared down digressions, deleted secondary characters, compressed plot develop-ment, and wrote the summary narrative passages in a condensed mono-tone when he revised the original screenplay.[28] The high-speed narrative, sound-deadened imagery, distortions of perspective, and occasional slow-motion effects create such a surreal atmosphere that the text mimics one's dreams and has the therapeutic effect of liberating the reader's repressed fantasies, ultimately to induce a catharsis that reorients one to a healthier norm. Hughes in his first "Myth and Education" essay (1970) writes at length about this very technique as stopgap therapy for our neurotically repressive culture. By activating the energy content of these repressed feel-ings as they are brought to consciousness, the reader may be able to achieve, at least temporarily, a greater equilibrium in the management of psychic energies. "A man freed of neurosis is a man whose intuition works for him rather than against him," according to Hughes. At the same time, reading a literary work of this type can liberate a person in a way that assists in developing an imagination that "can deal with both the outer world and our inner life."[29]

The thematic motif of music also reinforces the dreamlike atmosphere of the central section; it underscores Jung's emphasis upon the necessary re-lease of libido in dreams. Music in *Gaudete* releases chthonic energies in the women of the parish; the release begins with Jennifer's cloying sen-suality as she plays her piano sonata, swells through Mrs. Walsall's coital "animal gurgles" (p. 96), and climaxes in the "music of slogging, deaden-ing, repetitive labour" (p. 139) as Lumb prepares to mount Felicity at the Institute meeting. The music ends with the birth motions of Maud pulling Felicity out from between her legs, only to stab her to death, while "The women are crying out in the hoarse pulse of the music" in Dionysiac frenzy. Maud kills Felicity as the "archaic music of pipes and drums" (p. 132) on the stereo "tears away the membranes," torturing the women "As if they were being torn out of their bodies" (p. 146). At the very moment that the loglike Lumb mounts Felicity, Hughes equates the music-induced frenzy with somnambulism:

> The music inside their bodies is doing what it wants at last
>
> As if they were all somnambulist
> They are no more awake than leaves in a whirlpool. (p. 146)

At this point the music is also likened to "the tumbling and boiling of a cauldron" (p. 145), which recalls Dionysus as victim being torn apart by the Titans and thrown into a cooking pot.[30] The ritual death of Felicity, and then of Lumb's loglike Double, is a climax of the real Lumb's personality dissolution in the underworld, as the unconscious completely overtakes the rational ego. According to Jung, "Dionysus is the abyss of impassioned dissolution, where all human distinctions are merged in the animal divinity of the primordial psyche—a blissful and terrible experience."[31]

The motif of music in *Gaudete* has variations, all of which Hughes links to the release of libidinal energy and its analogues in the cycle of birth, growth, and death in humans and in nature. The music at the Women's Institute meeting seems "bolted into the ground" (p. 139) and further conflated with human physiology, primitive ritual, and the deathly in modern warfare. Lumb hears the "rendings and caressings" of the earth's music as it beats "at the soles of his feet" (pp. 49–50). In Lumb's daydream of the burning cathedral, he envisions the edifice as "humming the chord / Of all those cries and the drum-pulse" of a tribal ritual that soon becomes a "hard banging" in his brain (pp. 121–23). Even Estridge, bastion of a defunct culture, is not immune: as he views Garten's fatal photograph, a "raving fantasy" of "Pulping Lumb's skull with an axe" arrives "like a lump of insane music" (p. 128). All these variations derive from Hughes's application of *enantiodromia* to chart the violent consequences of repressed instinct in the individual and in a culture:

> But still the enraged
> Albeit ephemeral music goes on
> Like a materialized demon
> Vandalizing the ponderous ill-illumined Victorian house,

Beating at the faded ochre prints of imperial battles,
Re-animating
The arsenals of extinguished tribesmen
That trophy the walls.
It grips the cellars, feeling for the earth beneath
As if to lift the whole ungainly pile and shake off the chimneys. (p. 44)

The motif of music as expressing the instinctual portion of unconscious life originated in Hughes's *Orghast* experience in the months directly preceding his reworking of the original *Gaudete* screenplay. Hughes has affirmed that in *Orghast* he strove to create a dramatic "language of tones and sounds, without specific conceptual or perceptual meaning," an "animal music" of melodies that we instinctively apprehend as delineating the mental states beneath discourse.[32] A few months after *Orghast* Hughes hints at the connection between this music and the unconscious, the psychic life that operates prior to rational discrimination and ethical differentiation, when he states that music gives us "access to a deeper world," a language "below the levels where differences appear, close to the inner life."[33] Hughes's dislike of conventional English during his *Orghast* period drew him to Lévi-Strauss's *The Raw and the Cooked*, where myth is defined as having both the structure (themes and variations that operate upon us unconsciously) and the undetermined meaning of music, and also the tendency of music to make us conscious of our "physiological rootedness."[34]

The formal device of simultaneity, presented through a juxtaposition of visual images, also encloses the loglike Lumb in a dreamworld atmosphere. Our first glimpse of Lumb's Double in the central narrative occurs as he stares into the "tough-looking lilies" of Hagen's lake, after hasty lovemaking with Hagen's wife, Pauline. Hagen, having watched the pair through his binoculars, shoots a ringdove through the head and hands its freshly killed, dripping frame to Lumb, with malevolent laughter (pp. 23–28). The remainder of the lengthy central narrative is, as Martin Greenberg once wrote of Kafka's surrealistic art in *The Trial*, a "steady deepening toward a conclusion already known at the beginning";[35] Lumb's loglike replacement acts out what the real Lumb, hypothetically experiencing this on the subliminal level, must gradually realize as his own spiritual deadness. This process of recognition begins with Hagen's ringdove offering and culminates with a bullet through the loglike Lumb's head, directed from the telescopic lens of Hagen's rifle, while Lumb prepares to dive into the same lake where he met Pauline, complete with its "oily fringe of lilies" that earlier were so "tough-looking" (pp. 166, 25). Thus Lumb's Double's demise is simultaneously present in the tableau at the outset of the central narrative, enhanced as it is with the dead marriage symbol, the ringdove, and the lilies, offerings to the departed soul in the hope of rebirth. As Joseph K.'s conscience presents him with surreal images of his spiritual malaise at the outset of *The Trial*, in his arrest and first interrogation, so Lumb's Double experiences images of spiritual inertia as the central narrative of *Gaudete* opens. Jung counsels that "the dream describes the inner situation of the dreamer" and that the dream images convey "the inner truth and reality of the patient as it really is: not as I conjecture it to be, and not as he would like it to be, but *as it is*."[36] Kafka similarly writes that "the dream reveals the reality, which conception lags behind. That is the horror of life—the terror of art."[37] The dream images of *Gaudete* also reveal the truth without discursive commentary or a definitive tone that predirects interpretation; the reader must become the dreamer and interpret the dream. The "Epilogue" poems constitute the poetic record of the real Lumb's struggle to interpret the substance of this dreamed central narrative.

Simultaneity also reveals a soul in the state of dissolution when one considers the characters of the central narrative as the components of the real Lumb's psyche. While Jennifer's turbulent music "elbows nakedly" (id) and Estridge (superego) flees to his telescope to create a barrier against it, and then to confer an impossible ideal upon the decidedly unideal Mrs. Holroyd, Janet (collapsed ego) is hanging herself in the attic, releasing the birds of her soul to fly unconfined by her father's stifling, antiquated values (pp. 41–46). The Estridge family members are estranged from each other; they operate disjunctively, and in complete isolation. Simultaneity through image juxtaposition reveals a fragmented, constricted soul in its death throes.

Another use of simultaneity to create an image of death occurs when Maud, the loglike Lumb's housekeeper, strangles a pigeon in the room below the one where Lumb is recuperating from his cattleyard slurry daydream (p. 116). Maud, having read Lumb's diary (p. 62), knows of his intention to escape into a conventional marriage with Felicity. When Maud daubs her naked body with the pigeon's blood, she becomes a primitive warrior ritually dedicating herself to her appointed task—the death of Felicity, the interloper—and efficaciously willing its success. At the same time, Lumb's Double has a daydream of a cathedral engulfed with flames and the cries of women, with he and Maud about to be married. The woman-filled cathedral is a dream image of Lumb's original project, the Women's Institute and its goal of producing a savior. The flames in part signify his decision to abandon that project and at the same time signify his being engulfed by his own erotic abandon (he is unaware of this second level of significance).

The juxtaposition of Maud's warrior preparations and Lumb's cathedral daydream constitutes the seldom-taken opportunity for repentance, a staple of Greek tragedy, that defines the self-willed portion of *hubris* while revealing how character is indeed fate or destiny, as in the Heraclitus fragment.[38] In this case the visual juxtaposition reveals that Lumb's Double is dead either way. If he persists in his escape plan, he activates the vengeance of Maud. But the collocation of the flames and the women's cries in the cathedral vision also indicates that by continuing his original Institute plan the loglike Lumb also becomes the victim, in this case of the hot drum-pulse of instinct and its predestined round of birth, suffering, and death—in the supplicating arms and the emotional needs of his female flock. When Lumb's Double ministers to his women, he becomes, to borrow Smayle's analysis (p. 65), both the one crucified to the world of the flesh ("Christ in his mammy's arms") and the women's hope for the time-bound future (the "babe at the tit"). Nevertheless, even after Lumb takes his own initiative and settles upon his plan for escape with Felicity, Maud's subsequent vengeance proves that he will *still* recapitulate the pattern of the dying vegetation god, male consort of the White Goddess. Erotic compulsion is erotic compulsion. As Lumb decides to place his own erotic desires above the needs of his flock, Hughes gives him an appropriate fate in the chase scene—that of the stag god Cernunnos. Here the hunter becomes the hunted in the foredoomed sexual cycle.[39] The frustration behind this simultaneity of foredoomed fates surfaces in the composite visual image of *coitus interruptus* at the end of Lumb's cathedral dream: at this point Lumb's Double lies unconscious on the floor above, and Maud lies naked and face upward on the floor below, with Felicity's knock interrupting Maud's designs (p. 123). Hughes characterizes Maud as an underworld double of the woman the real Lumb is to cure in the spiritual world. But both Maud and the loglike Lumb are inadequate to the task.[40]

Two further instances of simultaneity cap the Maud/Lumb/Felicity triangle. The first concerns Hughes's insertion of two passages between Maud's warrior preparations and Lumb's cathedral daydream; both portray Felicity learning the truth about Lumb's ministry from Garten's fatal photograph. As carnal knowledge becomes general knowlege and truth begins to pervade this dreamworld, a recognition of the import of the sexual cycle begins to become available to the real Lumb, who will interpret these juxtaposed visual images, at the same time that the explosion of repressed libido in the male townsfolk cancels the loglike Lumb's ministry. From this point on the real Lumb needs his Double no more than Lear needs the Fool after act III, for the process of psychological reclamation has begun. The demise of the love triangle in Felicity's death at the very moment when the loglike Lumb first sees the men in the churchyard coming to kill him (p. 151) should instruct the real Lumb of the limitations of his Double's erotic compulsiveness. Felicity, an allegorical figure like Goethe's Care, represents a state of mind that Lumb's Double would like to attain, but cannot: image juxtapositions suggesting death surround her every appearance.

One learns how little self-awareness Lumb's Double has by examining his daydream of fishing with Felicity (pp. 77–83). Felicity, the state of bliss or happiness, is the fish Lumb hopes to catch. But the hooked fish, normally a symbol of sustenance won from the unconscious,[41] yields instead a simultaneous scream from Felicity in this surreal context. She is being abducted by what the loglike Lumb fails to understand—his own compulsive animal instinct projected into the form of yet another "double" (p. 81). Like a play within a play, this dream within a dream reveals truth. The "thin leaping figure, moving like a monkey," is a standard expressionist device used to convey alienated instinct, as with the bandy-legged student Berthold, who abducts the usher's wife in chapter 3 of *The Trial*.

The image of the hands wrestling against each other ("freeing his left hand he grips his own right wrist," p. 82) in the fishing daydream, a stock motif of trickster literature that indicates an infant stage of self-awareness, also refers to the epigraph passage from book XV of *Parzival*. The *Parzival* reference is complex, but nonetheless central to the meaning of *Gaudete*. The epigraph quotation is spoken by Eschenbach's narrator, who knows, as the hero does not, that Parzival's opponent in single combat is his own long-lost brother Feirfiz. During the combat Feirfiz out of knightly courtesy suggests a truce after Parzival's sword, taken from Ither, breaks. Only at this point does each recognize the other's true identity. The broken sword thus cues an expansion of self-awareness in Parzival, and its history in the novel underscores the depth of this expansion of self-awareness. Earlier in the novel Parzival failed to win Condwiramurs because of his excessive self-regard; his self-centered obsession with becoming a knight caused the death of his own mother from a broken heart, the death of Ither from Parzival's own armor-coveting hands, and the initial failure to show compassion for Anfortas. But after Trevrizent awakens Parzival to Adam's sin— innate selfishness—Parzival learns humility, accepts Christianity, and wins Condwiramurs. The sword breaks in the later fight with Feirfiz not by accident, but as an influx of God's grace to one who is gradually trading his former selfishness for self-mastery.[42]

Conversely, the loglike Lumb gains no awareness of his compulsive need for self-gratification from his fishing dream. The dream ends without illumination; Lumb simply squeezes Felicity more tightly to his "sodden body / Under the hammering of the rain." Felicity is as near to drowning in Lumb's uncontrollable eroticism as she was when caught in the grip of the "double" who finally disappears into the lake. The fishing dream, however, helps to explain Lumb's strange silence when Felicity later suggests that they escape before what proves to be the fatal Institute meeting (pp. 124–25). Lumb's silence reveals that he remains locked in a fatalistic compulsiveness: immediate sexual gratification in his Institute ministry is as far as his vision reaches. To fuel this compulsion he responds to Felicity's escape idea by stooping to deceiving her with the lie that Garten's photo was faked, and then even lowers himself to a sleazy moment of undisguised rakishness:

> She wants to leave now, this moment.
> Why can't he just cancel that meeting tonight.
>
> He kisses her, overpowering her with his kisses and easy smiles.
> He starts to unzip her dress. (p. 124)

One can see why Hughes chose not to develop the inordinate phallicism of the trickster myths in *Crow*: he saved this rich lode for *Gaudete*, already in progress before the Crow material solidified. Lumb's imagination is also as anemic as Crow's, but fitted with the distorting lens of eroticism rather than scientific objectivity. When Lumb's Double tries to "imagine simple freedom," he finds every conceivable world fitted "with a bed at the centre. A name. A pair of shoes. And a door" (p. 50). The door of Lumb's Double's eye opens onto unvarying erotic vistas, arid and impersonal. As in "Crow Alights," catalogues of unrelated objects reveal the lack of any imaginative life to infuse them with purpose, warmth, spirit. Unlike Hughes's directives in the epigraph statements to this chapter, the loglike Lumb's mind is anything *but* a "great theatre" where a strong imagination can reconcile inner and outer worlds.

Like Ither's sword in *Parzival*, Lumb's Double's characteristic dependence upon the earth for strength—the world of trees, mud, and temporality— defines his *hubris*. Lumb fails to recognize the "chemical limits" of his energy (p. 155) and deludes himself into believing that earth's power alone will forever ensure his survival. This is the central revelation of the chase scene. Lumb plugs "his energy appeal into the inexhaustible earth" and "sinks his nerves into the current of the powerline" (pp. 163, 156), but soon feels utterly abandoned when his exhaustion reveals to him that the individual organism has distinct limits. Lacking any imaginative resources to promote self-awareness or a reconciliation to his fate, Lumb reverts to a fatalistic extreme; he suddenly considers the earth a futile "ignorance" and his own future that of a doomed conversion into the "mud from which plants grow and which cattle tread" (p. 165). Without imaginative powers to comprehend the Western mythic round of birth/death in temporality, and to raise his plight to the level of understanding and spiritual illumination, Lumb's Double rationalizes one last escape from the world of his own limited vision as he prepares for his final dive into Hagen's lake:

> He collects himself, and concentrates
> On the small target, the small carefulness
> Of liberating himself
> From this crux of moments and shouts and water-margin
>
> . . . .
>
> He balances,
> Narrowing himself to pierce a disappearance, to become infinitesimal
> To slip through the crack of this place
> With its clutching and raging people, its treacherous
> lanes, its rooted houses. (pp. 165–67)

Lumb habitually avoids and evades, to keep his psyche an untroubled *tabula rasa*, a passive receptor where imagination could never develop.

Freedom to Lumb's Double is freedom *from* thinking. When Felicity demands an explanation why Lumb will not escape with her before the fatal Institute meeting, she finds him "Explaining without explanation" (p. 125). And when Felicity counters by demanding that she attend the Institute meeting, Lumb tries to reconcile his world with Felicity and his world of the Institute ministry, but finds himself utterly incapable; he "Gazes blankly toward a reassessment / Impossibly beyond him." Maud knows that the loglike Lumb's planned escape with Felicity to live as "an ordinary man / With his ordinary wife" is a prosaically unimaginative cop-out (p. 147). Lumb similarly evades the consequences of his cattleyard slurry dream, by keeping his mind a blank, in a state of negative freedom:

His only effort now
Is pushing ahead and away the seconds, second after second,
Now this second, patiently, and now this,
Safe seconds
In which he need do nothing,
And in which nothing whatsoever can happen. (p. 108)

A well-developed imagination could raise Lumb's Double's suffering to the level of wisdom and spiritual enlargement, but he lacks precisely this power. Early in the chase scene the loglike Lumb tries "to feel back to the sure root of guidance" after having embraced a beech tree (a near sub-stitute for the oak) to restore his power (pp. 160, 156).[43] Yet Lumb does not comprehend that his chosen oak, the oracular tree and the tree of Zeus's lightning bolt power, is also the tree where humans and animals—all males—were sacrificed to Thor and Odin.[44] The oak symbolizes both his physical strength and its limits, including of course his mortality. When Lumb reexamines his plans to escape with Felicity, he prays to an ash tree, the prototype of Odin's Yggdrasil, the Druidical wand, divination, rebirth, and the triumph of Christianity over paganism (pp. 50–53). The ash, however, is also the tree where the White Goddess dispenses justice, which always entails death for her male consorts.[45] Lumb's loglike Double, like all of us, is crucified to the world of birth and death; his relegation to this unending cycle is the "tree / Of what he cannot alter" (p. 50). Like Malory's Gawain, Lumb's Double's energy level varies with the sun's diurnal cyle, and in Lumb's case this defines the natural limits of his purely physi-cal energy. Lumb makes love to Pauline Hagen in the "midmorning light" (p. 23), and his "communion" with Mrs. Garten at noon is "especially deep and good" (p. 68), but he dies "As the sun touches the skyline, under the red-plumed sky" (p. 165). Because he lacks self-awareness and a strong imaginative life, he is incapable of grasping his finite limits and becomes purely a victim of the vegetative cycle. Lumb's fortunes deteriorate slowly but unswervingly from noon on, as Garten's freshly developed photograph, the townsfolk's increasing comprehension of the nature of his ministry, Lumb's own troubled daydream visions, and

the sun crossing one more degree
Bring the reaching of the landscape roots
A fraction closer
To the vicar's body. (p. 67)

Physical needs motivate Lumb's Double's every activity in *Gaudete*; he always responds freely and unreflectively to the earth energy that beats against the soles of his feet (p. 49). As he tries to manage the "difficult child" of the flesh ("The Perfect Forms," *Lupercal*), Lumb becomes both consort of the White Goddess and a type of Christ, but in each case without a consciousness of his role. Maud brightens his room with apple blossoms, the tree whose fruit signifies sexual consummation with the White Goddess and also the possibility of immortality through wisdom.[46] But after she learns of Lumb's perfidy, Maud places apple blossoms at a lonely gravestone near the unoccupied grave where she will soon drop Lumb's car keys. "*Gaudete*" (rejoice), the sole word chiseled on the gravestone, alludes to a Latin hymn in the *Piae Cantiones* (1582) that celebrates Christ's birth.[47] Betrayed, and given a Christ-like pitchfork wound in his left side, the loglike Lumb at the end of the chase scene yet fails to attain any consciousness of mission or understanding of purpose. Though consort to the White Goddess, Lumb's Double also fails to gain wisdom from his experience in this surrealistic dreamscape. He lacks the imaginative ability to generate the self-knowledge and spiritual capacities that could liberate him from purely physical responses. His function is that of the Shadow archetype in the real Lumb's individuation process: he liberates the real Lumb's libido and offers him a pattern for contemplation—the inevitable round of all organic matter in the Western mythic portion of Hughes's two-way journey toward Reality.

A mandalalike visual image of the psychic wholeness that Lumb's substitute lacks appears in the Baskin drawing on the dust jacket and paperback cover of *Gaudete*. The bottom portion of the skull bulbs out of the earth, as plantlike as the sunbathing Mrs. Holroyd or as charged with earth's energy as the loglike Lumb himself. But the upper portion of the skull reaches the sky and contains free, open space, precisely that "great theatre" of the imagination that can liberate through a "large, flexible grasp, an inner vision."[48] The Baskin drawing provides a visual equivalent of a major seventies theme that Hughes first articulated in his pivotal *Orghast* mythology. In his *Orghast* outline Hughes depicts humans as halfway between animal instinct and godly immortality, figures whose salvation resides precisely in that power that neither extreme possesses—imagination. "Orghast" or "spiritfire" can reconcile humans to their lot as it transforms suffering into illumination. According to the *Orghast* mythology, the loglike Lumb is an Agoluz, a Hercules figure, and the real Lumb of the "Epilogue" poems becomes a Sogis figure who can transform suffering into wisdom and spiritual illumination. Like Agoluz, Lumb's Double in the central dream narrative is "too thoroughly materialized in time."[49] His sexual obsessions pervade his daily life to such an extent that he will never develop an adequate imaginative life.

Hughes's choice of the Heraclitus epigraph (CXVI) further reinforces this instinct/spirit distinction in *Gaudete*. The *Fragments* constantly emphasize the value of wisdom, of clear-eyed understanding. A few quotations from the dozen or so fragments that extol lucidity will suffice: "But other men are oblivious of what they do awake, just as they are forgetful of what they do asleep" (from I); "Whatever comes from sight, hearing, learning from experience: this I prefer" (XIV); and "It belongs to all men to know themselves and to think well" (XXIX). Charles Kahn considers the equation of Dionysiac ritual mania with sensuality and with Hades to be the most significant area of interest in fragment CXVI, the one Hughes quotes in his epigraph. Hades (*Aides*) is the "unseen," the god of death, a darkness of the soul at the furthest extreme from wisdom.[50] Lumb's Double's compulsive instinctuality keeps him spiritually ignorant and therefore lacking in wisdom. Kahn believes that a significant gloss on fragment CXVI is fragment XCVII: "The best choose one thing in exchange for all, everflowing fame among mortals; but most men have sated themselves like cattle." To be afflicted with *Aides* is to live like the cattle of the fields.

This is precisely Lumb's Double's predicament. His lengthiest and most important daydream in the central narrative presents him as cattlelike—a stolid, bovine figure slogging through the mud of animal instinct. The loglike Lumb envisions himself in a cattleyard slurry during a rainstorm (pp. 98–106); here the "thick sludge grips his feet" and cattle press upon him, bellowing and lurching, while men "deformed by oilskins" rain blows upon him with sticks. When he asks for an explanation, he is given a sodden, illegible paper, a typical expressionist device, and next finds himself "buried in mud, / His face into mud, his mouth full of mud," along with his parishioners. Finally he helps to pull out of the mud a woman with "A face as if sewn together from several faces. / A baboon beauty face, / A crudely stitched patchwork of faces"—as in "The Disquieting Muses," the surrealist painting by de Chirico that inspired Plath's eerie poem of the same title. Then the loglike Lumb becomes both the baboon woman in labor and the child of that labor. Both Sagar and Faas interpret this as a rebirth motif,[51] but Hughes himself demurs: "in *Gaudete* the women are being put together in a mistaken, wrong and limited way."[52] Hughes identifies his baboon symbol as referring to "the sacred Thoth baboon of the upper Nile,"[53] normally a symbol of healing, knowledge, vision, and the founding of the fine arts—the imaginative life.[54] But the surreal context and Hughes's own remarks indicate that the baboon symbol exists ironically in the cattleyard slurry daydream; it points toward what loglike Lumb fails to perceive and attain.

Again we are faced with the question of the degree of Lumb's Double's self-awareness. Jung writes that personality growth can only be achieved by "the thorough and conscious assimilation of unconscious contents" and that the menacing aspects of the archetypes diminish "the moment the patient begins to assimilate contents that were previously unconscious."[55] Similarly, in her undergraduate honors study of the double in Dostoevsky, Plath found that Ivan Karamazov may ultimately achieve sanity because he begins to recognize the Smerdyakov (devil) in himself, whereas Golyadkin in the earlier *The Double* ends in schizophrenia because he cannot attain sufficient self-awareness to recognize that his double is an aspect of himself.[56] But in the loglike Lumb's cattleyard slurry daydream, the surrealistic distortions continue. Soon after the mimed childbirth, Lumb's Double sees the baboon woman bellowing and screaming and feels his own body being twisted apart. Though at the end of the dream he glimpses her face "undeformed and perfect," the dream itself has no positive effect upon him. He remains one of those who, according to Heraclitus, have "sated themselves like cattle" instead of seeking illumination. Indeed, four pages later Lumb rivets his gaze upon a primitive stone carving that reflects a very low level of culture. Here a woman with "wide-splayed, artless knees," and with her hands beneath her buttocks, is "pulling herself wide open." Once again Lumb's Double indulges in blunt animal instinct. He is incorrigibly the Shadow. It remains for the real Lumb to lift the unconscious contents of his dream to consciousness, in the "Epilogue" poems.

In its positive manifestations the Thoth baboon in Egyptian symbology signifies the divine intelligence of creation, especially through the efficacious power of words. As scribe of the gods, Thoth invented language and the fine arts, uttered the words that formed the world, gave Isis the magical words to resurrect Osiris, and even provided Osiris with the words he needed to survive the judgment trial and win eternal life.[57] As the real Lumb begins his attempt to comprehend the significance of his central narrative dream in the "Epilogue" poems, however, faith in the power of words is precisely what he lacks. These forty-five short, allusive prayers to the White Goddess record the real Lumb's struggle to reconcile his lot as lover/victim in a quest to unite with his vision of eros-amor. Now that his libido has been released therapeutically in the central narrative dreamscape, he can begin to probe the significance of the Western round of the virtuoso bacteria. In the "Epilogue" Lumb's words record his pain and torment candidly, unsparingly, and with a deep humility. His persistent self-examination and his struggle to clarify his relationship to the Goddess in words finally succeed in attaining a new level of awareness, a knowledge of self that liberates his imagination and lifts his experience from the mud of temporal decay into the healing realm of spirit.

Lumb in the "Epilogue" progresses from a passive state of helplessness at what he perceives to be the overwhelming destructiveness of the Goddess to an acceptance of the temporal round of death and rebirth; then to a more balanced focus that recognizes the sensual, creative, and spiritual aspects of the Goddess, and finally to the role of healer/seer *actively engaged* in reviving Cerridwen and in transmuting the essence of the experience into imaginative vision. In the process Lumb attains sufficient consciousness to affirm a faith in the power of words as a unique helpmeet in transmuting experience into enlightenment. Near the end of the sequence a more perceptive Lumb expresses pity for those whose awareness is insufficient to invoke the power of the Goddess through words and whose grounding in the elemental earth is too complete to develop a strong imaginative life (#37).[58] Those who are "trying to tell" the name of the Goddess are incapable of attaining sufficient culture and self-consciousness. They only bequeath a "gagged yell," and "libraries / Of convalescence," for they remain too rooted to the earth that bore them.

The "Epilogue" begins with disarmingly candid self-assessment. The cryptic admissions of the first poem reveal an intense self-scrutiny at a level of consciousness already beyond the capacities of Lumb's Double. The real Lumb confesses that his former posture toward experience lacked directness and personal involvement in the moment. He has found refuge in escapes, consequences, and after-the-fact rationalizations. The last stanza may even contain self-criticism of Hughes's own sixties Orientalism as potentially a casuistical retreat from the temporal world, with *śūnyatā* and *satori* as varieties of ascetic withdrawal that merit the reproof of the White Goddess.

In the second poem Lumb approaches the center of his problem. How can he articulate in words his complex emotional life and subtle affective states? Words reflect a culture's experience, values, and perceptions, and Western civilization has narrowed to the passivity of Hagen's binocular vision and the violence of his gunsights. The second "Epilogue" poem intimates a cultural context that George Steiner discusses in the opening essays of *Language and Silence*—that contemporary civilization has cheapened language through overkill. Gossip, advertising, information vending, public relations puffs, media image making and unmaking, and public words that mask and hasten private savagery are the common fare today.[59] Like Steiner, Hughes feels that poetic silence is an honest response to our post-Auschwitz culture and that honesty and economy are paramount considerations when using language at all today. Whereas words in the Thoth world of ancient Egypt were valued so highly that correct enunciation of a god's name or point of ritual could grant the speaker salvation,[60] the second "Epilogue" poem maintains that speech today is a charlatan, a quack that prevaricates and defers.

To create a climate for psychic reclamation and spiritual enlargement in the "Epilogue," Hughes prefaces the poems with a three-page interlude designed to create an almost prelapsarian, Eliadian *illud tempus* context where humans have converse with animals and the natural world and where words are efficacious. Here a rejuvenated Lumb calls up an otter from the lough and himself becomes enraptured when he demands that the three girls *name* all the loughs and mountains in sight. As Evans-Wentz notes in his field work on the changeling, remnants of Celtic rebirth doctrines still exist in the west of Ireland, the locale of this interlude; they are preserved in oral tradition and removed from corrosive contact with contemporary urban civilization. In this context, words amplify nature's healing and transformational powers: when the girls take Lumb's poems to their parish priest, and *recite the story* of raising the otter, the cleric too becomes entranced, "carried away by his words," and launches into a paean about the beauty of God's creation. Once again the girls become mesmerized by speech and remain so until "the moment his words passed." By the end of the interlude, words become nearly synonymous with creation itself.

Hence Lumb in the "Epilogue" exists in an environment where words have the power to facilitate spiritual renewal. But at the outset of his meditations his words only reveal his limited perceptions. Lumb dotes only upon suffering and destruction, and despair becomes a possibility. In the third poem of the sequence Lumb recognizes that responses at the level of automatic instinct leave one as chained to the earth as the Double of the chase scene; each response when "the blood jumps" merely engages one in a dreary, repetitive cycle as old as the earth and procreation. Lumb at this point cannot see how it can be otherwise. Yet his unsparingly steady observation of the destructive in nature in the first dozen poems of the "Epilogue" ultimately yields positive results.

Hughes's main sources for the "Epilogue" poems emphasize the necessity of firsthand knowledge of pain as instructive of the actual human condition—a necessary prerequisite for self-development. As both the Occidental and the Oriental paths of his two-way journey toward Reality open for the first time in Hughes's poetry, it is fitting that the central influences upon the "Epilogue" poems derive from both Western and Eastern sources: the poetry of the Hungarian János Pilinszky and south Indian *vacanas* dedicated to the Hindu god Śiva, lord of destruction. These two sources function as guides to the form and content of the "Epilogue." In 1975–1976, at the time he composed the *Gaudete* "Epilogue," Hughes also collaborated with János Csokits in translating a volume of Pilinszky's poetry and wrote an eloquent introduction praising the poet's "mystically intense feeling for the pathos of the sensual world."[61] Pilinszky, captured by the retreating German army, spent the last year of World War II moving from one prison camp to another. Hughes realized that the experience created poetry where "words escaped, only with great effort, from an intensifying, fixed core of silence" to create a vision of "humanity stripped of everything but the biological persistence of cells." Hughes concluded that Pilinszky's unflinching gaze upon the elemental suffering of prisoners ravaged by pain and hunger finally wrought a redemptive vision, "in some all-too-human sense, somewhere in the pulsing mammalian nervous-system, by a feat of human consecration." Like those of Pilinszky, Lumb's honest perceptions of the virtuoso bacteria's sufferings are his best assurance that he too will achieve a redemptive vision. In Pilinszky's *Selected Poems*, shortly before a poem about surviving intense hunger by foraging on all fours for food scraps in refuse dumps ("Frankfurt 1945"), the persona of "World Grown Cold" perceives the "eternally unknowable" in a world limited to biological compulsion and organic decay:

> This world is not my world.
> Merely my body's compulsion
> as I worm, like a maggot,
> deeper and deeper into its bowels.
>
> So I feed on death,
> And so death too gets his fill of me.
> . . . .
> And this is how the eternally unknowable
> gets its homely look.
> As with the leaves in their withering,
> my decay embalms me.

Lumb too must learn to consecrate the compulsions of the virtuoso bacteria in a world where the teleological comforts of traditional religion do not apply. Only then will he be capable of reviving Cerridwen.

As in his sixties poetry, Hughes's surrealism in the first twelve "Epilogue" poems reflects the persona's distorted perceptions. As he apprehends only a world of destructive instinct, Lumb initially perceives Cerridwen surrealistically. He sees her as "The woman who wore a split lopsided mask," recollecting his Double's cattleyard slurry dream of the baboon woman (#10). Early in the sequence Lumb is only furtively conscious of her as "some female groaning / In labor" (#4). In the sixth poem Lumb becomes conscious of animal and vegetable life, but he lacks knowledge of its animating principle—the White Goddess "stayed outside" him. Lumb "assailed" her (#7) when he grew mature enough to possess the apple, symbol of consummation. Aggressiveness blinds him; he does not comprehend that this apple of experience also contains immortality through wisdom.[62] Surreal images dominate as a forlorn Lumb wonders how he can reconcile himself to the Goddess when sex arrives with explosive energy, "Like the electrocuted man / Banged from his burst straps" (#9), or with a screech like the scraping of steel or an "abortionist's knife" (#10). Lumb's honesty couples with a disarming, Pilinszky-like accuracy as he confesses how often his biological needs arrive with a clamorous, numbing urgency. By the twelfth poem Lumb recognizes that his energies derive from the Goddess and that she commands their exercise. In some unaccountable way his actions are directed toward her, and this condition is anterior to satisfying his private needs (the music motif carried over from the central narrative). Unlike Pilinszky, however, Lumb at this point is a passive figure with a negative perspective. He finds little in life worth consecrating.

Following the thread of Lumb's changing relationship with Cerridwen does not do justice to the haunting beauty of the poems, their richness of imagery, subtlety of tone, and economy of statement; but it does clarify their highly elliptical content by establishing a thematic continuity in the "Epilogue" and a coherence of form and meaning in *Gaudete*. Poems 13 through 19 disclose Lumb growing to accept his lot as lover/victim of Cerridwen in the Western round of death and rebirth. Correspondingly his attitude toward nature and the Goddess becomes more benign. In poem 13 Lumb envisions Cerridwen as supportive—rescuing him, in almost pietà-like fashion, from the sea of dissolution that makes him conscious of the gray in his hair. Cerridwen looms gigantic in this poem as an "unearthly" figure whose strength creates the very waves, whereas Lumb views himself as subordinate, a helpless child in her arms. Without surrealistic fright or disgust, poem 14 takes a more objective, circumspect view of appetite as a blind force incapable of uniting lover and beloved. The next poem presents Lumb as having a vision of the union of White Goddess, the oak's bride, with her consort/victim. Lumb sees that both the bliss and the pain are preordained, that cellular biology is encoded with a pattern as old as that found in the couplings of prehistoric insects. The four concluding one-line stanzas indicate that Lumb, however, is too weak to participate actively in this cosmic round; he lies passively beneath the oak in "A perilously frail safety." Nevertheless the vision of the nuptials of oak and bride is positive, intense, sustained, and mature enough to encompass both the bliss and the pain.

Poem 17 contains Lumb's dawning realization that the problem may lie within rather than without. Through a simple, humble synecdoche he asserts that self-examination is a necessary agony that he now chooses deliberately to undertake. The poem ends with an elegant simplicity of quiet affirmation where words stand firm and clear:

> The one I hunt
> The one
> I shall rend to pieces
>
> Whose blood I shall dab on your cheek
>
> Is under my coat.

Like "Glimpse" in *Crow*, poem 18 brings the realization that Lumb still feels alienated, far removed from any direct knowledge of nature: "A primrose petal's edge / Cuts the vision like laser." Lumb still feels the compulsions of blood banging in his brow and admits perplexity, but the few surrealistic images (the "skin of terror" and the bottomless hole) are more subdued in the poem, subordinate to the greater strength of Lumb's inquiring mind now actively engaged in puzzling out his problems.

The highly allusive poem 16 is the most affirmative of this second section. Lumb is gradually gaining in knowledge of the Western cosmic round and asserts his new insights in words formed into straightforward declarative statements. For the first time Lumb affirms the possibility of rebirth. The poem conflates Western and Eastern mythological symbols to state the possibility of transcending the temporal through an enlargement of consciousness in the realm of spirit. The first two lines readily acknowledge the destructive aspect of the Goddess, without surrealistic flinching. As Isis she conspires with Set, whose theriomorphic counterpart is the wild ass, in the yearly murder of Osiris.[63] And the destructive wrath of both the Egyptian Sekmet and the Hindu Devi, consort of Śiva, are figured forth in their lion counterparts.[64] Lumb has seen enough of this destructive earth energy already. The last two lines of the first stanza, however, present a union of opposites on a transcendent plane—the Goddess riding the white bull (her consort) across the heavens. The white bull, theriomorphic counterpart of Dionysus, is both a sacrificial animal and a symbol of divination in Greek, Cretan, and Celtic cultures.[65] In heaven Śiva and Devi ride Nandi, the milk-white bull, signifying the transcendent union of male and female.[66] In the second stanza Lumb recognizes that pain and suffering must inevitably occur to gain this superior understanding: whoever strives for the apple of consummation with the Goddess must nail his heart to the "leafless tree"—the cross of suffering. For the first time Lumb acknowledges that suffering may function as just one part of a purposive cosmic cycle.

Poem 16 introduces Oriental symbolism for the first time into the "Epilogue." Hughes will again draw upon symbolism from the Oriental path of his two-way journey for other poems to follow (#s 21, 25, 27), and especially for the climactic dancer image in poems 42 and 44. Hughes told Faas in 1977 that an important source for the content and the confessional/devotional form of the *Gaudete* "Epilogue" was A. K. Ramanujan's Penguin translation of south Indian *vacanas*, devotional lyrics to Śiva, first published in 1973.[67] These *vacanas* ("sayings" or "things said" in Kannada, a Dravidian language) form a portion of medieval wisdom literature directed toward the protest of orthodox Hindu religious practice. Written in the vernacular, they emphasize the personal devotion (*bhakti*) of the *jaṅgama*, the wandering ascetic, for Śiva, venerated as a monotheistic deity. These antiestablishment poems oppose knowing through orthodox Hindu emphases upon caste, sacred places, artifacts, and rituals, to knowing through cultivating the mystical moment of experience (*anubhāva*), the unmediated and unpredictable inrush of the moving spirit. When articulating this spiritual visitation in poetry, the devotee often borrows from the traditions of yogic psychology and Tantric philosophy and esthetics.[68] (According to Tibetan tradition, Nagarjuna, a native of Andhra, in southern India, introduced Tantrism in the second century A.D. into the heart of Dravidian southern India.)[69] *Vacanas* are typically short poems that borrow the epi-

grammatic three-line stanza from oral tradition, employ domestic metaphors, and incorporate sophisticated formal devices such as parallelism,
oppositions, and extended metaphors. *Vacanas* may attain a simple lyric
grace or the complexity of metaphysical riddles—as in the poems of
Allama Prabhu, a favorite of Hughes.

The purpose of these devotional poems to Śiva is quintessentially Indian
in its mystical Oriental austerity. Śiva in Hindu religious symbology has his
creative and his preserving aspects, but his destructive aspect often dominates in Indian culture. Yet destruction in Indian philosophy is not a purely
negative occurrence. When Śiva assumes his destructive aspect, his purpose is to dissolve time, obliterate the phenomenal world, and thus prove
that destruction is but one aspect of *unending life*, an Absolute of world
process that can be apprehended in contemplation as an image of total
activity.[70] In the *vacanas* the *jaṅgama* strives for spontaneity, directness of
personal involvement, and intensity in devotion to Śiva. The goal is to apprehend the presence of Śiva in the present moment, the mystical NOW, to
transcend the phenomenal world through an intense experience that takes
place on the inner plane of an awakened spirit, as in the following *vacana*
by Dasimayya:

> To the utterly-at-one with Śiva
>
> there's no dawn,
> no new moon,
> no noonday,
> nor equinoxes,
> nor sunsets,
> nor full moons;
>
> his front yard
> is the true Benares,
>
> O Rāmanātha.[71]

Such a moment of mystical transcendence does not occur early in the
Gaudete "Epilogue," but Hughes's use of the form and techniques of *vacana*
poetry announces the possibility of such a moment happening later in the
sequence.

The effect of yoking the suffering spirit (the Pilinszky influence) with the

196 · The Poetry of Ted Hughes

possibility of transcendence (the Indian *vacanas*) in poem 16 and in subsequent "Epilogue" poems must have been liberating for Hughes, for it unlocked his private past in a beautifully creative way. Readers of the poetry of Hughes and Plath must have experienced astonishment in reading poem 19—Hughes's first direct treatment of Plath's suicide, almost a decade and a half after the event. In this poem Plath becomes a type of the White Goddess who merged with her own destructive aspect. Poem 19 opens with the broken marriage and the lapse of sexual relations (the "banked hospital bed") and then articulates the irrevocable finality of the suicide through the image of the flower vase smashing after having been knocked over a third time. The number three refers to the third death alluded to in Plath's "Lady Lazarus," after her father's death when she was eight (1940) and her first, unsuccessful suicide attempt while an undergraduate at Smith College (1953). The Hughes poem continues with the persona kissing the Goddess's (Plath's) forehead in the morgue, in a mood that combines deep sadness with an infinite tenderness. The following image of alienation, the "defunct" pillar in "sun-darkness," is honorific of Plath's art, for it recollects the metaphysical landscapes of de Chirico, an important influence in her poetry.[72]

With tenderness and pity Lumb in poem 28 again meditates upon the Goddess in her destructive aspect. The poem refers to Susan Allison, a friend of Hughes's who died a slow, painful death of Hodgkin's disease.[73] The "not infallible" Goddess manages her own beauty imperfectly and has an intimate knowledge of the pain that often attends her cyclic processes. Hughes presents the pain of the disease as the Goddess's weary attempt to reclaim her beauty, to lift it away from its human container.

Poems 20 and 21 initiate a major change in direction in the "Epilogue": in poems 20 through 40 Lumb becomes *actively* engaged in undergoing the ordeal of suffering and gradually ascends to a spiritual level of understanding. Poem 20 announces his decision, and both 20 and 21 present visionary foreshadowings of future success in the light and sun imagery. From this point on Lumb *acts* and meditates upon the positive significance of his suffering. He enters Cerridwen's cave (#22), receives nourishment from the Goddess as the Egyptian sky deity Tefnut (#23), undergoes shamanic ordeals of suffering and death (#s 24, 32, 38), becomes a warrior for the Goddess in a destructive world (#26), and finally revives Cerridwen through an outpouring of sympathetic, selfless love (#34). In the process Lumb becomes more philosophical about the necessity of action and suffering in a world of strife (#s 26, 31), recognizes the joy that paradoxically exists in undergoing the painful round of suffering and death (#35), affirms the positive aspects of the Goddess as all-powerful guide (#s 25, 36) and lover (#s 27, 29, 30, 36), and even assumes the positive role of healer in breathing life back into his sixties satiric stereotype of the scapegoat soldier (#39). By the end of poem 40 Lumb has realigned his universe in a way that places the creative energy of the tiger, Blake's Los, in its rightfully superior place. Poems 41 through 45, the final poems of the "Epilogue," present a transformation of his knowledge onto the plane of mystical vision.

At the left center of the 1969 Gavin Robbins broadside, the original printing of poem 20 ("I said goodbye to earth"), Robbins drew the equal-armed cross of the four elements, the symbol of Malkuth, the lowest and most earth-bound of the ten Sephiroth, the stages of upward ascent in the Cabbala toward mystical Kether, the realm of pure, shadowless light.[74] Here Lumb affirms very decisively the commencement of an ordeal that will begin with the four elements of earth and hopefully end in the light of spiritual vision, a superior understanding of both the Oriental (the *śūnyatā* "nails of nothing") and the Occidental (the broken, bleeding atoms) paths of Hughes's two-way journey toward Reality. In poem 20, and in other "Epilogue" poems that articulate specific mental visions, Hughes employs a *vacana* technique borrowed from Tantric yoga—of realizing (*sādhana*) or interiorizing a religious state of transcendence by meditating upon visual icons that are self-constructed upon the inner screen of the creative imagination.[75]

Poem 21 announces a shifting of the poetic landscape onto the plane of Lumb's newly awakened imaginative life, that "great theatre" of the imagination. Lumb leaves the world of appetite and temporal decay; only his absence and an obituary remain. The sun image at the poem's end is a magnet for half of world mythology, for the sun is the premier symbol of transcendence. It is the abode of power and enlightenment for Ra, Osiris, Viṣṇu, the *ātman* of the Upanishads, the fiery creative energy of Los in Blake's *Milton*, and for dozens of other mythological figures and systems.[76] The "keeper" seen in the sun is obscure, but may allude to Graves's observation that Hercules as oak-god became doorkeeper of the gods after his death.[77] The falcon is the self-begetting solar falcon Horus.[78] The poem does not present an achieved mystical moment, but only a visionary foreshadowing of such a moment. The pain must first be suffered and comprehended.

Recoil from visionary moments occurs in poem 22. "A voice quaking lit heaven / The stone tower flies" possibly alludes to Yahweh's crushing of the Tower of Babel (Gen. 11). In fear of this Lumb rushes to Cerridwen's wolf cave for protection. Steiner believes that events of this sort articulated in dreams express a recurrent fear in poets that speech is a "miraculous outrage" that apes the gods and breaks the silence of matter.[79] Lumb is not entirely confident of his visionary powers as yet; he requires more support from the Goddess. This he receives in the next poem: a turbulent annunciatory dream ends with Lumb drawing sustenance from sky goddesses such as the Egyptian Nut or the lioness Tefnut.[80]

"A doctor extracted," poem 24, presents the first extended instance of Lumb willfully undergoing pain. Here imagery of shamanic initiation combines with a decision to cleanse himself of the aggressive behavior that he inherits from patriarchal mythological systems where a hero creates the world violently, by ripping open the female dragon of all-space, as Marduk ripped open the belly of Tiamat in the Babylonian *Enuma Elish*. Poem 25 continues this willingness to undergo pain, as Lumb experiences the ritual death of Osiris. By now he has learned only to trust the Goddess, not antiquated religious orthodoxies, the "creaking heavens." The striking images of needle and axle present the Goddess in the positive role of being the center of Lumb's world-orientation, organizing and stabilizing his universe. These two images are used toward similar ends in the *vacanas* of Allama Prabhu translated by Ramanujan (see #s 42, 431).

Lumb expresses complete loyalty to the Goddess in poem 26, where he offers himself as a warrior in the service even of her wrathful raven form of battlefield destruction and evil omen, as with the Morrigu in the Celtic *Táin Bó Cúalnge*. Willing to do his duty in a universe of destruction, Lumb achieves some of the detachment one finds in the *Bhagavad Gita*. What matters most to Lumb, as poems 27 and 30 reveal, is the continued presence of the Goddess in his personal life. Poem 27 combines the *vacana* preference for the personal presence of the deity over conventional worship in the religious edifice with Lumb's first positive treatment of the erotic potential of the Goddess. The personal experience of the Goddess in the flux of daily living is more enduring. Lumb contemplates the erotic potency of the Goddess in a *vacana* philosophical backdrop. Here the self-purifying river bespeaks both a continuing world process, and the ability of the Goddess to reconcile opposites on a transcendent plane of unity:

> Churches topple
> Like the temples before them.

> The reverberations of worship
> Seem to help
> Collapse such erections.
>
> In all that time
> The river
> Has deepened its defile
> Has been its own purification
>
> Between your breasts
>
> Between your thighs

Poems 31 and 32 return to the willing endurance of pain and add the earlier theme of the efficacy of words. Lumb here achieves a much more self-conscious awareness of the arduous act of writing as painful payment for the ability to write honestly, accurately, and truthfully (#31). In poem 32 Lumb furthers his meditations upon his artistic role by confessing that words are really a poor substitute for union with the Goddess. In Egyptian symbology divine beings alight in the wide-branching, shady sycamore,[81] but Lumb feels acutely the "weeping letters" of his words, a poor replacement for actual union. He characterizes his artistic role as a kind of invisibility symbolized by the fern;[82] the very ephemerality of his artistic office strikes him as being a poor substitute for the lived experience. Hence Lumb affirms that his Apollonian artistic endeavors by themselves are insufficient; he must merge with the drunken singer, the consort/victim Dionysus, in order to find the proper mode for apprehending the Goddess. To earn his poetic office and his union with Cerridwen he must utterly give himself over in selfless, ecstatic devotion.

In poem 33 he does exactly that. With complete abandon he removes the crutches of intellect (the "handful of hair") and emotion (the "handful of flesh"); defenseless, he "reaches both hands into the drop." In complete self-surrender and loving devotion he finally succeeds in reviving Cerridwen, in the very next poem:

> When the still-soft eyelid sank again
> Over the stare
> Still bright as if alive

> The chiselled threshold
> Without a murmur
> Ground the soul's kernel
>
> Till blood welled.
>
> And your granite—
> Anointed—
> Woke.
>
> Stirred.

A central image in the poem, that of the "chiselled threshold"—the cold, barely conscious forehead of Cerridwen fast becoming a tombstone, suggesting her immanent death—becomes in Lumb's consciousness a millstone that grinds his soul like grain until sympathy wells up from the intense pain. His pain (blood) articulates a selfless love that anoints and stirs the Goddess. Words may be a poor substitute for experience, but if the experience is lived at a depth of intensity and feeling, the poetic imagination will intuitively seize upon the right words to convey it. Here the utter simplicity and rightness of the images, and the economy of statement, combine with a post-Auschwitz restraint—the spareness of phrase and the silence of the bare space surrounding the poem. Through his devotion and his words Lumb conveys a great deal of reverence for the Goddess.

The following three poems, along with poem 43, could be classified as the love poetry of one who has become hypersensitive to the oscillations of the Goddess's presence and absence in an otherwise meaningless and destructive world, a world that produces plantlike people with so little consciousness that they have no awareness of her, and no power to articulate her presence in words. In poem 36 Lumb becomes a troubadour who expresses his love through confessing his insignificance. This he articulates in verse that is reminiscent of the *Rig-Veda* passage that depicts Viṣṇu as an aloof, all-powerful deity who enveloped the entire universe in the dust created from his three steps.[83] Lumb's version of this is similar, but more humane:

> Each of us is nothing
> But the fleeting warm pressure
>
> Of your footfall

As you pace
Your cage of freedom.

Poems 38 through 40 present Lumb in the active role of shaman and healer, witness and priest of the creative energy of the Goddess's world. Poem 38 reveals Lumb as shaman attending to his own microcosmic universe. He officiates at his own shamanic initiation rite as he learns to absorb the pain and separate the decayed parts from the living flesh. Stanzas I, II, and IV begin with the affirmative "I," revealing Lumb in complete control of his actions. "Eat," the single word injunction that ends the poem, indicates that Lumb has accepted the limits of the Western round of the virtuoso bacteria. The central image of the molten metal and the metal mold in poem 39 recollects the furnaces of the creative imagination of Blake's Los in book I of *Milton* (plates 22, 24). Lumb breathes life into the "steel man" as Los did to Milton: "Los had enterd into my soul: / His terrors now posses'd me whole! I rose in fury & strength" (plate 22). Hughes's poem suggests a more humane attitude toward the scapegoat soldier of his sixties poetry. Los, the tiger of Blake's creative imagination, can rest quietly in poem 40, for his energies now pervade both heaven and earth, making Lumb's universe whole.

In the last five poems of the *Gaudete* "Epilogue," Lumb, having achieved personality integration, receives an experience of Reality, the goal of Hughes's all-suffering pilgrim's two-way journey, in a timeless moment of sustained mystical vision. Poem 41 reveals Lumb having vaulted from the mud of temporality onto a new spiritual plane, with a rainbow "silking" his body and with new wings fitted for spiritual ascent. Poem 42 continues the revival of the pilgrim as soldier, as in 39. Here Lumb bears witness to the Goddess's animating energy through his words, and presents this energy much more positively than the electrocution imagery of poem 9. When this energy arrives,

> the dead man flings up his arms
> With a cry
> Incomprehensible in every language
>
> And from that moment
> He never stops trying to dance, trying to sing
> And maybe he dances and sings
>
> Because you kissed him.

> If you miss him, he stays dead
> Among the inescapable facts.

The influx of energy from the Goddess's kiss again recollects Blake's *Milton* (book I, plate 22), where Los kisses Milton and infuses within him a prophetic imagination that makes him whole: "but he kissed me, and wished me health. / And I became One Man with him arising in my strength."

After this influx of the creative imagination, Lumb experiences the mystical moment of illumination in the realm of spirit, realized in his creation of a complex Tantric icon sustained in his inner world by his now highly developed imaginative powers. Poem 44 begins with a guard/dancer uniting with a lightning-blasted oak in a dance:

> Your tree—your oak
> A glare
>
> Of black upward lightning, a wriggling grab
> Momentary
> Under the crumbling of stars.
>
> A guard, a dancer
> At the pure well of leaf.

The paradoxical black lightning is a favorite alchemical symbol for the mystical, transcendent unity wrought by the union of opposites, as in Boehme and Paracelsus. For Paracelsus especially, dark lightning signified the *lumen naturae*, the divine spark buried in darkness, and the *hieros gamos* or sacred marriage of Sol and Luna.[84] For Frazer and Graves, the black or lightning-blasted oak revealed the sacred inrush of Zeus's power into the phenomenal world; such trees were consecrated and set aside as shrines to Zeus the Descender.[85] Lightning itself is a favorite symbol of liberation and transcendent illumination in alchemy, Zen, and the Upanishads.[86] The upward-thrusting lightning may allude to the Lightning Path, the twenty-fourth path in the ascent of the cabbalistic Tree of Life, signifying the death and rebirth of the personality through the Imaginative Intelligence.[87]

Lumb conflates Occidental and Oriental sources in his yoking of the guard and dancer images. The guard, of course, is Frazer's King of the Wood, who could reign supreme so long as he could guard the Sacred Wood of Diana at Nemi and prevent his successor from plucking a Golden

Bough and slaying him.[88] The dancer is the Śiva of *vacana* poetry: a Cosmic Dancer who dissolves time and the phenomenal world in a dance that symbolizes the Absolute as a relentless flow of world process, incorporating at every moment a dynamic union of all five of Śiva's activities—creation, maintenance, destruction, concealment, and favor.[89] As Lumb's pain is transfigured into mystical illumination, Hughes appears to suggest that in some respects at least the Eastern Self and the Western virtuoso bacteria are ONE in the NOW moment of exalted vision.

The complex image of the guard/dancer dancing around the lightning-blasted oak reconciles the agony and the ecstasy of Lumb's "Epilogue" meditations through a visionary knowledge that his Double, rooted so completely in the earth, could never attain. Poem 44 also unifies the four earthly elements—first the conjunction of lightning (fire) with the "clay, water and the sunlight," and then the lightning, the thirsting seas, and the flying, earth-straddling oak—by lifting them to the level of awareness in Lumb's imaginative vision. As the black oak dances, Lumb sustains his meditative gaze upon "the centuries of its instant" and achieves a mystical moment of liberation when he envisions that "The oak is flying / Astride the earth."

For the first time in Hughes's poetry, the esemplastic power of Coleridge's primary imagination apprehends a higher Reality beyond the world of sense. The oak itself is a symbol of wholeness and maternal renewal in life and a vehicle of mystic ecstasy for the shaman climbing it.[90] As the oak belongs to the Goddess—Lumb identifies it as "your oak"—his union with it in the form of guard and dancer signifies a union of Goddess and consort/victim, an energizing, revitalizing experience for all inspirational poets. The flying oak reveals that the real Lumb has liberated himself from his Double's world of erotic compulsion and earth-bound decay, by comprehending its significance in the airy realm of an awakened imaginative life. The straddling of the earth by the oak signifies that the oak (Lumb and the Goddess united) controls the temporal world, a far cry from the tremulous surrealism of the "Prologue," the central narrative, and the first dozen "Epilogue" poems of *Gaudete*.

The synthesis of Western guard and Eastern dancer at the climax of the *Gaudete* "Epilogue" reveals that Hughes in his third period believes that in some respects the Occidental and Oriental paths of his two-way journey work in consort. But the merging of these two mythic modes does have its limits, for they are essentially opposites in many fundamental ways. Yogic philosophy, according to Eliade, ultimately aims at denying the value and meaning of suffering as something that only affects the psychomental life of the personality (*asmitā*), whereas the goal of Patanjali in his *Yoga Sutras*, for instance, is to liberate one by awakening to the fact that the spirit (*puruṣa*) is autonomous, free, impassive, and existing entirely apart from the life of the senses. Eliade does list the devotional mysticism of the antiestablishment *bhakti* poets as an important exception, for these clearly prefer the felt presence of Śiva as recompense for real suffering.[91]

The evidence of *Gaudete* and other volumes in his third period indicates that Hughes follows the moderate way of the *bhakti* poets and is not a world-denier. In his third period Hughes reaffirms solidarity with the cyclic round of the suffering spirit, the Western virtuoso bacteria. The final poem of the *Gaudete* "Epilogue" underscores this point unequivocally. As Lumb merges with the flaming darkness in a moment of mystical oneness, he ends *Gaudete* with lines that reaffirm the Western mythos of periodic suffering as necessary to achieve wisdom and personality growth, not personality annihilation: "So you have come and gone again / With my skin." Śiva's doctrine that each instant contains all possibilities for growth and destruction is conformable to Hughes's insistence that perception creates or denies possibilities, and the intense devotion of the *bhakti* poets suits the inspirational poet in Hughes; but his poetry reveals that he does not subscribe to the world-denying withdrawal of the orthodox yogin.

The *Gaudete* "Epilogue" records the fruits of what happened to the real Lumb in the spiritual world. Through significant suffering Lumb transforms the libidinal energy that his Double released into an expansive "great theatre" of the imaginative life—for future guidance, self-realization, and personality growth. Lumb's central narrative dream was therapeutic in the Jungian sense: it healed him as he interpreted its significance, and the act of interpretation raised his self-knowledge. The form of *Gaudete* is a purposive and coherent *paideuma*. As Lumb unites with his Goddess and Muse, Hughes reaffirms the efficacy of words and gains a new faith in the Western portion of his two-way journey.

CHAPTER 7

Taking
Each Other
to the Sun
Cave Birds
1978

*the outer world is only one of the worlds we live in.
For better or worse we have another, and that is the
inner world of our bodies and everything pertain-
ing. It is closer than the outer world, more decisive,
and utterly different. So here are two worlds, which
we have to live in simultaneously. And because they
are intricately interdependent at every moment, we
can't ignore one and concentrate on the other without accidents. Probably fatal accidents. . . . We can
guess, with a fair sense of confidence, that all these
intervolved processes . . . —our glands, organs,
chemical transmutations and so on—are striving to
tell about themselves. They are all trying to make
their needs known. . . . because all these dramatis
personae are really striving to live, in some way or
other, in the outer world. . . . A person's own inner
world cannot fold up its spirit wings . . . just because [modern science] requires it to. As the religion
was stripped away, the defrocked inner world became. . . . a hell. Religious negotiations had formerly embraced and humanized the archaic
energies of instinct and feeling. They had conversed
in simple but profound terms with the forces struggling inside people, and had civilized them, or attempted to. Without religion, those powers have
become dehumanized. The whole inner world has
become elemental, chaotic, continually more primitive and beyond our control.*

—Hughes, 1976[1]

In *The Place of Poetry* (1981) Christopher Clausen
asserts that most modernist poets have lost their audience by neglecting
both the *dulce* and *utile* of Horace. Instead of delighting their audience
with comprehensible themes and events, modernists regularly alienate
through excessive formal experimentation. They use archaic myths, complicated metaphors, and heterogeneous fragments of non-Western history
and culture as formal devices to organize their wide-ranging poems, and
these methods of organization are beyond the ken of the average reader.
Furthermore, instead of instructing readers in ways that may strengthen

the moral sense and apply to problems in contemporary living, modernists accept the Romantic elevation of the imagination and consequently adopt theories of the nonreferentiality of pure art or preoccupy themselves with formal craft. Clausen finds most modernists deficient in implementing two principles: that "important poetry conveys significant ideas normally intended to apply to the world outside the poem, and that the profundity and coherence of those ideas are a legitimate and important part of the reader's concern."[2] Though Pound's use of myth and history in a pointless longing for a world without *usura* is exceptional, and though a few modernists may similarly be tempted to raid history and mythology to support private emotional or political positions, Clausen still has his finger squarely on a central issue: does modernist poetry educate and delight in ways that pertain to "the world outside the poem"? Pound certainly thought so, in his educational theory of *paideuma*, but his practice in the *Cantos* entails such esoteric associations and specific, non-Western arcana as to give instruction and delight only to the most fervent Pound expert, not to the average undergraduate or even the average university professor.

Cave Birds (1978) might almost appear to have been written in response to Clausen's charges, some three years prior to their appearance. The single persona of *Cave Birds* has a sufficiently developed imaginative life to save his soul; his progress in the volume reveals a heightened capacity for suffering and illumination that pertains to himself *and* the world outside the poem. The persona is able to indict *himself*, not just his received culture, for moral callousness to human suffering and then carry the reader through a process of self-examination and final resolution that not only includes a sense of responsibility toward human suffering in the real world, but also offers a paradigm to the reader that is directed toward alleviating some of that suffering. It is a measure of Hughes's extraordinary commitment to life and art that the central persona of *Cave Birds* is himself an artist, an alter ego in some very limited ways for Hughes, who riddles himself with accusations and guilt about an aloof professionalism, a "cold business" ("In these fading moments I wanted to say") that can lapse into moral indifference and rationalizations that insulate him from caring.[3] Only a superior poet could bare himself in print with such candor and courage, and only a great poet could carry it off with the depth, integrity of feeling, and the intensity that Hughes sustains in *Cave Birds*.

The formal principles that bring coherence to *Cave Birds*—the arcana of alchemy, individuation and the compensatory nature of the Jungian psyche, the solar eagle symbolism, and the revelation of guilt and self-examination of the poet-persona—are inseparable from a content that applies both to the individual reader and to the world outside the poem. Hughes, like Jung, finds in alchemy a rich repository of important medieval Christian cultural patterns for expressing and disciplining inner world needs and for managing and directing what both believe to be a compensatory relationship between the conscious and unconscious portions of the Western psyche. In the solar eagle symbolism of *Cave Birds* Hughes articulates the drive of the Western psyche toward illumination and an enlarged self-comprehension. These formal devices, plus the pilgrim's progress of the poet-persona, organize the A, B, and C groups of *Cave Birds* poems into a coherent statement of how an aware adult can lead a responsible, self-directed life. The A group reveals the persona's guilt at a transgression against the feminine principle and suggests future rebirth; the B group provides an alchemic/shamanic paradigm for earning the rebirth through significant suffering and death to the former self-concept; and the C group specifies the exact nature of the transgression, personalizes and intensifies the suffering, and supplies a moral framework that applies to the world beyond the poem.

Cave Birds began when Hughes in 1974 saw nine of Leonard Baskin's weirdly anthropoid *Cave Birds* drawings. Hughes wrote a poem for each—the nine A group poems.[4] These are static cameo portraits of a persona and allegorical figures in a plot that reveals that persona's guilt for some unnamed transgression against the feminine in nature. This persona, once convicted, is then reborn as a falcon in "The risen." Baskin, taken by these nine poems, produced another ten bird drawings, and Hughes another ten companion poems—the B group poems of the Scolar Press limited edition, sold at the Ilkley Literature Festival in May· of 1975, where Hughes read many *Cave Birds* poems. Originally Hughes intended *Cave Birds* to be a sequence of cryptic hieroglyphs for bibliophiles, published in a limited edition by Baskin at the Gehenna Press. But after the Ilkley Festival offered Hughes a commission to present *Cave Birds* as a stage reading, he developed a psychodrama plot in the B group poems, to add dramatic emphasis. Then Hughes revised and discarded a few of the poems and interspersed another twelve poems (the C group) not linked to any Baskin drawings. Hughes read thirty of the thirty-one total poems, skipping only the two-line "Finale," for the BBC Radio 3 immediately after the Ilkley Festival (recorded 26 May 1975), with helpful but short introductory comments.[5] Though Hughes revised some of the poems, deleted short stanzas in several others, and retitled a few before and after the BBC reading, the only differences in the *ordering* of the poems between the BBC transmission and the final trade editions are the reversing of the first two and the exclusion of the third (A-2: "The advocate") and eighth (C-4: "Your mother's bones wanted to speak, they could not"). Hughes's interleaving of the A, B, and C groups into the twenty-nine poems of the final trade editions of *Cave Birds*, significant for the content and form of the sequence, becomes the following:

1. C-1 "The scream"
2. A-1 "The summoner"
3. C-2 "After the first fright"
4. A-3 "The interrogator"
5. C-3 "She seemed so considerate"
6. A-4 "The judge"
7. A-5 "The plaintiff"
8. C-5 "In these fading moments I wanted to say"
9. A-6 "The executioner"
10. A-7 "The accused"
11. C-6 "First, the doubtful charts of skin"
12. B-1 "The knight"
13. C-7 "Something was happening"
14. B-4 "The gatekeeper"
15. B-3 "A flayed crow in the hall of judgment"
16. B-2 "The baptist"
17. C-8 "Only a little sleep, a little slumber"
18. B-5 "A green mother"
19. C-9 "As I came, I saw a wood"
20. B-6 "A riddle"
21. B-7 "The scapegoat"
22. C-10 "After there was nothing there was a woman"
23. B-8 "The guide"
24. C-11 "His legs ran about"
25. B-9 "Walking bare"
26. C-12 "Bride and groom lie hidden for three days"
27. B-10 "The owl flower"
28. A-8 "The risen"
29. A-9 "Finale"

Analyzing *Cave Birds* according to the A, B, and C groups of poems has the advantage of isolating significant themes and formal devices; it demonstrates the richness of the text at the same time that it reveals Hughes's probable intentions in developing the final organization. One can see in the chart of the table of contents that the eight remaining A group poems form an envelope that introduces the reader to static cameo portraits of the protagonist and portions of his Jungian unconscious. A-1 and A-3 through A-7, occurring among the first ten *Cave Birds* poems, reveal the guilt of the persona; A-8 and A-9, at the end of the sequence, present the hero's rebirth and reentry into the mutable world. What the initial sequence lacked—a dramatic sense of process, a convincing agon or struggle that grants credibility to the rebirth imagery of "The risen" (A-8)—Hughes added when he composed the B and C groups. These last two groups aid in understanding Hughes's subtitle for *Cave Birds*—"An Alchemical Cave Drama." The "cave" of *Cave Birds* is the Platonic cave of the physical, material world, not the ideal world (*Republic*, book X). It is a cave especially in the sense of the material reality of the body, Hughes's inner world, with its biological processes, nervous system, and conscious and unconscious forces. Likewise it is the sacred cave of primitive hunting peoples, a place where one can summon psychic forces in order to preordain a successful outcome for the hunt. In *Cave Birds* Hughes also draws upon the metaphysics of cave rituals, that primitive intuition of complicity and unending participation in a natural round of birth and death where both hunter and hunted are but ever-changing receptacles for an undying life force that forever demands rebirth.[6]

The A group introduces some of the psychic participants in this drama of rebirth, but no more. Hughes may have originally conceived *Cave Birds* as another Jungian individuation drama and combined his very perceptive and imaginative visual responses to Baskin's original nine drawings with descriptions of a protagonist encountering Jungian archetypes as his self-image disintegrates. Alchemical imagery does not dominate until the B group appears. In the A group legalistic imagery of a courtroom interrogation predominates. After an essentially static revelation and acceptance of guilt, the protagonist rises as a falcon in "The risen." Hughes must later have realized, as he began the B group, that his original arrangement proved to be a solid outline, but could not convince by itself because the reader never observes the persona enduring the requisite suffering that would make the final transformation earned. The B group contains sufficient stages in the process of self-annihilation and articulates the pain experienced in undergoing this process; it also draws from the repository of medieval Christian symbolism that alchemists attributed to their ostensibly material process, to reveal the significance of the transformation as one of spiritual enlargement. The A group envelope contains only the legalistic, Kafkaesque revelation of guilt (a sort of *Eat Crow* with very muted surrealism) followed by a sudden change to a falcon once the hero accepts his guilt. In the A group cave the hero's Jungian unconscious erupts into his conscious self-image and introduces him to its energy-bearing personalities, the archetypes.

"The summoner," the first A group poem, introduces the Jungian Shadow, a familiar figure from *Crow* and *Gaudete*, the ambivalent, unrecognized darker forces from the personal unconscious. Lines in the opening stanzas such as "Protozoic, blood-eating" combine Hughes's responses to the girth and bulk of the Baskin drawing with the physicality of a bodily process that operates beneath the threshold of consciousness. The legal imagery of words such as "foreclosure" and "arrest" signifies both the termination of the hero's former self-image and a severing of that self's relationship to the outer world. The setting of the poem, the moment between sleep and waking, is a stock introduction to a surreal (i.e., psychological) drama; as the soul slides into sleep, conscious control relaxes, yielding the leavings of a formidable presence. The title Hughes gave to Baskin's drawing, "A Hercules in the Underworld Bird," is significant, for it introduces us to the strength and perseverance of a psychic force capable of enduring many labors and much suffering—the potent though morally ambivalent energies of the unconscious.[7] Though initially he grips the persona menacingly, the Summoner becomes a "protector" as the hero works his way through the encounter. The Summoner's disarray ("rinds and empties") and spectral bedroom presence suggest the first appearance of Golyadkin's Double in Dostoevsky's *The Double*, a work Plath discussed in her Smith undergraduate honors thesis. The unconscious first breaks in upon conscious life when too much life has been left outside in the unconscious, and when a withdrawal of libidinal energy signals a sundering of one's old self-image, after which the psyche becomes temporarily schizoid and tosses up the archetypes in dream image projections.[8]

"The interrogator" (A-3) is the anima archetype in her predatory aspect as the vulture-headed Isis. Hughes, from his *Orghast* acquaintance with Egyptian mythology, connects Isis with Baskin's drawing, calling it "A Titled Vulturess," for Isis has a predatory vulture aspect in *The Egyptian Book of the Dead*.[9] The anima appears after the patient recognizes the unsavory Shadow aspects of his personality and begins to accommodate the psychic energy of that archetype. The anima, the nixielike soul that corresponds to the subordinate feminine personality traits in the male, can at first appear as a menacing lamia or succubus that drains the life out of the patient; in "The interrogator" she picks his bones clean and then leaves with a "dripping bagful of evidence" after she confronts him with his complacent self-centeredness. The opening image of the vulture homing in from above upon a man too mulishly obstinate to move is very effective, as are the auditory effects in the gruff images that convey her anger. Her interrogation proceeds "By grapnel" as "Some angered righteous questions / Agitate her craw."

In "The judge" (A-4) Hughes introduces the abstracting intellect in human consciousness as a paradoxical faculty that devours all phenomena it perceives, yet is itself not a physiological organ. It is a "garbage-sack of everything that is not." This Judge digests all that it catches in its webs and translates it into abstract systems governed by an "Absolute." Hughes responds to the oafishness of the Baskin drawing by figuring forth the abstracting intellect as a faculty that has physiological roots, but whose only "leavings are guilt and sentence." One is reminded of Kafka's existential description of consciousness in his aphorisms (#38) as an ever-present Judgment Day within the self, a "summary court in perpetual session." The heart of the poem, however, resides in the satiric allusion to Blake's Urizen exploring his dens with a trailing web on plate 25 of *The Book of Urizen* and in Night the Sixth of *The Four Zoas*. As Urizen in Night the Sixth of *The Four Zoas* systematizes and measures out the universe and attempts to account for all phenomena through laws (webs) of uniformity and conformity developed by the deistic or Lockean abstracting intellect, he spins a dire, cold web:

> And the Sciences were fixd & the Vortexes began to operate
> On all the sons of men & every human soul terrified
>
> . . . .
>
> For Urizen lamented over them in a selfish lamentation
>
> . . . .
>
> Clothed in aged venerableness obstinately resolvd
> Travelling thro darkness & whereever he traveld a dire Web
> Followed behind him as the Web of a Spider dusky & cold
> Shivering across from Vortex to Vortex drawn out from his mantle of
>   years
> A living Mantle adjoined to his life & growing from his Soul [10]

As it digests all into abstract system and objective fact, the Judge receives its just deserts—the eerie emptiness of "solar silence." Elsewhere—plate 91 of *Jerusalem*, for instance—Blake presents the abstracting intellect as a "Swelld & bloated Form," a Polypus-like aggregate of dissected particulars that fits perfectly the omnivorous obesity of Hughes's Judge.

Jung describes the anima as capable of a spritelike proliferation of manifestations, a changing "into all sorts of shapes" with "an unbearable independence."[11] In his introductory remarks to the BBC reading of "The plaintiff" (A-5), Hughes corroborates this fact: "His victim takes on a form which is progressively more multiple and serious, progressively more personal and inescapable." The "victim" is the feminine in nature, a crime against which caused the anger of "The interrogator." "The plaintiff" describes a more positive anima as the power of love within the protagonist, his "heart's winged flower" that he has nursed so long. The flame imagery derives in part from the flaming fire of love in the second valley of the Sufi fable *The Conference of the Birds,* by Farid ud-Din Attar, a text Hughes worked on for more than a year with Peter Brook's actors.[12] Hughes may also have drawn upon Christian sources, given his title for Baskin's drawing—"A Hermaphroditic Ephesian Owl." St. Paul's Epistle to the Ephesians contains numerous metaphors developing the idea that love joins together all parts of the body and that we are all one body and one spirit in our love of one another through Christ (4:16; 4:2ff.). The Church Council of Ephesus in 431 A.D. raised Mary, the maternal, material principle, to the status of Mother of Christ and an indivisible part of the godhead. This power, rooted in the body of the protagonist of *Cave Birds,* gives him the potential to speak in tongues, to direct his heart's affections toward others. From this point on in the sequence, the anima will become an increasingly positive force, though not without the side effect of occasionally producing illusions.

At this point the persona's unconscious floods his mind in "The executioner" (A-6). Jung writes that this flooding is often depicted in terms of an invading darkness or blackness.[13] When the island of one's conscious self-image shrinks to the point of leaving too much out of life, it can lead to an inundation by the surrounding sea of the unconscious, for the unconscious "yields an endless and self-replenishing abundance of living creatures, a wealth beyond our fathoming."[14] Hughes extends an allusion to Socrates' cup of hemlock to convey this inundation. The purposeful repetition of the verb "fills up" becomes cloying overstatement, an objective correlative for the feeling of a paradoxically revitalizing death by drowning. The poem concludes with a beautiful image of freshened perception, the attaining of a new perspective where life "feels like the world / Before your eyes ever opened."

The persona's acceptance of his guilt occurs in "The accused" (A-7). He "confesses" the various parts of his body, heaping them up for a judgment "On a flame-horned mountain-stone, in the sun's disc." Acquiescence is likened to submission to an Aztec ritual sacrifice, complete with sun-drenched stone temple, ritual daggers, and the skin of a "bedaubed, be-gauded / Eagle-dancer." The persona becomes both the captive warrior to be slain and the slayer, the painted, gaudily dressed dancer of the select solar Eagle Knights. The judgment tableau occurs on the sun's disk atop an Aztec temple, possibly that of the awe-inspiring Pyramid of the Sun, rising two hundred feet above the sacred city of Teotihuacan. George Vaillant describes a typical ritual sacrifice in ways that closely parallel images in "The accused":

> At dawn a captive dressed as the Sun God, Tonatiuh, ascended to the platform in front of the temple. Four priests spread-eagled the victim, and a fifth opened his breast to tear out the heart as an offering to the god. The populace then feasted until noon, gashing their ears and parts of their bodies with blades of obsidian. In the afternoon the Eagle and Tiger Knights, votaries of the solar cult, took part in a dance dramatizing the sacred war wherein the sun is slain, to be reborn the following day. The dance culminated in a gladiatorial sacrifice. Selected Eagle and Tiger Knights, armed with real weapons, slew a captive warrior, chosen for his military distinction, who was tethered to a circular stone representing the sun's disk and who defended himself with dummy weapons only.[15]

Here one can apply Hughes's comments in the epigraph to this chapter: if Christian morality no longer has significance for moderns, perhaps the more elemental, less civilized morality of guilt and sacrifice can touch the lapsed soul.

In the logic of the A group, once the persona has submitted to his fate and accepted his guilt, he dies and is reborn as a solar falcon, the theriomorphic counterpart of Horus, whose eye contains the light of the morning sun—heavenly illumination.[16] In "The risen" (A-8), at the end of the final trade edition, the persona soars with new wings in a "burning unconsumed." His new shape is that of "a cross, eaten by light, / On the Creator's face," the shape of psychic wholeness and the acceptance of pain.[17] The final lines of "The risen" and those of the closing "Finale" (A-9) indicate that this new self is no guarantee of permanent well-being and perpetual self-control; the process of personality growth will recur when needed in the mutable world.

When the Ilkley Festival offered Hughes a commission to produce a dramatic reading, he improved upon his A group structure by writing poems that show the painful stages in the process of death and rebirth. The al-chemical symbolism in the B group presents the persona learning the transport from the pain in a more dramatically compelling way. In his BBC introductory remarks Hughes writes that after "The accused" (A-7), the last poem in the first part of the A envelope, the hero is swallowed by a raven and begins a "new adventure." The B group adventure begins two poems later with "The knight" (B-1). Two motifs organize Hughes's B and C groups: the alchemical process of dissolution, purification, and liberation; and the shamanic journey to the heaven of the eagles.

According to Jung, the obscure and (from our point of view) useless pseudoscientific attempts of alchemists to produce gold, the tincture, the philosopher's stone, or whatever from dross metals should be understood as an adventurous wish fulfillment by highly imaginative people as they tried to comprehend the principles of matter long before any of the laws of modern chemistry were discovered. We should understand their spirit of adventure much as we understand the visions of those who hoped for flight centuries before Kitty Hawk.[18] The significance of alchemy for Jung lies in the fact that the alchemist in reality projected conscious and uncon-scious psychological contents derived from the late medieval Christian tra-dition. In seeking to understand the world of matter the alchemist, accord-ing to Jung, "projected the unconscious into the darkness of matter in order to illuminate it. In order to explain the mystery of matter he projected yet another mystery—his own unknown psychic background—into what was to be explained."[19] The alchemist "experienced his projection as a property of matter; but what he was in reality experiencing was his own unconscious."[20] What the alchemist really attempts to liberate is Mer-curius, or Christ, the world-creating deity imprisoned in matter.[21] Thus the alchemical process at root is both a type of the divine mythos of the God-man (Christ) temporarily imprisoned in mortal form (in matter), who by a sacrificial death redeems humankind and reconciles us with God,[22] and a paradigm of the Jungian individuation process, the evolution of the new self from a dissolution of the old personality.[23]

Hence what many critics may perceive in Cave Birds to be obscurantism and arcana-fetish is really a serious modernist attempt to recover worth-while cultural gold from the dross of the past—from one of the great West-ern cultural expressions of spirit—because that past culture contains im-portant statements about what constants are civilizing, enduring, and necessary for psychic health. Most of the specific alchemical allusions in Cave Birds have already been uncovered by Hirschberg and in an essay by Graham Bradshaw, after a pioneering chapter from Sagar.[24] Jung's three and

a half volumes on alchemy are of course the common source for the alchemical allusions of *Cave Birds*. The alchemical transformation in *Cave
Birds* repeats the central mythos of Hughes's third period, the lifting of
matter into spirit through the auspices of the creative imagination. As in
the "Epilogue" of *Gaudete*, the transformation encompasses both the Eastern and Western paths of Hughes's two-way journey toward Reality; the
aforementioned Sufi *Conference of the Birds*, written by the medieval Persian
poet Farid ud-Din Attar, functions as an Eastern source that often parallels
and enriches the motifs of *Cave Birds*.

Though alchemical texts vary enormously in the chemical substances
used, the method, and the goal to be achieved, Jung finds a commonality
in the stages of the process. After specifying a *prima materia* or matter containing the potential for spiritual development, the alchemist separates the
ore into parts, just as the psyche experiences a split when the old self-
image no longer functions. The second stage contains a two-part *nigredo* or
confrontation with blackness: first the experience of libidinal withdrawal,
and a confrontation with the Shadow, and then a descent of the fallen ego
into the unconscious, a killing (*mortificatio*) of the material or old self-
image and an experiencing of its decay (*putrefactio*), just as Osiris was dismembered and enclosed in a coffin. The third stage concerns an ascent as
the animus and anima (*sponsus* and *sponsa*) are made conscious. A *destillatio* follows, a purification (*mundificatio*) of the personality so that a *coagulatio* or union of *sponsus* and *sponsa* can occur. This yields a sublimation into spirit, the whiteness (*albedo*) and the rich redness (*rubedo*) of
liberation, illumination. The process ends with the realization of the alchemical *lapis* or philosopher's stone, which Jung interprets as the psychological event of acquiring the gemlike hardness of the new self as a creative
tension of conscious and unconscious contents.[25] The alchemical transformation primarily applies to the person in the second half of life, already
having consolidated and stabilized the ego and acquired security and social position, who then is naturally concerned with the larger cultural aims
of comprehension of self and world through spiritual enlargement.[26] Loose
parallels occur in Eastern sources like Attar, in the sense that Sufis must
divest themselves of material possessions and needs, vanquish fears related
to their former habituation to material desires, and then awaken the inner
self. They must die to their old materialistic selves in order to experience
an illumination characterized by being lost in an ardent love for God and
all creation—*faná.*[27]

"The knight," the first B group poem of *Cave Birds*, presents an initial
stage in this transformation process. The Knight conquers by divesting

himself of material spoils and becoming himself the *prima materia* capable of liberation as he fuses with the earth—with roots, rain, and "mineral stasis." To grow as adults Jung counsels that we must learn to *let go* (Lao Tzu's *wu wei*), to "let things happen in the psyche" and trust in our own knightlike integrity, devotion to self-development, and patience.[28] Through his flawless submission, the patience of Hughes's Knight "grows only more vast." His remaining weapons are his inner powers—his intuition and his reason, a faculty often misused for analysis and rationalization. Through his submission the Knight can glimpse ever-stronger intimations of his future self: the sun that "Strengthens its revelation" at the end of the poem is an alchemical symbol for the *rubedo* as the final goal of illumination.[29] The Knight's divestiture corresponds to the first valley of Attar's Sufi quest, disencumbering oneself of all material cares and attachments, surrendering all, possessing nothing.[30] Unlike the aggressive Knight in section III of "Gog" (British *Wodwo*), Hughes's Knight in *Cave Birds* remains in a receptive state of nonaction, wrapped only in the banner of his own integrity.

"The gatekeeper" (B-4) alludes to the castle Porter or gatekeeper in Johann Christian Andreae's *Chymical Wedding of Christian Rosencreutz*, a seventeenth-century alchemical romance that Hughes originally worked on for over a year just after Plath's suicide.[31] The Gatekeeper is a sort of wounded Fisher King who has mistaken the erotic in nature for the spiritual goal of the alchemical opus; this earns him banishment from the King and Queen (the alchemical *sponsus* and *sponsa*) and a lowly position outside the castle as gatekeeper until another offender relieves him of his duty. In Andreae's romance the hero, Christian Rosencreutz, makes that same mistake: he succumbs to viewing the naked Venus in a room of the castle he was expressly forbidden to enter.[32] Rosencreutz berates himself for his ignorance and for confessing his offense when the previous gatekeeper enters to demand his freedom; here Rosencreutz speaks of his "tormented," "wretched," "miserable condition."[33] To arrive at the castle Rosencreutz originally chooses one of several paths while being preoccupied by a raven attacking a white dove. The raven and dove both signify his desire for the alchemical transformation, for the raven is the *caput corvi* or raven's head (the skull or psyche as the vessel of the alchemical transformation), and the white dove is Mercurius or Christ as Holy Ghost (the spirit to be liberated from matter).[34] Rosencreutz by taking this path expresses his zeal to become transformed, but his progress later in the *Wedding* indicates imperfect dedication and flawed self-discipline.

The persona of Hughes's "The gatekeeper" appears to be experiencing the moment of revelation of his imperfect self-discipline. He has chosen his path, the "simple fork in the road," but he has erred and is in the process of coming to grips with his transgression. He is both the offender preoccupied with eros *and* the "stranger who wails out your name"—the gatekeeper (his own conscience) about to convict him. "Remorse" then arrives "Blurting from every orifice." In *Cave Birds*, however, the confession earns the persona a second chance. In his BBC poem introductions Hughes writes that the convicted persona is swallowed by a raven, emerges as a crow, and is accepted for new trials and adventures in the heaven of the eagles. Here Hughes conflates the eagle flight of shamanic magical powers with the eagle as the final form of the freed Mercurius, the liberated spirit in alchemy.[35] At the conclusion of "The gatekeeper" the eagle that nails the persona with his talons conveys the violence of shamanic initiation, the imperative to experience the total death of the ordinary self in order to acquire the shaman's visionary powers. The shamanic/alchemic drama of personal suffering begins, with the hope of spiritual liberation.

"A flayed crow in the hall of judgment" (B-3) presents the persona of *Cave Birds* undergoing the requisite pain. The darkness of self-annihilation in the poem describes a consummation by raven, the *nigredo* state of total blackness in alchemy that parallels the dissolution of the personality in the individuation process.[36] The "globe of blot" is the black sun, the *putrefactio* of decomposition.[37] Yet even in total dissolution the persona anticipates a future ascent: the eagle feather talisman, kept beside the initiate on his first night, ensures the North American Indian shaman the future attainment of healing powers and magical flight.[38] In Hughes's poem the feather is more ambivalent: it is both a hope for success—"What feathers shall I have?"—and an expression of anxiety, a weighty fear that is paradoxically as light as a "feather on a hand." At the conclusion of the poem the persona experiences the violent shamanic initiatory pain of having his skin flayed, as in offerings of captive warriors' skins to the flayed Aztec god Xipe.[39] The hall of judgment in the poem title refers to the pervasive sense of moral culpability in primitive cultures, often expressed in crude rituals of human sacrifice. One finds judgment scenes, including imagery of scales, weighing, and punishment, in the *Bardo Thödol*, *The Egyptian Book of the Dead*, and even in the *Chymical Wedding of Christian Rosencreutz*. The persona undergoes his judgment and annihilation of the old self-image with a Knightlike equanimity: "I shall not fight / Against whatever is allotted me."

"The baptist" (B-2) extends the *putrefactio* state of personality dissolution by combining alchemical allusions with imagery of the coffin-enclosed

Osiris. Both water and salt are ambivalent symbols in alchemy; they first further the process of dissolution and then assist in the transformation. *Aqua permanens* first dissolves the *prima materia* into the four elements and then transforms the elements into the *albedo* by animating the inert matter, just as the officiant of the Christian baptismal ceremony first divides the water into four parts as he makes the sign of the cross over it prior to performing the rite of rebirth into Christ.[40] Hughes also connects the water with the Osiris-like mummy bandages suggested by Baskin's drawing for this poem, which Hughes titled "A Maze Pelican." We know from Shakespeare (*Hamlet*, IV:v:146; *King Lear*, III:iv:73) that the Pelican suckles its young with its own blood, a nourishing water. The bitter salt of alchemy ultimately transmutes metals into spirit, but initially expresses the imperfections of the *prima materia*.[41] The Hughes poem dramatizes how the Knight undergoes the imperative to "dissolve, in the cool wholesome salts . . . drop by drop." In the *Chymical Wedding* Rosencreutz exchanges his water and salt for tokens of entrance into the castle.[42] The water and salt in Andreae and in "The baptist" adumbrate both the human imperfections in need of transmutation and obscure psychic powers within the self that purge and then nourish, providing the tenacity needed for personality development. Ultimately they fructify the "seed in its armour," a symbol for the *lapis*.[43]

Hughes underscores the importance he places upon suffering to earn illumination in "A green mother" (B-5). The hero must reject what Hughes calls in his BBC introductions an "easy option"—easy because this illusory anima projection minimizes the pain necessary for transformation. Every corner of the earth contains a cradling "heaven," according to this mother; it is almost as if by repeating the word "heaven" nearly a dozen times she expects to bewilder the hero into submission. Personality transformation is a much more complex matter than simply developing a symbiotic attachment to a maternal figure, however; it necessitates a clear understanding of the paradoxical truths contained in "A riddle" (B-6). Enduring real suffering also demands that the hero relinquish aspects of the conscious self-image directed toward public show. "The scapegoat" (B-7) drives out the showman in the self through ridicule, overstatement, and an absurdly long catalogue of disparaging terms: the "frilled lizard of cavort," the "baboon of panoply," the "comedian," "joker," and "champion of swoon."

As in the epigraph quotation to this chapter, the wings of the spirit rise from one's inner world once inner and outer worlds are reconciled and the psyche has achieved wholeness. "The guide" (B-8) presents a positive anima image speaking with strength in forthright declarations:

Where the snow glare blinded you
I start.
Where the snow mama cuddled you warm
I fly up. I lift you.

Tumbling worlds
Open my way

And you cling.

The content and mood of "The guide" are similar to Attar's fourth valley, the discovery of self-sufficiency and personal resources. Often Attar presents the attainment of these personal resources in imagery of a blazing fire.[44] The red and black winds that emanate from the "flame wind" in "The guide" cleanse the hero of attachment to worldliness by emptying and scouring. Hughes may have been alluding to the red and black imagery associated with the karmic winds of the *Sidpa Bardo*; *nirvana*—liberation through release from phenomenal existence in the *Bardo*—is literally translated from the Sanscrit as "blown-out," a cessation of wind, as in the "non-wind" of line 18 of "The guide." In the breath control of yoga the "non-wind" would certainly be "a least breath." The concluding image of the magnetic needle perfectly conveys the anima's power to orient the male and point the way toward self-reliant toil and effort. The earlier Scolar Press edition of "The guide" contained an extra stanza that emphasizes the arduous labor needed to attain a state of self-sufficiency: "The chick ruptures its shell, then stops, dazzled. / I have not stopped." The anima aids in motivating the effort and toil that ultimately raise consciousness from the birth stagger of nature to the knowledge and illumination of culture.

Hughes in his BBC radio introductions to *Cave Birds* poems connected the wings imagery of "The guide" with a stage in the hero's adventure in the heaven of eagles: "It seems as if his real journey through the heaven of eagles were only just beginning." Actually, a careful reading of these introductory notes reveals that Hughes intended the hero's adventure in the heaven of the eagles to be a central motif, a modernist organizing of a complex text through an extended metaphor. Hughes specifically directs his radio audience to the eagle world adventure in no less than ten of his last sixteen poem introductions. In the poems and the BBC introductions Hughes connects the eagle adventure with the solar symbolism. His introductory comment for "Walking bare" (B-9), for instance, is "At the same time he seems to be journeying into the sun." This helps the radio audience to key upon the wings imagery of "Walking bare" at the same time that it clarifies the poem's concluding image. The hero has just achieved the "gem" of himself—what Sagar in a perfect turn of phrase calls the hero's "irreducible core of selfhood."[45] The gem image recollects the shaman's achievement of magical powers and the yogin's diamond body of permanent, achieved selfhood.[46] Paralleling this is the wings imagery of ascent to illumination, with the hero merging with the sun in the concluding image, becoming "a spark in the breath / Of the corolla that sweeps me."

Hughes draws upon alchemy, shamanism, and primitive and Oriental art for the solar eagle symbolism that aids in knitting together the A, B, and C groups of poems. In alchemy the eagle signifies the spirit liberated from matter; it symbolizes Mercurius in his final spirit form and also the anima in its creative aspect.[47] Jung notes that in the *Rosarium Philosophorum* eagles flying upward with flaming feathers repeat "the miracle of the phoenix, of transformation . . . of the *nigredo* into the *albedo*, of unconscious into illumination."[48] Graves observes that the mythical phoenix was actually an eagle as calendar beast, representing the Sun-God at the Sun Temple of On-Heliopolis; it was burned alive with spices in a nest of palm branches to inaugurate a new Phoenix Age every 1,460 years, for the Egyptians had no leap year and the extra quarter day accumulated until it produced an entire Phoenix Year of leap days (365×4 equals 1460). This bird became entirely mythical, later becoming a type of Christ's rebirth, after Augustus stabilized the Egyptian calendar in 30 B.C.[49] Jung also links the eagle with Sol, a spirit that, when united with Luna or body, produces an alchemical union of opposites—spirit and body, consciousness and unconsciousness—in the marriage of *sponsus* and *sponsa*.[50] The resurrected Hercules becomes an eagle sitting in the sun (cf. the *Gaudete* "Epilogue" poem #21), and Ezekiel in visionary rapture perceives a sun with eagle's wings.[51] Shamanic initiation, as in "The gatekeeper," often commences with the initiate being carried aloft or to an underworld by an eagle.[52] In "The gatekeeper" the eagle expresses the violent power of initiatory seizure.

The ur-source for all eagle symbolism is probably the solar eagle of Sumerian art that signified both the predatory power and the revitalizing energy of the sun, the great hunter who vanquishes all carrion in the cosmic round.[53] Joseph Campbell, discussing the solar eagle on a Sumerian cylinder seal of c. 3500 B.C., interprets it to mean in context a "life-in-being-through-mutual-killing," a "self-consuming, ever-dying, ever-living generative energy that is the life and death of all things."[54] This insight, set beside Hughes's comment in the epigraph to this chapter about how contemporary Western civilization's repudiation of Christian myths merely returns life to the elemental world of primitive cultures, explains (to skip forward a moment) the enigmatic ending of "Something was happening" (C-7):

> And when I saw new emerald tufting the quince, in April
> And cried in dismay: 'Here it comes again!'
> The leather of my shoes
> Continued to gleam
> The silence of the furniture
> Registered nothing
>
> The earth, right to its far rims, ignored me.
>
> Only the eagle-hunter
> Beating himself to keep warm
> And bowing towards his trap
> Started singing
>
> (Two, three, four thousand years off key.)

The persona has reached such a cul-de-sac that he is completely numb, unable to respond to the suffering woman in the poem and unable to relate even to the ordinary furniture of his environment. The eagle-hunter begins singing because the hero's psyche, given the abandonment of Christian myths by contemporary civilization, reverts to primitive myth to heal him. Four thousand years ago he would have been singing on key in the primitive belief system. Hughes's introductory comment to "Something was happening" is that "While the hero undergoes his vigil a helper begins to work for him calling on the eagles." This "helper" is both the eagle-hunter and the eagle he summons, a helping spirit of the shaman.[55] High in the mountain cold the eagle-hunter generates body heat vicariously to keep warm and to begin his ecstatic journey. He bows toward his trap to signify his reverence for that principle of immortal life that forever emanates and returns and to appease his moral sense through the shared sympathy in mutual killing that he senses in the eye-stare of the game he captures.[56]

Bradshaw voices reservations about the applicability of the shamanic journey to contemporary civilization, for shamans operated in a shared community of belief, may have been highly neurotic or even schizophrenic, and may have taken great liberties with truth and the laws of nature to convince the audience that their bodies actually experienced dismemberment and flight.[57] But from a modernist standpoint these comments are imperceptive. The important point is that whole communities for many centuries and in very different geographical areas—from Siberia to Sumatra, Nepal to North America—found shamanic techniques psychologically efficacious and demanded these healing techniques at times of crisis or of spiritual impasse. The paradigm and its effects are important, not the performer or methods. Shakespeare knew that it makes no difference whether Gloucester actually falls off a cliff or falls six feet onto the stage boards; what is important is that he believes in himself again, that he experiences the feeling of psychological renewal.

Hughes emphasizes the sun energy of rebirth in his BBC introductory comment to "The owl flower" (B-10): "The sun being in its aspect of benevolence is an owl which is also a flower. The judgment of the eagles, evidently, is that he should be reborn." Hughes entitled this drawing "An Owl Flower," and we can see Hughes finding in the flowerlike circularity and completeness of the Baskin drawing a mandala of psychic integration and wholeness, as in Jung's discussion of mandalas.[58] The poem functions as a magnet that draws together many recurrent images: the coffin and seed images of "The baptist"; the plumes or feathers of "The plaintiff" and "A flayed crow in the hall of judgment"; the flower of "The plaintiff"; the skin imagery of "The accused," "First, the doubtful charts of skin," and "A flayed crow in the hall of judgment"; the egg imagery of "A flayed crow in the hall of judgment"; and earth and sun imagery from *Cave Birds* poems too numerous to mention. We can appreciate the pyrotechnic craft of welding these disparate images together, but none of the images themselves are sufficiently extended to arrest and give pleasure. The poem becomes a catalogue that attempts to combine so much through the fusing power of conscious craft that the metaphoric enjambment becomes transparent, as in "The mummy grain is cracking its smile / In the cauldron of tongues," or "The egg-stone / Bursts among broody petals." Smiling in a cauldron and broody petals are contrived; they smack of that heterogeneous yoking of ideas through conceits that Dr. Johnson in his *Life of Cowley* believes does not move the affections. We can see how "bursts" relates to flowers and how "broody" refers to egg-hatching, but the transposition is too unusual and insufficiently sustained to matter, even though the formal welding does suggest the content, an achieved integration of the personality.

A comparison of the early and final versions of "A riddle" (B-6), the only remaining B group poem not discussed thus far, reveals other organizational motifs Hughes developed as he integrated the twelve C group poems into *Cave Birds*. The early Scolar Press version, entitled "A Monkey-Eating Eagle: Incomparable Marriage," is completely different from the final trade version; only the final stanzas of each and some similarities in content mark them as two versions of the same poem. Hughes read the early Scolar Press version in his BBC radio reading of 26 May 1975, though this broadcast contained all twelve C group poems and a near-final ordering of the sequence. Hence the revision of "A Monkey-Eating Eagle: Incomparable Marriage" into "A riddle" must have been one of his final major changes in organizing *Cave Birds*.

The early Scolar Press version begins with the legal imagery typical of the A group poems. But stanzas III and IV introduce a theme not developed in either the A or B groups—the self-indictment of the professional artist for callous indifference. This motif, one of the central themes in the C group poems, may have originated in these stanzas, even though Hughes did not revise "A Monkey-Eating Eagle: Incomparable Marriage" until after he completed the C group poems:

> The thought behind your eye, so lightly fleeting,
> Wrought a question
> In hooked letters of iron
> From which you now hang. I am that shape.
> And you are all I have.
> Just as I am all you can see.
> A forged face of brass perforce ravenous
> For its creator.[59]

Here Hughes adds a new dimension to his hero-persona. Stanza III identifies the process of composition as self-examination, a theme developed only in the C group poems, a questioning where the very words shackle the persona to the page as if to dungeon torture. The nixielike anima, not yet a completely positive figure at this juncture, takes the poetic shape of his suffering. But from here on, the early version of the poem lapses into the sort of directness and bald statement that Hughes regularly edits out of his poems. The C group poems personalize *Cave Birds* by adding a level of introspection and emotional candor that reminds one of the Camera Eye sections in Dos Passos's *U.S.A.* trilogy, except that in the C group poems of *Cave Birds* the moral sensitivity derives from self-indictment instead of social analysis or expressions of moral outrage.

The final version of B-6, "A riddle," uses paradox extensively as a means ot presenting what Jung calls transconscious facts, facts too deep for normal conceptual logic.[60] Paradox underscores another theme developed primarily in the C group, the compensatory nature of the unconscious.[61] In "A riddle" the hero's psyche authors or fathers the anima, and in personality integration the anima becomes his bride. As an archetype of healing energy the anima mothers his rebirth. This approximates the mythic paradox embodied in Isis as sister, bride, and mother of Osiris, with the only difference being that between daughter and sister. Stanzas III through XI of "A riddle" reinforce in both form and content the compensatory nature of the anima as an archetype from the unconscious. The first line of each stanza indicates progress in consciousness only; this leads to aggressive self-interest, with the unconscious compensating by absorbing the damage. But when stripped of these willful activities, as in the conscious choice of "The knight," the anima in the last three stanzas takes on a maieutic function, assisting the hero in the process of rebirth. The compensatory activity of the unconscious in the C group poems supports the New Critical principle that form and content are inseparable. It is as if Hughes, having already composed the C group poems, decided to make one of his last major thematic revisions a central organizational statement for *Cave Birds*. The twin themes of composing poems as self-examination and the compensatory nature of the unconscious pervade the C group poems. In this last group of *Cave Birds* poems Hughes's poet-persona wrestles with self-incrimination and guilt for having neglected what Clausen calls "the world outside the poem."

The C group poems articulate the exact nature of the crime against the feminine that the static A group poems only hint at. "The scream" (C-1), the opening poem of the trade editions of *Cave Birds*, introduces a persona lolling at ease, complacent in the happy miracle of life, where everything in nature is "doing a good job." Stanzas V through IX, however, introduce something between sardonic self-deprecation and dramatic irony, for here the persona indicts himself for moral callousness at the suffering of others. The persona of "The scream" exhibits a Parzival-like lack of *caritas* especially for those who suffer in the real world beyond his doorstep:

> And the inane weights of iron
> That come suddenly crashing into people, out of nowhere,
> Only made me feel brave and creaturely.

> When I saw little rabbits with their heads crushed on roads
> I knew I rode the wheel of the galaxy.

Calves' heads all dew-bristled with blood on counters
Grinned like masks, and the sun and moon danced.

And my mate with his face sewn up
Where they'd opened it to take something out
Raised a hand—

He smiled, in half-coma,
A stone temple smile.

The persona's culturally trained feelings of superiority over nature lead to insensitivity and indifference while a manic egotism reigns. "The scream" concludes with an enantiodromic eruption of the unconscious in a way that automatically convicts the persona of his guilt. The "stone temple smile" of the lobotomized mate leads to a painful recognition of guilt metaphorically presented as an Aztec torture sacrifice, where atop a stone temple obsidian daggers assisted in cruel acts of maiming, flaying, or tearing out the heart of a victim.[62] Again Hughes's comment reprinted in the epigraph to this chapter applies: "Without religion. . . . the whole inner world has become elemental, chaotic, continually more primitive and beyond our control."

The primitivized inner world rears up in protest in "After the first fright" (C-2). The "he" of the poem is the Summoner of A-1, the previous poem in the trade editions. As in "A riddle," attempts to use logic and rational thinking inevitably lead to self-serving rationalizations in an obstinate attempt to maintain one's innocence. The unconscious responds with typical primitive attempts to recognize the guilt and appease one's sense of morality through mourning—chopping off one's fingers or committing harakiri—while consciousness evades. Finally, when the conscious self becomes completely bewildered and lapses into apathy, the unconscious appears to die. The conscious mind, locked in the vise grip of rational logic, refuses to allow the unconscious its compensatory activity, and the unconscious gives up, exhausted with ever more extreme manifestations of primitive morality that go entirely unrecognized. This is the substance behind Hughes's BBC introductory comment to "After the first fright": that the hero "cannot understand the sequence of cause and effect." The cause-effect form of these unrhymed yet almost closed coupletlike tropes intersects perfectly with the content.

The real brilliance of the poem, however, resides in the Browning-like self-revelation through dramatic irony. The persona's protestations mark him as an erudite man of letters, the same one we encountered in the first version of B-6. His protestations about "Civilization" amount to an elaborate screen to mask moral turpitude. He simply does not care about real human suffering. Dante would place this persona in one of the lower bolgias, as a conscious deceiver lacking in love. His complaints about the need for "Sanity" and his strident appeals to "Civilization" sound all too familiar: they are the clichés of the university address. "A Tumbled Socratic Cock," Hughes's title for the drawing that parallels "The accused," and the hemlock allusion in "The executioner" indicate that Hughes through his poet-persona is satirizing the development of Western civilization since the time of Socrates as one where utility, dialectical logic, and the love of learning have deluded us into believing that the advancement of consciousness can by itself solve the riddles of existence. Nietzsche similarly criticizes Socrates in sections 12 through 18 of *The Birth of Tragedy*. Plato in his *Dialogues* relies upon Socratic dialectics and analytic reason to develop distinctions between body and soul, substance and accident, form and content, and so forth. Nietzsche goes so far as to state that the Socrates created by Plato in the *Dialogues* is the "archetype and progenitor" of science.[63] Hughes, before reading "After the first fright," informed his radio audience that the hero "protests as an honorable Platonist, thereby re-enacting his crime in front of his judges." The reverberations of "After the first fright" definitely encompass the world outside the poem.

The anima tries to revive the rationalizing persona by confronting him with his offense in "She seemed so considerate" (C-3). The puzzled hero does not understand why he sniffs decadence in the comments of his coterie of admirers. The persona as poet appears to be satisfied with past successes; he rests on his laurels like the "Famous Poet" in *The Hawk in the Rain*, but his anima, here in its aspect of poetic intuition, tries to lure him back into life—like Ripley's anima in *The Wound*. Her statement that "your world has died" at once relates to both the moral and the esthetic realms. The comment makes the persona realize that the sanguine optimism voiced in the opening stanzas of "The scream" is morally shallow and really reveals the lack of any supportive relationship between self and nature at the same time that it reveals the lack of any recent forward progress in his art. Hughes deliberately links the two worlds of reference in a sort of moral gestalt to underscore the position that art must relate to the world outside the poem.

The dead "pet fern" of line 11 reinforces the persona's esthetic limbo. The "pet fern" relates to the persona's self-concept as artist through a very personal, oblique allusion to the dying and reviving vegetation spirit Jack-in-the-Green in Frazer.[64] Hughes's poem "Fern" (*Wodwo*) presents the poet as orchestra conductor of a surrealistic concerto, and in the 1975 Ilkley Festival exhibition program Hughes comments that "Fern" relates to an old childhood photograph of "the 'Jack in Green' or Green Man, with his two attendant garlands and bearers, the bringers of spring." Art, a product of the psyche, also needs periodic revitalization. The persona's art has become a house pet to be stroked—a lovepet—not an art that grapples with significant human suffering. The hero feels that life has canceled him, but he has just enough honesty and intuition left to follow his anima's lead.

"In these fading moments I wanted to say" (C-5) continues the anima's arraignment of the persona's moral turpitude, alleging that his craft has been a "cold business" of landscapes, not of people and their pain. The hero protests his innocence again and makes a facile attempt to convince her that he has sensitivity to human suffering. But his use of the famous incident of the Buddhist monk who committed suicide by pouring gasoline over himself and lighting it to protest the Viet Nam War only proves his hollowness. He coopts impeccable moral virtue to suit his comfortable circumstances, and the shift in context has all the telling dramatic irony of Browning at his best:

> How imbecile innocent I am
>
> So some perfect stranger's maiming
> Numbs me in freezing petroleum
> And lights it, and lets me char to the spine

By the end of the poem the persona has lost every bit of his artistic integrity by protesting his innocence, and with it any sense of meaningful relationship with the natural world: "The whole earth / Had turned in its bed / To the wall." After much suffering and personality realignment, the hero finally regains a satisfactory relationship with his environment near the end of the sequence, in "Walking bare" (B-9): "The stones do not cease to support me. / Valleys unfold their invitations."

"First, the doubtful charts of skin" (C-6) presents the hero's personal realization of his guilt. Echoes of the quest journeys of Odysseus and the Grail Quester combine with imagery of the human anatomy to suggest that the real journey here is an interior one: from the hero's extremities through his digestive tract, into the blood and up to the brain and the bestialized unconscious, the "skull-hill of visions and the battle in the valley of screams." His unconscious reveals the truth of the matter, in a vision of his own gravestone. On the gravestone his unconscious chisels the truth—that he has used the world for his own selfish purposes. The "weapons" of the epitaph recollect the "useful-looking world, a thrilling weapon" in the *Gaudete* "Epilogue" poem #4, and the weapons produced by the visor slits of aggressive utility in "O White Elite Lotus."[65] The analytic ego has been his principal weapon; a utilitarian attitude toward the world has produced the moral callousness. This is the substance of the transgression against the feminine in nature. The quest imagery also introduces the new adventure of the persona as a crow in the world of eagles, as Hughes notes in his BBC introduction to this poem.

The doubt expressed in "Something was happening" (C-7) appears once again to parallel the persona's neglect of the sufferings of an unidentified female figure. The doubt at one level indicts the persona of negligence in the development of his craft and at another indicts him for his moral complacency. The poem appears to contain oblique biographical allusions. Plath had no sister to get "the call from the hospital," but the dedicatory poem to *Remains of Elmet* indicates that Hughes's mother Edith Farrar Hughes died around 1973, about two years before the Ilkley Festival. In "Something was happening" the admission of failure to attend the sufferings of a female figure merits a very positive event—the appearance of the previously discussed shamanic helper, the eagle-hunter of primitive cultures.

The dropped poem C-4, "Your mother's bones wanted to speak, they could not," printed in *The Achievement of Ted Hughes*, considers the mother's death as a reminder that both heredity *and* moral culpability appear in one's every action. The poet-persona's words imprint the state of his soul in every line; they carve his "signature in the papery flesh," and any coldness or moral turpitude will show. The dead bones of his mother reprimand every lax line of verse. Her death may be "unarguable" fact, but the poem argues that she suffers for his every failure to heed her moral imperatives.

More than any other poem in *Cave Birds*, "Something was happening" foreshadows Hughes's third period in important nonbiographical ways. The poem intimates that artistic doubt contributes to the death of the feminine figure. The persona vacillates in his quest and wonders "'Ought I to turn back, or keep going?' / Her heart stopped beating, that second." This is readily understood in Jungian psychology as an artistic impasse causing an atrophied anima. But Hughes's lines probe deeper, revealing a Blakean attitude toward the act of perception that becomes a cornerstone of the third-period works. For Blake, who prefers Berkeley over Locke, the act of perception is an imaginative one, an organizing and interpreting of the world. "Reality" for Blake is mental; it is the "Imaginative Form" accorded the object in the mind of the perceiver.[66] Hence in "The Mental Traveller" Blake writes that "the Eye altering alters all," and, in the "Annotations to Reynolds," "As the Eye—Such the Object."[67] The imaginative organization of reality into art is the only true reality for Blake; thus the famous lines in the letter to Trusler: "to the Eyes of the Man of Imagination Nature is Imagination itself. As a man is So he Sees."[68] In the "Auguries of Innocence" Blake ridicules the doubt of Descartes and the empiricists that can only separate subject from object: "He who Doubts from what he sees / Will neer Believe do what you please."[69] By questioning his progress the persona of "Something was happening" can only experience numbness as his imaginative vision splits into inner world doubt and the cold objectivity of outer world empiricism.

The surgical metaphor of "Only a little sleep, a little slumber" (C-8) presents the removal of the persona's former self-concept, after which progress occurs. Hughes writes in his BBC introductory comments that once the hero recognizes his "total dependence on the help of the Eagles" he begins to feel the "first stirrings of humanity again." By questioning the eagle at the end of the poem the persona finally shows concern for another. "As I came, I saw a wood" (C-9) reminds him to be wary of delusory anima projections in his very vulnerable state. He must earn salvation through further suffering, not through accepting easy solutions. As in Attar's third valley of Understanding, effort is all-important.[70] The paradise offered in "As I came, I saw a wood" is that of the visionary unitive moment, an Eliadian prelapsarian communion with animals and nature. But the poem ends with the persona's realization that survival through suffering in a postlapsarian world of carrion is a prerequisite for such visionary moments.

The last three C group poems reveal gradual progress in the hero's attempts to find the right relationship with the feminine portion of his personality. "After there was nothing there was a woman" (C-10) presents a feminine figure just learning to care for herself and to understand her surroundings. She has worked her way up the evolutionary scale to liberate consciousness from the *prima materia*, yet she still has strong memories of her origins in the elemental world of excrement and the predatory. The parts of her body connect and unify from various places, as in the reconstitution of Osiris through the ministrations of Isis, or as in Attar's fifth valley, where a broken reality once again unifies and all existence partakes of a single wholeness.[71] The persona's vision is beginning the delicate task of personality reintegration.

The ascent toward the alchemical marriage of *sponsus* and *sponsa*—body and spirit, conscious and unconscious life—continues in "His legs ran about" (C-11). Here the masculine and the feminine in the hero grope toward mutuality and unity like two teenage lovers fumbling through their first sexual encounter. In the afterglow of their final peace the hero resumes his right relationship to the earth. The first influx of this resumption appears in a splendid image of wonder, a "Rushing through the vast astonishment." Attar in his sixth valley would call this living in the state of imagination.[72]

The perfected *sponsus/sponsa* union occurs in the lovely "Bride and groom lie hidden for three days" (C-12), the concluding C group poem. The imagery of mechanical refurbishing indicates a mutual sharing and an infinite care for the other that is very different from the possessive love of "Lovesong" and the one-way giving of "The Lovepet," two *Crow* poems similarly concerned with changes in self and other in the love experience. This sharing brings the arrival of psychic reintegration. *Sponsus* and *sponsa* become the phoenix/eagle vaulting toward the sun; unconscious energies have become conscious in a new selfhood as the liberated spirit soars in illumination and renewed power:[73]

And he has fashioned her new hips
With all fittings complete and with newly wound coils, all shiningly oiled
He is polishing every part, he himself can hardly believe it
They keep taking each other to the sun, they find they can easily
To test each new thing at each new step

Hughes succeeds at what otherwise might be considered a catalogue of anatomical and mechanical parts by emphasizing an innocent freshness and amazement in the ministrations of the marriage pair:

He gives her her skin
He just seemed to pull it down out of the air and lay it over her
She weeps with fearfulness and astonishment

She has found his hands for him, and fitted them freshly at the wrists
They are amazed at themselves, they go feeling all over her

He has assembled her spine, he cleaned each piece carefully
And sets them in perfect order
A superhuman puzzle but he is inspired

The poem ends as the couple "bring each other to perfection" in the reciprocal caring and mutual sharing of a love directed beyond the self.

The art critic Kenneth Clark has written that the twelfth-century cult of the Virgin was typical of the Catholic Church's ability to civilize ordinary peasants through harmonizing their emotional life and instilling the virtues of tenderness and compassion. Aggressive, nomadic societies—Clark names Israel, Islam, and the Protestant North—developed paternalistic gods and little religious imagery. Clark concludes that "the great religious art of the world is deeply involved with the female principle."[74] In the White Goddess devotional poetry of the *Gaudete* "Epilogue" and in the anima poems of *Cave Birds*, we can see Hughes working his way out of the analytically oriented surrealism of his sixties poetry and harmonizing his own psyche as he accords the feminine greater importance as a healing, civilizing influence. *Remains of Elmet* and *River* are deeply civilizing volumes in their ability to reawaken in readers the feminine qualities of beauty, receptivity, and acquiescence to change. Neither volume could have been written, however, without the White Goddess meditations of the *Gaudete* "Epilogue" or the anima visions of *Cave Birds*.

What is really astonishing in *Cave Birds* is the naturalness and even the inevitability with which Hughes links the esthetic and feminine impulses with a moral sense that he apparently believes is indigenous (though in need of development) to the psyche. In the male the anima nurtures and strengthens this innate moral sense. The persona of *Cave Birds* achieves personality integration and compassion for the world of suffering beyond the self by paying attention to the ethical imperatives of the anima's early appearances—in "The interrogator" and the C group poems "She seemed so considerate" and "In these fading moments I wanted to say." Because Crow naively accepts the repression and quantification of his Western cultural myths—his "mishmash of scripture and physics"—he cannot perceive nature as his bride; the vision he realizes of his anima in "Crow's Undersong" is weak and dim, with a tank parked on his voice and Manhattan weighing on his eyelid. The persona of *Cave Birds* is more successful at achieving wholeness, because his imaginative life is more extensively developed. The gradually more perfect and arresting visions of the anima near the conclusion of *Cave Birds*—in "A riddle," "After there was nothing there was a woman," "The guide," "His legs ran about," and "Bride and groom lie hidden for three days"—ought to receive recognition by feminist readers and critics of Hughes. The connection between a reverence for the feminine in *Gaudete* and *Cave Birds* and the civilizing emotions aroused as a result of this reverence should command the attention of especially those British critics of Hughes who chronically bemoan the lack of any moral and ethical applicability to what Clausen calls the world outside the poem. Nevertheless the stale, disparaging tags continue: Alan Brownjohn finds no unity in form or conception in *Cave Birds*, and Calvin Bedient, Robert Nye, and Julian Symons glibly denounce the volume as a misanthropic, nihilistic flogging of the imagination with savage diction and imagery.[75]

Hughes's interleaving of the A, B, and C groups of *Cave Birds* poems creates a rich text where motifs from each group respond to each other in alternating rhythms of unity and polyphonic harmony. Yet the thematic progression conforms to a basic dramatic outline. The anima convicts the strutting cockerel of a prideful moral callousness; then he is swallowed by a raven, reborn with the tenacity and survival instincts of a crow, and carried aloft for humanizing trials in the spirit world of the eagles. The more studied motifs from alchemy and the solar eagle of primitive art complement the mysticism of Attar and the intense introspection and self-examination of the C group poems with graceful counterpoint. Main themes intersect near the end of the volume through the motifs of the *sponsus/sponsa* alchemical union, the wings imagery, and the eagle flight to the sun of renewed power and achieved selfhood.

"Something was happening" anticipates Hughes's third-period drama of perception, where the persona organizes reality through the power of a Blakean and Coleridgean imagination. The analytical surrealism and the criticism of Western culture in the main narrative of *Gaudete* is of a piece with Hughes's sixties surrealism, and both *Gaudete* and *Cave Birds* contain the sixties mythos of the Jungian visit to the underworld to heal the psyche. But the muted, restrained surrealism of the Gaudete "Epilogue" and *Cave Birds* and the elevation of the feminine in both works herald Hughes's third-period lifting of matter to spirit, and nature to culture, through the powers of the creative imagination.

In *The Conference of the Birds* only thirty birds survive the quest through seven valleys of toil and suffering to arrive at the door of His Majesty the Simurgh, who is more radiant than the sun. As they experience the intoxicating self-annihilation of Sufi *faná* in an outpouring of love for His Majesty, inner and outer worlds merge in a mystic consciousness of enlarged selfhood. They comprehend that the Simurgh (literally "thirty birds") is none other than themselves.[76]

Hughes's use of Attar, as with his use of *vacana* poetry in the *Gaudete* "Epilogue," is important but limited. According to Cyprian Rice, the *faná* of the Sufis comprises a mystic living "in and for another, in a sort of perpetual ecstasy . . . an absorption in God . . . accompanied by complete abstraction from the sense world and utter obliviousness to time and place."[77] Hughes in the last stanza of "The risen" and in "Finale" asserts very definitely that he adapts his Oriental sources to a predominately Western quest in time and human experience—for selfhood, spiritual renewal, and the enlargement of consciousness. Complete ascetic withdrawal from the world is too severe for his Western roots; he will soon favor the mysticism of Taoism because of its intense absorption in the natural world. Yet in the concluding image of merging with the sun in "Walking bare"— becoming "a spark in the breath / Of the corolla that sweeps me"—and in the astonished congruency of self and other in "Bride and groom lie hidden for three days," the Sufi beliefs of Attar coexist in moderated form with the alchemy and the solar eagle symbolism. As in the *Gaudete* "Epilogue," Hughes in *Cave Birds* reaches toward his third phase mythos of attaining an at-oneness in Being through either or both the Eastern and the Western portions of his two-way journey toward Reality.

CHAPTER 8

From
Emptiness to
Brighter
Emptiness
Remains of Elmet

1979

*The most impressive early companion of my child-
hood was a dark cliff, or what looked like a dark
cliff, to the South, a wall of rock and steep woods
half-way up the sky, just cleared by the winter sun.
This was the memento mundi over my birth: my
spiritual midwife at the time. . . . The first half of
the climb was over fields. . . . The second field be-
longed to the farms above. It was poorer, wilder,
steeper, and in it you began to feel a new sensation,
the volume of space, the unaccustomed weight of
open sky, and you saw that the ridge of Scout Rock
was a ridge below the further ridge of moor, and
moor was friendly. In the third much steeper field
you began to feel bird-like, with sudden temptings
to launch out in the valley air. . . . At that point
you began to feel the spirit of the moors, the pecu-
liar sad desolate spirit that cries in telegraph wires
on moor roads, in the dry and so similar voices of
grouse and sheep, and in the moist voices of curlews.*
—Hughes, 1964[1]

Some fifty or so miles northeast of Manchester
lies the Calder Valley, nestled in a cleft of the Yorkshire Pennines' jagged
spine. An hour's drive through the bleak industrial towns that envelop
Manchester reveals a valley of windswept grassland, terraced stone dwellings, and abandoned factories surrounded by the gentle slopes of the high
moors and separated from all else by tyrannical Pennine foothills. Here, in
Mytholmroyd, a village on the textile route but also near the Brontë country, Ted Hughes lived the first seven years of his life (1930–1937). Trips
back as an adult, after his parents returned to settle there once again in the
early fifties, periodically renewed Hughes's memories of his Yorkshire
childhood. This is the locale of the deeply meditative landscape poetry of
Remains of Elmet (1979).

Remains of Elmet comprises some sixty-two short meditative poems that
Hughes wrote in response to Fay Godwin's photos of the Calder Valley
landscape, mills, chapels, and graveyards. For Hughes the experience of
seeing these photos became a *recherche du temps perdu*, initiated in the introductory poem by a teacup conversation with his uncle, and dedicated

to the memory of his mother, Edith Farrar Hughes, now *"Six years into her posthumous life."*[2] Whereas Hughes fleshed out Baskin's *Cave Birds* drawings with the abstract organization of an alchemical individuation journey, Godwin's photos of concrete locales in his childhood opened deep wells of feeling and unlocked significant memories. Hughes articulates these feelings and memories in a rich context that entails an evaluation of the nurture and culture of his youth, and this produces a volume far superior to *Cave Birds*. Hughes informs us in a prefatory note that the Calder Valley in the early eighteen hundreds was "the cradle of the Industrial Revolution in textiles, and the upper Calder became 'the hardest-worked river in England.'" Throughout his lifetime Hughes "watched the mills of the region and their attendant chapels die" and observed the population, once "rooted for so long," change rapidly. Today the area is a clean air zone and the looms, factories, and pulpits remain only as remnants of Industrial Revolution culture suitable for viewing by tourists. Amid the soot-blackened stone dwellings of Heptonstall, just above Mytholmroyd, one can still visit the octagonal chapel where Wesley preached, and view the cottage of John Sutcliffe, the last hand-loom weaver of Heptonstall, who worked a seventy-hour week for 6s. 6d. until his death in 1902.

Hughes, however, grew up in the early thirties, when this Industrial Revolution culture still had enough impact upon the North Country to engrave its values upon the customs and habits of his relatives and neighbors. As Hughes meditates upon Godwin's photos, he assesses the effects of that culture and the maternal nurture of the moors upon his character. In *Elmet* Hughes's memories of his youth emerge in contrapuntal fashion, the good oscillating with the bad, and this opposition parallels and merges with a landscape opposition between the maternal nurture of the gentle moors and the paternal, authoritarian Pennine foothills that walled out the sun and trapped the smog of grimy machinery. In the poems Hughes often connects the soft feminine moor lines with the artistic, the liberating, and the imaginative in his childhood memories, and the stark Pennine hills with the rigidity of the Protestant ethic and the mechanistic science that produced the Industrial Revolution. Inevitably the paternal portion of Hughes's meditations deepens to connect once again the religion and the science with the violence of World War I, for the gravestones and cenotaphs of the Lancashire Fusiliers dot the hillsides and bring back memories of conversations with relatives about the Great War. *Remains of Elmet* does not, however, simply reiterate the sixties *enantiodromia* monomyth; instead the formal and thematic progression of the volume concern the muting and then the elimination of this monomyth as Hughes's spirit soars above the rock to a liberating, bird's-eye spiritual comprehension of the moors and his childhood.

As in a sonata, the form of *Remains of Elmet* entails developing a counterpoint between a dominant (Western science and religion) and a tonal (the nurture of the moors). The two clash throughout the volume within individual poems and in groups of poems until a resolution in the concluding poems of the volume finally eliminates the power of the dominant. This resolution occurs through applying the Oriental portion of Hughes's two-way journey, in this case by rejecting the analytic ego's obsessive desire to objectify and interpret a dead cultural past, and by releasing the spirits of Edith Farrar Hughes, Sylvia Plath, and other departed relatives into a heaven that becomes in part an extension of an awakened self's inner serenity.

The actual facts concerning the composition of *Remains of Elmet* support both the sonata form emphasis and the spiritual resolution. Hughes chose the opening and closing poems for *Elmet*, and then he and Fay Godwin together decided how to organize the sequence of photographs. Finally they decided which poems should appear next to which pictures; at this point Hughes most often accepted Godwin's choices. Though Hughes himself ordered the earlier Rainbow Press edition differently, the ordering of the trade editions does suit him. *Remains of Elmet* could not have reached its present trade edition form without his express consent. Hughes responded warmly to an earlier draft of this chapter that contained both the sonata form discussion and the ensuing spiritual resolution.[3]

By divesting himself of his analytic ego, the unvarying persona of *Elmet* soars in a birdflight release of imaginative vision. Once again form and content are inseparable in Hughes's poetry. By the end of the volume the persona smiles beneficently upon his past as he considers events and shifting landscapes chiefly as means to apprehending a Reality beyond the world of sense. An awakened self sees that beyond the flux of opposites the Light of ultimate Tao shines brightly. The spirit flight of a liberated imagination is possible in *Remains of Elmet* because the persona's perspective is supported by the animism and philosophy of the primitive and Taoist Chinese.

"Think often of the silent valley, for the god lives there," the opening line of the second poem, "Hardcastle Crags," and the only quoted passage in all of *Remains of Elmet*, is a Taoist proverb.[4] The proverb reinforces a mood of receptive meditation, an activation of the creative unconscious, by invoking the intuitive, shadowy, receptive, holistically perceiving *yin* principle of primitive and Taoist Chinese thought. The proverb specifically recalls the mysterious Valley Spirit of Lao Tzu (especially VI, XXV, XXVIII, LII, LXI) and Chuang Tzu (XXXIII).[5] The Tao—the eternal, unvarying Absolute, the order of things and the undifferentiated substance from which all derives— is likened to the Valley Spirit or the Mysterious Female when it enters the manifest world, particularly because of similarities concerning a dark, mysterious, womblike emptiness that houses all potential for renewal and rebirth.[6] In *Elmet* the persona's unassertive cultivation of an intuitive grasp of reality and his perception of the yielding, maternal qualities of earth as the locus of all transformation and renewal indicate an empathy with the Valley Spirit.

The earth in *Elmet* regularly manifests the traditionally female attributes of soft receptivity, mystery, change, renewal, and sympathy with creation. In "The Big Animal of Rock" the enigmatic "Festival of Unending" is the dynamic, ceaseless Taoist flux, the constant interplay of feminine *yin* and masculine *yang* in the phenomenal world, in which the "Mourning Mother / Who eats her children" simply represents a principle of decay and change. The presence of the Valley Spirit in *Elmet* assures the possibility of renewal in this flux; here "soil deepens" and decaying matter inevitably falls "into the only future, into earth" ("Lumb Chimneys"). The soft curves of the land are worshipped as a "Hill-sculpture," a "prone, horizon-long / Limb-jumble of near-female" ("The Weasels We Smoked Out Of The Bank"). Creation begins where the mothers "Gallop their souls" ("Where The Mothers"), and curlews rise "Out of the maternal watery blue lines" ("Curlews Lift"). New creation redeems the carnage of war when the "whole scene, like a mother, / Lifts a cry / Right to the source of it all" ("Long Screams").

Hughes's heightened sensitivity to the feminine principle in the Yorkshire landscape creates a positive context for those childhood memories that concern nature. Memories of smoking weasels from a river bank lead to a personification of the electric frenzy of the frightened animals as excess energy from demonic laborers who toil in the service of the "near-female" hill-sculpture ("The Weasels We Smoked Out Of The Bank"). From a Taoist perspective even memories of "The Sluttiest Sheep In England" on their "worthless moraines" can provide intuitions of an angelic power operating in nature:

> This lightning-broken huddle of summits
> This god-of-what-nobody-wants
> In his magnetic heaven

> Has sent his angels to stare at you
> In the likeness of beggars.

Under a main route bridge, below the rumble of textile lorries, Hughes in "The Long Tunnel Ceiling" recollects a face-to-face childhood encounter with a huge trout as a Taoist epiphany, a vision "Brought down on a midnight cloudburst / In a shake-up of heaven and the hills." Hughes articulates his vision with a genuinely childlike astonishment and innocent joy at an unexpected glimpse into the heart of nature amid the clatter of machinery. The trout becomes a treasured lily surviving under "tortured axles" and "A seed / Of the wild god now flowering for me."

The respect for nature in Chinese culture derives from the fact that the ancient Chinese developed their religious concepts from direct observation of natural phenomena. According to Mai-Mai Sze,

> The great unifying aim [of Chinese painting] has been to express *Tao*, the Way—the basic Chinese belief in an order and harmony in nature. This grand concept originated in remote times, from observation of the heavens and of nature—the rising and setting of sun, moon, and stars, the cycle of day and night, and the rotation of seasons—suggesting the existence of laws of nature, a sort of divine legislation that regulated the pattern in the heavens and its counterpart on earth.[7]

When one ceases to analyze nature and becomes absorbed in it and resigned to its cycles, one heeds Chuang Tzu's advice to "listen with [the] spirit." In a state of perfect stillness, of oneness with nature, Chuang Tzu believes that one can "fly . . . without wings," for then "the spirit is empty and waits on all things" (IV). Spirit flight, including returns to the pristine childhood intimations of the sacred, is possible when the persona attains a state of *tz'ŭ* sympathy so deep that he identifies with the maternal roots of love and compassion at the heart of nature. Hughes observed in conversation that the wings imagery in *Elmet* derived principally from discerning an icon of esthetic flight (✕✕) in the soft, undulating lines of the high moors, where "mown fields escape like wings" ("Hardcastle Crags").[8]

The primitive, pre-Taoist Chinese, according to Arthur Waley, developed a very strong belief in a reciprocal sharing between the heavenly and earthly realms. They developed a concept of soul based upon the primitive idea of a spirit entering an individual and residing there until death, after which it returns heavenward. Each individual functioned as an emanation of the divine, a link in an unending round of return to and exit from *T'ien* or heaven. The *ch'i* or "life-breath" and *hun*, the "cloud" or exhalation of breath on frosty mornings, signified to the predynastic Chinese the participation of the individual in the heavenly.[9] Chinese painting, especially from the Sung dynasty forward, often employs mists, clouds, and vast stretches of sky to convey the belief that the world of the spirit may unfold at any moment, or that the earthly may momentarily intrude upon the heavenly. The shifting cloudscapes of many *Elmet* poems convey just this sense that spiritual insight may be possible at any moment. Ancestral landscape spirits in "The Big Animal Of Rock" solemnly "visit each other in heaven and earth." The moors of *Elmet* "Are a stage for the performance of heaven" ("Moors"). The changing configurations of clouds tease the persona's imagination into visions of endlessly changing cycles of kings, queens, and champions. The "chapel of cloud" provides a pulpit and altar for the light-energy of masculine *yang*, "The Word That Space Breathes."

Significantly, the culture that influenced Hughes's youth—the Protestant ethic and mechanistic science—affords no moments of cleansing elevation. Rock and stone imagery in *Elmet* have both positive and negative values, but whenever Hughes alludes to the effects of the Industrial Revolution and the Protestant ethic in the context of this imagery, the values are negative: it conveys obstinacy or a heavy, exhausting weight or a ruthlessness in the employment of abstractions as mechanistic levers to pulverize stone or convert it to a rigid sameness. The pioneer hope of New World Puritans "squared stones" into rigid Euclidean forms, and the Industrial Revolution blackened stones with an obstinate "dogged purpose" ("Top Withens"). The people become "fixed" in attitudes as compulsively repetitious as their machines and architecture as they convert "their stony ideas / To woollen weave," taming the "Wild Rock" of the landscape. The effort to remake the land after the fashion of their "foursquare scriptures" tires the Christian soldiers into passive postures of television viewing—the contemporary expression, for Hughes, of an utterly exhausted cultural spirit ("When Men Got to the Summit"). The monotonous regularity of factory machinery is equally deleterious; it hypnotizes generation after generation into a "four-cornered, stony" rigidity ("Hill-Stone Was Content"):

> And inside the mills mankind
> With bodies that came and went
> Stayed in position, fixed like the stones
> Trembling in the song of the looms.

Rock and stone imagery in *Elmet* reveals the pervasively negative effects of a repetition-compulsion machine ethic upon even the landscape of the Calder Valley and the customs of its citizens. The "Happy work-hum of the valley mills" becomes "a fierce magnet" that pulls all into an "indrag of wet stony death" ("The Sheep Went On Being Dead"). The farms that sprang up beyond the "sunk mill-towns" become "stony masticators" that digest all into cemeteries ("Remains of Elmet"). Hughes describes the ubiquitous rock walls that divide the farmland into private property as "Spines that wore to a bowed / Enslavement" the labor of generations of men ("Walls"). And the "Forbidding forbidden stones" of graveyard cenotaphs characterize the local Council's authoritarian suppression ("Rhododendrons").

Hughes extends his cultural analysis in *Elmet* to include an interpretation of the historical roots of the Reformation and mechanistic science in England as a series of destructive conquests that ultimately lead to the Great War. The primitive, pre-Christian Celts with their Druidical spells, highly developed art, and their comparatively sedentary, loosely organized society, are supplanted by aggressive, overly rational, and anal retentive invaders—the first-century Romans, the fifth-century Angles and Saxons, and the ninth-century Vikings. In the character of such invaders, reasons Hughes, lie the seeds of our contemporary Western science and religion and the violence of modern warfare. The first sentence of the prefatory note to *Remains of Elmet* provides an important clue that relates this theme to many poems in the volume: the Calder Valley was the "last ditch of Elmet, the last British Celtic kingdom to fall to the Angles." The *Wodwo* poem "The Warriors of the North" is paradigmatic of the historical outlook that pervades *Elmet*. The "frozen swords" of "The Warriors of the North" are thawed by bloodshed and anal acquisitiveness: the conquering nomads covet "The fluttered bowels of the women of dead burghers, / And the elaborate, patient gold of the Gaels." Their reckless urges for conquest and booty perpetuate themselves, according to Hughes, in a utilitarian "cash-down, beforehand revenge" that flows into "the iron arteries of Calvin."

Hughes metaphorically presents the derelict factories of the Calder Valley in *Elmet* as a more recent variety of Viking invasion that has spent itself, ending in a plundering of towns and a rape of the environment by sullen progeny. After a debased "shuttle's spirit" wandered off to Japan and the cloth rotted on the looms, the battered, abandoned factories became in "Mill Ruins" the leftovers of roaming bands of Viking/English children who "Smashed all that would smash," "Levered loose and toppled down hillsides," and

Then trailed away homeward aimlessly
Like the earliest
Homeless Norsemen.

In "For Billy Holt," a poem commemorating a native resident of nearby
Todmorden whose wanderlust, involvement in the cloth trade, and social-
istic fervor elevated him to the status of local folk hero, Hughes locates the
genetic inheritance of the Viking invaders in an obstinate determination
seen even in the facial features of today's North Country English townsfolk:
"The longships got this far. Then / Anchored in nose and chin." From this
legacy arises a penchant for treating the environment with calculating abstractions and a menacing utilitarianism, "A far, veiled gaze of quietly /
Homicidal appraisal." The results are a ruthless reordering of nature
through conquest and abuse, a cutting of "rock lumps for words" and a
"requisition[ing]" of rain and hills, ultimately leaving a devastated "graveyard / For homeland." One is left to conclude that the icily calculating,
hardnosed progeny of continental invaders ultimately spawned the Industrial Revolution.

The obsessive regularity of the Protestant ethic and mechanistic science
leads to cries of pain and enantiodromic eruptions of violence. In "Hardcastle Crags" the landscape of "leaf-loam silence / Is old siftings of sewing
machines and shuttles" where a healing nature is engaged in the process of
repairing cultural wounds. Here the "beech tree solemnities / Muffle much
cordite," and

                                    the air-stir releases
        The love-murmurs of a generation of slaves
        Whose bones melted in Asia Minor.

The entire region appears to lament both "the bottomless wound of the
railway station / That bled this valley to death" and the countless cenotaphs
that dot the hillsides ("First, Mills"). Factory machinery drugs the landscape to a murderous pulse; in "The Sheep Went On Being Dead" the
"throb of the mills and the crying of lambs" rises to a fever pitch so that it
becomes too much "Like shouting in Flanders."

Not all cultural ideas are debilitating in *Remains of Elmet*. Hughes praises
the expansive, adventurous, exhilarating spirit of the Spanish and English
Renaissance that colonized America in "There Came Days To The Hills." He
analogizes this Renaissance spirit as a taut, sleek, heroic vessel leaving port

"Urgent and important" with "fluttering pennants" on a fine, "wind-slapped" day. In "Heptonstall Old Church" Hughes also admires the civilizing culture of medieval Christianity. The Church of St. Thomas à Becket, erected in Heptonstall in 1260 and a ruin since its roof collapsed in 1847, becomes in Hughes's words and in Fay Godwin's photographs the shrine where an uplifting cultural idea landed like "a great bird." The bare arches of the church, which stand so nakedly in Godwin's photograph, coax from the poet's animated spirit an image of a huge bird's carcass.

The culture created by the Industrial Revolution, however, does not draw the living out of rock with uplifting cultural ideas; it misdirects them toward "the wage-mirage sparkle of mills" and "the veto of the poisonous Calder" ("Sunstruck") and finally wears them down into early graves. The progress of the Industrial Revolution is from railway station to sacked villages, gravemounds, and "an empty helmet / With a hole in it" ("First, Mills"). Hughes's central assertion in his criticism of this culture is that it lacks vision: instead of raising people from the level of nature to the level of culture, it myopically drains them of whatever creative energy they possess and then erases their lives with the anonymity of cemeteries ("Walls"):

> Eyes that closed
> To gaze at grass-points and gritty chippings.
>
> Spines that wore into a bowed
> Enslavement, the small freedom of raising
> Endless memorials to the labour
>
> Buried in them. Faces
> Lifted at the day's end
> Like the palms of the hands
>
> To cool in the slow fire of sleep.
> A slow fire of wind
> Has erased their bodies and names.
>
> Their lives went into the enclosures
> Like manure. Embraced these slopes
> Like summer cloud-shadows. Left
>
> This harvest of long cemeteries.

Most of Hughes's memories of his childhood concern puzzling out the problematic effects of this dying Industrial Revolution culture upon his formative years. A childhood expedition becomes a learning experience when the young Hughes decides not to confine the loach (a small, minnowlike fish), but instead to return them to their natural habitat. The presences of Manchester and Mount Zion in the background seem to precipitate the realization that confining the loach to a two-pound jam-jar is cruel ("The Canal's Drowning Black"). Initially he removes the loach from their "ocean-shifting aeons" with a makeshift net of kitchen curtain and then drops them

> Into a two pound jam-jar
> On a windowsill
> Blackened with acid rain fall-out
> From Manchester's rotten lung.
>
> Next morning, Mount Zion's
> Cowled, Satanic Majesty behind me
> I lobbed—one by one—high through the air
> The stiff, pouting, failed, paled new moons
>
> Back into their Paradise and mine.

Each day Hughes walked to school guided by the predawn illumination of factory lights. Five hundred glass skylights became "Five hundred stones" that "Gave my school-going purpose" ("Under the World's Wild Rims"). The light, however, is artificial, eerie: it falls on the "horns" of flowers and allows Hughes's boots to progress through a catastrophically surrealistic landscape. His boots trod "Ankle-deep through volcanic talc / Kicking up magical objects / For futuristic knobkerries." Inside the factories "wagepackets / Had leaked a warm horror, like Pompeii." The mood of the poem and the choice of imagery suggest that the guidance provided by the factory light is sinister.

"Mount Zion" and "The Ancient Briton Lay Under His Rock" specify much more directly how the Protestant ethic and mechanistic science became constricting influences upon Hughes's early years. The home of Hughes's birth was caught in the shadow of Mount Zion Church, which blocked out the moon and darkened "the sun of every day / Right to the eleventh hour." Here the "convulsed Moses mouthings" and "mesmerized commissariat" of Christian soldiers standing at attention beside "Wesley's foundation stone" evoked childhood memories of bigots "Riving at the religious stonework / With screwdrivers and chisels." With sardonic humor Hughes suggests that their purpose was to crucify a heretical cricket, an upstart from the natural world that broke the atmosphere of prison silence and submissive gloom with a song from a crack in the wall. Like the machine regularity of the Industrial Revolution, the obstinate self-righteousness of Protestant orthodoxy walls out any possibility of experiencing communion with nature or the spirit flight of an awakened imagination. The poet can only remember his youthful terror at Mount Zion admonishments recited to armies of dumb, cowed recruits when one day he was "Marched in under, gripped by elders / Like a jibbing calf" awaiting ritual sacrifice. In "The Ancient Briton Lay Under His Rock" the Mighty Hunter, fortified with his primitive sense of the sacred in nature, only burrows deeper when village boys "Laboring in the prison" of their "Sunday bells" try to dig him out with minds tooled by the dogged obstinacy of Newtonian mechanistic science—those "Stinging brows, Sunday after Sunday. / Iron levers."

From childhood Hughes has always associated World War II, another cultural influence upon his youth, with an important break in family ties and a complete loss of the child's intuitive communion with nature. In *Poetry in the Making* (p. 16) Hughes describes how he developed his youthful passion for nature by functioning as a retriever for his older brother Bert, a gamekeeper, on hunting expeditions. But Bert left home in 1938 and joined the armed services a year later. Since then Hughes has seen his brother only on short holidays, for Bert settled in Australia after the war. Hughes recounts his joy at one such morning hunting expedition in the *Elmet* poem "Two" and also reveals how in his young mind the war ruined this *illud tempus* communion with nature. In "Two" Bert and Ted "stepped down from the morning star," arms laden with freshly killed game, and into a war where the guide (Bert) suddenly disappeared, "flew up from the pathway." Hughes relates his loss in simple, poignant statements:

> The other stood still.
>
> The feather fell from his head.
> The drum stopped in his hand.
> The song died in his mouth.

"Tick Tock Tick Tock" contains Hughes's most complex, philosophically dense treatment of his childhood memories and then presents a way out of the cultural constriction he endured as a child. In the J. M. Barrie story Peter Pan severs Captain Hook's right arm and throws it to a crocodile; soon afterward the crocodile swallows a clock. The apparently accidental clock tick that subsequently emanates from the crocodile as it chases Hook thus associates his misdeeds and mechanistic time with deformation. But Peter and Hughes mean to reverse this temporal process of degradation. As Peter prepares for his final confrontation with Hook, he notices that the crocodile's clock has recently stopped ticking; nevertheless Peter mimics the tick (figuratively swallows time) to shatter Hook's confidence. Peter resides in the ageless realm of Neverland, so his mimicry indicates that he is absorbing profane time into the Sacred. Neverland supplants the environmental degradation that Hook's piracy symbolizes as Peter kicks Hook off his pirate ship. This serves simply as background to the *Elmet* poem.

In "Tick Tock Tick Tock" Hughes unites with the endlessly creative, ageless child Peter Pan, a soaring spirit, in order to redeem and transcend an exploitive attitude toward the environment that fits both Captain Hook's villainy and the culture that created the pollution of Yorkshire mill chimneys. By becoming the crocodile (as Peter did), whose ticking swallows the deformations of history, Hughes asserts that forty years later, through the study of social anthropology and patient toil at his craft, he has lifted nature to culture and comprehended the significance of his childhood. Forty years after playing the crocodile and toiling from "prehistory," Hughes lifts his comprehension to awareness in the mediatory realm of the imagination. The articulation of the final poem proves that the "great theatre" of his imagination has redeemed the cultural degradation:

> Peter Pan's days of pendulum
> Cut at the valley grove.
>
> Tick Tock Tick Tock
> Everlasting play bled the whole unstoppable Calder
> And incinerated itself happily
> From a hundred mill chimneys.
>
> Tick Tock Summer Summer
> Summer Summer.
> And the hills unalterable and the old women unalterable.
> And the ageless boy
> Among the pulsing wounds of Red Admirals.

> Somebody else acted Peter Pan.
> I swallowed an alarm clock
> And over the school playground's macadam
> Crawled from prehistory towards him
> Tick Tock Tick Tock the crocodile.

Schoolroom repetitions of the Barrie play must have bored Hughes to tears, but forty years later he redeems the experience by recognizing that certain elements in the story may have had a subliminal effect upon him as a child in a way that foreshadowed his artistic career. As Hughes unites with the creative energy of Peter Pan, he lifts his childhood experience to the level of articulation and awareness, as Lumb did in the *Gaudete* "Epilogue." Spirit flight is possible through tapping the energies stored in childhood memories, and through the artistic process that creates an "ageless boy" from the "pulsing wounds" of his environmental shell. As Peter himself says, "I'm youth, I'm joy . . . I'm a little bird that has broken out of the egg." [10]

The essence of Hughes's third phase, the desire to rise from the mud of temporality through lifting experience into vision and transforming nature into culture, is actually present in a 1964 essay that he composed for the BBC Home Service. "The Rock" is a fine example of Hughes's prose style, and provides a glimpse of just how deeply the landscape and culture of his youth affected him. Scout Rock, a sheer cliff of the obdurate Pennines that towered hundreds of feet over Hughes's back yard (see the Godwin photo on page 71 of *Elmet*), "constricted life in some way, demanded and denied." It elicited feelings of "oppression" from Hughes, of being "trapped" in some disaster: "It was a darkening presence, like an over-evident cemetery. Living beneath it was like living in a house haunted by a disaster that nobody can quite believe ever happened, though it regularly upsets sleep." Escape for Hughes was "north and upwards, up the north slope" to the "gentle female watery line" of the moors, where you can hear "the moist voices of curlews." [11] The first line of "Curlews Lift" in *Elmet* reveals that Godwin's photos caused Hughes to meditate once again upon his BBC essay, for the curlews lift "Out of the maternal watery blue lines."

"Curlews Lift," however, ends in a state of Taoist awareness. The curlews attain a state of ontological purity as they drink "the nameless and naked / Through trembling bills." It is not so much that Hughes simply adopts the nameless, the Tao, as his philosophical first principle in *Elmet*, but that his insights into natural cycles he has meditated upon for decades deepen to a point where they often mesh with those of Taoist philosopher-poets who lived some twenty-three hundred years earlier. One small passage about the moors from "The Rock," for instance, indicates how close was Hughes's affinity with the Taoist *yin* principle a decade before his poetry reveals a consciously adopted Taoist influence:

> The rock asserted itself, tried to pin you down, policed and gloomed. But you *could* escape it, climb past it and above it, with some effort. You could not escape the moors. They did not impose themselves. They simply surrounded and waited. They were withdrawn, they hid behind their edges showing their possessions only upward, to the sky, and they preferred to be left alone, seeming almost to retreat as you approached them, lifting away behind one more slope of rough grass or parapet of broken stone.[12]

The Taoist reverence for the feminine principle softens Hughes's stern criticisms of Western culture in *Elmet*. Only in "Mount Zion" and "Rhododendrons" does his tone become harsh; in most poems that discuss Western science and religion ("Hardcastle Crags," "Walls," "First, Mills," "Mill Ruins," "Remains Of Elmet," and others) Hughes accepts Industrial Revolution culture as just one malformed manifestation of the Tao in the world of *yin/yang* fluctuation, a world where, as the reborn Lumb learned, "all is temporary / And must pass for its opposite" (*Gaudete* "Epilogue" poem #7). In a world of change all must inevitably return to the earth for periodic renewal ("Lumb Chimneys," "Walls"). Few poems in *Elmet* are entirely critical of Industrial Revolution culture; most balance the criticism with the healing balm of Taoist reverence for nature. In "Walls" the stone walls enclosed the bodies of the men as the men enclose their private property, but the feminine slopes are pliant, willing to endure being embraced, and to take the failed bodies of the men like compost for further renewal. Similarly, the "soil deepens" to accept decaying cultural edifices such as "Lumb Chimneys." And the "beech-tree solemnities" of the valley "Muffle much cordite," soften the blows and heal the wounds of war ("Hardcastle Crags"). As in the organization of the volume, most individual poems in *Elmet* generate a contrapuntal opposition between the negative effects of Industrial Revolution culture and Taoist tenets.

If Hughes in the *Gaudete* "Epilogue" is able to remove the surrealism from his criticism of Western science and religion through the Western mythos of enduring pain and suffering and by wrestling with one's instincts in the unconscious, so in *Remains of Elmet* he is able to achieve serenity through his adoption of the Taoist process of divesting himself of analytic knowledge and impulsive action. Both Lao Tzu (XIX, XX) and Chuang Tzu (III, VI, XV) advocate the process of abandoning one's analytic knowledge as necessary for apprehending the workings of the Tao. Chuang Tzu is most eloquent in directing the initiate to become "vast in his emptiness" by listening with the spirit, not the mind (III, VI); his parable of the Woman Crookback and Pu-liang Yi (VI) and his advice in chapter XV most closely resemble the process by which Hughes first mutes and then eliminates the power of the dominant Western culture in the sonata form of *Elmet*. In chapter XV Chuang Tzu advises one "to lose everything and yet possess everything, at ease in the illimitable, where all good things come to attend—this is the Way of Heaven and earth, the Virtue of the sage. So it is said, Limpidity, silence, emptiness, inaction—these are the level of Heaven and earth, the substance of the Way and its Virtue."[13] Lao Tzu also advises "actionless action" (II, XXII) as a means of controlling aggressive impulses and absorbing hostility. By professing *wu wei* one avoids all unnecessary, hostile action, develops compassion and humility to keep willfulness in check, and trusts in intuitive powers and the internal action of the mind to make crucial modifications.[14]

In the *Elmet* poems "Tree" and "A Tree" Hughes divests himself of analytic thinking and impulsive action as he advocates a tranquillity that contains a criticism of his *Crow*-period verse. After smiting the horizon with language and fulminating against Western culture, as in *Crow*, the priest of "Tree," in utter exhaustion, empties himself of his action-prone Western inheritance and for the first time feels "Heaven and earth moving" in ceaseless, stately, *yin/yang* flux. He then feels cleansed, a "new prophet." The persona of "A Tree" abandons former attempts to confess or rationalize; the tree divests itself of even linguistic camouflage. "Stripped to its root letter, cruciform," the tree comprehends the elemental suffering of all men and

> Finally
> Resigned
> To be dumb.
>
> Lets what happens to it happen.

Other elements in the feminine landscape resign themselves to accepting change. Water in *Elmet* is a patient, toiling sufferer. As in Lao Tzu and Chuang Tzu, water is unassertive, placid, and takes the low ground.[15] Similarly hill-stone, anticipating future freedom, is content to be conscripted into the service of cultural ideas that play themselves out in time ("Hill-Stone Was Content," "Top Withens"). The effect of *wu wei* resignation is to merge with dynamic *yin/yang* movement—to *become* the changing, rather than be victimized by rigidity. Here a healthy element of relativism softens one's views, without necessarily leading to utter passivity and capitulation. Lao Tzu recognizes (XXX) that force is occasionally a regrettable necessity; but when one is flexible, develops an intuitional grasp of changing circumstances, and trusts in the inner activity of mind, one's purpose can often be effected with a quick, decisive stroke rather than by becoming distraught through anxious overinvolvement with circumstances.

The adept learns to appreciate change as the manifestation in the phenomenal world of a Tao that is both immanent and transcendent; the ontological disjunction between authoritarian creator and created world in Western religion is foreign to the Taoist. All manifestations of the Tao derive from an infinite continuum of possibilities; what is important is that the adept recognize the life-force of the uplifting spirit in the phenomenal world. Chinese and Japanese gardens, for instance, are designed according to a potentially infinite succession of relatively asymmetrical areas, with a fondness for the strangely shaped, waterworn *t'ai hu* stones, meandering paths, the occasional modifications people make to bring comfort to their environment, and the ubiquitous presence of streams to symbolize the influx of the Tao in the created world. The purpose is to provide an environment in which to enhance the human potential for developing the imagination and fusing it with a reverence for nature. Gardens in Western culture such as the English manor garden too often reflect an excessively "foursquare" ordering. Western gardens in literature are usually organized according to moral concerns to reflect with Christian symbolism a heavenly order, but are separated from people or from that celestial order by an ontological river or wall barrier.[16]

When the persona preoccupies himself with analyzing modern Western culture, he perceives rocks and stones as constricting, weighed down by a malformed, visionless system. But he is also capable of perceiving rocks and stones in a spiritual dimension, as animated with the life-force of the Tao, when he discards his analytic ego. As "Heaven glows through" the "High Sea-Light," the persona apprehends an animated "live wreathed stone." Nearby Haworth Parsonage, home of the Brontë sisters, contains the "Infatuated stones" of artists constricted by a narrow culture. "The Big Animal Of Rock" is personified as a cantor at prayer, communing with ancestral spirits. Outcrop rock in April becomes a huge "soft animal of peace," a theriomorphic visitation from a Mesozoic ancestor. Its trancelike mystic ecstasy heals and sweetens the land ("In April"). Perceiving with the animated spirit is common for the Chinese; John Blofeld observes that

> No matter where one goes in China, it is rare to find a mountain ridge or rocky eminence of any sort that has not been likened to something alive. At the very gateway to the country, the mainland facing Hong Kong, one finds Nine Dragons (Kowloon), Lion Rock, Nurse-Carrying-Child Rock and so forth. South China, especially, teems with rock formations suggestive of turning into living creatures . . . but it takes a Chinese eye to detect the likeness without it being pointed out. Then one perceives how these rocks lend vividness to the concept of a single universal substance forever undergoing cloud-like transformations from form to form.[17]

Cultivating the animated spirit at times leads Hughes to adopt Taoist esthetics as the very mode of perception of the creative moment. As in Taoist painting and *Ch'an* Buddhism, moments of ecstatic fusion of poet, audience, perceived landscape, and poetic artifact are possible when the *ching chiai* or inner mind of the poet is perfectly attuned to the subject matter, reveling in the suchness of nature *as it is*, without prior analytical scrutiny.[18] Consider Tao-chi's responses to paintings first of plum blossoms and bamboo and then of orchids:

> First it shows one or
>   two blossoms,
> Gradually we see five or
>   ten flowers;
> In a setting sun
>   with brilliant clouds glowing
>   in the distance,
> How the beautiful flowers
>   compete with my brush and
>   ink.
>
> .   .   .   .
>
> Words from a sympathetic heart
>   Are as fragrant as orchids;
> Like orchids in feeling,
>   They are agreeable and
>   always joyous;

> You should wear these orchids
>   To protect yourself
>   from the spring chill;
> When the spring winds are
>   cold,
> Who can say you are safe?[19]

In the *Elmet* poem "Bridestones," a psychopomp of outcrop rock officiates at a marriage of masculine sky (*yang*) and feminine land (*yin*). As he becomes absorbed in appreciating this natural event as a pure emanation of the Tao, Hughes fuses the very process of composing and typing the poem with the attention of the audience in reading it, as in Tao-chi:

> And marriage is nailed down
> By this slender-necked, heavy-headed
> Black exclamation mark
> Of rock.
>
> And you go
> With the wreath of weather
> The wreath of hills
> The wreath of stars
> Upon your shoulders.
>
> And from now on,
> The sun
> Touches you
> With the shadow of this finger.
>
> From now on
> The moon stares into your skull
> From this perch.

In correspondence during his *Elmet* period Hughes occasionally speaks of his artistic labors as getting "onto my perch."[20] The birdlike flight of the poet's visionary imagination in "Bridestones" accomplishes a clear, direct, *ching chiai* fusion of correspondences in the natural world, from landscape to audience, in one swoop.

Ideally the Taoist poet-philosopher hopes through patient meditation, absorption in nature, and the absence of analytic preoccupations to feel a *shên yün* spiritual rhythm in life that facilitates a mystic vision of a Tao that operates in a Reality beyond the world of sense objects.[21] As Lao Tzu says, "The largest square has no corners . . . The Great Form [the Tao] is without shape" (XLI). In a heightened state of receptivity the adept can apprehend the undifferentiated *ch'ang tao*, the absolute emptiness beyond the phenomenal world that contains everything. In "Open To Huge Light" Hughes personifies wind-shepherds in the high moor grass as apprehending *ch'ang tao* as they bend to accommodate every wind change. Mystic calm is the result of their yielding posture:

> Now hills bear them through visions
> From emptiness to brighter emptiness
> With music and with silence.

Light imagery in *Elmet*, as in Lao Tzu and Chuang Tzu, frequently symbolizes the *yang* of masculine energy, or a serene self-knowledge that merges objective and subjective worlds in a way that often induces a glimpse of the Heavenly Light of the Tao.[22] According to Chuang Tzu, "He whose inner being rests in the Great Serenity will send forth a Heavenly Light" (XXIII); unaware of dualities, such a person "illuminates all the light of Heaven" (II). Self-knowledge in this context refers to reacquainting oneself with one's creative unconscious, not revising one's persona or conscious self-image. It means developing an intuitive grasp of the harmony and wholeness of nature and merging with its animated spirit. "Heaven glows through" the "High Sea-Light" as the persona begins to apprehend nature as an emanation of the Tao. After centuries of "clog irons and looms . . . and biblical texts," nature reanimated by the Tao in "The Trance Of Light" opens "younger, fresher wings."

In "Widdop" the persona comprehends the *yin/yang* flux of the phenomenal world as but an intermediary stage in the continual process of emanation and return to *ch'ang tao*; when "a gull blows through" this world the persona perceives an intimation of the "nothingness" that lies before and after temporality. The persona of "Widdop," a late poem in the *Elmet* sequence, perceives nature redeemed through a Taoist spontaneity and imaginative vision. Here, as in other late poems in the sequence, the persona resides in the Great Serenity of a self-knowledge that eliminates earlier preoccupations with Industrial Revolution culture, leaving only the ethereal spiritual rhythm of nature. With a childlike wonder he views a photograph of a moorland reservoir as a miracle where out of nothing a lake suddenly appeared. The lake's temporal existence issues from a numinal "nothing-ness"; it is "A rip in the fabric" that in time will return to "nothingness." From here through to the end of *Elmet* the Industrial Revolution appears only in "Tick Tock Tick Tock," where Hughes asserts that he has tran-scended its negative impact upon his childhood through vision and art.

The final poems in *Elmet* present the spirit flight of an awakened Taoist imagination. When "Light Falls Through Itself" the persona loses his iden-tity as a being distinct from the environment and merges with the impover-ished winter landscape in a state of *Tz'ŭ* sympathy. Soon afterward Hughes relates a moment of union with a vitalistic *yang* energy in nature as farm-yard roosters, "Brightening the underclouds" with fire-crests and "bursting to light" with their daybreak shouts, boil over in the "valley cauldron" be-low Scout Rock ("Cock-Crows"). The *yang* energy of "The Word That Space Breathes" is a light that joins the landscape and the buried dead in a "huge music / Of sightlines." This word, expressed through the *hun* or ani-mated spirit, redeems the dead and opens sightlines to the world above as if the rock of all-space were cleaved at the horizon line into a new heaven and a new earth. Now that the persona has become one with the spiritual essence that pervades the Taoist universe, he can affirm in "Heptonstall Cemetery," the penultimate poem of the volume, a birdflight benediction to the spirits of Edith Farrar Hughes, Sylvia Plath, and other deceased rela-tives as "Living feathers / Where all the horizons lift wings." The interment of close family, seen with this pure, childlike vision, only reminds the per-sona that their spirits have returned to *T'ien*, the heaven of the ancient Chinese.

By becoming one with the Tao through harmony with its manifestations in the cycles of nature, Hughes experiences a new freedom that allows him to alter his perspective toward the past. "The Angel," the final poem of *Re-mains of Elmet*, is a revision of "Ballad from a Fairy Tale" in *Wodwo*. Both poems recount dream premonitions of Sylvia Plath's death some two years before the event. In the dream the white square of satin foreshadowed the white square of satin covering Sylvia's face when Hughes first viewed the body.[23] The swan/angel of both poems derives from the swan maiden, a folklore motif of worldwide distribution that develops the primitive ani-mistic belief in the influx of the heavenly into the earthly. In the swan maiden motif a mortal male is able to possess a goddess or divine princess only until she recovers her feather garment from his possession or until he breaks a taboo. The swan maiden motif reminded primitives both of celes-tial origins and of the inevitable transiency of all earthly things, for the feather garment is usually recovered or the taboo broken by the imperfect mortal.[24] Hughes created an atmosphere of apocalyptic foreboding in the earlier "Ballad from a Fairy Tale," in part through the recurrent use of the valley of the shadow of death motif from Psalms 23:4. At the conclusion the persona realizes his dread, and he is left standing in a valley so dark and deep that he cannot touch the satin square. The attempt to touch it remains in the subjunctive ("I could have reached and touched it / But. . . ."), and the reader is left with the dominant imagery of darkness and the colossal, apocalyptic departure of the swan/angel.

The *Remains of Elmet* version, though less powerful, is more tranquil and accepting, and the ending more positive. The imagery of the dark valley, used only once, becomes a minor element. Here Hughes emphasizes the persona's clarity of vision and attempt to comprehend the dream event. The diction is more straightforward and assertive, and the persona affirms a positive identification with the deceased: "When next I saw that strange square of satin / I reached out and touched it." Time the healer removes the earlier need for the distancing imagery and subjunctive mode, while the animated Taoist landscape places supportive ground under the poet's feet. In contrast to the darkness at the conclusion of the *Wodwo* poem, the persona at the conclusion of "The Angel" has the words of this mother "under [his] feet." The receptive Valley Spirit, incarnated in the spirit and memories of the deceased mother, assures further flowering in the realm of Hughes's imagination. Here especially her *"posthumous life"* will continue, even as her swanlike soul wings heavenward.

The very sophisticated use of rock, water, light, and wings imagery in *Remains of Elmet* supports a complex modernist formal design. All depends upon whether the persona views the landscape with the negative effects of Industrial Revolution culture filtering his perceptions or whether he views the landscape with the reverence for nature promoted by Taoist culture organizing his perceptions. The latter finally heals the psyche, liberates the imagination, and eliminates the power of the former to constrict vision, through *Elmet's* pervasively contrapuntal design. The individual poems, so impregnated with Hughes's characteristic New Critical welding of form and content, become presentational. The Wellek and Warren definition of form developed in chapter 1 applies perfectly here: in *Elmet* the form "aesthetically organizes its 'matter'"; form, content, and stylistic effects "are pulled into polyphonic relations by the dynamics of aesthetic purpose."[25] Landscape does not become subordinate setting for representational action; it meshes with form and content to liberate the poet's imaginative eye.

Instead of adhering to a present-day historical context, Hughes activates what Auerbach dubbed the "omnitemporality" of the modernist perceiving consciousness as he moves through hundreds of years of Industrial Revolution and Taoist culture to plumb the significance of childhood memories that are some forty years old.[26] As he writes in a 1980 BBC talk on *Elmet*, Hughes distills the whole history of the area into a single omnitemporal lens, a single modernist formal *paideuma*:

> I use Elmet then to signify not just a rather vaguely-featured Celtic and criminal and nonconformist inheritance, but a naturally-evolved local organism, like a giant protozoa, which is made up of all the earlier deposits and histories, animated in a single glance, an attitude, an inflection of speech. If you imagine all those things distilled into a lens, with filters and distortions peculiar to the ingredients, then the characteristics of this lens would be, in a sense, *Remains of Elmet*.[27]

Ultimately Hughes inspects Industrial Revolution culture to deny its hegemony, to show how time and the elements of geologic change are wearing away its hold on humankind. As a major preoccupation in his intellectual and emotional life, at least, the cultural suppression of the Industrial Revolution "is all one. It is over" ("Rhododendrons"), and its exploitation of the environment "is all over" ("Top Withens").

The landscape poetry of *Elmet* is much more mature and positive than the earlier *Season Songs* (1975), a minor volume that began as a 1968 sequence of songs for children's voices.[28] This earlier work contains many light touches of myth and personification to enhance the content, but Hughes restricts the organization to a simple four poems per season. The poems often contain a Schopenhauerian pessimism, a sense of nature as a deceptive, blind will more suited to the sixties surrealism than to the positive perception of the feminine qualities of nature in Hughes's third period. The last of "The Seven Sorrows," for instance, occurs when "the year packs up / Like a tatty fairground / That came for the children." "A March Calf" is doomed to the slaughterhouse; the "Swifts" fly directionless and nearly blind; the "Sheep" are powerless; and spring arrives as an express train that blurs through or as wind and rain wrecking partytime spirits ("Deceptions"). The "Hay" is giddy in its empty unconcern; winter is reserved for suffering ("Solstice Song"), and even in spring the crocuses of "Spring Nature Notes"

remind you the North Sky is one vast hole
With black space blowing out of it

> And that you too are being worn thin
> By the blowing atoms of decomposed stars.

In Taoism, however, one achieves the Great Serenity by participating in the Allness of nature and penetrating beyond sense objects to glimpse a higher Reality (the Tao) orchestrating the panoply of change in the phenomenal world. This exalted vision in *Remains of Elmet* liberates Hughes's mind from any lingering resentments he may have had concerning events in his past. Having attained an enlarged perspective, Hughes can conclude the volume with a benediction, blessing his past as he blesses the spirits of his departed family members. Geoffrey Thurley's comment about Hughes's inability to submit to the law of the feminine may apply to the sixties surrealism, but it certainly does not suit the *Gaudete* "Epilogue," *Cave Birds*, or the landscape poetry of *Remains of Elmet* and *River*.[29] Taoism moderates the driving intellectual force in Hughes's poetry that often in the past gathered up diction and kinetic energy like a storm gathering clouds.

Adopting Taoist esthetics allows Hughes to become influenced by the reverence for nature of Chinese literature and to organize his meditations upon nature purposefully, without the world-denying flavor of Indian persuasions such as yoga. Achieving the Taoist Great Serenity and merging with the objective world to gain exalted visions of a Reality operating beyond sense objects is very far from realism, but very close to Coleridge's description of the primary imagination, that consubstantiality of matter and spirit that "brings the whole soul of man into activity" in the act of symbol-perceiving, not symbol-combining (the secondary imagination).[30] The liberation of the persona at the conclusion of *Remains of Elmet* brings Hughes to moments best understood by Coleridge's famous description of the primary imagination: communion with "the living Power and prime Agent of all human Perception . . . a repetition in the finite mind of the eternal act of creation in the infinite I AM."[31]

CHAPTER 9

No Wing
to Tread
Emptiness

Moortown

1979

*It's extremely difficult to write about the natural
world without finding your subject matter turning
ugly. In that direction, of course, lie the true poems,
the great complete statements of the world in its
poetic aspect. . . . [Poetry] seizes upon what is de-
pressing and destructive, and lifts it into a realm
where it becomes healing and energizing. . . .*
                                    —Hughes, 1978[1]

Gaudete and *Cave Birds* are transitional volumes
not in substance or in depth but in terms of
Hughes's emerging vision; they delineate a renewed reverence for the feminine and successful
transformations of suffering into spiritual illumination, but only after a sixties descent to a surreal underworld. Taoist esthetics in *Remains of
Elmet* extends Hughes's regard for the feminine
while presenting a sustained example of the persona as seer, a figure whose
imagination penetrates beyond the discrete object to glimpse a transphenomenal Reality governing events. *Moortown* (1979), Hughes's second
third-period volume, celebrates a renewed confidence in Western attitudes
toward nature as a revived Adam treads firmly on world-rock, announcing
that he is "no wing / To tread emptiness."[2] The imagination manifests itself
in *Moortown* chiefly in the persona's capacity to apprehend a higher Reality, but this Reality is not the Tao; it is a more Western energizing principle
that extends vision beyond the discrete object to encompass and redeem
the environment and to reconstruct time and space. This energizing principle resembles the generative capacity of the Hindu *ātman* in Hughes's
sixties work, but its real source derives from the active imagination and the
emanationism of Blake. In *Moortown*, as in Blake's late prophetic works,
poetic utterance functions as an analogue of this inspiriting, constitutive
force.

The form of *Moortown* at first appears to be one of convenience—a
bindery device collecting works already available in private press editions,
interspersed with previously uncollected poems that span more than a
decade. *Prometheus on His Crag* (1973), *Moortown Elegies* (1978), and *Adam
and the Sacred Nine* (1979) appeared in limited editions from Rainbow
Press; a few *Moortown* poems originally appeared in the Rainbow Press
Orts (1978); and the "Earth-numb" section collects magazine publications

from 1966 through 1978. But Hughes offered Sagar a telling insight that suggests significance embedded in the organization of *Moortown*. Of the two Baskin dust cover drawings—the snake on the front (and paperback cover) and the phoenix on the back, reprinted on page 183 of the text—Hughes writes that "the whole drift is an alchemizing of a phoenix out of a serpent."[3] Through a modernist metaphoric overlay Hughes embeds significant content in the formal organization of *Moortown*, content that aids interpretation of individual poems.

Moortown contains four major sections: "Moortown," a revised "Prometheus on His Crag," "Earth-numb," and "Adam and the Sacred Nine." The alchemical structure of *Moortown* concerns the transformation of the serpent energy of a farmer figure, a fallen Adam laboring in a fallen world in the opening "Moortown" sequence, to his phoenix rebirth into the cabbalistic Adam Kadmon, the primordial man, in the concluding "Adam and the Sacred Nine." In *Mysterium Coniunctionis* Jung discusses at length the alchemical Adam as a Mercurius/Christ figure who begins as the *prima materia* and then develops into the *lapis*, in the end realizing his inner world resources.[4] *Adamah* in Hebrew means "earth" and is related to *dam*, "blood." Adam is therefore he who is "made of red earth"—clay or mud.[5] "Adam and the Sacred Nine" begins with a fallen Adam who is "Too little lifted from mud." The farmer in the opening "Moortown" section, "Skull-raked with thorns" and toiling "in the knee-deep mud of the copse ditch" ("A Monument"), is quintessentially the fallen Adam. Hughes in a BBC Radio 3 reading suggests a growth toward spiritual illumination in the organization of "Adam and the Sacred Nine": "The idea is that Adam has, as usual, fallen. Originally all the creatures of the world come to him, telling him to pull himself together and get moving, but he just lies there, getting limper and limper. At last, his creator can't stand it any longer, and so he sends down nine divine birds to become his guardian exemplary spirit. They are actually just ordinary birds, except for one, which is a Phoenix."[6]

Unlike *Cave Birds*, however, no significant alchemical imagery exists in the middle sections "Prometheus on His Crag" and "Earth-numb." The "alchemization" Hughes alludes to is largely metaphorical. Hughes had already accomplished a rigorously alchemical drama in *Cave Birds*, and in more than two decades of a prolific career he has never repeated an earlier success. A more profitable approach concerns investigating the emanationism and world-creating visionary imagination of the cabbalistic Adam Kadmon and his one significant literary incarnation—the myth of the fallen Albion in *The Four Zoas* and *Jerusalem*. The visionary epistemology that Blake constructs around his Albion myth applies very directly to the middle sections of *Moortown*. The revised "Prometheus on His Crag" fore-shadows the Blakean visionary rebirth of "Adam and the Sacred Nine," while "Earth-numb" primarily presents a static limbo of fallen vision. Through specifying Blakean tenets and applying them to all four sections of *Moortown*, one can once again observe how form and content intersect in Hughes and also chart the alchemical transformation of the farmer's Orc-like serpent energy into the seer's visionary imagination, the phoenix voice of poetry, in "Adam and the Sacred Nine."

The Baskin serpent on the dust jacket of *Moortown* represents a stylized version of the cabbalistic Serpent of Wisdom whose three and one-half coils wind around the Tree of life in the Cabbala and direct the ascent from Malkuth, the most mundane Sephirah or contemplative state, to glimpses of the Unmanifest in Kether, the most spiritual Sephirah.[7] According to the Cabbala the ten Sephiroth first took shape in Adam Kadmon, with lights from his forehead precipitating the primordial world. The Dead Sea Scrolls and Jewish Gnostic sects that influenced cabbalistic tradition denied dualism and emphasized the unity of God and primordial humans. Though Adam separated himself from God through sin, cabbalistic tradition emphasizes that through ascending states of spiritual understanding he can trace the emanational path and once again develop an awareness of his true essence.[8] The precipitation of the world from lights emanating from Adam Kadmon parallels the central cabbalistic creation of the world as a series of progressively more material emanations downward from the Primordial Light of Ain into Kether and the lower nine Sephiroth.[9] The key to unlocking many of the poems of *Moortown*, including many of the most obscure—such as "Four Tales Told by an Idiot," "A Citrine Glimpse," and "Seven Dungeon Songs," among others—derives from a use of the Albion/Adam Kadmon myth that in many ways parallels that of Blake.

Keith Sager affirms the strong influence of Blake upon Hughes in a recent essay that interprets Hughes's entire corpus according to the fourfold vision concept articulated by Blake in the famous 22 November 1802 letter to Butts.[10] But similarities in *Moortown* to Blake's epistemology of vision and his adaptation of Gnostic or cabbalistic emanationism in the Albion myth also need clarification. The cabbalistic Adam Kadmon, as Northrop Frye observes, is one of Blake's central sources for his myth of the fallen Albion in *The Four Zoas* and *Jerusalem*.[11] More recently, Thomas Frosch in *The Awakening of Albion* interprets Albion's fall in Blake's work as a process of externalization caused by *tabula rasa* passivity.[12] As Albion becomes passive, he objectifies nature, and in so doing abstracts the natural from the human and rigidifies it, producing an autonomous landscape that becomes ever more remote and cold and dividing the integrated body into the fragmented, disputatious Zoas of the emotions and smell (Orc/Luvah), imagination and hearing (Los/Urthona), analytical reason and sight (Urizen), and touch (Tharmas).[13] According to Blake, Albion's fall derives from a lapse in his imagination's duty to create reality anew at each moment according to the authentic individual's desires. Albion's sickness can be remedied through the energy and effort of Los, Blake's figure for the shaping imagination. Los must refashion the "ratio" of the five reduced senses that shackle "cavern'd Man" (*Europe*) to his dungeon or Mundane Shell (*Four Zoas*, II:32).[14] This prisonlike existence is a self-created Ulro, an alienating cosmos, mapped by Urizen's mechanistic science, where all matter weeps at its distance from the beloved.[15]

According to Frosch, Los reawakens Albion by making him aware of certain Blakean tenets: that his imagination is active and autonomous, that his perceptions are fluid and flexible, and that he has greater capacities for sensual experience than the five sense "ratio."[16] In Blake, human perceptions need not be chained to Newtonian mechanistic science or Lockean empiricism; they can expand and contract at will: "Earth was not: nor globes of attraction / The will of the Immortal expanded / Or contracted his all flexible senses" (*Urizen*, 3:36–38). Humans bear the responsibility to organize and create for the self, to extend the energies of their bodies to encompass all. The road of libidinal excess leads to a moral dimension, the human family, through acts of forgiveness. As the imagination humanizes reality, an Edenic vision arises that obliterates any dualistic distance between subject and object.

Frosch concludes that redeemed vision manifests itself in many ways in Blake's poetry: in "the deep forgiveness of sexual energy," in a Beulah-like innocence and intimacy with nature, in a synesthetic reorganization of the senses, in "an eye capable of multiple perspectives at any given moment," and in an Edenic vision where "there is no longer any disparity between the visible and the demands of feeling and imagination."[17] The prime symbol for the energy and fluidity of transformed vision in Blake is fire; here Blake may have been influenced, Morton Paley notes, by Paracelsus and the alchemical tradition.[18] The ever-changing contours of fire and its consuming strength make it the perfect vehicle for the Divine Vision in Blake; and this fluid fire has its microcosmic counterpart in the eye's ability to transform reality at will:[19]

Then the Divine Vision like a silent Sun appeared above
Albion's dark rocks: setting behind the Gardens of Kensington

On Tyburn's River, in clouds of blood: where was mild Zion Hills
Most ancient promontory, and in the Sun, a Human Form appeared
And thus the voice Divine went forth upon the rocks of Albion [20]

The Sun has left his blackness & has found a fresher morning
And the mild moon rejoices in the clear & cloudless night
And Man walks forth from midst of the fires the evil is all consumd
His eyes behold the Angelic spheres arising night & day
The stars consumd like a lamp blown out & in their stead behold
The Expanding Eyes of Man behold the depths of wondrous worlds [21]

When Albion in an act of friendship enters the furnace flames at the conclusion of *Jerusalem* to save Los from the Covering Cherub, he becomes
Jerusalem, the vision of his complete freedom and fulfillment; at this point
he is indistinguishable from his environment, with the Zoas of his senses
and faculties reintegrated and multiplied within him. [22]

For Blake "all-powerful Human Words" (*Jerusalem*, I:24:1–2) provide
the perfect analogue for the power of Los's fiery transformations, for the
words of poetry transmute reality into vision. According to Paley, Los's creativity, the province of the poetic imagination in Blake's late work, is so
active that it actually constructs time and space and reveals in its intuitive
strength the power of Coleridge's primary imagination to penetrate into
the innate ideas behind phenomena, to participate in the "infinite I AM" of
existence. [23] Frosch concurs:

> For Blake, eternity and infinity involve not an emancipation from, but
> a reorganization of the sense of space and time. They signify the lib-
> erty to invent space and time, in the way that art does, and so to be
> alive in an immediate present that is delineated by the perceiver's
> imagination.
> The visionary conversation is thus the making of life, now analo-
> gous to the making of a work of art. . . . [24]

To facilitate his renovative work Los creates four orders of perception:
Ulro, Generation, Beulah, and Eden. Ulro is the passive state of dualism
and objectification that distances nature and reduces perceptual powers to
a five sense "ratio." Generation is the world of organism and environment,
genital sexuality, and struggles for power and dominance that often express themselves, as Frye observes, through a preoccupation with money. [25]
Beulah is the innocent vision of nature as a nourishing female, a reverent

but passive contemplation of the pleasures of nature, divided into a lower realm of childhood perception and an upper realm of sexual fulfillment. Eden is the only realm where the imagination actively creates reality; it is a fiery state of powerful forces clashing and transforming themselves, where the perceiver cannot be distinguished from the environment because imaginative vision has extended itself outward to create one risen body.[26]

These four orders of perception mark stages in the reintegration of Albion's fallen body. Albion's progress through these four orders and the consequent reintegration of his Zoas and awakening of Edenic vision illuminate the relationship of persona to perceived landscape in *Moortown* and provide an adequate paradigm for understanding the movement from the farmer (the fallen Adam/Albion) to Adam Kadmon in "Adam and the Sacred Nine"—a transformation of serpent energy to phoenix rebirth. In a BBC Radio 3 talk Hughes reveals that he consciously employed levels of awareness in organizing the poems of the "Earth-numb" section of *Moortown*: "the general theme running through all the pieces under this title concerns events and confrontations along a certain boundary. . . . The boundary, if it can be called that, runs between awareness, and unawareness, between the life of the one and the mere circumstances of the other, and the baffled sort of collision between them."[27] One can usefully discuss the formal organization and the liberation of the seer's active imagination in *Moortown* through comparing Hughes's "boundaries" with those of Ulro, Generation, Beulah, and Eden.

The poems of the opening "Moortown" section are startlingly fresh and vivid accounts of Hughes's early seventies labor on a Devon farm owned by himself and his second wife, Carol. Hughes's father-in-law, Jack Orchard, also worked the farm. In his BBC *Moortown* talk Hughes states that in the great majority of the poems he deliberately sought to copy down the details fresh, as near as possible to the day of the actual occurrence, in a rough, pocket journal sort of verse. He soon learned that reworking the poems later involved "imposing patterns" and styles that were "familiarly [his] own," whereas he preferred not to destroy the "fresh, simple presence of the experience."[28] Except for the elegies to Jack Orchard and the four poems "Orf," "Coming down through Somerset," "Tractor," and "Roe Deer," Hughes did exactly that: he confined himself to reproducing the unadorned experience sympathetically and vividly, but rigorously limiting himself to the boundary of the actual events. Here he deliberately chose not to recreate reality through applying his considerable imaginative powers.

The persona of the farming poems of "Moortown" perceives reality with the freshness, wonder, and receptivity of Blake's Beulah. The poems are striking in their highly evocative imagery. "Rain," the very first poem of *Moortown*, inundates the reader with vivid sensual imagery driven by Hughes's muscular verbs. Sleet-soaked rain pulses "across purple-bare woods / Like light across heaved water" (sight). It spatters on the ground and drums on roofs amid the "squelching cries" of snipe (sound), while cows sniff at the boundary wire that Hughes and the farmer erect (smell). Verbs of sinking and soaking confront the reader every few lines to portray a nature restricted to elemental processes and animal behavior, a nature that has not been lifted to the realm of spirit through imaginative powers. Imagery of the birthing of sheep and calves in "Moortown" is rich in its exactness and attentiveness to detail, but always limited to the boundary line of the actual: each birth ends in its "mess / Of puddled tissues and jellies" ("Struggle") or its "blue plastic apron" of afterbirth ("Surprise"), otherwise presented as that "banner of thin raw flesh that / Spinnakered from her rear" ("Birth of Rainbow"). Nature for the animal life of the farm is a perpetual "Confusion of smells / And excitements" ("Last Night"), anxieties and bafflements about the weather and the sexual cycle. At best the persona of the "Moortown" section realizes a vision of Beulah, of nurturing mother nature, as in the healing of the "Little Red Twin":

> The smell of the mown hay
> Mixed by moonlight with driftings of honeysuckle
> And dog-roses and foxgloves, and all
> The warmed spices of earth
> In the safe casket of stars and velvet
>
> Did bring her to morning. And now she will live.

"March Morning Unlike Others" contains a beautiful image of nature healing itself in the early spring sun after the operation of winter. Yet "Happy Calf" asserts that animal life can only appreciate nature's sunshine with a stolid languor, however sympathetically presented. At best nature seen with a fresh and sensitive eye produces a Beulah-like elation and innocent absorption in natural processes, as at the conclusion of "Last Load":

> Your sweat tracks through your dust, your shirt flaps chill,
> And bales multiply out of each other

All down the shorn field ahead.
The faster you fling them up, the more there are of them—
Till suddenly the field's gray empty. It's finished.

And a tobacco reek breaks in your nostrils
As the rain begins
Softly and vertically silver, the whole sky softly
Falling into the stubble all round you

The trees shake out their masses, joyful,
Drinking the downpour.
The hills pearled, the whole distance drinking
And the earth-smell warm and thick as smoke

And you go, and over the whole land
Like singing heard across evening water
The tall loads are swaying towards their barns
Down the deep lanes.

"Last Load" captures just the right feeling of release and sensual gratification in the easy, uncomplicated rhythm, upbeat tone, and the highly sensual imagery that flows smoothly and inevitably, without an excess of craft that could strain sense and syntax as it compresses.

The opening section of *Moortown* is memorable especially for its unsentimental, antipastoral insider's view. The poems convince us that this is what farm life is really about. We feel the wire's tension as bulls are dehorned, the press of weather as cattle are fed at midnight, the anxiety of the animals in rough weather, and the limits of human assistance in birthing. We nod at the tractor's "Shackle pins bedded in cast-iron cow shit" in the winter's cold, the unromantic urgency of cattle mating, and the balked hauteur of the bull in "While She Chews Sideways." After reading "Last Night" we may want to congratulate nature for taking the ewe's mind off her dead twins by having the greyface and the blackface vie to mount her; yet the ewe simply hurries and nibbles, while simultaneous attempts by the two males to mount her lead to awkward jostling and bafflement. "While She Chews Sideways" achieves uniqueness in its unsparing portrait of male machismo at the animal level. The addition of the pathetic fallacy at the end of the poem teases us into wondering just how much of this unlovely instinctual swagger resides at the base of the male's responses at the human level:

He sniffs the length of her spine, arching slightly
And shitting a tumble-thud shit as he does so.
Now he's testy.
He takes a push at the crazy Galloway with the laid back ears.
Now strolling away from them all, his aim at the corner gate.
He is scratching himself on the fence, his vibration
Travels the length of the wire.
His barrel bulk is a bit ugly.
As bulls go he's no beauty.
His balls swing in their sock, one side idle.
His skin is utility white, shit-patched,
Pink-sinewed at the groin, and the dewlap nearly naked.

. . . .

Today none of that mooning around after cows,
That trundling obedience, like a trailer. None of the cows
Have any power today, and he's stopped looking.
He lays his head sideways, and worries the grass,
Keeping his intake steady.

Hughes finds a great deal of beauty in the ugly or sad events of farm life, but he keeps the poetic rearrangement of the experience at a minimum. Absolute faithfulness to the actual has its power and its charm, but does not open the furnace door of Los's active imagination. Nevertheless, attentiveness to the actual can render nature with a touch so close that the reader feels an awed reverence for the pain and the pathos, as when the "needle jet" of blood squirts from the dehorned bull's "white-rasped and bloody skull crater" ("Dehorning") or in the unforgettable portrait of the stillborn lamb in "Ravens":

Born dead,

Twisted like a scarf, a lamb of an hour or two,
Its insides, the various jellies and crimsons and transparencies
And threads and tissues pulled out
In straight lines, like tent ropes
From its upward belly opened like a lamb-wool slipper,
The fine anatomy of silvery ribs on display and the cavity,
The head also emptied through the eye sockets,
The wooly limbs swathed in birth-yolk and impossible
To tell now which in all this field of quietly nibbling sheep
Was its mother.

"Moortown" unsentimentally chronicles the limits or boundary lines of nature unredeemed by imagination in the successful births of four animals and the unsuccessful births of seven others.[29] The drama of "February 17th" is easily the most unforgettable in the volume, a straightforward account of the "to-fro futility" that often characterizes purely physical efforts to make nature manageable. Without its front legs forward at the moment of birth, a large lamb in a small ewe faces impossible odds, even with the total concentration and dedication of a sympathetic farmer. All one can do is save the mother:

> No hand could squeeze past
> The lamb's neck into her interior
> To hook a knee. I roped that baby head
> And hauled till she cried out and tried
> To get up and I saw it was useless. I went
> Two miles for the injection and a razor.
> Sliced the lamb's throat strings, levered with a knife
> Between the vertebrae and brought the head off
> To stare at its mother, its pipes sitting in the mud
> With all earth for a body. Then pushed
> The neck stump right back in, and as I pushed
> She pushed. She pushed crying and I pushed gasping.
> And the strength
> Of the birth push and the push of my thumb
> Against that wobbly vertebra were deadlock,
> A to-fro futility.

The lamb's head may have "all earth for a body," but the metaphor obscures a fate that opens astonishingly in the knifelike caesura of the poem's last line: "And the body lay born, beside the hacked-off head."

The dominant motif of "to-fro futility" lies hidden within the sensuous imagery and the occasional pleasures of husbandry in "Moortown." The boundary post holes that the farmer digs in the opening poem "Half fill with water before the post goes in." The dehorning wire moves "Left right left right" as the men lean "Backward full weight, pull-punching backwards." After the agony of birth a soon-to-die calf and its mother "lay face to face like two mortally wounded duelists" ("Struggle"). At their twilight feeding the cows in winter "Jostle and crush," "Battling the hay bales" from the farmer. Chase and escape is the law in "Fox Hunt"; death and procreation bump in uneasy contiguity in "Last Night"; and auctioning a bull leads to "a table-tennis to-fro-strife" ("She Has Come to Pass"). The inner world of conscience and the outer world of necessity strain in opposite directions in "Orf," and a "baffled, stamping, storming" ewe ready to give milk cannot comprehend a son too weak to take it ("Sheep").

Similarly, the farmer, who at times resembles Hughes's own father-in-law, endures the "to-fro lurching" of wire and boundary posts ("A Monument"). He becomes so habituated to struggling against natural obstacles that Hughes presents him metaphorically having to push his way into his own funeral pyre, just as in life he "loved to push the piled live hedge boughs— / Into a gathering blaze." Mud provides the only competition for dominant imagery in "Moortown." Hughes's sympathetic recovery of the quintessentially human saves the farmer from becoming one with the

> snaggle of faces
> Like pulled-out and heaped-up old moots,
> The natural root archives
> Of mid-Devon's mud-lane annals,
> ("The Formal Auctioneer")

If the persona views nature unsentimentally in the opening section of *Moortown*, he does characteristically view it sympathetically, assisting as much as possible and revering the labors of the farmer. Amid the "Barbarous wire" of the farmer's labors Hughes learns how nature "comes to be manageable" ("Hands"). The "appalling stubbornness" of the farmer's chain-smoking, gruff labor endears him, as does his broad-backed strength, though too often he expended it with careless abandon. The persona's final memory is of a sudden elegance in the farmer's hands, now folded in death. In life these hands were utility devices, McLuhanesque extensions of a rural technological will. Hughes depicts the farmer's hands as utilitarian "dung forks" and twice describes them as tractorlike. Under his "tool-worn" face his hands appear as "old iron tools"—instruments that amplify his "hawser and lever strength" ("Now You Have to Push," "Hands"). Hughes draws a poignant portrait of the farmer as a fallen Adam in a world not as yet redeemed by the imagination. He cares about how the farmer used his life up setting wire "through impassable thicket, / A rusting limit."

The limits of the Beulah-like innocent gaze of the persona in "Moortown" reveal themselves in "Orf," "Coming down through Somerset," "Tractor," and "Roe Deer." Here outer world experience invades the persona's inner world, to question his responses to nature. In the first two poems the inner world refuses to capitulate to outer world mutability, causing to-fro conflict. In "Orf" conscience will not consign the "lamb life in my care" to the necessity of euthanasia. The persona of "Coming down through Somerset" brings the slain badger "close / Into my life" and refuses to let go; the animal's "rankness, his bristling wildness, / His thrillingly painted face" appear to be such a momentous intrusion of life into his routine that he wants the badger to "stay as he is" and "stop time." Yet the boundaries of the "Moortown" section do not really allow for such inner/outer complexity—a telling qualification. Neither experience is successfully resolved; the whole point is to remind the reader of what complications a Beulah-like innocent absorption in nature fails to include.

In his Radio 3 reading of *Moortown* poems Hughes singles out "Tractor" as one of the few poems in the first section that he did rework into a carefully crafted literary product.[30] Through opening oxymorons of "molten ice and smoking snow," Hughes reinforces the unnaturalness of the tractor in the frozen countryside. Becoming involved with this machine prepares the persona for the "Earth-numb" section of *Moortown*, for the tractor exists in an Ulro world of machines—nature cut off and externalized from the self in an alienating "space-cold." Using this machine consigns the persona to a world of "condemned obedience" to machine repetition, without imaginative freedom. Here fingers become tormented and eyes weep in a chloroform wind. The sweating tractor is directionless and draws out a negative will to dominate: "I drive the battery / As if I were hammering and hammering / The frozen arrangement to pieces with a hammer." By driving the tractor the persona has stepped into a "trap of iron stupidity."

More than any other single poem in the opening "Moortown" section, "Roe Deer" reminds the reader of what the innocent Beulah gaze of the persona fails to include—the visionary imagination. One winter dawn the auto-driving persona sees two deer and anticipates a visionary moment when

> for some lasting seconds
> I could think the deer were waiting for me
> To remember the password and sign
>
> That the curtain had blown aside for a moment
> And there where the trees were no longer trees, nor the road a road
>
> The deer had come for me.

Like the young Ike McCaslin in Faulkner's "The Old People," the persona of "Roe Deer" hopes for a numinous instant that would cleanse him and direct his future. Sadly enough, such visionary moments are universally absent throughout the opening section of *Moortown*. The deer of the "Roe Deer" have not come for the persona, and snow soon obliterates their tracks, "Revising its dawn inspiration / Back into the ordinary."

The three poems Hughes changed in his revision of *Prometheus on His Crag* for section II of *Moortown* reveal subtle changes in emphasis toward the more Blakean concerns of fallen and redeemed vision, the regathering of the environment into the imaginative awareness of Prometheus, and the fashioning of the poems themselves as the product of a transforming imaginative power. The original 1973 Rainbow Press version articulated the typical early seventies theme of the enduring of suffering to gain illumination—the Aeschylean influence from the 1971 *Orghast*. In this early version Prometheus has important encounters with Pandora's box of diseases (#5) and with Io, still in painful flight from the gadfly (#12). Finally Prometheus recognizes that disease and pain are the mortal's lot and that his compensation for the pain is illumination in the realm of spirit. He gradually comprehends that the vulture who daily picks apart his liver is an emissary of this purposive pain, "the Helper / Coming again to pick at the crucial knot / Of all his bonds" (#20). With this knowledge Prometheus gains the illumination of the last poem in the sequence (#21): the man-mountain erupts into a new level of awareness, and the poems themselves, the "Puddled, blotched newsprint," become the record of his bloody suffering. Prometheus now knows that he is his own source of creative fire and that the vulture (his suffering) is the "burrowing double tongue" that rekindles his flame (#17).

The later version, section II of *Moortown*, contains three new poems. Hughes also deleted both the earlier encounters with Pandora's box and Io's suffering, along with Prometheus's new understanding of the fire theft. The effect of the additions and deletions is to place greater emphasis upon the Titan's decision to become completely mortal as a *mistake*, a lapse in creative power that causes an externalization of the environment and self-inflicted chains. The way back is through the fire of artistic creation, through developing the "gobbet of sun" he plucked. The new axis of interpretation is very much like Albion's fallen vision and his final reintegration through the fire of Los's creative furnace. The new poems Hughes added to the *Moortown* version (#s 5, 7, and 17) move the sequence away from resignation to a principle of suffering *in nature* and toward a problem within Prometheus's own consciousness—a lapse in his Albion-like imagination's ability to encompass reality and transform it into vision.

In #5, the first new poem in the revised *Prometheus on His Crag* (henceforth all poem numbers refer to the revised version), Prometheus dreams of exploding the sun's mass and emerging mortal. At the same time "He had resolved God / As a cow swallows its afterbirth." "Resolved," in context with the minimal consciousness of animal instinct, indicates a purely cerebral resolution to his problem—the limited, fallen vision of Urizen and Ulro. The result is an externalized nature and a diminished vision where the elements weep and the imaginative energy that had sustained a universe-for-the-self collapses into the shut jar of the heart—a *self-created*, neurotic Pandora's box. The poem ends in weeping and in total division among members of the human family: "The infant's bottomless cry, the mother's lament, / The father's curse."

Poem #5 sheds new light on #3, for it reveals that the "world's end shout" of Prometheus is an abdication of responsibility to create reality for the self. It brings him the peace of the sleeping Albion and dehumanizes creation into diminished forms, whereas they were once a world of "holy, happy notions"—a Blakean world of infinite perceptions where everything that lives is holy, as in the concluding chorus of *The Marriage of Heaven and Hell* and the conclusion of *A Vision of the Last Judgment*. Weeping in Blake is often a function of fallen perception, the sound of an alien environment that longs for humanization, reintegration, as in the weeping that follows the division of Tharmas (the sense of touch) from Albion, and his further division into emanation (Enion) and Spectre at the opening of *The Four Zoas*. Here the environment weeps continually, defeating Enion's every activity. This weeping also occurs in many poems in the "Earth-numb" section of *Moortown*, in the limbo of Generation and Ulro.

Poem #7, the second new poem added to the revised *Prometheus on His Crag*, presents Prometheus chaining himself by digesting his fire into diminished analytical vision. The vulture's pain becomes the sun's revenge, and the earth once again weeps at its distance from the perceiver. Hence the flowers that Prometheus sees are self-created, withered perceptions: "Flowers of a numb bliss, a forlorn freedom."

Hughes offers a Blakean redemptive path for this fallen vision in #17, the third new poem in the revised *Prometheus*. On plate 12 of *The Marriage of Heaven and Hell* the prophet Isaiah finds no God in "finite organical perceptions," but is moved to write when his senses "discovered the infinite in everything." Writing offers the path for the redeemed vision to form; the fire of Los hammered into words reinvents reality; it opens the eyes, unites the senses, and reconciles humans with the environment. This is the message of #17. As in the deleted #17 from the earlier sequence, Prometheus is himself the fire; but the new poem is more specific, better-focused. In

the new poem Hughes links the fire not with the vulture and his capacity
to transmute suffering, but rather with the autonomous creative imagination's power to expand beyond the self-inflicted chains of limited Ulro
vision:

> No God—only wind on the flower.
>
> No chains—only sinews, nerves, bones.
>
> And no vulture—only a flame
>
> A word
> A bitten-out gobbet of sun
>
> Buried behind the navel, unutterable.
> The vital, immortal wound.
>
> One nuclear syllable, bleeding silence.

Prometheus now comprehends the Blakean/Buddhist doctrine that "All deities reside in the human breast."[31] Expanded vision returns Prometheus's
body to himself as unchained "sinews, nerves, bones."

The new poem #17 throws added emphasis upon the relationship between the blood-puddle of newsprint and the volcanic eruption in the last
poem of the sequence. For Blake, creative activity is a titanic clash of
powerful energies. Prometheus's desire to relax into a helpless peace in
poems #2 and #3 causes his problem. In the concluding poem Hughes
presents the resumption of Prometheus's creative labors as a volcanic eruption of dormant energies, where the bubbling magma becomes the puddled blood of newsprint. When Albion awakens at the conclusion of *Jerusalem* (plate 98), Blake presents him as "Eyed as the Peacock," a man whose
vision encompasses the globe with hundreds of eyes in all directions.
Prometheus on His Crag also ends with the peacock of infinite vision:

> And Prometheus eases free.
> He sways to his stature.
> And balances. And treads
>
> On the dusty peacock film where the world floats.

At the close of *Prometheus on His Crag* the poet as seer extends his imaginative energies beyond the discrete object to encompass an integrated whole of self-and-world. The fallen Adam of "Adam and the Sacred Nine" undergoes the same process of psychic reintegration, though in presenting the arrival of guardian bird-spirits Hughes offers a more sustained example of writing impelled by the active imagination. Before arriving at "Adam and the Sacred Nine," however, the reader must traverse "Earth-Numb," a collection of poems spanning more than a decade of encounters primarily with the boundaries of Ulro and Generation. The emanationism and active versus passive imagination in Blake's Albion myth provide an especially fruitful critical perspective for interpreting the poems of "Earth-numb."

The man living in Ulro is Blake's "cavern'd Man" (*Europe*), a passive *tabula rasa* dependent on a "ratio" of five diminished senses, who looks out through the cavern chinks at remote objects in an autonomous environment. Helplessness and fears of the void result, not the "spirit confidence" in nature that Hughes prizes. Many poems in "Earth-numb," the third section of *Moortown*, depict this fallen state, including some of the most obscure. The speaker of "Four Tales Told by an Idiot," for instance, is Macbeth himself, a passive figure totally dominated by the destructive Lady Macbeth. His famous soliloquy alluded to in the title voices a dead-end despair that Hughes could never agree with. In the first three sections of "Four Tales Told by an Idiot" Macbeth has nightmare visions of the elements tormenting and torturing him. He remains entirely passive in these nightmares, a victim of self-created pain. By the fourth section nature becomes so distanced from him that he prophesies doom, with anxieties of stellar space at the heart of his final neurotic admonition to "KEEP ON DIGGING AWAY AT THAT HOLE." Just as the "stars flee remote" when Albion's Human Form fails,[32] so Macbeth conceives of the stars as active menaces in a universe neurotically feared as a void. He crawls into a hole as stars surround him "far into infinity."

Frosch agrees with Robert Gleckner that the fallen mortal must multiply the chinks in the cavern, expand the visionary rays of light entering the inner world, until inner world and moment-to-moment perception coalesce.[33] "A Citrine Glimpse" is one such shaft of visionary sunlight entering a cavern chink, bringing hope to the alienated elements of the fallen body. But in the second section of the poem the hoped-for liberator has not acquired enough visionary power to expand the chinks and reintegrate the elements back into the self. The weeping continues. The final line of the poem, "And a wolf cried in its deformity," echoes the "howling in the

Wolf," the last cry of Albion's divided, scattered body in *The Four Zoas* (VIII:110a:22).

The Divine Image in *Jerusalem* (III:plates 60ff.) descends at one point to the Dungeons of Babylon to begin the work of revivification by making Jerusalem, the emanation of Albion's risen body, aware of the sanctity of the self. It finds Jerusalem dumb and insane, living in a worldly chaos. In "Seven Dungeon Songs" a similar rebuilding of the body's divinity and an expansion of its senses occurs, with the help of visionary sunlight, in stages that ebb and flow. The sunlight, emphasized repeatedly as a "crack of light," a "Tree of light," and a "crystal of light," gradually heals the persona's madness. This leads to an attempt in sections V and VI to attach the self to an environment that reciprocally becomes steadier, less surrealistic. In the final section the persona hopes for a reintegration of senses, bodily members, and environment. Were this successful, the risen body would in no way be differentiated from its environment. Divided self and externalized environment would then unite. Then "The speech that works air / Might speak me." Each stanza links bodily parts with alienated elements to mimic a reintegrated, risen body, but in "Earth-numb" such a reintegration must remain in the subjunctive mode as a possibility, not an achieved reality. This foreshadows the achieved reintegration of "Adam and the Sacred Nine," where the active imagination combines with the creative act of poetic speech in a way that "works air" to bespeak the risen self.

Reductive Ulro vision dominates other poems in "Earth-numb." In "Old Age Gets Up" Hughes reveals that old age is especially sad when the mind has been conditioned throughout life to lean on the window frame of Ulro vision for support. Living under this "fatal, real injury," old age can only pull "its pieces together" and attend to bodily needs. Passive acceptance of the limited vision of our mechanistic culture leaves us in old age without sufficient inner world resources or self-comprehension to build a self-reliant wisdom. Here the only recompense for old age is a fuzziness that leads to an amnesiac condition where ideas "collapse / At the first touch of attention."

The estranged, dehumanized environment that attends Ulro vision appears in "Life Is Trying to Be Life" and "Song of Longsight." The figure Death in "Life Is Trying to Be Life" is the distancing eye of objective vision that estranges self from environment and insulates that self from the human family, as in the allusion to the Ancient Mariner's killing of the albatross in lines 2 and 3. Death in this poem cannot integrate self with experience. In "Song of Longsight" Hughes satirizes the universally valid laws of modern science as causing a fearful alienation of consciousness. Paradox, reversal, and transmutation also operate in this world, as in the yin/yang flux of *Remains of Elmet*, and can lead to redeemed vision, or at least the Zen-like No-bird's *satori* vision of wholeness in stanza I. But the poem gradually progresses into the world of modern science, with its rigid cosmos where laws like the action/reaction opposition of Newton's Third operate irrespective of the perceiver. In the long view or longsight of cultural development in the history of *Homo sapiens*, modern science appears as a devolutionary reversal. When surgeons in stanza III cut out (externalize) a star from the body of Yes, she is left "Living in uplooking fear."

Blake's champion Ezekiel defines the presence of God within us as a face-to-face encounter (*Ezekiel*, 39:29), a personalized, humanized relationship.[34] Hence Blake presents the risen body of Albion in terms of integrated faces, the four Faces of the Four Eternal Senses on plate 98 of *Jerusalem*. "Acteon" and "Deaf School," possibly the two best poems of "Earth-numb," present the inability to achieve an integrated body as producing defective vision and defective faces, both of which preclude any chance of friendship. Here faces become concealing masks, two-dimensional blanks, or enigmas wrapped in clouds of inference. Acteon, lacking an integrated self, cannot develop a personalized relationship. He stares at Diana, but he "could not see her face" with his limited vision. His eyes analyze into particulars with Ulro inevitability; he perceives even the maiden's hair as "a sort of furniture" and her hands as "useful gadgets." In the stare of his nonvision her face becomes a jigsaw puzzle that explodes into the hounds of alienated instinct. As the demonized animals tear the flesh from his limbs, "the blank of his face / Just went on staring at her / Talking carpet talking hooverdust."

The faces of the deaf children in "Deaf School" "lacked a dimension"— the dimension "of sound and responses to sound." Blake in Night the First of *The Four Zoas* presents the "Auricular Nerves of Human life" as socializing, whereas Urizen's building of the Mundane Shell of caverned man in Night the Second is depicted entirely in terms of the individuating eye of single vision.[35] Hughes's deaf children lack the sympathetic dimension of the human voice and its "assertion in doubt." (Doubt in Blake, as in "Auguries of Innocence," typically refers to the philosophy of Descartes and describes a rational process that separates self from world.) Without the humanizing dimension of sound, the deaf children rely too heavily on a machinelike sign language and a faculty of sight that creates an "alien space / Separated from them." The face of each child becomes a camouflage of "simple concealment" where a withdrawn self cannot develop or reach out to encompass the human family. Denied the faculty of hearing, the children remain "unaware" and "separate"; they lack a sensitivity for kindred feeling that the spoken word's self-reflexive capacity for generating "its own public and audience" inspires. Hughes conveys the effects of the deaf children's overreliance upon sight with images of mechanical, marionettelike jerkings, and images of a machinelike separateness and concealment (lines 14–17, 22, 25–28). Their frenetic communication through sign language alternates very effectively with other images that describe their eerily simple watchfulness. The odd combination makes the deaf children appear otherworldly—distant relatives of *Homo sapiens* from a remote star of impassable separateness.

Other poems in the "Earth-numb" section treat experience at the level of Blake's Generation, the ordinary fallen world of dualism, with its struggles for survival, power, and possession, often expressed through images of genital sexuality and concern for money. These poems are mimetic and have realistic settings, but they only satirize the historical/cultural influences portrayed. The myth of Adam Kadmon/Albion that knits the volume together, of course, is a modernist formal device, a metaphoric overlay that does not depend upon realism. The need for a maxi-coat motivates "That Girl." Her need for this coat impels her forward, motivates her to "hurry . . . Down that lane" to a future tryst with a well-heeled lover. In the concluding stanza Hughes asserts that the need for the maxi-coat masks a more fundamental biological itch that the "Earth-numb" world of generation can satisfy through the auspices of "Young Mother Nature" and "Old Father Nature, Too, / Hairy Old Man."

In "Here Is the Cathedral" the excavation of the Roman garrison bath house and the plague burials at Exeter Cathedral is of a piece with creature comforts and conspicuous consumption. The "headlamp chromes / Of Peugeots, Toyotas, Volkswagens, Jaguars, Saabs" that ring the cathedral witness and even invite the spadework. This culture suppresses its desecration of the dead under the motive of providing a tourist attraction: "And this is the House of the Dead / Open to everybody." Even the tramp's conduct is infected by this sham cultural value; his only interest in the persona is utilitarian, the need for a handout. Like the cathedral, the tramp needs "Cash for renovations," but two officials shout him off the premises. Religion should inspire compassion, but here both tramp and cathedral officials manipulate people according to personal needs and inimical socioreligious codes. They dispossess themselves of Eden with proscriptive commands: "OUT / OUT OUT OUT." Similarly, the tramp in "A Knock at the Door" manipulates the persona by using conversation for self-seeking purposes. While the tramp hides his embarrassment behind a dualistic face of concealment, he unctuously uses each bit of conversation as a probe to satisfy physical needs. "MONEY" motivates his conversation; it is an anesthetic fittingly translated later in the day into church worship in a dead-drunk alcoholic stupor. The tramp sadly sleeps in the cathedral of values he tacitly accepts by virtue of his passivity—a sad waste of human potential.

When Albion lapses into fallen vision and his senses separate into Zoas and their emanations, all projects fail because of competition for dominance and favor. Similarly, the female office worker of "Nefertiti" uses her physical endowments to possess, to entice men at the bar. Her body becomes a consciously employed extension of a will to manipulate, with knees and wrists a "trip-wire menace" and "eyelids and lips / Machined to the millionth." In the world of Generation sexual desire ends inevitably in the death-cries issuing from "dividing steel." In her utilitarian hands even her office pen becomes a tool that separates people. The world of Generation also motivates the hauteur of the young German in "Postcard from Torquay." His "Continental sportswear" and brilliant glass yacht fuel his arrogance. The aloof materiality is as menacing as in William Carlos Williams's "The Yachts." The young German of the Hughes poem epitomizes an entire culture's will to power and corresponding utilitarian vision. Once again the possibilities of life diminish. Hughes undercuts the Occupation swagger of the German with a sardonic conclusion: his yacht is being lowered into a "swell of tourist effluent / And holiday turds."

"A Motorbike" offers a perfect illustration of Hughes's BBC comment about "Earth-numb" dealing with "the boundary . . . between awareness and unawareness, between the life of the one and the mere circumstances of the other, and the baffled sort of collision between them."[36] As postwar England settles into a "horrible privation" of peacetime, the possibilities of life appear to dwindle to the limits of resorts and dance halls. The quiet young man who buys the motorbike, a six-year relic of the war, apparently wants to commune with greater life energies than are possible, to return to the zesty "thunder, flight, disruption" of wartime. Yet in the limited world of Generation he can only exit into death, for at this level of perception spiritual enlargement simply is not possible. He and his motorbike escape into the technological energy of a South Yorkshire telephone pole.

Embedded in the "Earth-numb" section of Moortown are a few poems that offer glimpses of states of being beyond Ulro or Generation. In the three sections of "Photostomias" Hughes presents first a predatory energy in the outer world, then a fiery inner energy awakened and controlled through yogic meditation, and finally a chiasmic union of inner and outer worlds through imaginative vision engaged in creating poetry. Section I depicts these predatory fish of the great deeps as exemplary of an energy in nature so fierce, obscure, and isolated that it has survived natural selection. This fish is a "Quiet little Einstein / Of outer darkness"—a force that has solved its survival problems through employing a "baleful perspective." Section II reverses section I by focusing upon an analogous power within the self capable of being developed and mastered through yogic concentration. "Buddha-faced, the tiger / In his robe of flames" signifies this energy within the self. The reference concerns the yogic meditation upon glowing coals to awaken and master an inner fire, and/or the awakening of the fiery Kundalini serpent of Tantric yoga that transmutes sexual energy into the union of inner and outer worlds that delivers the adept from the world of birth and death into *nirvana*.[37] Both the beetle (the Egyptian scarab) and the peacock suggest transmutation to a higher plane of awareness. Through meditative concentration the inner world awakens and unites with the outer world at the end of section II: "Earth is gulping the same / Opium as the heart."

Section III of "Photostomias" presents a paradoxical unity of opposites sustained through imaginative energy. The photostomias are both a Los-like "Creation's hammer" and an Oriental "Anvil of Nothing," Western "Glassy digits" and the Oriental "Bottomless zero," a Urizenic "space-computer" and the dumbstruck Eros of Kundalini transformation. The both/and logic of section III suggests that Hughes is fusing inner and outer worlds through the active imagination to articulate an energy that penetrates both and to affirm that we can master this energy and enlarge our vision. The last two lines are pure Blake: the photostomias are both a Urizenic decalogue, a prescriptive set of universal laws, and a rainbow, an image Blake uses to underscore the promise of a revived Jerusalem (*Jerusalem*, IV:86:21), or to express one of the mind's "Images of wonder" on page 82 of *A Vision of the Last Judgment*.

"Tiger Psalm" also presents an approach to experience that surpasses the fallen vision of Ulro and Generation. Hughes has told Sagar that the poem was originally composed as a dialogue between Socrates and the Buddha,[38] and the poem's content and date of original composition (1971) reflect Hughes's *Crow*-period opposition of Western and Oriental cultural orientations.[39] The poem argues that the to-fro dialectic of Socratic reason must end in a murderous technology, a final expression of human distance from nature and of the neurotic fears that ensue. In contrast the Buddha-tiger kills expertly, economically; he blesses his victim and grants him an enlarged sense of the inner self, the "tiger within the tiger." Developing and disciplining the inner life, the Oriental path of Hughes's two-way journey, is preferable to disputatious rational discourse. The killing done by the Buddha severs the appetitive self—the wants, desires, and ego-dependency upon a material world—through yogic meditation. The death and resurrection motif of the poem concerns ancient shamanic practices involving the mastery of fire that influenced the development of Buddhism.[40]

Not all of the poems of "Earth-numb" fit Blakean modes of interpretation. Many of the poems of "Orts," which Hughes translates as "leavings" in the sense of "the lady's leavings are the dog's dainties," are leftovers from an early attempt at the *Gaudete* "Epilogue" in the mid-seventies.[41] They present the possibilities of communion with the White Goddess of nature in our everyday contemporary culture and are not planned specifically according to the Adam/Albion epistemology of fallen and reintegrated vision. "Speech out of shadow," however, expresses the dilemma of limited vision in the world of Generation, and "Buzz in the window" introduces "Intelligence, the spider," Blake's abstracting intelligence, as in "The judge" from *Cave Birds*. The first two poems of "Orts" do present the promise of Edenic vision for the seer, but the remainder of the twenty-five poems, with the single exception of "Night arrival of sea trout," only detail the inhibiting effects of contemporary Western culture. The first poem of "Orts" is particularly Blakean in its assertion that each new moment offers an opportunity to recreate reality according to the seer's changing impulses and desires. The last stanza conveys a Los-like clash of energies in the process of artistic creation. Beyond the brain's cerebrations lies the imagination, that rises swanlike with a "Convulsion of wings, snake-headed / Uncoilings, conflagration of waters."

"Earth-numb," the title poem of section III of *Moortown*, presents the psyche's imaginative energies reaching out into the environment in a primitivistic way that has some points of similarity with Blakean Edenic vision. Hughes wrote a lengthy introduction to this poem for his 1978 Norwich Tape reading. He analogizes his success in catching a large salmon, the subject of the poem, to the magical thinking primitives practiced before the hunt to ensure success. Through a prayerlike projection of healing energy a primitive hunter could self-induce a heightened state of alertness, concentration, and confidence that would substantially enhance the chances for success in the hunt. Hughes suggests in the Norwich Tape that the poet in crafting a poem similarly creates that heightened aura. He "finds and fixes an image of his own imagination" such that "his imagination would heal itself," while leaving a vivid and powerful record to influence his and his readers' future thoughts and actions.[42]

Like "Pike" in *Lupercal*, "Earth-numb" records that moment of stillness before the arrival of inspirational energy, and then the shock of its actual arrival—the salmon's strike. In "Earth-numb," however, Hughes is less interested in fishing a pond "as deep as England" than he is concerned with specifying within and beyond the concrete experience the numinous visitation of inspirational power, and how it fuses psyche and landscape in one electrified current. Somewhat like Edenic vision, the primitive hunter's expenditure of libido in searching out and hypnotizing the prey leads to moments when ordinary dualistic modes of vision vanish in an exalted participation in the godly:

> A piling voltage hums, jamming me stiff—
> Something terrified and terrifying
> Gleam-surges to and fro through me
> From the river to the sky, from the sky into the river
> Uprooting dark bedrock, shatters it in air
> Cartwheels across me, slices thudding through me
> As if I were the current—
>
> Till the fright flows all one way down the line

"Adam and the Sacred Nine," the fourth and concluding section of *Moortown*, presents a sustained example of the unifying Blakean imagination glimpsed in the third section of "Photostomias," the last poem of "Prometheus on His Crag," and the seventh of the "Seven Dungeon Songs." Unlike the opening farmer's journal, vision in "Adam and the Sacred Nine" is not limited to the actual, objective occurrence. The fallen Adam's faculties and the elements of this environment reintegrate as he is transformed into Adam Kadmon. A solar flight to the source of creative imagination parallels this reintegration in a way that also unites persona, perception, and environment. As a result the poet as seer emerges, with powers to penetrate to a monistic Reality beyond the discrete object. The seer's vision is particularly Blakean in its fiery energy, and in its flexibility—its ability to expand and contract according to the pulsations of feeling and desire.

The invocatory "Song" begins the sequence by emphasizing a central motif in Hughes's third period, the lifting of matter to spirit. The song searches not for any of the divided elements of the earth, but for "what did not exist"—the yet to be attained spiritual awakening of Adam. "Song" ends with the assertion that this spiritual self is "not yet born." According to Jung, a preliminary stage in the alchemical awakening of Adam is the reintegration of the elements and faculties to achieve a quaternity.[43] In "Adam and the Sacred Nine" the guardian exemplary spirits sent by God will first unify the four elements as they reintegrate the four Jungian faculties of intuition, intellect, feeling, and sensation. A very earthy, undeveloped Adam manages a spark of intuition; the Falcon arrives to ignite the fires of intellectual comprehension; the airy oscillations of the Skylark free the affects or feelings; and the Wild Duck returns to Adam the fluid changes of his sensory life. All of the visiting birds that become Adam's collective "guardian exemplary spirit" are imbued with a Los-like energy that reorganizes the world into one ontologically different from the worlds of Ulro, Generation, or even Beulah. The birds follow Blake's directive to

> renew their brightness & their disorganized functions
> Again reorganize till they resume the image of the human
> Cooperating in the bliss of Man obeying his Will
> Servants to the infinite & Eternal of the Human form[44]

Adam in the second poem of the sequence begins being "Too little lifted from mud." He exists with the vegetable consciousness of Generation as just another sodden growth of the natural world. But he does manage sufficient intuitional power to desire development: his capacity to dream draws the guardian spirits to him. With their aid he can generate enough inner world strength and energy to reclaim the alien world of his environment. At this point, however, his dreams lack direction and guidance. He dreams Taoist/cabbalistic visions of "the tower of light," and the "diamond body" of Tantric Buddhism,[45] but interspersed with dreams of warplanes and machinery. He remains too weak and vulnerable to extend his energies beyond his epidermal "peach skin and bruise."

"And the Falcon came" revives the fiery power of the intellect in Adam. The power of intellectual comprehension appears in two manifestations that are similar to Coleridge's secondary and primary imagination. First the Falcon divides and reformulates; it engages its energies in "stripping down the loose, hot flutter of earth / To its component parts / for the reconstitution of Falcon," as in the conscious craft of Coleridge's secondary imagination. Then the Falcon fuses his physical body with the environment through an explosive outpouring of energy. His "bullet brow" and "tooled bill" arrive with the instantaneous impact of gunfire. All is fed into the Falcon's "eye flame," a flame that continually shifts from division to holistic comprehension in order to convert material tinder to visionary utterance, as in Coleridge's primary imagination. Urizenic reason transformed into intellectual understanding is a crucial state in reviving Adam/Albion. As Hughes raises matter to spirit in his third-period works he agrees with Blake that "men are admitted into Heaven . . . because they have Cultivated their Understandings. The Treasures of Heaven are not Negations of Passion but Realities of Intellect from which All the Passions Emanate Uncurbed in their Eternal Glory."[46]

In the fourth and fifth poems of "Adam and the Sacred Nine" a Skylark reclaims the element of air and the faculty of feeling, and the Wild Duck the element of water and faculty of sensation. The Skylark's effort and labor lift it toward the sun in swells of "bird joy." The crest of its song decorates the earth with an energy that partakes of the sun's corolla. The Skylark commands the air, alternately "Thatching the sun" and cresting the earth with its songswell. Its vision expands to its sunward limits and contracts to its earthly foreground at will, according to the "swinging ladder" of desire.

The Wild Duck in the following poem reclaims the world of water and the faculty of sensation. It rises from the "ooze before dawn" and comes "spanking across water," "Calling softly to the fixed lakes." The Arctic imagery in the poem connects the Duck's mission with the earth's daily rise out of the "frosty dark" and the evolution of organic life from the zero of space cold, impelled by the inspiriting warmth of "the precarious crack of light."

The reintegration of the four elements and the four faculties reverses Adam/Albion's fall into four alien elements in *Jerusalem* (III:59:19–20). In Blake the four elements of the environment are finally humanized into an Edenic reinstatement of our total substance on plate 98 of *Jerusalem*. The same recapitulation occurs in "Adam and the Sacred Nine." Behind this regathering in Blake's work Frosch finds the quintessentially Romantic impulse of attaining an exalted state of consciousness where inner/outer, subject/object distinctions vanish.[47] Imaginative vision in poetry can recapture this unitive state through its fiery transformations, through its metaphoric and synesthetic ability to connect elements with faculties, and through its liberating activity of reinventing space and time according to the ever-shifting impulses of desire. In the *Gaudete* "Epilogue," *Remains of Elmet*, "Adam and the Sacred Nine," and *River* Hughes develops the seer's ability to extend imaginative capacities beyond the discrete object to encompass and redeem reality through a holistic vision that fuses psyche and object in the moment of perception. Here Hughes comes full circle, for what began as a New Critical principle of poetic craft in *Hawk* becomes the foundation for a renovated spiritual plane of imaginative vision, with the addition of an essentially Blakean epistemology of the act of perception. To appreciate this one need only contrast the fiery, fusing energy of Falcon and Skylark that welds psyche and landscape, with the pain, the alienated machinery of isolated elements, and the anxious searchings for a passive safety in "Poor Birds," from the opening "Moortown" section:

> In the boggy copse. Blue
> Dusk presses into their skulls
> Electrodes of stars. All night
> Clinging to sodden twigs, with twiggy claws,
> They dream the featherless, ravenous
> Machinery of heaven. At dawn, fevered,
> They try to get some proper sleep without
> Losing sight of the grass. Panics
> Fling them from hill to hill. They search everywhere
> For the safety that sleeps
> Everywhere in the closed faces
> of stones.

With elements and faculties reintegrated within Adam, God sends the Swift, the fastest flier among birds, to lift Adam from the world of matter to that of spirit. The swift puts off body to ascend to spirit; he "Casts aside the two-arm two-leg article— / The pain instrument / Flesh and soft entrails and nerves, and is off." His flight encompasses the limits of the earthly and the spiritual, both "mineral limit" and "dream and number," in an expansion of vision. The Swift generates energy for both a *descent* to pluck "the nymph of life / Off the mirror of the lake of atoms," and an *ascent* "into the sun's retina," as in the solar eagle symbolism of *Cave Birds*. Vision is not limited to the actual events in an alienated landscape, for the Romantic visionary eye is hunting the exalted moment of spiritual enlargement. The inexhaustible energy of the Swift becomes a Los-like imaginative fire, an "uncontainable burning" that transforms matter to spiritual illumination in each moment of perception.

In the last of the "Seven Dungeon Songs" the persona hopes to integrate his senses and faculties so that "The speech that works air / Might speak me." The Wren of "The Unknown Wren" achieves exactly this return of the world into the risen body. Here psyche and environment unify in each moment of visionary perception. This Wren "sings only Wren," and alternately "His song sings him." His activity creates a communality of self and world; all is Wren's song, with no dualistic distance between subject and object. Hughes repeats this motif in stanza IV: "Wren is singing Wren—

Wren of Wrens!" The Wren represents Adam's achieved prophetic voice, his ability to transform the world into Edenic vision. The Wren's singing actually constructs space and time for the self, for when his attention lapses into sleep the world dissolves: "the star-drape heavens are a dream / Earth is just a bowl of ideas." Imagery of tongues and of the risen sun present the Wren as a risen body energetically engaged in reconstituting the world for the self through his "blur of throbbings."

As Adam reabsorbs the world into the self and activates his spirit and his prophetic voice, he reawakens his soul, the central core of self. "And Owl" opens with the device of chiasmus used in section III of "Photostomias." The purpose is the same, to fuse inner and outer worlds through a formal cross-stitching: the Owl is "a masked soul listening for death. / Death listening for a soul." Hughes portrays the Owl in a deeply meditative state, a yogalike attaining of the "diamond body" of the Tantrists through "ripping the bandages off"—abandoning the physical body and dependence upon the phenomenal world of death. Adam's dream of the "religion of the diamond body" in the second poem of "Adam and the Sacred Nine" comes true. The *Kālacakratantra* expresses the Tantric Buddhist doctrine that through meditation and an excess of sensual pleasure the cosmos can be contained within the body. Tantric *sādhana* or realization concerns the unification of opposites within the body to achieve the diamond body of the indivisible, impenetrable, unified self, the goal of the Indian alchemist.[48]

The Owl's vision in "And Owl" is multidirectional, a totalistic comprehension comparable to that of Albion's peacock eyes, for "Nothing is neglected, in the Owl's stare." Blake on plate 4 of *The Marriage of Heaven and Hell* wrote that "Man has no Body distinct from his Soul"; for Adam at the conclusion of *Moortown* the same truth applies, for body and soul are now one. The final chiasmus at the conclusion of the poem depicts the merging of heaven and earth through imagery suggesting the sacrificial eating of the god among primitives. The purpose is the same in each case—to participate in the power of the divinity.[49] The Owl has exchanged his physical shape of throat, face, and talons for an all-inclusive astral body where circumference does not exist and where "Only the center moves."

If all individuality reunites within Adam Kadmon's risen body, then all are equal and all is forgiven. "The Dove Came" articulates the outpouring of mercy and compassion that an active imagination in a unified self necessarily demonstrates. The Dove arrives with "Her breast big with rainbows," recollecting Los's song of the fullness of Jerusalem, where he envisions her as a dovelike bird descending from heaven "Clear as the rainbow, and the cloud of the Sun's tabernacle" (*Jerusalem*, IV:86:21). Renovated vision holds the promise of the human family, of redemptive respite from the pain and limitations of the purely physical body. The Dove alights "In the body of thorns," redeeming the farmer's pain instrument—the purely physical body, "Skull-raked with thorns" ("A Monument"), with its narrow boundaries.

In "The Dove Came" this emissary of the spirit is repeatedly knocked down and finally consumed before being able to nest in the human heart. Hughes introduced "The Dove Came" in his BBC reading of "Earth-numb" poems by noting that the "gentle Dove" has a difficult time "Forcing herself through all the opposition."[50] Does this "opposition," along with the "to-fro futility" of the opening "Moortown" section, indicate that for Hughes matter has become accurst? Could his work with Manichean and Zoroastrian sources in Iran have convinced him of an irreconcilable chasm between matter and spirit? Or does the opposition derive from a Taoist yin/yang flux in a phenomenal world "where all is temporary / And must pass for its opposite" (Gaudete "Epilogue," poem #7)? Is the emanationism that Hughes shares with Blake tainted with Gnostic/Manichean beliefs in matter as an eternally evil principle?

Sagar is correct in asserting that Hughes has an even greater reverence for nature than Blake.[51] All of Hughes's third-period landscape poetry attests to a celebration of nature through an opened visionary eye. The emanationism of Taoism and the Cabbala best fits the poetry, with a parallel in the neo-Platonic emanationism of Plotinus. We do know from Cave Birds that Hughes studied Jung's three volumes on alchemy, and Jung believes that in the alchemical tradition Gnostic material undergoes a transformation, as in Zosimos, so that both Physis and Nous, the hylic and the pneumatic human, reside in matter.[52] The evidence of the poetry suggests that through honesty, respect for nature and the self, and the fiery expenditure of energy in effort and concentration, one can purify the body so that it may become "the vehicle for the spirit"—the goal of Hughes's training regimen for his Orghast actors.[53] The inner world of consciousness allows humans to aspire beyond the limits prescribed for animal and vegetable nature, as in the Gaudete "Epilogue." The imagination is that divine spark from a transcendent Reality that humanizes and elevates matter. Stuart Curran's conclusion from his study of Blake's Gnostic sources applies to Hughes: poets are mythographers, not scholar-researchers, and can borrow elements from a given philosophy for their unique mythologies, without necessarily adopting all tenets, as Blake adopted Gnostic emanationism without ascribing to the Gnostic belief that matter is inherently evil.[54]

The Crow next whispers survival news to Adam, but survival in the sense of a complete journey onto a spiritual plane of existence. His news is unspeakable—matter for divination, not intellectual apprehension. Adam then becomes a fully aware, spiritually awakened Adam Kadmon in "And the Phoenix has come." He takes on a risen body of spiritual understanding that echoes the Pauline dictum that "the first man Adam was made a living soul; the last Adam *was made* a quickening spirit" (1 Corinthians, 15:45). For both Blake and Hughes, the renovated spiritual individual is manifested primarily through the prophetic voice of poetry, the record of the imagination's active recreation of the world. The Wren's oracular voice becomes a first principle of fiery energy in a Phoenix world of never-ending transformations, a liberated Eden of vision:

> Its voice
> Is the blade of the desert, a fighting of light
> Its voice dangles glittering
> In the soft valley of dew
>
> Its voice flies flaming and dripping flame
> Slowly across the dusty sky
> Its voice burns in a rich heap
> Of mountains that seem to melt

As in Blake, Hughes connects fire, Blake's symbol of active imagination's energy and its ceaseless changes in visual perspective, with the prophetic voice of the poet. The poem ends when energy and vision unite in an image of the human form: "And naked the newborn / Laughs in the blaze."

The spiritual individual lives in a paradise of heightened awareness and fresh perception. Hughes conveys the purity and strength of Adam Kadmon's reconstituted vision in "The sole of a foot," the concluding poem of "Adam and the Sacred Nine." The sole is also the soul of a poetic foot, with imaginative perception reintegrated into the whole person, as when Milton enters Blake's left foot in *Milton* (15:49; 21:4). Adam has attained a "Comfortable" relationship with nature—the "spirit confidence" Hughes prizes.[55] The universe under renovated vision makes Adam once again "The first host, greeting it, gladdened"; it feels to Adam like "the world / Before your eyes ever opened," the concluding image of "The executioner" in *Cave Birds*. The healing energy of poetry has lifted matter into spirit, ending its dungeon days of weeping.

The inner person has flowered into a totality, a synthesis of all necessary psychic powers, reabsorbing Reality into the self. Jung's citation of a passage from the cabbalistic treatise *Tractatus de Revolutionibus Animarum*, by Christian Knorr von Rosenroth, applies here: "From En Soph, from the most general One, was produced the universe, which is Adam Kadmon, who is One and Many, and of whom and in whom are all things."[56] Adam's final affirmation that he is "no wing / To tread emptiness" expresses a preference for an absorption in the concrete and the sensual, as opposed to the voids of stellar space; no imagery exists in the poem to suggest that the "emptiness" refers to Buddhist *śūnyatā*, though Hughes appears to be expressing a preference for a Western immersion in the particulars of temporal experience.

The epistemology of vision deriving from a use of the Albion/Adam Kadmon myth in Blake and the Cabbala best explains Hughes's comment that the form of *Moortown* concerns "an alchemizing of a phoenix out of a serpent."[57] The subject matter and imagery in individual poems are Hughes's own, but the emanationism and the active imagination in Blake's Albion myth help to clarify many obscure poems and to locate significance in a volume that at first appears randomly organized. Hughes wrote in a 1980 letter that "I seem to have spent quite a bit of [the seventies] recovering from the sixties, & it's only now that certain essential things are coming back into focus." This comment introduces *River*, his most recent volume of poems.[58] The strong Blake influence in *Moortown* brought Hughes firmly back to the Western ground of the concrete and the sensual; in *River* the poet as seer gradually extends his visionary capacities throughout the entire landscape.

CHAPTER 10

Sanctus
Sanctus
River
1983

There are two kinds of simplicity, after all. The common type belongs to simplifications made this side of the experience of the complexity of the subject; and is achieved by retreating from it. The rare type belongs to the observations made on the other side of the subject, when the experience of having gone through the complexity has changed the observer, and brought him to a direct grasp of the inner sources of the subject, which are always simple. The first common type has the simplicity of excluding all but a few salient effects. This other rare type has the simplicity of an inclusion of everything in a clear solution. . . . [In Stephen Crane's poetry one finds] not quite a simultaneous vision of some spiritual truth of things, behind and different from the material truth, though it is that too. Whatever it is, it's a vision of a world of strange forms, and strange doings, within the observed one, and it leaks through to us—when it does—with a shock. . . . To succeed in any degree in producing [this simplicity], a writer needs a strong imaginative grasp, and exhaustive accurately imagined experience, of common reality at many levels—as well as tenacity, and a good compass. . . . That sort of simplicity—so deep and impersonal and somehow all-inclusive—cannot be faked. It is natural to the spiritualized morality of the statement. . . .

—Hughes, 1980[1]

                                                    But after
The warm shower
That just hazed and softened the daffodil buds
And clotted the primroses, a gauze
Struggles tenderly in the delighted current—
Clambers wetly on stones, and the river emerges
In glistenings, and gossamer bridal veils,
And hovers over itself—there is a wedding
Delicacy—
                            so delicate
I touch it and its beauty-frailty crumples
To a smear of wet, a strengthless wreckage
Of dissolving membranes—and the air is ringing.

It is like a religious moment, slightly dazing.

It is like a shower of petals of eglantine.[2]

River (1983) began with Peter Keen's desire to photograph a river, source to mouth, through an entire twelve-month cycle. Unlike *Remains of Elmet*, however, in *River* Hughes did not limit himself to the photographs.[3] He developed a *paideuma* that works in both directions at once: toward a Taoist sympathy (*tz'ŭ*) with creation, and its end in mortality's mouth, and toward communion with creation's source—a combination of the ascetic spirit of the Tao and the imaginative energy of Blake. The latter two principles inform the events that occur in the phenomenal world of *River*, and the poet-persona's ability to penetrate beyond the events to their spiritual source generates religious moments as fine as any in English poetry. Hughes achieves a startlingly fresh simplicity, a "direct grasp of the inner sources of the subject"—like Coleridge's primary imagination—in modernist fashion, through spatial arrangements of extended metaphors. The river and light images become metaphors that reveal a transphenomenal energy and sustenance descending from a Blakean/Taoist heavenly realm. The snake imagery represents a corresponding energy in the phenomenal world, while the salmon typify the wisdom within the survival struggle of all creatures.

The double journey outward toward mortality's mouth and its spiritual source is simultaneously the poet's inward journey toward self-knowledge the acceptance of mortality, and the surety that the poetic imagination has the power to raise nature to culture. The central persona of the poems is closest ever to Hughes himself (the poems frequently use the first-person pronoun), and the real Gulkana salmon he quests for is not the "small, crazed" eye, sunk in Arctic cold and crawling like the *Elmet* crocodile toward him from prehistory, but self-knowledge, a lifetime's affirmation of the power of poetry, and a penetration to the spiritual source of it. Hughes achieves this only after abandoning the ironical, abstracting intellect that informs many of the poems before "After Moonless Midnight" and sympathetically identifying with the visitations of theriomorphic energy and White Goddess inspiration that transpire in many of the poems that occupy the second half of the volume. The message of "Go Fishing"—to let "brain mist into moist earth"—foreshadows a process of modifying the analytical intellect that the persona achieves in the second half of the volume. At the close of *River* Hughes sustains a Blakean Edenic vision by reintegrating the intellect into the whole, the Jungian quaternity of thought, feeling, sensation, and intuition. In "Salmon Eggs" the subjective self, its act of perception, and the perceived become one personalized, humanized substance. *River* fuses Hughes's Oriental and Occidental interests, while at the same time it recapitulates all of the themes of Hughes's third period, and many of the earlier ones.

River offers readers such a profusion of lush imagery, vividness and accuracy of observation, rightness of feeling, and delicacy of mood that one can praise the volume as superb landscape poetry. An accomplished angler himself, and at the height of his poetic powers, Hughes captures the unique raiment of each river he plies in England, Scotland, Wales, Ireland, and Alaska. Each poem bedazzles the reader with refreshed feeling and intense absorption into nature—with showers of eglantine petals. The riverscapes are visually arresting; they regularly oscillate from a Keatsian sensuousness to a Taoist visionary austerity. The initial motivation is pure. The poems are not *exempla* of Taoist metaphysics or Blakean imaginative energy, but originate in the clear observations of a circumspect angler perfectly at home in his native environment, and as cravings of the poetic sensibility for those moments of congruence with nature when the senses savor the honey of its nourishing wealth:

> The current
> Hauls its foam-line feed-lane
> Along under the far bank—a furrow
> Driving through heavy wealth,
> Dragging a syrupy strength, a down-roping
> Of the living honey.

> It's an ancient thirst
> Savouring all this, at the day's end,
> Soaking it all up, through every membrane
> As if the whole body were a craving mouth

("River Barrow")

Passages as lush with nature's concrete particularity as this one occur often in *River*.

Yet, as we observed in *Remains of Elmet*, the philosopher in the poet cannot help but probe deeper, into the "inner sources of the subject." In the early sixties Hughes wrote that "if any word could be found engraved around my skull . . . it would probably be the word 'horizon.'"[4] Twenty years later Hughes follows the river to its source, where riverline meets horizon at a point that vanishes into the transphenomenal. If one views the river as an energy source, the center of a spatial composite, and focuses upon the point where it meets the horizon, the river can become an avenue for a philosophical "down-roping / Of the living honey," where the visionary eye perceives a metaphysical first principle being drawn down from the sky into the water. Li Po, the masterful Chinese Taoist poet, often dwells upon the river/horizon vanishing point as the place where phenomena reveal their numinous source:

> The lonely sail in the distance
> Vanished at last beyond the blue sky.
> And I could see only the river
> Flowing along the border of heaven.

(from "On Seeing Off Meng Hao-Jan")

> Faring far across the river-narrow of Ching-men
> I have come with you into the land of Chu.
> Here ends the mountain-range that stretches along the plain,
> While the river flowing on, enters the distant heavens.

(from "Parting at Ching-Men")

> Do you not see the waters of the Yellow River
> Come flowing from the sky?

(from "An Exhortation")[5]

Like Li Po, Hughes often apprehends a controlling spiritual presence behind the clarity and simplicity of his riverscapes. The title poem of *River* presents the river as a channel or culvert for the influx of spirit, ultimate Tao, into the impermanent phenomenal world. Pietà-like, "River" has

> Fallen from heaven, lies across
> The lap of his mother, broken by world.
>
> But water will go on
> Issuing from heaven
>
> In dumbness uttering spirit brightness
> Through its broken mouth.

Allusions to the river as gateway to the supratemporal world of spirit occur often in the poems. The "long pool tail" that the persona seeks in "Milesian Encounter on the Sligachan" contains a "superabundance of spirit." In "Low Water" Hughes personifies the river as an idle woman who "eyes you steadily from the beginning of the world." The seatrout, emissaries of the mystical sublime in *River*, "inhale unending" through their gills in "August Evening."

Joseph Campbell observes that the river "is throughout the literature of the Orient symbolic of the pouring of divine grace into the field of phenomenality."[6] In Indian literature the river as symbolic of divine sustenance occurs in the *Mahabharata* and in the *Ramayana* story of Ganga (the Ganges) descending from heaven to quell the devouring fire of Agastya.[7] Often Hughes associates the river's divine grace with light imagery. One can readily find analogues for light imagery in Boehme and others and a river of light in "Canto XXX" of the *Paradiso*. Taoist literature, more sensitive to nature and less rigid in its orthodoxy, best parallels the mystical qualities evoked by Hughes. As we observed in chapter 8, light is symbolic of the Tao.[8] Hughes opens the Harper and Row edition of *River* with the river as "Flesh of Light." In "West Dart" the river "spills from the Milky Way, pronged with light." The "piled flow" of the river in "Salmon Eggs" becomes a "ponderous light of everlasting." "Unending river" in "The Vintage of River Is Unending" swells from a winepress tightened "with golden light." The mystical seatrout in "Strangers" experience the unitive *samādhi* state of yoga as they first "Hang in a near emptiness of sunlight" and then "Lean in the speed of light." The "real samadhi" occurs because the seatrout have the capacity to become so absorbed in their contemplation of the river's light that they enter a trance: they "Absorb everything and forget it / Into a blank of bliss."

Spirit and light imagery converge in "Under the Hill of Centurions" and "That Morning." In the former poem Hughes depicts the minnows as laboring in the river's "wheel of light." The river buffets the minnows with "Ghostly rinsings / A struggle of spirits." Hughes presents an Eliadean encounter with salmon and bears while fishing in Alaska in "That Morning." As father and son fish while standing waist-deep in a river incredibly flooded with salmon, two bears wade in nearby and prong salmon with their talons. Just before that moment, the abundance of salmon causes the persona to drop his "doubting thought" and become a "spirit-beacon," at one with nature's plenitude. The prelapsarian communion with animals that follows leaves the persona at the end of the poem feeling "alive in the river of light / Among the creatures of light, creatures of light."

Spirit and light images accrete throughout *River* to present a steadily deepening penetration into what Hughes in the epigraph quote to this chapter calls the "spiritual truth of things." This process culminates in "Salmon Eggs," the last and most philosophically dense poem in the volume. The poem contains light imagery, but not the word "spirit." Yet spirit is omnipresent in the poem; it manifests itself primarily in imagery of silence—the point of mystical union with the source. This is the moment when description falters and words cease, as when Dante, aware of the sacred having broken in upon the profane world, realizes that speech has left him, in "Canto XXXIII" of the *Paradiso*. Lao Tzu describes the mystical experience of oneness with the Tao as a rarefied state of soundlessness, an experience that cannot be grasped by the ear's sensual aperture (XIV). Similarly, he describes the Tao, the state of original oneness, as without sound (XXV). Chuang Tzu also counsels instruction in silence as "the substance of the Way" (XIII) and as conducive to achieving communion with "the root"—the "undifferentiated chaos" of the One (XI).[9] In two of the more significant parables in his writings, those concerning Dragon Vision (XI) and the Yellow Emperor (XIV), Chuang Tzu equates silence with the mystical state of unity with ultimate Tao, with that "clouded obscurity where there is no sound."[10]

Similarly, the climax of *River* contains a mystical moment of silence. While meditating upon the spawning salmon one year after the time of the volume's opening poem (Faber edition), Hughes suddenly grasps the metaphysical truth of the river and delivers his revelation in a rapt moment of silent vision. Through an instantaneous seizure of the "spiritual truth of things"—an instance of Coleridgean primary imagination—Hughes attains his deepest penetration into a supratemporal Reality beyond the world of sense:

Something else is going on in the river

More vital than death—death here seems a superficiality
Of small scaly limbs, parasitical. More grave than life
Whose reflex jaws and famished crystals
Seem incidental
To this telling—these toilings of plasm—
The melt of mouthing silence, the charge of light
Dumb with immensity.

· · · · · · · · · · · · · · · · · · ·

It is the swollen vent
Of the nameless
Teeming inside atoms—and inside the haze
And inside the sun and inside the earth.

It is the font, brimming with touch and whisper
Swaddling the egg.

Only birth matters
Say the river's whorls.

And the river
Silences everything in a leaf-mouldering hush

Hughes also conveys the experience of the ineffable in "Salmon Eggs" through imagery other than that of silence. The river as "the swollen vent / Of the nameless" recollects the Nameless, Lao Tzu's term for the Tao in his first chapter. Frequent liturgical imagery underscores the sacredness of the experience. Paradoxes, as at the conclusion of the *Gaudete* "Epilogue," also convey the ineffable. The river's action is at once "More grave than life" and "More vital than death." A paradoxical stasis within movement appears, a frequent Taoist motif for articulating the inner experience of the Tao within the creative artist;[11] hence "The river goes on / Sliding through its place, undergoing itself / In its wheel."

River also contains a subjective, microcosmic thematic level: the penetration to a transphenomenal source is also the artist's reunion with creative energies. Like Eliot's "trilling wire in the blood," the river is a "solid mystery with a living vein" ("River Barrow"), a fusion of "spirit and blood" ("West Dart"), a "womb of lymph" ("Go Fishing"), and the throbbing aorta of creative spasm ("In the Dark Violin of the Valley"). The central persona, as we shall see later in this chapter, achieves a reunion with a creative source in "Salmon Eggs" by moderating his Western tendency to indulge in excessively analytic observation. Then he links up with his creative unconscious, becomes one with the theriomorphic energy of the world beyond the self, recognizes the hand of the White Goddess, and professes a deep sympathy for all created being. Like the *Elmet* poems "Tree" and "A Tree," "Go Fishing" presents Chuang Tzu's advice of "losing" (XV), of divesting oneself of the analytic intellect in order to cultivate the immediacy of first-hand experience. Hughes finds immersion in the suchness of precognitive, concrete experience at once refreshing, healing, and necessary. To be "supplanted by mud and leaves and pebbles" in "Go Fishing," one must "Let brain mist into moist earth" and be "dissolved in earth-wave." To grasp the mind's creative flow one must "Lose words / Cease."

River contains more, however, than an austere Taoist penetration to a metaphysical and creative source. The volume crackles with the Western sounds of nature's energy, sometimes nourishing, at other times awesome, even fearsome. Hughes often compounds electrical imagery with the Blakean metallurgical/alchemical imagery of Los's forge to convey the power of nature, which has its cunning microcosmic counterpart in the poet's imaginative energy. Hence the river in "Flesh of Light" begins in the sun's "smelting," its "core-flash" that "brims out," spilling "boiling light" into "the river's magnetic descent." When Hughes wants to articulate the power of nature's springtime energy renewal, he presents a pool ("Stump Pool in April") as a cauldron

> simmering with oily lights. Deep labour
> Embodied under filmy spanglings. Oxygen
> Boils in its throat, and the new limbs
> Flex and loosen.

Spirit and earth-flesh in "West Dart" merge in a molten fusion as spirit "spills from the Milky Way" onto "the flash-gripped earth" and then into a "mould of quick moor water," to cool in a slag of thunder and rain. And light in "September Salmon" is a mercurial "molten palate."

Hughes also develops serpent imagery to describe nature's energy, especially that derived from the instinctual life of its creatures. In this respect he follows Blake, who frequently associated Orc with serpent imagery, to convey the body's assertive strength. Hence the cormorant's hunting prowess ("A Cormorant") resides in its "Body-snake," just as the heron's powerful flight ("Whiteness") derives from "Clang / Coiling its snake in heavy hurry." In "Last Act" Hughes presents the damselfly as dressed in sensuality, in her "snakeskin leotards."

Blake regularly qualifies his serpent imagery by associating it with time-bound, cyclic finitude—the limitations of Orc's willful, passional self.[12] Some of Hughes's serpent imagery similarly qualifies the powers of the instincts. In "The Gulkana" the persona, having finally ended his quest for salmon, recognizes in the gaze of a beached King Salmon an eye imprisoned in its instinctual life—"small, crazed, snake-like." The Mink of "The Merry Mink" also leads a life restricted to the expenditure of his furious bodily energy, in a "trapped, drowned snake-head."

On one occasion at least, at the opening of Night the Ninth in *The Four Zoas* (pp. 118–19), Blake suggests that humans can transmute the energies of the passional self into wholeness, vision, and the human community, through enlisting the aid of the imagination. Here Orc is reborn through fiery transformational flames; his serpent body transmutes to what Erdman calls "the expanded center of an awakened universe."[13] Hughes presents nature's power of renewal through serpent imagery in "Fairy Flood," but his most positive statement of the power, especially in the artist, to transform energy into awareness occurs at the opening of *River*, in "Flesh of Light":

> This is the sun's oiled snake, dangling, fallen,
> The medicinal mercury creature
>
> Sheathed with the garb, in all its inscribed scales,
> That it sheds
> And refreshes, spasming and whispering.

Hughes conflates the snake's skin-shedding power of renewal with the healing caduceus and with Mercury, both the alchemical agent of transformation and the spirit to be liberated from matter.[14] The "inscribed scales" of course refer to the poet's maieutic agency. On the psychological level, the river in this passage announces the potential for the influx of the imagination into the everyday.

The central persona of *River* does not, however, immediately take advantage of the potential in nature for the active development of imaginative vision. Many of the poems in the first half of the volume simply present sensual impressions of nature in its seasonal lushness—Blake's Beulah world—as in the opening section of *Moortown*. The persona observes and records, and embellishes with vivid diction, but his everyday rational ego often distances him from responding to nature with complete sympathy and openness. Often this distance produces a wry or self-deprecating irony and a corresponding emulous awe of the powerful in nature. In "A Cormorant" the persona admires the predator's ability, like that of the primitive hunter, to concentrate solely upon capturing its prey. The cormorant succeeds because it "becomes fish"; it captures its prey because its diving is a process of "Dissolving himself / Into fish, so dissolving fish naturally / Into himself." Meanwhile the persona frets over his status as an interloper, overequipped with culture's gear: his Barbour jacket is "proof / Against the sky"; his hat embarrasses him; and the cormorant's success leaves him "high and dry in my space-armour." In the last of the "Four March Watercolours" the persona emphasizes another disparity. The frigid water of early spring, with the salmon in coma, contrasts with the "morning-sleep lightness" of the airy human habitat and the persona's perceptual remove from the salmon.

The fisherman persona glances at his watch and frets over schedules in "Milesian Encounter on the Sligachan." As he traces the Sligachan River upstream on the Island of Skye, off the west coast of Scotland, the persona has grand expectations of communing with his treasured salmon, his "fellow-aliens from prehistory." A lengthy hike and an equally lengthy poetic meditation yield the ironic "supernatural fright" of "Only a little salmon." The disparity between grand expectation and meager event only reinforces the persona's distance from prehistory. A mythological allusion compounds the distance. The salmon's "disembodied" head peeps up from the pool, recalling an ancient Celtic tradition, once strong on the Island of Skye, of conferring fertility and healing upon wells associated with decapitated warriors' heads.[15] Many such wells still exist on Skye, and Hughes reinforces his mythological allusion in the penultimate line of the poem, "In the ruinous castle of Skye." The irony is intentional, for the belief structure of this mythology is itself in ruins in the contemporary present. The grand expectation of communing with a salmon, so carefully labored for and so carefully coaxed to fruition in the poem, is in actuality so very minimal and momentary an encounter as to leave the persona tinged with sadness at the insurmountable distance between ancient belief and present fact.

The "Milesians" of the poem's title refers to a legendary group of early invaders who told utterly incredible grandiose tales. Hughes uses the term in a half-comic sense to underscore the irony of the persona's laborious two-mile trek upstream in search of an ordinary salmon. Diction in "Milesian Encounter on the Sligachan" also reinforces the ironic disparity. As the salmon makes her fleeting appearance, the persona magnifies the event through the deliberate use of archaic language and regionalisms. A "Boggart" is a West Yorkshire dialect term for a specter that haunts a particular spot. "Gruagach" and "Glaistig" are Gaelic terms, the former referring to a young maiden or bridesmaid, and the latter denoting a beautiful female fairy, seldom seen except when washing clothes at a stream. All three uses of archaic diction aggrandize the event by placing it in a former mythological context where magic and supernatural visitations were possible. After the longed-for event, however, Hughes chooses the neutral zoological term for the Atlantic salmon species, the Latin "*Salmo Salar*," to heighten the ironic deflation. The persona cannot sustain the magical mythological context; the visitor is "Only a little salmon."

In other poems in the first half of *River*, Hughes attests to nature's momentary beauty, especially by pointing out rhythms that alternate in a temporal process of change and decay. These observations also signify a limited Beulah world context: the poetic consciousness does not suffuse the landscape with imagination in such a way as to humanize nature and create one Blakean Divine Body of Imagination, where body, mind, spirit, and the perceived unite in the act of perception.[16] Ironic disparities dominate. "Japanese River Tales," for instance, presents nature's alternate beauty and terror through a folktale device. The Japanese have a legend of Yuki-onna, the Snow Woman, about primitives' attempt to comprehend the contradictory beauty and deadliness of a blizzard. Yuki-onna, a variant of the swan maiden folklore motif, appears in the first beautiful flakes of a coming storm. Then she lulls men to sleep, to experience death in her terrifyingly cold embrace. In one instance Yuki-onna supposedly lulled to death an older man, but spared his younger companion when he promised never to speak her name. The survivor later married a woman named Yuki, a Japanese word for snow. Yuki proved a loving wife until one day her demeanor reminded him of the tragic episode of his youth. When he spoke her name she melted away forever, returning to her celestial abode.[17]

"Japanese River Tales" presents Hughes's poetic rendering of unredeemed nature's variability, through the device of the Snow Woman. The river at first appears beautiful at the onset of a storm, as the female spirit, "Glint-slippered" and bejeweled, enters the river's "grasping bed." The next night, however, the "snow princess" comports herself quite differently. Her kiss is a vise grip that "locks / On the dislodged vertebrae," and her fingers are talons that "open / The long belly of blood." At the end of the poem a ghastly Yuki-onna returns heavenward; she "flies / Through the shatter of space and / Out of being."

Other riverscapes present nature as a crux of disparate tendencies, unredeemed by an actively engaged imaginative effort to resolve antinomies by penetrating into the "spiritual truth of things." "The Morning Before Christmas," the opening poem in the Faber edition, celebrates nature's plenty and human stewardship over nature, without obscuring the cruel facts that motivate eight men in assisting its processes. The salmon's luck in the lottery of birth and death is "five thousand to one against survival," and the men sling out dead salmon as well as coax the clottings of eggs and milt. The experience "Dazzle-stamped" the persona's consciousness, but he refrains from investing the actual with deeper significance. The events are as delicate and as momentary as a fox's "touch-melted and refrozen dot-prints."

Events and riverscapes, however lush and beautiful, are distanced or restricted to momentary reactions to the actual in most of the poems before "After Moonless Midnight." Such is the case in "New Year," "Whiteness," "Four March Watercolours," "Ophelia," and "Dee." In "New Year" the persona sees the old year in the throes of a difficult cesarian. The hospital metaphor continues throughout the poem, emphasizing only an ordeal of pain, to the complete neglect of the "ticking egg" of rebirth. The antinomy remains unresolved. The fisherman of "Whiteness" becomes totally preoccupied with presenting the heron as a predator in search of filling his belly. Here Hughes uses the pathetic fallacy deliberately, to emphasize the heron's instinctively utilitarian analysis: the heron ponders, looks, and sees, finally becoming "an open question" to the fisherman. This mentalized distance creates a disparity: the river "nags to be elsewhere."

"Four March Watercolours," as the painterly metaphor implies, presents the fluid, kinetic changeability of the river—its Beulah world aspect. Throughout the poem's four sections the river is "Fully occupied with its callisthenics, / Its twistings and self-wrestlings." The only solution provided by the poem is that of death, an inevitable, never-ending "all-out evacuation / To the sea," presented in a dispassionate, neutral tone. The poem ends by affirming the river's "oldest commerce"—its cargo of deathly flotsam—but does not delve into specific applications to the human world. As in "Ophelia," the river's engine carries within its ghostly makeup the taint of death. Conversely, the controlling image of "Dee" is that of the snowcapped hills as "shining paps" whose springtime runoff nourishes the rivers. Hence the beautiful concluding metaphor of the river as a jeweled necklace dangling in "The high, frozen bosom" of the snowy hills. The purpose of "Dee" is restricted to celebrating the seasonal splendor of early spring in the riverscape surrounding the Scottish Dee.

A number of first-half poems in *River*, placed closer to the center of the volume, announce the possibility of grasping a spiritual dimension behind landscape and riverscape. "The Merry Mink" and "Creation of Fishes," for instance, take reader and persona back to primitives' playfully earnest attempts to locate spiritual significance in earthly events, in ways that satisfy the need to conform godly operations to the limits of human intelligence. The Mink, a trickster figure and culture hero for the Salish and other Northwest Coast American Indian tribes in the Puget Sound and British Columbia areas, announces his freedom from mimesis and realism. Hughes may be trying to account for the incredible energy of the Mink, who is "Aboil with lightnings / He can't get rid of," by alluding to the ending of an American Indian folktale of how the Son of the Sun shoots an arrow ladder to the sky to join his father. But the son, impatient and careless when given the opportunity to manage his father's duties, is condemned to revert to earth in the form of a mink.[18] Hughes intimates that the Mink's energetic playfulness is a reflex of divine power, allowing him the imaginative freedom, spontaneity, and obliviousness to the everyday, to make his life a charmed arena. Yet the persona carefully notes that the Mink lives in prosaic times, "lost from his mythology," and plays "As if he were deathless." The merry Mink, too much the optimist, at least announces the possibility of imaginative communion with a spiritual dimension.

"Creation of Fishes" is in part a "just so" story of why the salmon has red flesh (it has its Sun-father's "flame-beauty") and why it cannot live out of water (the Moon tricked the Sun because the earth was too hot under his paternalistic dominance). But the poem offers more; it equates the Moon's slyness with imaginative intelligence. The Moon, more regularly associated with the artistic in cultural history, is more subtle, imaginative, and humane than the plodding, simpleton Sun. Her offspring "spangled" in her less harsh, less direct rays, while the Sun's children burned and shriveled in his blunt energy. Hughes may or may not have been meditating upon a particular North American Indian or Eskimo folktale, but the poem's message is that only the cooler imagination accommodates and often resolves nature's antinomies.

Other riverscapes suggest the presence of the spiritual as a dimension within the everyday, could the doors of human perceptions be cleansed. The persona of "Salmon-taking Times" avoids the river when it is muddied by a flood-rain, but is moved to apprehend the possibility of a "religious moment" when a warm shower arrays the river in "gossamer bridal veils." In "Under the Hill of Centurions," the seasonal massing of cock minnows in a pool crypt, "All singing and / Toiling together" before mating, invites the persona's admiration of a solid wealth of bodies in solemn fulfillment of the demands of eros. A fleeting glimpse into the spiritual follows: "Ghostly rinsings / A struggle of spirits." The first greenery surrounding a stump pool suggests to the persona of "Stump Pool in April" that the river wishes to respond by sprouting wings and raising itself into a freedom-filled imaginary world, so to mate behind the hill-wood's violet bridal veil. "River Barrow" recounts the slightly dazed, almost cloyingly still moment just before a breakthrough into the spiritual. Hughes ingests the Barrow's honey-sweet savor, "All evil suspended." Light imagery, a sense of mystery, and paradoxes begin to accrete. The Barrow becomes a "Great weight / Resting effortless on the weightless." Past, present, and future begin to collect on the still point of the river's "thick nerve," its "solid mystery / With a living vein." But the poem stops just short of a visitation of the numinous.

"Go Fishing" and "Strangers" propel the persona into the reversal of "After Moonless Midnight." In "Go Fishing" the fisherman recognizes the need to lose the analytical persona that distances himself from nature and restricts his duties simply to registering and embellishing impressions. He must wade into the river and become immersed in experience in a much more direct, unself-conscious way, without the ready-made responses of his conscious artistry. He must "Be supplanted by mud and leaves and pebbles" and by the water's lighted "sun-melt." Here the Taoist imperatives to abandon analytic thinking, personal ego, and all the cultural gear that insulates one from perceiving nature directly help the persona to release his imaginative powers. Just before "After Moonless Midnight" the seatrout appear, in "Strangers." They are "bowed in preoccupation" with some deep spiritual presence, and thus oblivious to hogweed and water-skeeters. The seatrout, the more adventurous of England's brown trout population, return from feeding in the Atlantic and await their mating duties in silent contemplation. In a state of yogic *samādhi*, they have abandoned exactly what the persona of "Go Fishing" counsels one to abandon. Their "blank of bliss" gradually takes the persona and the reader out of the Beulah world by cleansing the doors of perception, to perceive the spiritual dimension.

"After Moonless Midnight" marks a change in direction in *River*. First-half poems like "The Morning Before Christmas," "New Year," "Salmon-taking Times," and "Milesian Encounter on the Sligachan" suggest that the fisherman persona stalks the treasured salmon in *River*. But in "After Moonless Midnight" suddenly the fish, in their "magical skins," stalk the fisherman. In beginning to divest himself of his analytic ego and his typical responses to nature, the fisherman opens his soul to uniting with visitations of numinous power. Now the fish world has "got him." The poem recollects many themes in Hughes's poetry: the theriomorphism of *Lupercal*; the hunter becoming the hunted in "The Harvesting" (*Wodwo*) and in the chase scene of *Gaudete*; the onset of *tz'ŭ* sympathy for creation, from *Remains of Elmet*; and *Moortown's* organizational movement from Beulah world to the Edenic realm where the imagination actively participates in grasping the spiritual in a flash and draws all into a humanized vision, a harmony of perception and environment. At the poem's end the river and its fish "held me deeper / With its blind, invisible hands."

In his "Introduction" to Sagar's *The Reef*, Hughes dwells a number of times upon Stephen Crane's ability, often present in his poetry, to perceive a spiritual dimension operating within observed nature. Crane, an iconoclast who abandoned conventional rhyme and religion, humanized the ironic clash of human isolation against indifferent nature and its often vengeful God. A pre-Kafka questioner of the lack of moral purpose in nature, as in "Blustering God" and "God fashioned the ship of the world carefully" (*The Black Riders*), Crane redeems human weakness by emphasizing the heroic but doomed suffering of the isolated individual, awash in a sinful frailty that can at best create a community of human suffering. The spiritual dimension is always present in Crane's poetry, though it often appears as a sham set of religious conventions to be arraigned as hollow. The only morality Crane can find is the courage of the individual who can suffer stoically the battle wounds that the vengeful God inflicts through nature, his handmaiden. In the process the doomed hero purifies himself through affirming an inner dimension, a code of personal honor, suffering, and honesty. In his discussion of "To the Maiden," from *War Is Kind*, Daniel G. Hoffman affirms that one of the illusions that Crane's personae must strip from their thoughts, in order to achieve honesty, is the one that assumes that "Nature, because occasionally beautiful, has any care for us in the vistas we admire."[19]

Many parallels exist between Crane's poetry and the poems of the second half of *River*, especially the emphasis upon suffering and the attempt to develop an inner dimension that can accommodate the spiritual potential of experience beyond the self. One significant difference exists: Hughes is far less eager than Crane to arraign the Creator or his handmaiden. Throughout *River* Hughes accepts the terms of the struggle, sees the majesty and beauty of it, and celebrates nature's "lime-bitter brightness." He does not expect the Tao or Blakean energy to conform to any anthropocentric categories of morality. Yet in the second half of *River* the central persona is far less apt simply to record vividly the impressions that nature offers; the poems reveal a Blakean imagination *actively* involved in resolving the actual and the spiritual dimensions in an instantaneous grasp of significance. A Coleridgean primary imagination creates one Blakean Divine Body of Imagination where nature is humanized, suffused with relevance for the world of the mortal perceiver. Spiritual perception and artistic creation become one. Often in the poems that follow "After Moonless Midnight" Hughes offers his readers the most complete celebration of the "war between vitality and death," the theme he announced in his very first (1957) statement on poetics, through revealing the spiritual dimensions of suffering. In many of the poems in the second half of *River*, Hughes generates examples of that rare type of simplicity he spoke about in the "Introduction" to Sagar's *The Reef*, the one where the observer has worked through the complexity of the experience.

"Last Act" is just one of many poems in the second half of *River* where the experience has changed the observer and led him to a direct grasp of the spiritual significance of the event. In the mating behavior of the damselfly or dragonfly,[20] which has survived since Mesozoic times, Hughes resolves the struggle of love and death in a Blakean last act of forgiveness. To comprehend the poem first requires some entomological exegesis. In most species of damselflies and dragonflies, the male stakes out a territory of a dozen or so square meters and attempts to mate with any female of his species that traverses his area during mating hours. The *Sympetrum striolatum* of southern England, for instance, mate for about fifteen seconds in air and then settle on a branch, continuing the love act for another fifteen minutes. Often the coloration of the female—what Hughes fancifully depicts as her "snakeskin leotards," "acetylene jewels," and "crazed enamels"—arouses the male to fly up to her and mate when she crosses his territory.

For the male's chance attentions the female pays dearly. Damselfly and dragonfly females normally oviposit the fertilized eggs immediately after copulation, in the male's territory, in most species (including *Sympetrum striolatum*) by gently lowering their abdomens or their entire bodies into the water. Here they deposit the eggs in a branch of a well-rooted water plant, after first serrating it. Though the male may remain in tandem, directly above her throughout oviposition, his typical role is one of guardian nearby. During the few minutes to a half hour when the female is ovipositing, she is very vulnerable to predation by surface-feeding fish, insects, birds, amphibians, and other male dragonflies. Or she may damage her wings irreparably through contact with water and abrasions from the branches of the plants in which she deposits the eggs. Few females of the New Zealand *Uropetala carovei*, for instance, survive their first underwater oviposition. Thus the damselfly of "Last Act" is portrayed as a Greek trage-dienne stepping "so magnetically to her doom."

Were Crane to write a poem about damselfly mating, he would empha-size the chance encounter and the foredoomed biological urge. Hughes rather focuses upon the beauty of love and death so completely inter-twined, recapitulating a lifetime's arc within minutes. The male also pays dearly, for the female's powerful embrace kills him. Having spent himself, he dies fittingly, wreathed in the "nightfall pall" of the erotically fragrant balsam. Fulfilling the reproductive demands of the species is the male damselfly's last act, as it probably also is the female's, since she is "lifted out of the river with tweezers." But the real last act of the poem is that of Hughes himself, as he raises this microtragedy to significance by focusing upon the stark interrelationship of love and death and by resolving the struggle through inferring the humanly satisfying act of forgiveness. A chance encounter and momentary amorousness may have caused the cur-tain to fall upon the damselflies, but "Everything is forgiven" in the per-sona's gaze as he celebrates a transfiguring "metamorphosis in love." Here the poetic imagination is actively involved in incorporating all essentials in a clear, simple solution, having recognized the spiritual dimensions of the event.

The river coaxes the persona's imagination into intimations of mortality and death in the riverscapes "Torridge," "Last Night," "August Evening," and "In the Dark Violin of the Valley." Images of darkness and of the music of instinctual life, a major motif in *Gaudete*, recur in these poems. The North Devon "Torridge" in the fall induces meditations upon the river's obliviousness to death. Hughes personifies the river's seasonal round as a woman who saunters and sings in carefree unconcern. She is a "novelty" from the red of mud (mortal) side of Adam. Venus warmth and Jupiter cold circle about her, forcing perennials like garlic and iris to endure a life cycle strained with seasonally contending opposites, but the river herself "has not once tasted death." Human implications for the "war between vitality and death" reside very near the surface of "Torridge." The persona of "Last Night" wades into the river and feels at first hand how its slimes, its old roots and holes, and its "blood-dark, old blood-dark" evil reminded him of the decay in all organic matter. The feel of this river is like being in a sick-bed or grave, and repetitions of the words "dark" and "evil" throughout the poem intensify this feeling. So do the images of the toxic hemlock, and of the alder and oak, trees associated with the sacrificial heroes Bran and Her-cules.[21] Images of oaks and alders similarly appear in "August Evening" to convey the first inklings of deathly winter, after summer fires and "the barley disaster" have spent their force and left the land charred and bare. The river's last "ghostly trail of smoke" completes an extended metaphor of summer's sacrificial blaze having reached its end, leaving the fumes of mortality. In these apparently easeful riverscapes the extended metaphors reveal decay, the fate of all participants in nature's seasonal cycle.

The extended metaphor of violin music becomes a synesthetic probe into the persona's nerves and aorta "In the Dark Violin of the Valley." The music has a "lancing" effect that cuts to both "bed-rock" and "earth-nerve," while it simultaneously sews body and soul with sky and earth. Persona and environment become one with mortality's sad tune played by the river on the valley floor's elongated violin. Even the dead are stirred into the role of a bowed chorus. Like a needle the river's music sews its water into the sea, its deadly mouth. Though a passage in the second of the "Four March Watercolours" speaks of the river's deathly evacuation of all substance into the sea, the tone and technique differ considerably from "In the Dark Violin of the Valley." The persona of "In the Dark Violin of the Valley" fixes a quiet, steady gaze upon his subject and develops the extended metaphors of music and sewing very deliberately; he becomes a participant, enveloped in the river's orchestration and stitchery. The persona of "Four March Watercolours" is self-consciously aware of his own shadow, while the river appears oblivious to his perceptions, preoccupied with its springtime calisthenics, its energy and movement. The second-half *River* poem reveals an eschatological dimension to ponder in every stanza; the first-half poem leaves the reader with fresh impressions of particular details and facts that sometimes move the persona to generalizations, but generalizations that do not enlist the feelings to contemplate a spiritual dimension.

Other poems in the second half of *River*, not concerned with the river's mouth of mortality, present the persona's more active attempt to use his imagination to fuse with the subject and to penetrate toward a glimpse of the transphenomenal or to satirize another for remaining secure in passive analysis. The Kingfisher's speed and energy, for instance, become vehicles for apprehending the spiritual in "The Kingfisher." His "sudden electric wire" is so powerful and instantaneous as to shatter the river's phenomenal mirror ("Erupts through the mirror") or to cut its material surface, and the persona's eye, with a diamond point. The Kingfisher probes deeper, behind the phenomenal event, to give the observer a glimpse of godly theriomorphic energy welding matter and spirit:

> Through him, God, whizzing in the sun,
> Glimpses the angler.

Through him, God
Marries a pit
Of fishy mire.

Just as instantaneously he is gone, a "Spark, sapphire, refracted / From beyond water."

In "An Eel" Hughes describes the eel's minimal orifices for sensing the phenomenal world as an attempt to wall out the profane everyday, to hoard a greater "Inward" apprehension, some "large awareness." The snout is "squashed," the mouth "perfunctory," and the pectoral fin its sole "concession / To fish-life." Even the eel's skin appears to be "insulation," a "rubberized weave . . . / Sealed from event." Alone and solitary, the eel, a leftover from less prosaic evolutionary times, seems to commune with the source, with a mystical vision from her inward eye.

"A Rival" contains an explicit judgment of the first-half poems "Whiteness" and "A Cormorant." In both earlier poems the persona insulated himself from experience by rational analysis or a self-effacing consciousness of culture's gear. But in "A Rival" the persona actively engages his imagination in humanizing the event—in applying animal behavior to human behavior. Here the cormorant is revealed in his naked predatory truth, as one who mutilates the river with the eye of a "commissar" who draws an "iron curtain" of appetitive self-interest over it. The cormorant's head is a Hitlerian "Sound-proof cellar of final solutions." Stanzas III and IV remind one of the amoral hawk of "Hawk Roosting" (*Lupercal*), and stanza VII of the rationalizing intellect of "The judge" in *Cave Birds*. The cormorant's strength resides in his ruthless reduction of all to his will-to-power and its hedonistic imperatives. His power to "reduce / All the blood in the world, yet still taste nothing" appears in humans also; the poem reminds us of a "Cancer in the lymph" to which our species is vulnerable.

The gentle irony of "Riverwatcher" reproves both birdwatcher and angler as imperfect appreciators of what nature can offer. The angler should not keep his "head clear" of the "river-fetch"; he should not "Cling to the gnat" in "dry difficulty." And the birdwatcher should not "sit brambly still" while peeping at nature through binoculars. Of course they must remain quiet, but they should open their imaginations to the ecstasy of the river-fetch that flashes from "The river's polished key-hole." Communion with river-fetch means uniting body, soul, and environment, including their spiritual dimensions, in one unitive dance, one ecstatic cry of the awakened spirit. In his "Glossary" to *The Conference of the Birds*, Nott translates *Bismillah*, an Arabic word used by Attar, as "in the name of God." The ecstatic dance that

Hughes longs for when he uses *Bismillah* in "Riverwatcher" recalls the dancer images in Yeats and Eliot, where dancer and dance cannot be distinguished or, to follow Blake's Edenic vision, one where spirit, body, mind, perception, and environment liquify "in the river of its own music"—in a total atonement of communion.

This is precisely the message of Hughes's 1984 children's volume *What Is the Truth?*. In this fable God the Father and God the Son visit earth, to satisfy the Son's curiosity about humankind. To learn something really significant about humans, the Father suggests that they visit at night, when the editing, calculating intellects of the village folk are asleep and when their souls are free to speak the truth about their relationships to nature. A Farmer and his family, a Vicar, Schoolteacher, Poacher, and Shepherd sing the praises of the animal world, each from his or her own perspective and knowledge, in vivid children's verse. At the end of the volume, when God the Son becomes impatient to know which person's account is the truth, God the Father, beaming beatifically, reveals that *all* versions together are the truth, because his substance suffuses all of their enthusiastic accounts, in one dance of the quickened spirit: "As I am, I am. I am that Foal. And I am the Cow. . . . I am each of these things. The Rat. The Fly. And each of these things is Me. It is. It is. That is the Truth."[22]

The most important difference between the *River* poems placed before "After Moonless Midnight" and those placed after concerns the salmon poems. The salmon are briefly mentioned often enough in first-part poems such as "New Year," "Dee," "Salmon-taking Times," and "River Barrow," but occupy the center of only four poems: "The Morning Before Christmas," the fourth of "Four March Watercolours," "Milesian Encounter on the Sligachan," and "Creation of Fishes." Only "Creation of Fishes" announces in a very oblique, folktale way the spiritual potential of salmon. As we have seen, "The Morning Before Christmas" celebrates the actual struggle and generative capacity of the salmon, from a Beulah world perspective, and "Milesian Encounter on the Sligachan" reveals the salmon as restricted to a prosaic world of zoological nomenclature, though they may swim in wells once supported by beliefs that were more sensitive to the workings of the spirit. Hughes introduces the reader of *River* to the spiritual potential of salmon in first-half poems, but these salmon are cut off from any deeper relationship to the persona, as in the fourth of "Four March Watercolours":

the snow-melt
Is an invisible restraint. If there are salmon
Under it all, they are in coma. They are stones

Lodged among stones, sealed as fossils
Under the grained pressure. I look down onto the pour
Of melted chocolate. They look up
At a guttering lamp
Through a sand-storm boil of silt
That scratches their lidless eyes,
Fumes from their gill-petals. They have to toil,
Trapped face-workers, in their holes of position
Under the mountain of water.

Here the salmon remain distanced, in a coma of objective fact, trapped like miners under the weight of the actual, unchanging elements, while the analytical eye of the persona is a "guttering lamp." The actual becomes a limit of opacity in restricted vision: the persona looks into the obscuring "melted chocolate" of muddy water, and the churning silt scratches the eyes of the salmon. Even when the persona empathizes with the scene and considers himself in the second watercolor as a tree that has survived another winter, perception remains limited: the human is naturalized, not the natural humanized.

The salmon in the history of North American Indian folklore and Celtic mythology have a richer tradition that is more substantively connected to humans. The importance of salmon for the survival of the Pacific Coast Indians cannot be doubted, but these Indians also saw the salmon as a gift from a spiritual realm. The culture heroes Raven, Coyote, Txa'msem, and Mink introduce salmon in their travels. Shared tales of the salmon as the gift of Bright-Cloud Woman or Salmon Woman reveal a reverence for nature as the source of life, for the salmon are available in abundance only so long as Trickster reveres Bright-Cloud Woman as wife. In these tales the salmon are a special expression of sustenance from the source.[23] Finn mac Cumhal in Celtic mythology received his supernatural wisdom and his prophetic powers from sucking his thumb, which had been burnt when cooking the salmon of knowledge for his master in the arts of poetry and magic.[24] In *The Mabinogion* story *Culhwch and Olwyn*, only the Salmon of Llyn Llyw, oldest and wisest of animals, knows where Mabon resides; without Mabon's help Culhwch cannot complete the series of tasks that would win him Olwyn's hand.[25]

Though Hughes does not allude to this rich heritage of salmon lore in *River*, the salmon as symbolic of wisdom and of sustenance from the source underlies much of the second half of the volume. Once the fish have "got him" in "After Moonless Midnight," the organizational progression of

River becomes an ever-deepening understanding of what wisdom and sustenance the salmon can impart to the fisherman. The central persona gradually comprehends what wisdom the salmon hold for his concerns—what the salmon mean to humans. Gradually the distance between self and other collapses, while the epic sweep of the returning salmon enacts a drama of mortality that calls out the poet's soul toward a synthesis of animal energy and human imagination. The persona's deeper involvement in reality transforms *River* into a personalized universe suffused with spiritual sight. In the process human mortality, the river's mouth, is transfigured—elevated to sacrament, an outward, visible sign of inward spiritual grace.

"An August Salmon" directly follows "After Moonless Midnight" and initiates a growing awareness in the persona of what wisdom the salmon have for him. The persona responds sympathetically to the salmon as a "holed up gangster" or a "bridegroom, mortally wounded / By love and destiny," a god on earth suffering "the clock of love and death in his body." Humbly and thankfully the salmon kneels, a bridegroom worshiping his river bride, the necessary and "ceaseless gift / That unwinds the spool of his strength." In the liturgical and marriage imagery of the poem, fish body and water spirit merge, aided by the great fund of sympathetic feeling Hughes establishes in the tone of the poem, while the fisherman persona moves magnetically toward communion with the plight of the salmon. Though he may try to muscle free, the salmon will inevitably drop his bodily weight, the martyrdom of his "riveted skull," into his oxymoronic "wedding cell," there to await "execution and death / In the skirts of his bride."

The river in "An August Salmon" has become not only a limiting condition for the salmon's survival, but also an instance of White Goddess worship. "Alone, in a cellar of ashroots," the male salmon waits for the female to arrive and stir the water—to hollow out a crevice, create a grotto for their tryst, a safe repository for the fertilized eggs, and (Hughes intimates) a grave for the male lover. By the end of the poem the objective eye of the persona has evaporated in poetic vision's teardrop. The conclusion of "An August Salmon" approximates what Blake called "Spiritual Sensation,"[26] where the imagination reveals the world without and within, as John Middleton Murry once noted, a place where the river bathes "the sentient soul . . . in the waters of the spirit."[27] Blake knew this Edenic state as one where man's "perceptions are not bounded by organs of perception. He perceives more than sense . . . can discover."[28]

The very title of "That Morning," the next salmon poem in the second half of *River*, recollects the Eliadean *illud tempus* moment of participation in godly energy and a prelapsarian communion with all created beings. Both "That Morning" and "The Gulkana," the subsequent salmon poem, relate the experiences of Hughes and his son Nicholas while on a fishing trip in southern Alaska in the summer of 1980. In "That Morning" the two men, waist deep in an Arctic river, feel the press of an entire school of salmon sliding past them. Here "doubting thought" retreats, while the body becomes "a spirit-beacon / Lit by the power of the salmon." The walls that divide man from man and man from all other orders of creation slide away as the fish elevate the fisherman's perceptions "toward some dazzle of blessing." The experience reconstitutes reality for Hughes. And when the gold bears enter and sport, and eat salmon as if sharing their dinner with the fishermen, the entire event becomes a paradisal journey's end, a moment of participation in the allness of being, lit by the beams of spirit brightness. So the men stand "alive in the river of light / Among the creatures of light, creatures of light." Mind, body, the moment of perception, and the perceived are transfigured into one unity, one Divine Body of Imagination.

"The Gulkana" has two versions: the earlier "Gulkana" in the Faber edition and "The Gulkana" in the Harper and Row, enlarged by about forty-two lines of new verse. Both poems recount the same experience of temporarily beaching a huge Chinook salmon in the "express torrent" of the Gulkana River in southeastern Alaska, near where it meets the Copper River, whose waters flow south into the Gulf of Alaska. Yet the two poems are very different in emphasis, and the revisions are significant. The earlier version takes an ironic stance much like "Milesian Encounter on the Sligachan." In the earlier poem the persona battles his disinherited *Doppelgänger*, one whose tastes revert toward a lost paradisal communion with prehistory and who laughs at the interloper fisherman preoccupied with his gear. The irony continues through the central passage where the persona observes the King Salmon's eye. Its dwarf, refrigerated lens further undercuts the quest for the prehistoric encounter. Like Lumb and his female parishioners in *Gaudete*, this salmon seems possessed by the music of limited instinctual existence. The fisherman concludes that the Gulkana salmon are "drugged victims" of the torrent's "drums and flutes," with a future restricted to "The actual, sundering death."

The revised version contains the same *Doppelgänger* passage, but the dismissively objective fisherman who limits himself to the actual is completely changed with the expansion of thirty lines at exactly the point where this persona meets the salmon's eye. In the revision the persona takes a much more compassionate position and celebrates the sacramental "orgy of eggs and sperm, / The dance-orgy of being reborn" in a necessary ritual that tears the masks off the salmon and leads to a healing communion "In the mercy of water, at the star of the source." The salmon are "somnambulists," but not in the surreal world of Lumb's musical orgy. This dance is positive, fulfilling; the sacramental imagery added by Hughes in the revised version suggests a spiritual purpose and links "The Gulkana" thematically with the later "September Salmon" and "Salmon Eggs." Another addition later in "The Gulkana" reveals the persona sympathetically recognizing his kinship with the salmon's dance of mortality:

Word by word

> The burden of the river moved in me
> Like lovesickness.
> Woke deeper, a secret bleeding of mourning,
> In my cave of body.
> While I recorded
> The King Salmon's eye.

While the original "Gulkana" conclusion presents the persona sadly leaving a decayed culture whose salmon remain "drugged victims" of instincts they cannot rise above, the revised conclusion in "The Gulkana" presents the persona's imagination actively engaged in humanizing the objects it perceives. The tone of Hughes's homeward departure at the conclusion of the revision is completely changed to one of attesting to the bravery of all life and the necessity of celebrating the fittingness of mortality's love orgy. The memory of the "one-rose rose" near the tent becomes in the revision one of "brave exposure," not the earlier "mock aperture." The experience is no longer an ironically sobering reminder of the folly of human expectations and designs, but a testament to the potential for spiritual renewal within and beyond the actual. In the revised version we are offered a "simultaneous vision of some spiritual truth of things. . . . within the observed one." The vision redeems the drab setting of the "comatose" Indian village and the "Arctic landslide of the Copper / Which was the colour of cement." The message of "After Moonless Midnight" becomes clear: the fisherman stalking the prelapsarian salmon is himself stalked by a fish that reveals to him his own mortality and his complicity in the drama of love and death—a truth Achilles learned when he viewed his own armor on the dead body of Patroclos in The Iliad.

Having recognized this complicity, the fisherman in "September Salmon" attains a greater reverence for life. The poem celebrates the salmon's return to his spawning grounds as a humble submission to nature's demands. In a simple reversed image on the river's surface, the persona sees the salmon performing in tragic glory "In the upside-down cage of a tree." The salmon gains a dignity in his suffering through the flexing lens of the persona's Edenic imagination: the salmon's patient endurance is highlighted by the implied allusion to Odin's upside-down sacrifice of himself to himself in *The Poetic Edda*, to gain prophetic inspiration and an enlarged inner life. The liturgical imagery of the penultimate stanza is the direct result of the persona's freedom-filled lens flex discerning spiritual truth behind the actual event. In the last stanza the salmon achieves an apotheosis into spiritual significance, as the imagery incorporates the actual and penetrates behind it. The salmon leaps in the September sun and into transfigured vision—into a recovery of what Blake called the "Golden Age" of imaginative delight: [29]

> Over the sky the skeeters traffic, godlike and double-jointed.
> He lifts
> To the molten palate of mercurial light
> And adds his daub.

The full recovery of the persona's imagination has enlarged his inner vistas. The octogenarian fisherman depicted in "Eighty and Still Fishing for Salmon" fishes in the stillness of his awareness, "Loyal to inbuilt bearings." Though the poem contains no actual salmon, it enriches and expands, like "An Eel," the parallel inner dimension, where the aging fisherman's sensitivity for the angler's art still plays, and where again and again "His fly will come round on the vacant swirl" because his intuitions apprehend a larger reality than the fishless nets outside the hotel. The *Nōh* dancer allusion in the last stanza fits this inner world emphasis perfectly. The octogenarian's stillness exhibits the artistic restraint and control, the outer economy of movement and inner concentration, that Zeami Motokiyo desired in his treatises on the art of the *Nōh* drama. [30]

Every exclamation point in "October Salmon" expresses a sympathetic outcry against death—for man as well as for the aging salmon. At an average of four years and six pounds, according to Hughes, the salmon returns to his birth pool to spawn, the birth pool then becoming his graveyard. Though only the Pacific salmon dies after his first spawning, and the penultimate stanza definitely places this salmon in the canals of England, "Under a mill-wall," a note to a photograph on page 126 of the Faber edition reminds us that few Atlantic salmon survive the spawning run. They are preyed upon by sport fishermen; by commercial nets, seines, and weirs; by low water in the spring or by the winter cold that follows spawning; and by otters, seals, and sea lions near the river's mouth. For all practical purposes, a close collocation exists, as in "Last Act," between birth and death in the salmon's life. The exclamation points mark an outcry against death that applies to the salmon, to humankind in general, and to Hughes in particular. Hughes was born in a West Yorkshire terraced house whose rear bordered upon a canal; he fished there regularly as a child. Once again the fisherman persona humanizes nature. How short is life, whether for four finny years or for the poet's three score and ten:

> What a change! from that covenant of Polar Light
> To this shroud in a gutter!
> What a death-in-life—to be his own spectre!
> His living body become death's puppet,
> Dolled by death in her crude paints and drapes
> He haunts his own staring vigil
> And suffers the subjection, and the dumbness,
> And the humiliation of the role!

The central tension in "October Salmon" derives from the opposition between the river and its flow, and the aging skin of the salmon, his "death-patched" embroidery. The river represents both the moment-to-moment flow of phenomenal experience, and a "she"—the White Goddess as the poetic and spiritual possibilities within the phenomenal flow. Though the salmon's skin shows the dignity of age, "The flow will not let up for a minute." The river tires out the hero as his skin becomes ever more wizened and pitiable—"patched with leper-cloths," the "clownish regimentals" of death, his "whole body / A fungoid anemone of canker."

The fisherman resolves the opposition in the last five stanzas, through expanded vision. The individual body is finally understood as a mere vehicle, an "armature of energy," and the salmon rides that energy for his allotted time as if on a roller coaster "surge-ride" of nature's power. More importantly, the persona ends the poem in complete identification with the salmon, inferring that the salmon values deeply his loyalty to genetic code, home, and river mother. At this point the poem achieves an epic grandeur, as the tragic salmon awaits his end in "epic poise," in full awareness of his fate, with a full knowledge of how what was "inscribed in his egg" is also

"stitched into his torn richness." The poem concludes with no distance between the persona's mind and feelings, or between perception and the object it contemplates. The seemingly simple, artless use of the pathetic fallacy resolves a great deal in a solution that reveals a spiritual dimension.
All is gathered together in Blake's "Spiritual Sensation."

River began with a celebration of the salmon's actual "five thousand to
one" struggle for survival in nature's lottery of birth and death. From this
beginning the central persona developed an ironic distance and a relatively
passive recording of impressions of nature's richness. Gradually this persona penetrated toward an apprehension of the spiritual significance of the
"war between vitality and death" and a deep sympathy for those involved
in this ultimately tragic homage to the White Goddess of the river flow.
"Salmon Eggs," the concluding poem of *River*, presents Hughes's deepest,
most clairvoyant insights into the spiritual significance of nature's cycle of
love and death. The use of silence and paradox to convey a mystical apprehension of a metaphysical first principle has already been discussed at
the opening of this chapter. But now one can fully appreciate the completeness of the fisherman's embrace of both river and salmon. As he meditates upon the river, and the salmon's deathward return to the sea after
"Emptying themselves for each other," the persona divests himself of his
ego, his "me," and merges with the perceived in one complete embrace,
alive to the spiritual dimension within the "piled flow" of moment-to-
moment experience:

> my eyes forget me
>
> And the piled flow supplants me, the mud-blooms
>
> All this ponderous light of everlasting

Like the salmon, the fisherman acknowledges his dependency upon the
ceaseless gift of the river's flow and becomes one with it. He grasps the
mutuality of suffering and extinction, the intertwining of love and death, in
the salmon's yearly spawning ritual and undergoes a baptism with a chrism
of water, now perceived as emanating from a holy font.

"*Only birth matters*" is a mystical moment of visionary assent to ontological purpose. In animal master rituals of primitive hunting tribes, death signifies only a return to new birth of a primal essence involved in an endless
process of creation.[31] Similarly, in Taoism the Tao manifests itself as a

creatio continua flux, a continual process of birth, return, and transformation—a swelling, perfect embryo in primordial amniotic water, forever engaged in fertile stirring.[32] Thus in "Salmon Eggs" the sun is a "veined yolk," the river water is the nourishing fluid that swaddles the egg of creation, and the male salmon are sperm on their errand. With transfigured vision the persona glimpses the dimensions of stasis and process, flux and return, to a metaphysical source.

The Blakean energy of the river's whorls in "Salmon Eggs" unites with Taoist light, as an awakened, Los-like imagination forges a complete union of mind and body, perceived and perceiver. Just as Albion becomes one with Jerusalem in the reintegration of his senses, during his entrance into the furnace flames at the end of *Jerusalem*, so Hughes becomes one with the river, and one with its human and animal spawn, in one baptism of water. The actual is no longer a limit of opacity, but a Blakean opportunity for a vision of "an Innumerable company of the Heavenly host crying Holy Holy Holy is the Lord God Almighty," as in the conclusion of *A Vision of the Last Judgment*.[33] In the original Latin of the Roman Catholic Mass, the hymn "*Sanctus Sanctus*" ("Holy Holy / Lord God of Hosts / Heaven and earth are filled with your glory / Hosanna in the highest") occurs directly before Holy Communion, the closest a practicing Roman Catholic comes to the Body of Christ. Hughes, no orthodox believer in any particular religion, understands the spiritual truth behind the hymn, and the holy communion of life, in the final embrace of "Salmon Eggs." The quest of nearly three decades to celebrate the "war between vitality and death" ends where it began, but with transfigured vision. The font of the river water nourishes the egg, swaddles it like Mary breastfeeding the infant Christ. These elemental images are the closest we can come to understanding life. The rest is a mystical sublime of silence, a privileged glimpse of the source:

> Sanctus Sanctus
> Swathes the blessed issue.
>
> Perpetual mass
> Of the waters
> Wells from the cleft.
>
> It is the swollen vent
> Of the nameless
> Teeming inside atoms—and inside the haze
> And inside the sun and inside the earth.

It is the font, brimming with touch and whisper
Swaddling the egg.

Only birth matters
Say the river's whorls.

And the river
Silences everything in a leaf-mouldering hush
Where sun rolls bare, and earth rolls,

And mind condenses on old haws.

NOTES

1. A Two-Way Journey toward Reality (Introduction)

1. Ted Hughes, "Quitting," rev. of *Vagrancy*, by Philip O'Connor, *New Statesman*, 6 September 1963, pp. 293–94.
2. The length of this study does not permit discussion of the three minor adult volumes *Recklings*, *Season Songs*, and *Orts*, the dramas, the children's works, or the Rainbow Press limited editions. The publications summary refers to 1980 totals gleaned from Keith Sagar and Stephen Tabor, *Ted Hughes, A Bibliography: 1946–1980*, plus the children's volumes *Under the North Star* (1981) and *What Is the Truth?* (1984), and the adult poetry of *River* (1983).
3. Terry Gifford and Neil Roberts, *Ted Hughes: A Critical Study*.
4. Keith Sagar, *The Art of Ted Hughes*, pp. 1–5.
5. See note 2 above.
6. Stuart Hirschberg, *Myth in the Poetry of Ted Hughes*; Ekbert Faas, *Ted Hughes: The Unaccommodated Universe*. Henceforth the Faas volume is abbreviated as Faas I.
7. See note 1 above.
8. Joseph Campbell, *The Masks of God: Creative Mythology*, pp. 428, 647, 650, 665, 678. Henceforth abbreviated as *Masks: Creative*.
9. Faas, "Ted Hughes and Crow," *London Magazine*, 10 (January 1971), 15; rpt. Faas I, p. 204. Since Faas reprints this important interview in its entirety in his book, subsequent citations refer to both sources.
10. See Sagar, *Art of Ted Hughes*, pp. 9–10. Hughes, born 17 August 1930 in Mytholmroyd, Yorkshire (near Halifax), won an Open Exhibition to Cambridge when he completed Mexborough Grammar School in 1948. He was first conscripted to serve for two years as a ground wireless mechanic for the RAF. Hughes attended Pembroke College, Cambridge, from 1951 through June 1954. In the last year before his graduation he switched from English to anthropology.
11. For a full discussion of Hughes's contact with the *Bardo Thödol*, see chapter 4 of this study.
12. For Hughes's observations on Western science and religion, see the "Ted Hughes and Crow" interview, pp. 5–20, rpt. Faas I, pp. 197–208; and two different essays written by Hughes with the same title: "Myth and Education," *Children's Literature in Education*, 1 (1970), 55–70; "Myth and Education," in *Writers, Critics and Children*, ed. Geoff Fox et al., pp. 77–94. Henceforth abbreviated as "Myth I" and "Myth II," respectively.
13. Faas I, p. 37.
14. See Hughes, *Poetry in the Making*, pp. 121–22; Hughes, "Superstitions," rev. of *Astrology*, by Aldus, and *Ghost and Divining-rod*, by T. C. Lethbridge, *New Statesman*, 2 October 1964, p. 500. The incident occurs on page 51 of Jung's autobiography *Memories, Dreams, Reflections*, trans. Clara and Richard Winston.
15. See note 12 above.
16. Carl Jung, *Psychology and Alchemy*, trans. R. F. C. Hull, pp. 7–8.

17. Mircea Eliade, *Yoga: Immortality and Freedom*, trans. Willard R. Trask, pp. 70, 160. See also Robert E. Hume, "An Outline of the Philosophy of the Upanishads," in his translation of *The Thirteen Principal Upanishads*, pp. 30, 50–53, 68.

18. Faas, "Ted Hughes and Crow," p. 19; rpt. Faas I, p. 207.

19. Jung, *Psychology and Alchemy*, pp. 81, 123, 430.

20. Donald Davie, *The Poet in the Imaginary Museum*, ed. Barry Alpert, p. 49.

21. M. L. Rosenthal, *The Modern Poets*, p. 9.

22. For the best summary of Jung's individuation process, see Jolande Jacobi, *The Way of Individuation*, trans. R. F. C. Hull, pp. 42–48, 60–81.

23. See Carl Jung, "Psychological Commentary," in W. Y. Evans-Wentz, ed., *The Tibetan Book of the Dead*, trans. Lama Kazi Dawa-Samdup, p. xliv: "The archetypes are . . . organs of the pre-rational psyche. They are eternally inherited forms and ideas which have at first no specific content. Their specific content only appears in the course of the individual's life, when personal experience is taken up in precisely these forms." In Jung's own thinking archetypes are not deterministic; they are formal categories that contain human wisdom, but the plot and the content are the dreamer's own. Henceforth this *Bardo Thödol* edition is abbreviated *Bardo*.

24. Campbell, *The Hero with a Thousand Faces*, pp. 35–38, 245–46; Campbell, *The Masks of God: Oriental Mythology*, p. 77. Henceforth abbreviated as *Hero* and *Masks: Oriental*.

25. Hughes, in a BBC Radio 3 broadcast, "Poetry Now," recorded 24 June 1970; summarized in part in the *Listener*, 30 July 1970, p. 149.

26. Jung, "On the Psychology of the Trickster Figure," in Paul Radin, *The Trickster*, pp. 195–211. See also Hughes, "Tricksters and Tarbabies," rev. of *Literature among the Primitives*, and *The Primitive Reader*, by John Greenway, *New York Review of Books*, 9 December 1965, pp. 33–35.

27. Allen Tate, "Tension in Poetry," rpt. in Tate, *Essays of Four Decades*, pp. 56–71; John Crowe Ransom, "The Concrete Universal: Observations on the Understanding of Poetry," rpt. in Ransom, *Poems and Essays*, pp. 159–85; Cleanth Brooks, *The Well Wrought Urn*, pp. 22ff.

28. T. S. Eliot, "The Metaphysical Poets," rpt. in Eliot, *Selected Essays*, p. 247.

29. Ezra Pound, "A Retrospect," rpt. in Pound, *Literary Essays*, ed. T. S. Eliot, p. 4.

30. Charles Olson, *Human Universe and Other Essays*, ed. Donald Allen, p. 4.

31. Sylvia Plath, *The Journals of Sylvia Plath*, ed. Ted Hughes and Frances McCullough, p. 216.

32. Bram Dijkstra, *The Hieroglyphics of a New Speech: Cubism, Stieglitz, and the Early Poetry of William Carlos Williams*, pp. 67–70.

33. Brooks, *Well Wrought Urn*, pp. 213–14.

34. William K. Wimsatt, Jr., and Cleanth Brooks, *Literary Criticism*, p. 748.

35. René Wellek and Austin Warren, *Theory of Literature*, p. 241.

36. Donald Davie, "As deep as England," rev. of *Wodwo*, by Ted Hughes, *Guardian*, 25 May 1967, p. 14.

37. Joseph Frank, "Spatial Form in Modern Literature," rpt. in Frank, *The Widening Gyre*, pp. 3–62 (the comments on Worringer and naturalistic versus nonnaturalistic form occur on pp. 50ff).

38. David Lodge, *Working with Structuralism*, pp. 3–16; see also pp. 68–75. Lodge acknowledges a major debt for his modernist and antimodernist distinctions to the

metaphorical and metonymical modes developed in the work of the structuralist critic Roman Jakobson.

39. Ibid., p. 15.

40. See Ian Hamilton, "Ted Hughes: *Crow*," in his *A Poetry Chronicle*, pp. 165–70; Calvin Bedient, "On Ted Hughes," *Critical Quarterly*, 14 (Summer 1972), 103–21; David Holbrook, "Ted Hughes's *Crow* and the Longing for Non-Being," in *The Black Rainbow*, ed. Peter Abbs, pp. 32–54. Hamilton's review of *Crow*, originally appearing as an unsigned *TLS* review (8 January 1971), set the tone for some of the most vicious attacks on Hughes's poetry. Yet Hamilton simply exaggerated an already pronounced tendency among one group of British critics who drew personal inferences about the source of Hughes's creative impulse, after complaining about the violence of his diction in his animal poems. See, for instance, J. M. Newton, "Mr. Hughes's Poetry," *Delta*, 25 (Winter 1961), 6–12; Sydney Bolt, "Ted Hughes: Laureate of Leucotomy," *Delta*, 42 (February 1968), 4–11. After *Wodwo*, Newton became a Hughes supporter. See Newton, "Ted Hughes's Metaphysical Poems," *Cambridge Quarterly*, 2 (Autumn 1967), 395–402.

41. Ezra Pound, *Guide to Kulchur*, p. 57; Pound, *ABC of Reading*, p. 104.

42. Pound, *Literary Essays*, p. 76.

43. Lodge, *Working with Structuralism*, p. 5.

44. Hughes, "Myth I," p. 66.

45. Albert Einstein, *Relativity*, trans. Robert W. Lawson, p. 142.

46. Hughes, "The Environmental Revolution," rev. of *The Environmental Revolution*, by Max Nicholson, *Your Environment*, 1 (Summer 1970), 81–83.

47. Hughes, "Wings," in *Wodwo*, pp. 174–76. The following subtitles for the three sections of "Wings" appear only in this Faber and Faber edition: "M. Sartre Considers Current Affairs," "Kafka Writes," and "Einstein Plays Bach."

48. Erich Auerbach, *Mimesis*, trans. Willard Trask, pp. 136–38, 391, 457, 472–90.

49. Ibid., pp. 484–85, 481.

50. Faas, "Ted Hughes and Crow," p. 15; Faas I, p. 204.

51. See A. C. H. Smith, *Orghast at Persepolis*, p. 96; see also pp. 50, 91, 181.

52. See Sylvia Plath, *Letters Home*, ed. Aurelia Schober Plath, p. 235. Note also the Blake allusion in "The Perfect Forms" (*Lupercal*), reprinted in this chapter.

53. William Blake, "Annotations to Berkeley's *Siris*," in David V. Erdman, ed., *Poetry and Prose of William Blake*, p. 652. Throughout this study, citations from the poetry and prose of Blake derive from the Erdman edition.*

54. Blake, *Jerusalem*, in ibid., p. 146.

55. See J. Robert Barth, *The Symbolic Imagination*, pp. 12, 27–28, 100–103, 134–35.

56. Gareth Knight, *A Practical Guide to Qabalistic Symbolism*, I, 250; Gershom Scholem, *Kabbalah*, pp. 130, 137, 152, 155, 162.

57. Chang Chung-yuan, *Creativity and Taoism*, pp. 8, 19–21, 203.

58. Ibid., pp. 5, 35, 49, 80.

59. Konrad Lorenz, *On Aggression*, trans. Marjorie Kerr Wilson, pp. 141–42.

60. See Jerome Klinkowitz, "Vonnegut in America," in Klinkowitz and Donald L. Lawler, eds., *Vonnegut in America*, p. 13.

61. Alvin Toffler, *Future Shock*, p. 13.

62. Faas, "Ted Hughes and Crow," p. 7; rpt. Faas I, p. 198.

63. Faas, "Ted Hughes and Crow," p. 10; rpt. Faas I, pp. 200–201.

64. Einstein, from a letter to Queen Elizabeth, dated 12 August 1939; quoted in Otto Nathan and Heintz Norden, eds., *Einstein on Peace*, p. 285.

2. A Craftsman Calm (*The Hawk in the Rain*)

1. Hughes, "Ted Hughes Writes," *Poetry Book Society Bulletin*, 15 (September 1957), 1.
2. Conquest, "Intercontinental Missiles," *Spectator*, 11 October 1957, p. 488.
3. Hough, "Landmarks and Turbulences," *Encounter*, 9 (November 1957), 83–87; (unsigned), "Poems of Substance," *Times Literary Supplement*, 18 October 1957, p. 626.
4. Carr, untitled review of *The Hawk in the Rain*, *Delta*, 14 (Spring 1958), 25–27.
5. Hough, "Landmarks," p. 87.
6. Sagar, *Art of Ted Hughes*, p. 11.
7. Edward Butscher, *Sylvia Plath: Method and Madness*, p. 202. Myers and Hughes were friends and contributors to *St. Botolph's Review*, which was founded by David Ross. It lasted one issue. Myers subsequently reviewed *Lupercal* for the Spring 1962 issue of *Sewanee Review*.
8. Conversation with Ted Hughes, 27 August 1979, at Exeter, Devonshire.
9. Faas, "Ted Hughes and *Gaudete*," in Faas I, p. 211.
10. Faas, "Ted Hughes and Crow," pp. 13–14; rpt. Faas I, p. 203.
11. Ransom, *The New Criticism*, pp. 279–336.
12. Ibid., pp. 279–336. See also chapter 1, note 27.
13. For irony in Ransom, see Robert Penn Warren, "John Crowe Ransom: A Study in Irony," *Virginia Quarterly Review*, 11 (January 1935), 93–112; rpt. Thomas Daniel Young, ed., *John Crowe Ransom: Critical Essays and a Bibliography*, pp. 24–40.
14. Ransom, *The World's Body*, pp. 111–42, esp. pp. 112–13, 123–24, 140–42. See also Thomas Daniel Young, "Ransom's Critical Theories: Structure and Texture," *Mississippi Quarterly*, 30 (Winter 1976–77), 71–85.
15. Hughes, "Ted Hughes Writes," p. 1.
16. Ransom, *Poems and Essays*, p. 3. Subsequent citations from Ransom's poetry are as found in this edition.
17. Tate, "Tension in Poetry," pp. 59–62.
18. See Tate, "Tension in Poetry"; Ransom, "Concrete Universal." Tate's use of the word "tension" is specialized: it concerns the tension between the intensional verbal world and the extensional world of concrete objects, in general semantics.
19. Warren, "John Crowe Ransom: A Study in Irony," in Young, *John Crowe Ransom*, p. 38.
20. Hughes, *The Hawk in the Rain*, p. 17. Subsequent citations from *Hawk* are as found in this American edition. Lines and sequence are identical to the 1957 Faber and Faber edition; pagination differs.
21. Muir, "Kinds of Poetry," *New Statesman*, 28 September 1957, pp. 391–92.
22. Ransom, *The New Criticism*, pp. 76–85.
23. Hughes, "Myth II," p. 66.
24. Williams, *The Poetry of John Crowe Ransom*, p. 52.
25. See Alan Brownjohn, "The Brutal Tone," *Listen*, 2 (Spring 1958), 20–23; David

Holbrook, "The Cult of Hughes and Gunn," *Poetry Review*, 54 (Summer 1963), 167–83. See also chapter 1, note 40.

26. Ransom, "Concrete Universal," p. 171; Ransom, *The New Criticism*, p. 76.
27. Hughes, "Ted Hughes Writes," p. 1.
28. Brooks, *Well Wrought Urn*, p. 203.
29. Ibid., pp. 212–14.
30. Freud, *Group Psychology and the Analysis of the Ego*, in the *Standard Edition*, ed. and trans. James Strachey, XVIII, 123.
31. Stewart, *The Burden of Time*, p. 228.
32. Jung, *Archetypes and the Collective Unconscious*, trans. R. F. C. Hull, part I, 20.
33. Brooks, *Well Wrought Urn*, pp. 213–14.
34. Osborne, *Look Back in Anger*, pp. 8–9.
35. Conversation with Ted Hughes, 27 August 1979, at Exeter, Devonshire.
36. Hughes, "Myth II," p. 92.
37. Coleridge, *Biographia Literaria*, II, 11.

3. Mouths Clamped Well onto the World (*Lupercal*)

1. Hughes, "Creatures," *BBC Home Service*, prod. Owen Leeming, recorded 5 May 1960, pp. 1, 3–4. These unpublished scripts reside at the BBC Written Archives Center, Caversham Park, Reading, and at the BBC Script Library, The Langham, Portland Place, London WIA IAA.
2. Faas, "Ted Hughes and *Gaudete*," in Faas I, p. 208.
3. Lowell, "On 'Skunk Hour,'" in Anthony Ostroff, ed., *The Contemporary Poet as Artist and Critic*, p. 108.
4. Faas, "Ted Hughes and *Gaudete*," in Faas I, p. 209.
5. Ibid.
6. Hughes, *Poetry in the Making*, pp. 21, 60–61. A shortened version of this text was later published in 1970 by Doubleday under the title *Poetry Is*.
7. Again, this "style of meditation" applies to Hughes's *Lupercal* period, for the BBC talk was recorded 24 February 1961. The passage later reappears on pp. 60–61 of *Poetry in the Making*.
8. This passage actually conveys a sense of the poet wrestling with the experience, to bring it under control. It is consonant with the conception, developed later in this chapter, of the poet as Luperci priest, the controller of theriomorphic energy and maker of wolf masks.
9. Ransom, *The New Criticism*, pp. 297ff.
10. Hughes, *Poetry in the Making*, pp. 18, 58, 100.
11. Faas, "Ted Hughes and Crow," p. 12; rpt. Faas I, p. 202. For Hughes's statement about memorizing Yeats's poems, see John Horder, "Desk Poet," interview with Hughes, *Guardian*, 23 March 1965, p. 9.
12. Yeats, "A General Introduction for My Work," in Yeats, *Essays and Introductions*, p. 521.
13. Yeats, letter to a friend, dated 22 January 1939, in Richard Ellmann, *Yeats: The Man and the Masks*, p. 285.

14. Parkinson, *W. B. Yeats: The Later Poetry*, p. 4.
15. Citations from *Lupercal* are as found in the American edition. Lines, sequence, and pagination are identical to the 1960 Faber and Faber edition.
16. Kunitz, "The New Books," *Harper's*, 221 (September 1960), 103.
17. Jones, untitled review of *Lupercal*, *Critical Quarterly*, 2 (Summer 1960), 185; Holmes, "A Poet Seeks the Limits of His World," *Christian Science Monitor*, 25 August 1960, p. 8.
18. Myers, "The Tranquilized Fifties," *Sewanee Review*, 70 (Spring 1962), 219.
19. Horder, "Desk Poet," p. 9.
20. Campbell, *The Masks of God: Primitive Mythology*, pp. 300ff. Hereafter cited as *Masks: Primitive*.
21. Eliade, *Shamanism*, trans. Willard R. Trask, p. 98.
22. Ibid., pp. 89–94.
23. Ibid., pp. 94, 171.
24. Rose, *Ancient Roman Religion*, pp. 57–58; Kerényi, "Wolf und Zeige am Lupercalienfest," in *Niobe: Neue Studien über antike Religion und Humanität*, pp. 136–47.
25. Harrison, *Prolegomena to the Study of Greek Religion*, pp. 49–55, esp. p. 53. Hughes professes familiarity with Harrison's work in a 1965 review. See Hughes, "Tricksters and Tarbabies," p. 34.
26. Michels, "The Topography and Interpretation of the Lupercalia," *Transactions of the American Philological Society*, 84 (1953), 35–59. Michels lists six scholars who wrote on the relation of the rites for the dead in the Lupercalia, from the years 1895 to 1951 (p. 48, note 20).
27. Sir James G. Frazer, *The Golden Bough*, abridged ed. (1922; rpt. 1951), pp. 268–69.
28. Eliade, *Shamanism*, p. 89.
29. Frazer, *Golden Bough*, abridged ed., pp. 541, 581.
30. E. O. G. Turville-Petre, *Myth and Religion of the North*, pp. 60–61, 280–81.
31. Faas, "Ted Hughes and Crow," p. 9; rpt. Faas I, p. 200.
32. Jung, *Symbols of Transformation*, trans. R. F. C. Hull, pp. 179–80.
33. Ibid., pp. 275–82.
34. Campbell, *Masks: Oriental*, pp. 37, 53 ff.
35. See John Press, *Rule and Energy*, pp. 27–28; G. Ingli James, "The Animal Poems of Ted Hughes: A Devaluation," *Southern Review*, 2, iii (1967), 193–203. See also chapter 1, note 40; chapter 2, note 25.
36. Eliade, *Myths, Dreams and Mysteries*, trans. Philip Mairet, p. 62.
37. Jane Harrison, *Themis*, pp. 110–11.
38. See Peter Elfred Lewis, "The New Pedantry and 'Hawk Roosting,'" *Stand*, 8, 1 (1966), 58–65.
39. See the discussion in Gifford and Roberts, *Ted Hughes*, p. 70. In the real legend of the Barnburgh Knight the wildcat died. Gifford and Roberts point this out as a flaw in the poem, but miss the genetic inheritance theme.
40. Campbell, *Masks: Oriental*, pp. 3, 9ff.
41. Freud, *The Interpretation of Dreams*, in *Standard Edition*, V, 357.
42. Hughes, "The Crime of Fools Exposed," *New York Times*, 12 April 1964, pp. 4, 18, of Book Review section; untitled review of *Men Who March Away*, ed. I. M. Parsons, *Listener*, 5 August 1965, p. 208.
43. Hughes, "The Crime of Fools Exposed," p. 4.

44. Alan Moorehead, *Gallipoli*, pp. 360–61.
45. Conversation with Ted Hughes, 27 August 1979, at Exeter, Devonshire.
46. Frazer, *Golden Bough*, abridged ed., pp. 715–20; see also pp. 728–29, 756, 761.
47. Bush, *English Literature in the Earlier Seventeenth Century*, p. 354.
48. Browne, *Hydriotaphia: Urn Burial*, in *Sir Thomas Browne's Works*, ed. Simon Wilkin, V, 489–92.
49. Ibid., V, 481.
50. Ibid., V, 494.
51. Bergonzi, *The Situation of the Novel*, pp. 57–63.

4. Goodbye to the Cenotaphs (*Wodwo*)

1. Hughes, "Dylan Thomas's Letters," review of *The Selected Letters of Dylan Thomas*, ed. Constantine Fitzgibbon, *New Statesman*, 25 November 1966, p. 733.
2. See Louise Bogan, "Verse," *New Yorker*, 30 March 1968, p. 137; J. M. Newton, "Ted Hughes's Metaphysical Poems," *Cambridge Quarterly*, 2 (Autumn 1967), 401; John Ferns, "Over the Same Ground," *Far Point*, 1 (Fall/Winter 1968), 69; Anthony Hecht, "Writers' Rights and Readers' Rights," *Hudson Review*, 21 (Spring 1968), 211–13.
3. Hughes married Sylvia Plath on Bloomsday, 16 June 1956; they moved to Devon in early September 1961. Sylvia's letters to her mother in September and October of 1961 indicate that they enjoyed the change immensely, although much work was necessary both inside and in the garden. Hughes, the son of an expert carpenter, made some of their furniture. Plath wrote to her mother that "Snow" presents "the *feeling* of being lost and struggling against terrific unknowns and odds, something most people feel at one time or another. I find it the most compelling of Ted's stories because it *fits* one's own experience so beautifully" (Plath, *Letters Home*, pp. 427–32).

   The narrator of "Snow" does his dreaming (writing?) on a "farmhouse sort of chair," but hasn't dreamt much about his twenty-third and twenty-fourth years, and nothing at all from his twenty-sixth onward. Hughes, born 17 August 1930, was twenty-six when he married Plath. The narrator's discrepancy between his present age and his age when appearing in dreams may simply indicate that he hasn't yet achieved enough distance from recent events to make them available to his dreaming. But he also has the "working hypothesis" that he is a partly amnesiac survivor of a plane crash. Whether the crash that numbs recent memory has any clear reference to Hughes's marriage or his private life is uncertain, but at one point the narrator considers that his chair may be a "harness," "invented" between his twenty-sixth birthday and the crash. The clarity of the surreal dislocation invites biographical speculation.
4. Hughes, "Vasco Popa," *Tri-Quarterly*, 9 (Spring 1967), 204–5.
5. "Snow" was first published in *Introduction* (London: Faber and Faber, 1960); "The Rescue," *Observer*, 29 October 1961; *The Wound*, broadcast 1 February 1962; "Bowled Over," recorded 29 August 1962 for Argo Records' *The Poet Speaks*; "The Green Wolf," *Observer*, 6 January 1963 (as "Dark Women").
6. Translated by Anna Balakian in her *Surrealism: The Road to the Absolute*, p. 111.

7. Breton, "Manifesto of Surrealism" (1924), in André Breton, *Manifestos of Surrealism*, trans. Richard Seaver and Helen R. Lane, pp. 22–23.

8. See note 1.

9. Balakian, *Surrealism*, pp. 152ff.; Balakian, *Literary Origins of Surrealism*, pp. 14–37.

10. Hughes, "After Lorca," *Poetry*, 103 (December 1963), 154–55.

11. C. M. Bowra, *Primitive Song*, pp. 88, 92.

12. *Listener*, 3 May 1962, p. 781.

13. Hughes, "Tricksters and Tarbabies," p. 35.

14. Eliade, *Shamanism*, pp. 33–34, 64–65, 76, 95.

15. *Listener*, 29 October 1964, pp. 677–78.

16. Claude Lévi-Strauss, *Structural Anthropology*, trans. Claire Jacobson and B. G. Schoepf, pp. 181–83.

17. Campbell, *Hero*, pp. 30, 35–36; *Masks: Creative*, p. 362.

18. Hughes, *Wodwo* (New York: Harper and Row, 1967), p. 7. Subsequent citations derive from this edition.

19. Hughes, "A Fable," *Times Literary Supplement*, 9 September 1960, p. 70. The American and British editions of *Wodwo* contain slightly different poem selections. The Harper and Row edition contains "Root, Stem, Leaf" and "Scapegoats and Rabies," both of which are omitted in the Faber and Faber edition; the British edition contains "Logos," not printed in the American edition, and adds sections II and III of "Gog." Otherwise the two editions follow the same sequence of poems, stories, play, and poems, with no line variations. Pagination differs.

20. Campbell, *Masks: Creative*, pp. 121, 553, 636, 647.

21. Hughes, "The Poetry of Keith Douglas," *Listener*, 21 June 1962, pp. 1069–70; "The Crime of Fools Exposed," pp. 4, 18; untitled review of *Men Who March Away*, p. 208.

22. Hughes, "Modern Poetry," *BBC Talks for Sixth Forms*, prod. Tom Butcher, recorded 24 May 1963.

23. Hughes, "On Writing for Radio," an unscripted interview with Anthony Thwaite, recorded 16 January 1963 by the BBC, transcribed from a teledictaphone recording.

24. For well-documented summary discussions of Freud's thoughts on aggression and the thanatos death instinct, see Liliane Frey-Rohn, *From Freud to Jung*, trans. F. E. Engreen and E. K. Engreen, pp. 126–32; Richard Wollheim, *Sigmund Freud* (New York: Viking Press, 1971), pp. 206–13. The principal source for Freud's comments on the repetition-compulsion organic drive is the *New Introductory Lectures on Psycho-analysis*, trans. W. J. H. Sprott, pp. 133–39.

25. D. T. Suzuki, *Mysticism: Christian and Buddhist*, p. 28.

26. Hume, *Thirteen Principal Upanishads*, pp. 42ff.

27. Patanjali, *The Authentic Yoga*, trans. P. Y. Despande, pp. 41 ff.; Ernest Wood, *Yoga*, pp. 43–44, 72.

28. Suzuki, *Living by Zen*, pp. 46–88; Suzuki, "The Oriental Way of Thinking," *Japan Quarterly*, 11 (1955), 51–58.

29. Heinrich Zimmer, *Myths and Symbols in Indian Art and Civilization*, ed. Joseph Campbell, pp. 175–84.

30. Faas, "Ted Hughes and Crow," p. 15; rpt. Faas I, p. 204.

31. Reprinted in Hume, *Thirteen Principal Upanishads*, p. 142. The brackets are Hume's. See also Chāndogya Upanishad (2.21.4), in ibid., p. 199.

32. Wood, *Yoga*, pp. 60–61, 68ff.

33. Suzuki, *Essays in Zen Buddhism, Second Series*, ed. Christmas Humphreys, pp. 30–36; Suzuki, Erich Fromm, and Richard De Martino, *Zen Buddhism and Psychoanalysis*, pp. 17–18, 49–56.

34. Frazer, *Golden Bough*, abridged ed., pp. 628–29, 664.

35. Robert Graves, *The White Goddess*, pp. 169, 176.

36. Knight, *Practical Guide to Qabalistic Symbolism*, I, 90–94; Dion Fortune, *The Mystical Qabalah*, pp. 139, 156–57.

37. Suzuki, *The Essentials of Zen Buddhism*, ed. Bernard Phillips, pp. 327, 396, 400.

38. Eliade, *Shamanism*, pp. 58–64, 434–36; Campbell, *Masks: Primitive*, pp. 334ff.

39. Eliade, *The Myth of the Eternal Return*, trans. Willard R. Trask, pp. 6, 9, 12–17.

40. Campbell, *Masks: Primitive*, pp. 334–49.

41. Graves, *White Goddess*, pp. 401–2. The response portion of the first stanza of the chant, not reprinted in the epigraph to "The Harvesting," specifies the greyhound as pursuer. Graves interprets this as evidence of the White Goddess as hag-destroyer of the male—nature in its predatory aspect. In "The Harvesting" a white greyhound is mentioned early in the story; it is doubtless the same dog that in the last paragraph opens its enormous white head to attack Grooby.

42. Walter H. Sokel, *The Writer in Extremis*, pp. 33–35.

43. Patanjali, *The Authentic Yoga*, pp. 19–24; Wood, *Yoga*, p. 15.

44. Eliade, *Shamanism*, pp. 62–63.

45. Jung, *Archetypes, Part I*, pp. 26–27.

46. Jung, *Aion*, trans. R. F. C. Hull, pp. 36–183, esp. pp. 182–83.

47. Frazer, *Golden Bough*, abridged ed., pp. 709–17.

48. Faas, "Ted Hughes and Crow," pp. 16–17; rpt. Faas I, p. 205. See also Plath, *Letters Home*, pp. 354, 371, 399. Hughes's libretto has unfortunately not been published to date.

49. Lama Anagarika Govinda, "Introductory Foreword" to *Bardo*, pp. lx–lxi. In the *Bardo* itself, see also p. 151.

50. *Bardo*, pp. xxxix, xl, xlvi.

51. Ibid., p. 123.

52. Ibid., pp. 161–62, 166–67.

53. Suzuki, *Essays in Zen Buddhism, First Series*, ed. Christmas Humphreys, pp. 214–66; Suzuki, *The Essentials of Zen Buddhism*, p. 359.

54. Suzuki, *Zen and Japanese Culture*, p. 350.

55. Merton, *Mystics and Zen Masters*, p. 14.

56. Suzuki, *The Essentials of Zen Buddhism*, pp. 362–63.

57. Suzuki, *Mysticism: Christian and Buddhist*, pp. 100–102; *Zen Buddhism and Psychoanalysis*, p. 12; *The Essentials of Zen Buddhism*, pp. 360–61.

58. Hughes, "Superstitions," p. 500.

59. Suzuki, "Zen and the Modern World," *Japan Quarterly*, 5, 4 (October/December 1958), 458.

60. Suzuki, *The Essentials of Zen Buddhism*, p. 358. Similar poems using negations, written by other Zen masters, are reprinted in Lucien Stryk, ed., *World of the Buddha: A Reader*, pp. 311, 353.

61. Suzuki, *The Essentials of Zen Buddhism*, p. 357.

62. Suzuki, *Living by Zen*, p. 76.

63. Hughes, *Poetry in the Making*, pp. 62–63.
64. Eliade, *Myth and Reality*, trans. Willard R. Trask, pp. 85–86.
65. *Bardo*, pp. 171, 177, 186; see also Eliade, *The Myth of the Eternal Return*, pp. 98–99.
66. Trans. and rpt. Suzuki, *The Essentials of Zen Buddhism*, p. 236. The image of wiping clean the karmic mirror is one of the most common in all of Oriental literature. See, for instance, Śvetāśvatara Upanishad, 2:14, in Hume, *Thirteen Principal Upanishads*, p. 399; Yoka Daishi's "Song of Enlightenment" in Suzuki, *Manual of Zen Buddhism*, p. 107.
67. *Bardo*, p. 188.
68. Suzuki, *Essays in Zen Buddhism, First Series*, pp. 225–26, 191, 263.
69. See Kena Upanishad, 4:29, in Hume, *Thirteen Principal Upanishads*, p. 339; Suzuki, *Essays in Zen Buddhism, First Series*, pp. 261, 245.
70. Zimmer, *Myths and Symbols*, pp. 70, 183, and plate 53.
71. Jung, "On the Psychology of the Trickster Figure," in Radin, *The Trickster*, pp. 202–9.
72. Sagar, *Art of Ted Hughes*, p. 61.
73. Reprinted in Robert Sohl and Audrey Carr, eds., *The Gospel According to Zen*, p. 28.
74. Suzuki, *The Essence of Zen Buddhism*, pp. 13–14.
75. "O White Elite Lotus," *Critical Quarterly*, 4 (Winter 1964), 319; rpt. *Achievement*, p. 318.
76. Reprinted in E. A. Burtt, ed., *The Teachings of the Compassionate Buddha*, pp. 211–12.
77. Zimmer, *Myths and Symbols*, pp. 37–38, 89.
78. See chapter 1, note 47.
79. Faas I, pp. 18, 116–17.

5. Nothing Escaped Him (*Crow*)

1. Hughes, "The Environmental Revolution," pp. 81–83.
2. Hughes, *Crow* (New York: Harper and Row, 1971), p. 11. Unless otherwise noted, citations from *Crow* follow this American edition. This Harper and Row edition contains all of the selections in the first Faber edition (1970) except "Crowcolour," follows the same sequence, and adds seven more poems ("Crow's Fall," "Crow Tries the Media," "The Contender," "Crow Paints Himself into a Chinese Mural," "The Lovepet," "Crow Hears Fate Knock on the Door," and "Crow's Elephant Totem Song"). The first British and American editions total sixty-seven different Crow poems. In the sixth printing (1972) Faber augmented its first edition to include all of the poems added to the American edition except "The Lovepet." The second (limited) Faber edition (1973) added three new poems ("Crow Rambles," "Crow's Courtship," and "Crow's Song about Prospero and Sycorax"). Three previously uncollected Crow poems have recently appeared in *The Achievement of Ted Hughes*, ed. Keith Sagar, pp. 330–31: "Crow Fails," "Crow Compromises," and "A Lucky Folly." The first two were unpublished; "A Lucky Folly" first appeared in *Workshop*, 10 (September 1970).

Twenty-nine other Crow poems have appeared in limited editions and private press publications or lie uncollected in periodicals, poster poems, or broadsides. *Crow Wakes* contains eleven additions ("Crow Wakes," "Bones," "Amulet," "Crow's Table Talk," "In the Land of Lion," "I See a Bear," "Anecdote," "Song against the White Owl," "The Ship," "Lullaby," and "Snow Song"). *Poems: Ruth Fainlight, Ted Hughes, Alan Sillitoe* contains four additions ("Genesis of Evil," "Crow's Song about England," "Crow's Song about God," and "Crow the Just"). *A Few Crows* contains "Carnival." All three of the above private press publications print other Crow poems found in the American and the three Faber printings. *A Crow Hymn* contains "A Crow Hymn."

Achievement (pp. 326–40) reprints a few of the private press Crow poems listed above, and nine previously uncollected poems that Sagar (*Art of Ted Hughes*, p. 130) considers part of the Crow sequence: "The New World" (six short poems), "Existential Song," "In the Little Girl's Angel Gaze," and "Song of Woe." Three remaining Crow poems lie uncollected: "Three Legends" (two have never appeared elsewhere), *Journal of Creative Behavior*, 1 (July 1967), 18–20; "The Space-Egg Was Sailing," in *New Poems 1970–71: A P.E.N. Anthology of Contemporary Poetry*, ed. Alan Brownjohn et al., pp. 49–50. Hughes has stated that several poems from *Cave Birds* belong in the continued *Crow* story.

At this count the *Crow* sequence numbers 102 different poems, only two-thirds of which appear in the Faber and Faber or Harper and Row trade editions. For full bibliographical citations, see Sagar and Tabor, *Ted Hughes: A Bibliography: 1946–80*, pp. 39–53, 168–74. One final Crow item is *Eat Crow*; this surrealistic psychodrama was originally written in 1964.

3. Hughes, "The Environmental Revolution," p. 83; "Vasco Popa," p. 202.
4. Alfred Korzybski, *Time-Binding: The General Theory*, p. 20; *Science and Sanity*, pp. xxxii–xxxiv, 20–26.
5. See the discussion in chapter 1.
6. Le Guin, untitled, tape-recorded interview with Charlotte Reed, 1973 (taped at Le Guin's Portland, Oregon, home), PTC/813.54/L52zl.
7. Gifford and Roberts, *Ted Hughes*, p. 116.
8. Hughes, *With Fairest Flowers While Summer Lasts*, pp. v–xxiii. This "Introduction" appears as "Note" at the end of the 1971 Faber and Faber edition, *A Choice of Shakespeare's Verse*, pp. 181–200.
9. All quotations in this paragraph derive from "Myth I."
10. See Sagar, *Art of Ted Hughes*, pp. 106, 235; Gifford and Roberts, pp. 115–17.
11. Faas, "Ted Hughes and Crow," p. 7; rpt. Faas I, p. 198.
12. Reprinted in Gifford and Roberts, *Ted Hughes*, p. 256.
13. G. S. Kirk, *The Nature of Greek Myths*, pp. 59–116.
14. See Freud, *Inhibitions, Symptoms, and Anxiety*, trans. Alex Strachey, ed. and rev. James Strachey, pp. 6–7, 28–77, for the ego as a defense mechanism. On this point see also Reuben Fine, *The Development of Freud's Thought*, p. 182; Frey-Rohn, *From Freud to Jung*, pp. 51–52.
15. Hughes et al., *Poems: Fainlight, Hughes, Sillitoe*, p. 15.
16. Shah, *The Sufis*, p. 198. For Hughes's review, see "Secret Ecstasies," *Listener*, 29 October 1964, 677–78.
17. Cyprian Rice, *The Persian Sufis*, pp. 76–82.
18. Hughes et al., *Poems: Fainlight, Hughes, Sillitoe*, pp. 16–17.

19. A parallel exists in Genesis 9:20–27, where Noah, having become a husbandman, embarrasses himself in drunken nakedness and then curses Ham for telling.
20. Campbell, *Masks: Creative*, p. 154.
21. Radin, *The Trickster*, pp. 164–65.
22. John R. Swanton, *Tlingit Myths and Texts*, pp. 80–81.
23. Jung, *Alchemical Studies*, trans. R. F. C. Hull, p. 101.
24. Hughes, "Three Legends," p. 19.
25. See Richard Holmes, "Ted Hughes: A Brutish Metamorphosis," *London Times*, 17 December 1970, p. 15. See also notes 52 and 53 below.
26. One can find examples of *enantiodromia* in many of the volumes of the Bollingen *Collected Works*. Jung defines *enantiodromia* in *Psychological Types*, trans. H. G. Baynes, rev. R. F. C. Hull, pp. 425–26. Examples of *enantiodromia* used in conjunction with Jung's theory of psychic compensation occur in *Archetypes, Part I*, pp. 38, 229, 346, 348, 353; *Alchemical Studies*, p. 245. An example of *enantiodromia* used to analyze contemporary civilization occurs in *Civilization in Transition*, trans. R. F. C. Hull, pp. 81–83. Another such example is developed in the next paragraph of this chapter.
27. Conversation with Ted Hughes, 27 August 1979, at Exeter, Devonshire. In response to a general question about *enantiodromia*, Hughes agreed that he is aware of this concept.
28. Jung, "On the Psychology of the Trickster Figure," in Radin, *The Trickster*, pp. 206–11.
29. See esp. pp. xvi–xix.
30. Lorenz, *On Aggression*, pp. 241–42.
31. Sagar, *Art of Ted Hughes*, p. 122.
32. In Brownjohn et al., eds., *New Poems 1970–71: A P.E.N. Anthology of Contemporary Poetry*, pp. 49–50.
33. Swanton, *Tlingit Myths and Texts*, p. 37.
34. Letter from Leonard Baskin to this writer, 11 March 1977.
35. Franz Boas, *Tsimshian Mythology*, pp. 567–86, 621–723.
36. Radin, *The Trickster*, p. 168.
37. Jung, "On the Psychology of the Trickster Figure," in ibid., pp. 202ff.
38. See Alfred Alvarez, "Black Bird," *Observer*, 11 October 1970, p. 33; Alan Brownjohn, "On Survival," *New Statesman*, 16 October 1970, p. 490; G. S. Frazer, "Books," *Partisan Review*, 38 (Winter 1971–1972), 477; Tony Harrison, "Crow Magnon," *London Magazine*, 11 (January 1971), 86–88; Jascha Kessler, "The Inner World Where Poets Wander," *Saturday Review*, 2 October 1971, pp. 39, 50; Derwent May, "Bird Words," *Listener*, 29 October 1970, p. 603; Howard Sergeant, "Poetry Review," *English*, 20 (Summer 1971), 66–67.
39. Sagar, *Art of Ted Hughes*, p. 107.
40. Radin, *The Trickster*, pp. 168–69.
41. Jung, "On the Psychology of the Trickster Figure," in ibid., p. 203.
42. Karl Kerényi, "The Trickster in Relation to Greek Mythology," in ibid., pp. 173–91, esp. p. 185.
43. Greenway, *Literature among the Primitives*, pp. 71–105, esp. p. 90. See also Greenway, *The Primitive Reader*, pp. 59–62.
44. Swanton, *Tlingit Myths and Texts*, pp. 3–21; also pp. 80ff.

45. Lévi-Strauss, *The Savage Mind*, trans. anon., pp. 1–22, 40ff.

46. Bowra, *Primitive Song*, pp. 103, 88–92.

47. Blake, "Annotations to the Works of Sir Joshua Reynolds," in Erdman, *Poetry and Prose of William Blake*, p. 634.

48. Blake, letter to Trusler (23 August 1799), in ibid., p. 677.

49. *Bardo*, pp. 175ff.

50. Blake, *The Marriage of Heaven and Hell*, plate 14, in Erdman, *Poetry and Prose of William Blake*, p. 39.

51. Hughes, "Superstitions," p. 500.

52. Hayden Carruth, "Here Today: A Poetry Chronicle," *Hudson Review*, 24 (Summer 1971), 327–29.

53. See chapter 1, note 40. Also Peter Cooley, "New Beasts, New Blessings," *Shenandoah*, 23 (Winter 1972), 88–93.

54. Marjorie Perloff, "Poetry Chronicle," *Contemporary Literature*, 14 (Winter 1973), 121–23.

55. Blake, *The Marriage of Heaven and Hell*, plate 11, in Erdman, *Poetry and Prose of William Blake*, p. 37.

56. Suzuki, *Mysticism, Christian and Buddhist*, p. 28. In conversation with this writer at Exeter, 27 August 1979, Hughes replied to a question about śūnyatā by smiling and stating that "nothing" can sometimes indicate very positive things.

57. Jung, "Psychological Commentary," in *Bardo*, p. xl.

58. *Bardo*, pp. 166, 171.

59. Ibid., pp. lxii, 83.

60. *The Dhammapada*, trans. P. Lal, pp. 150–53.

61. Hughes et al., *Poems: Fainlight, Hughes, Sillitoe*, p. 18.

62. Suzuki, *The Essence of Buddhism*, pp. 10–13.

63. See note 10 above.

64. Faas I, p. 116.

65. "Poetry Now," *BBC Radio 3*; recorded 24 June 1970.

66. "Now Read On," *BBC Radio 4*; recorded 17 December 1970.

67. Suzuki, *The Essence of Buddhism*, p. 22.

68. See note 12 above.

69. *Achievement*, pp. 330–31.

70. See Anne H. Gayton and Stanley S. Newman, *Yokuts and Western Mono Myths*, pp. 1–109.

6. Flying Astride the Earth (*Gaudete*)

1. Hughes, "Myth II," pp. 80, 84, 91–92.

2. Hughes, *Gaudete* (New York: Harper and Row, 1977), p. 199. Subsequent citations from this American edition appear in the text. Except for the lengthier "Argument" on page 9 of the American edition, the Harper and the Faber British editions are exactly the same, with the same pagination and no line variations.

3. Blake, letter to Trusler, 23 August 1799, in Erdman, *Poetry and Prose of William Blake*, p. 677.

4. Sagar, *Art of Ted Hughes*, p. 187; Faas I, p. 214.

5. Smith, *Orghast at Persepolis*, pp. 181, 96–97.

6. Hughes, *Orpheus*, pp. 7, 17; rpt. in Hughes, *"The Tiger's Bones" and Other Plays for Children*, pp. 97, 107.

7. Hughes, *Prometheus on His Crag*, poem #20.

8. Hughes, "Asgard for Addicts," rev. of *Myth and Religion of the North*, by E. O. G. Turville-Petre, *Listener*, 19 March 1964, p. 485.

9. Hughes, "Myth I," pp. 66–67; "Myth II," pp. 82, 92.

10. Graves, *White Goddess*, pp. 222, 447–48.

11. Jung, *The Practice of Psychotherapy*, trans. R. F. C. Hull, pp. 139–61.

12. Ibid., p. 160.

13. Ibid., p. 155.

14. Ibid., pp. 12, 149.

15. Ibid., pp. 13, 15–16.

16. Graves, *White Goddess*, pp. 444–48.

17. Ibid., p. 222.

18. Ibid., p. 448.

19. Ibid., p. 125.

20. Jung, *Practice*, pp. 11–13, 153.

21. Ibid., p. 148; *The Structure and Dynamics of the Psyche*, trans. R. F. C. Hull, pp. 266–67.

22. Frazer, *Golden Bough*, abridged ed., pp. 351–52.

23. Graves, *White Goddess*, pp. 106, 134. The Apis bull of Osiris, however, is black.

24. W. Y. Evans-Wentz, *The Fairy-Faith in Celtic Countries*, pp. 104, 111–12, 128, 132, 136, 143, 146, 156, 171, 176–77, 182, 198, 204, 210–11.

25. Ibid., pp. 252, 490.

26. Ibid., pp. 358–96, esp. pp. 384, 386.

27. Jung, "On the Psychology of the Trickster Figure," in Radin, *The Trickster*, pp. 202–11; Jung, *Psychology and Alchemy*, pp. 29, 90–93; Jung, *Practice*, pp. 151–52.

28. Faas, "Ted Hughes and *Gaudete*," in Faas I, p. 214.

29. Hughes, "Myth I," p. 59.

30. Jung, *Alchemical Studies*, pp. 160–61, 317.

31. Jung, *Psychology and Alchemy*, pp. 89–90.

32. Hughes, as quoted in Tom Stoppard, "'Orghast,'" *Times Literary Supplement*, 1 October 1971, p. 1174.

33. Hughes, quoted in Smith, *Orghast at Persepolis*, p. 45.

34. Smith, *Orghast at Persepolis*, pp. 91, 117–18; Lévi-Strauss, *The Raw and the Cooked*, trans. John and Doreen Weightman, pp. 26–30.

35. Martin Greenberg, *The Terror of Art: Kafka and Modern Literature*, p. 124.

36. Jung, *Practice*, p. 142.

37. Gustav Janouch, *Conversations with Kafka*, trans. Goronwy Rees, p. 35.

38. "Fragment CXIV." Many different numberings and translations of Heraclitus's *Fragments* exist. Throughout I use that of Charles H. Kahn, *The Art and Thought of Heraclitus*.

39. See Sagar, *Art of Ted Hughes*, pp. 202–3. I am indebted to Sagar for locating the Cernunnos allusion in John Sharkey, *Celtic Mysteries*, p. 12.

40. Hughes, in Faas, "Ted Hughes and *Gaudete*," Faas I, pp. 214–15.

41. Jung, *Aion*, pp. 182–83.

42. See Hugh Sacker, *An Introduction to Wolfram's 'Parzival'*, p. 162. See also pp. 49–63, 93–111.

43. Graves, *White Goddess*, p. 177.

44. Frazer, *The Golden Bough* (1911), II, 361–65.

45. Graves, *White Goddess*, pp. 57, 68, 198–99.

46. Ibid., pp. 253–59.

47. Sagar, *Art of Ted Hughes*, pp. 188–89.

48. See note 1 above and the epigraph quotations to this chapter.

49. Hughes, reprinted in Smith, *Orghast at Persepolis*, pp. 96–97.

50. Kahn, *Art and Thought of Heraclitus*, pp. 73, 81, 263–66.

51. Sagar, *Art of Ted Hughes*, p. 207; Faas I, p. 127.

52. Faas, "Ted Hughes and *Gaudete*," in Faas I, p. 214.

53. Ibid.

54. E. A. Wallis Budge, *Osiris*, I, 10, 65–66, 82.

55. Jung, *Practice*, p. 152.

56. Plath, "The Magic Mirror," pp. 43, 58–60.

57. Budge, ed. and trans., *The Book of the Dead*, pp. 5, n6; 41, n3; 133, n1.

58. Sagar, *Art of Ted Hughes*, p. 209, lists forty-five poems in the "Epilogue" of *Gaudete*. The diamond-shaped poem dividers in both American and British editions, however, separate forty-four poems. The discrepancy occurs between pages 186 and 187 in both editions. The original Gavin Robbins broadside of poem #20, "I said goodbye to earth," ends with "On a dark sill, and to bleed"—at the bottom of page 186. See the Sagar and Tabor *Bibliography*, p. 38. I number the poems to simplify references in my discussion and consider the line "The swallow—rebuilding—" atop page 187 to introduce a separate poem, thus totaling Sagar's forty-five. The second Faber edition (1979) restores the missing diamond.

59. George Steiner, *Language and Silence*, pp. 3–54. Hughes mentions Steiner in "Myth II," p. 93.

60. Budge, *The Book of the Dead*, pp. lxxxii–lxxxiii, lxvi, 542.

61. Hughes, "Introduction," *Selected Poems*, by János Pilinszky, trans. Hughes and János Csokits, p. 13.

62. Graves, *White Goddess*, pp. 253–58.

63. Ibid., pp. 290, 317.

64. Campbell, *Masks: Oriental*, pp. 5–6, 90–91; Zimmer, *Myths and Symbols*, pp. 48, 70, 138, 189; Wendy Doniger O'Flaherty, ed. and trans., *Hindu Myths*, pp. 247–49.

65. Graves, *White Goddess*, pp. 105–6, 134.

66. Zimmer, *Myths and Symbols*, pp. 61, 137–38, 197–99.

67. Faas I, p. 137.

68. A. K. Ramanujan, "Introduction," *Speaking of Śiva*, ed. and trans. Ramanujan, pp. 19–55.

69. Eliade, *Yoga*, p. 201.

70. Zimmer, *Myths and Symbols*, pp. 115, 125, 131, 154, 167, 175.

71. Ramanujan, *Speaking of Śiva*, p. 105.

72. See Judith Kroll, *Chapters in a Mythology*, pp. 22–32.

73. Sagar, letter to this writer dated 28 October 1984.

74. See the Sagar and Tabor *Bibliography*, p. 38; Knight, *Practical Guide to Qabalistic*

Symbolism, I, 189–203. One of the seventy-five signed copies of the Robbins broadside can be seen in the Rare Book Room at the University of Wisconsin-Madison Memorial Library.

75. Eliade, *Yoga*, pp. 206–7.
76. See Budge, *Book of the Dead*, pp. 137, 408 (Ra); Budge, *Osiris*, I, 15 (Osiris); Zimmer, *Myths and Symbols*, pp. 36, 51 (Viṣṇu); Hume, *Thirteen Principal Upanishads*, p. 27 (*ātman*); Erdman, *Poetry and Prose of William Blake*, p. 116 (Los).
77. Graves, *White Goddess*, p. 177.
78. Campbell, *Masks: Oriental*, pp. 49, 53.
79. Steiner, *Language and Silence*, p. 36.
80. Campbell, *Hero*, p. 298; Budge, *Book of the Dead*, p. 50.
81. See Budge, *Osiris*, I, 37, 163; II, 259, 344. Also *Book of the Dead*, pp. 194, 204, 216.
82. See Graves, *White Goddess*, p. 42, and the Hughes poems "Fern" in *Wodwo* and "She seemed so considerate" in *Cave Birds*. The fern in the Welsh *Câd Goddeau* or *The Battle of the Trees* confers the kind of invisibility that allows the poet to "spy" into "all secrets."
83. W. J. Wilkins, *Hindu Mythology, Vedic and Puranic*, p. 125.
84. Jung, *Alchemical Studies*, pp. 160–61, 317.
85. Frazer, *Golden Bough* (1911), II, 361; Graves, *White Goddess*, p. 298.
86. Jung, *Archetypes, Part I*, pp. 295, 301–2; Suzuki, *Essays in Zen Buddhism, First Series*, pp. 245, 258n; Hume, *Thirteen Principal Upanishads*, p. 339.
87. Knight, *Practical Guide to Qabalistic Symbolism*, II, 97–98.
88. Frazer, *Golden Bough*, abridged ed., pp. 1–7.
89. Zimmer, *Myths and Symbols*, pp. 30, 131, 134–35, 154, 167. A photograph of a statue of the four-armed Śiva as Cosmic Dancer appears on the paperback cover of Ramanujan's *Speaking of Śiva*.
90. Jung, *Symbols of Transformation*, p. 258; *Archetypes, Part I*, p. 341.
91. Eliade, *Yoga*, pp. 33, 1–46.

7. Taking Each Other to the Sun (*Cave Birds*)

1. Hughes, "Myth 2," pp. 85, 86, 90.
2. Christopher Clausen, *The Place of Poetry*, p. 21; See also pp. 45, 88, 127.
3. Hughes, *Cave Birds* (New York: Viking Press, 1978), p. 20. Subsequent citations are as found in this edition. Poems and pagination are identical to the 1978 Faber and Faber edition.
4. See Sagar, *Art of Ted Hughes*, pp. 243–44, for a summary of the composition of the A, B, and C groups of *Cave Birds* poems.
5. Hughes, *"Cave Birds," BBC Radio 3*, prod. George Macbeth, recorded 26 May 1975, pp. 1–6. Subsequent citations in the text refer to this recording.
6. Campbell, *Masks: Primitive*, pp. 292–98, 336–42, 348. In the poems of *Cave Birds* we see this motif principally in the solar eagle symbolism.
7. Jung, *Practice*, p. 192.
8. Ibid., pp. 173–82.
9. Budge, *Book of the Dead*, pp. 523–24.
10. In Erdman, *Poetry and Prose of William Blake*, p. 343.

11. Jung, *Archetypes, Part I*, p. 25.
12. Farid ud-Din Attar, *The Conference of the Birds*, trans. C. S. Nott, p. 102.
13. Jung, *Practice*, p. 187.
14. Ibid., p. 177.
15. George C. Vaillant, *Aztecs of Mexico*, rev. Suzannah B. Vaillant, p. 166; see also pp. 32, 42–44. Hughes has used Aztec imagery before: see line 7 of "Second Glance at a Jaguar" (*Wodwo*)—"Like a thick Aztec disemboweller." In the first Faas interview Hughes characterizes the jaguar of this poem as "a precise historical symbol to the bloody-minded Aztecs."
16. Campbell, *Masks: Oriental*, p. 53; Budge, *Book of the Dead*, p. cc; Max Muller, *The Mythology of All Races*, ed. Louis Herbert Gray, XII, 24, 27.
17. Jung, *Practice*, p. 303.
18. Jung, *Psychology and Alchemy*, p. 241.
19. Ibid., p. 244.
20. Ibid., p. 245.
21. Ibid., pp. 293, 312.
22. Ibid., p. 306.
23. Ibid., p. 35; Jacobi, *The Way of Individuation*, pp. 59, 74–75.
24. See Sagar, *Art of Ted Hughes*, pp. 171–85; Hirschberg, *Myth in the Poetry of Ted Hughes*, pp. 152–77. Also Graham Bradshaw, "Creative Mythology in *Cave Birds*," in *Achievement*, pp. 210–38.
25. Jung, *Psychology and Alchemy*, pp. 227–483; Jacobi, *The Way of Individuation*, pp. 74–75, 59.
26. Jacobi, *The Way of Individuation*, pp. 25–29, 59.
27. Rice, *The Persian Sufis*, pp. 76–82.
28. Jung, *Alchemical Studies*, pp. 16–18.
29. Jung, *Psychology and Alchemy*, p. 232.
30. Attar, *Conference of the Birds*, pp. 97–101.
31. Faas I, pp. 81–210.
32. Johann Christian Andreae, *The Hermetick Romance: Or the Chymical Wedding of Christian Rosencreutz*, trans. E. Foxcroft (London: A. Sowle, 1690), p. 129. See Jung's comments on the *Chymical Wedding* in *Alchemical Studies*, pp. 183–84, 187, 230–31; and especially in *Practice*, p. 289.
33. Andreae, *Chymical Wedding*, pp. 224–25.
34. Ibid., pp. 23–25; Jung, *Psychology and Alchemy*, pp. 436–37 (white dove); *Mysterium Coniunctionis*, trans. R. F. C. Hull, p. 513 (raven's head).
35. Eliade, *Shamanism*, pp. 140, 204n; Jung, *Mysterium*, p. 295.
36. Jung, *Practice*, pp. 295–99; *Psychology and Alchemy*, p. 230.
37. Jung, *Mysterium*, p. 95.
38. Eliade, *Shamanism*, p. 302.
39. Vaillant, *Aztecs of Mexico*, p. 145.
40. Jung, *Alchemical Studies*, pp. 68, 84.
41. Jung, *Mysterium*, p. 193.
42. Andreae, *Chymical Wedding*, pp. 27–29.
43. Jung, *Practice*, p. 256.
44. Attar, *Conference of the Birds*, pp. 112, 118–19.
45. Sagar, *Art of Ted Hughes*, p. 182.

46. Campbell, *Masks: Primitive*, p. 255.
47. Jung, *Psychology and Alchemy*, pp. 417, 437; *Mysterium*, pp. 295, 141.
48. Jung, *Mysterium*, p. 77.
49. Graves, *White Goddess*, pp. 412–13.
50. Jung, *Mysterium*, pp. 144, 148, 323.
51. Graves, *White Goddess*, p. 126; Ezekiel, 1:4–10.
52. Eliade, *Shamanism*, pp. 204n, 218.
53. Campbell, *Masks: Primitive*, p. 298.
54. Campbell, *Masks: Oriental*, pp. 39–40.
55. Eliade, *Shamanism*, pp. 89–106.
56. Campbell, *Masks: Primitive*, pp. 342, 348ff.
57. Bradshaw, in *Achievement*, p. 212.
58. Jung, *Archetypes, Part I*, pp. 355–90.
59. Hughes, *Cave Birds*, n.p.g.
60. Jung, *Mysterium*, p. 82.
61. Ibid., p. 162; Jung, *Practice*, p. 182.
62. Vaillant, *Aztecs of Mexico*, pp. 26, 55, 166, 179, 189, 191.
63. Friedrich Nietzsche, *The Birth of Tragedy and The Case of Wagner*, trans. Walter Kaufman, p. 110.
64. Frazer, *Golden Bough*, abridged ed., pp. 129, 299–300.
65. *Critical Quarterly*, 4 (Winter 1964), 319; rpt. *Achievement*, p. 318.
66. Blake, "Annotations to Berkeley's *Siris*," in Erdman, *Poetry and Prose of William Blake*, p. 653. See also the discussion in Northrop Frye, *Fearful Symmetry*, pp. 14–27.
67. In Erdman, *Poetry and Prose of William Blake*, pp. 476, 634.
68. Dated 23 August 1799, in ibid., p. 677.
69. Ibid., p. 483.
70. Attar, *Conference of the Birds*, p. 107.
71. Ibid., p. 114.
72. Ibid., p. 123.
73. Jung, *Mysterium*, pp. 77, 144, 148, 323; *Practice*, p. 271; Eliade, *Shamanism*, pp. 70–71, 128n, 157.
74. Kenneth Clark, *Civilization*, pp. 175–77.
75. Alan Brownjohn, "Heads, Tongues & Spirits," *Encounter*, 51 (November 1978), 64; Calvin Bedient, "New Confessions," *Sewanee Review*, 88 (Summer 1980), 480–81; Robert Nye, "Poetry," *London Times*, 7 September 1978, p. 14; Julian Symons, "Grigson: A Long Look Back," *London Sunday Times*, 26 November 1978, p. 40.
76. Attar, *Conference of the Birds*, pp. 131–32.
77. Rice, *The Persian Sufis*, p. 77.

8. From Emptiness to Brighter Emptiness (*Remains of Elmet*)

1. Hughes, "The Rock," in *Writers on Themselves*, ed. Herbert Read, pp. 86, 91.
2. Hughes, *Remains of Elmet* (New York: Harper and Row, 1979), p. 7. Subsequent citations in the text derive from this edition. Poems and pagination are identical to the Faber and Faber edition (1979), with no line variants.

3. In a letter to this writer dated 14 June 1981, Hughes responded to an earlier draft of this chapter that contained both the sonata form discussion and the Taoist spiritual resolution. Hughes offered many clarifications about particular poems and then concluded that "the whole main part of the essay finds the kind of sense in the poems that I tried to put there." After reading the final manuscript version of this chapter, Hughes on 7 June 1985 responded to a query letter from this writer, in part to reconfirm his assessment of this chapter and to clarify the exact causal sequence that led to the final organization of the trade editions.

4. Conversation with Hughes, 27 August 1979, at Exeter.

5. References in this chapter to the eighty-one chapters of Lao Tzu and the thirty-three chapters of Chuang Tzu derive from the following: Arthur Waley, ed. and trans., *The Way and Its Power*; Burton Watson, trans., *The Complete Works of Chuang Tzu*.

6. Chang, *Creativity and Taoism*, pp. 34–35; Holmes Welch, *Taoism: The Parting of the Way*, pp. 54–55; John Blofeld, *Taoism: The Road to Immortality*, pp. 167–68.

7. Mai-Mai Sze, *The Tao of Painting*, p. 3.

8. In our conversation of 27 August 1979, Hughes stated that the soft, undulating feminine lines of the high moors were a major source for the wings imagery of *Remains of Elmet*.

9. Waley, *The Way*, pp. 26–28.

10. J. M. Barrie, *Peter Pan*, p. 188.

11. Hughes, "The Rock," pp. 90–91.

12. Ibid., p. 90.

13. In Watson, *Complete Works of Chuang Tzu*, p. 168.

14. Welch, *Taoism*, pp. 19–25; Sze, *Tao of Painting*, pp. 17–18.

15. Compare the use of water in Lao Tzu, VIII, LXI, LXXVII, and Chuang Tzu, XV, with the water imagery in the *Elmet* poems "It Is All," "Hill-Stone Was Content," and "Crown Point Pensioners."

16. Andrew H. Plaks, *Archetype and Allegory in the Dream of the Red Chamber*, pp. 127–77 (chapters on "Western Allegorical Gardens" and "The Chinese Literary Garden").

17. Blofeld, *Taoism*, p. 168.

18. Chang, *Creativity and Taoism*, p. 171.

19. Tao-chi, *Returning Home*, ed. and trans. Wen Fong, poems #2 and 4. Tao-chi (1641–ca. 1710) was a leading artist of the Individualist school of the early Ch'ing (Manchu) period.

20. Letter from Hughes to this writer, dated 21 December 1980.

21. Chang, *Creativity and Taoism*, pp. 24, 171; Sze, *Tao of Painting*, pp. 33–36.

22. See Lao Tzu, XXVII, XLI, LII, LVIII; Chuang Tzu, II, XXIII. See also Chang, *Creativity and Taoism*, pp. 5, 35, 49, 80. According to the Sinologist Richard Wilhelm, *yin* originally meant "the cloudy," "the overcast," and *yang* originally meant "banners waving in the sun." See Wilhelm's "Introduction" to his edition of *The "I Ching" or Book of Changes*, trans. Cary F. Baynes, p. xxxvi.

23. Conversations with Ted Hughes and Olwyn Hughes, August 1979, at London and Exeter.

24. See "The Story of Janshah," in Sir Richard F. Burton, trans., *The Book of the Thousand Nights and a Night*, V, 345ff.; Julius Eggeling, ed. and trans., *Satapatha-*

Brahmana, in Max Muller, gen. ed., *The Sacred Books of the East*, XLIV, 71–72. See also Stith Thompson, *Motif-Index of Folk-Literature*, II, 34.

25. Wellek and Warren, *Theory of Literature*, p. 241. See also the discussion in chapter 1.
26. Auerbach, *Mimesis*, pp. 484–85; 481. See also chapter 1.
27. Hughes, "Elmet," *BBC Radio 3*, prod. Fraser Steel, recorded 3 May 1980, p. 5.
28. Hughes, *Season Songs* (New York: Viking, 1975). Subsequent citations derive from this edition.
29. Geoffrey Thurley, *An Ironic Harvest*, pp. 187–88.
30. Coleridge, *Biographia Literaria*, II, 11; Barth, *The Symbolic Imagination*, pp. 11–12, 27–28.
31. Coleridge, *Biographia Literaria*, I, 295–96.

9. No Wing to Tread Emptiness (*Moortown*)

1. Hughes, *Ted Hughes and R. S. Thomas read and discuss selections of their own poems*, *The Critical Forum*.
2. Hughes, *Moortown* (New York: Harper and Row, 1980), p. 182. Subsequent citations derive from this edition. The 1979 Faber and Faber edition contains the same poems, and no line variants, with the single substitution of "The Lovepet" and the deletion of "Bride and groom lie hidden for three days." Pagination differs, however.
3. Sagar and Tabor, *Ted Hughes*, p. 90.
4. Jung, *Mysterium*, pp. 382–85, 393–94, 397, 454.
5. Ibid., p. 406.
6. Hughes, "Earth-numb," *BBC Radio 3*, prod. Fraser Steel, recorded 6 February 1980, p. 11.
7. Knight, *Practical Guide to Qabalistic Symbolism*, I, 250.
8. Scholem, *Kabbalah*, pp. 21, 100, 130, 137, 152, 155, 162, 164.
9. Knight, *Practical Guide to Qabalistic Symbolism*, I, 9, 30–37.
10. Sagar, "Fourfold Vision in Hughes," in *Achievement*, pp. 285–312.
11. Frye, *Fearful Symmetry*, pp. 44, 125, 287. See also Sheila Spector, "Kabbalistic Sources—Blake's and His Critics'," *Blake: An Illustrated Quarterly*, 17 (Winter 1983–84), 84–99. Spector concludes that, while a cabbalistic influence in Blake is undeniable, his only possible sources in eighteenth-century England were inaccurate and distorted interpretations of Latin cabbalists, written by non-Jews and Christians. The main textual evidence concerns the resemblance of the myth of Albion to the cabbalistic Adam Kadmon. Spector refers readers to Blake's "To the Jews" on plate 27 of *Jerusalem*: "You have a tradition, that Man anciently containd in his mighty limbs all things in Heaven & Earth."
12. Thomas R. Frosch, *The Awakening of Albion*, pp. 17–20.
13. Ibid., pp. 33–34, 38, 62.
14. All quotations and line citations from Blake's work in this study derive from the Erdman edition.
15. Frosch, *Awakening of Albion*, pp. 40, 57.
16. Ibid., pp. 23, 28, 66–67.

17. Ibid., pp. 92–93, 124; 42, 80, 151, 176, 179; 123, 135; 118; 127.
18. Morton D. Paley, *Energy and Imagination*, p. 14.
19. Frosch, *Awakening of Albion*, pp. 144, 181–82.
20. *Jerusalem*, II:43:1–5.
21. *The Four Zoas*, IX:138:20–25.
22. Frosch, *Awakening of Albion*, pp. 92, 100, 34.
23. Paley, *Energy and Imagination*, pp. 200–201, 24–25.
24. Frosch, *Awakening of Albion*, p. 151.
25. Frye, *Fearful Symmetry*, pp. 76, 235, 251, 262.
26. The foregoing paragraph represents a distillation of Frye's and Frosch's descriptions of Ulro, Generation, Beulah, and Eden.
27. Hughes, "Earth-numb," *BBC Radio 3*, p. 1.
28. Hughes, "Moortown," *BBC Radio 3*, prod. Fraser Steel, recorded 6 February 1980, pp. 7, 2, 1, 4.
29. Successful births occur in "Surprise," "Birth of Rainbow," and "Little Red Twin" (two); unsuccessful births occur in "Struggle," "Last Night" (two), "Ravens," "February 17th," "Orf," and "Sheep."
30. Hughes, "Moortown," *BBC Radio 3*, p. 4.
31. *The Marriage of Heaven and Hell*, plate 11; *Bardo*, pp. 121–23.
32. *Jerusalem*, III:66:81.
33. Frosch, *Awakening of Albion*, p. 29. See also Robert Gleckner, "Blake and the Senses," *Studies in Romanticism*, 5 (Autumn 1965), 1–15.
34. See the discussion in Frosch, *Awakening of Albion*, pp. 143, 150, 156.
35. Ibid., pp. 105–6.
36. See note 27 above.
37. Eliade, *Yoga*, pp. 72–73, 106, 246.
38. Sagar, "Fourfold Vision in Hughes," in *Achievement*, p. 307.
39. "Tiger Psalm" originally appeared as "Crow's Table Talk" in Hughes, *Crow Wakes*.
40. Eliade, *Yoga*, pp. 220, 320.
41. Sagar, catalogue note to the 1980 Manchester City Art Gallery Exhibition of Hughes's work.
42. See note 1 above.
43. Jung, *Mysterium*, pp. 389, 421ff.
44. *The Four Zoas*, IX:126:14–15.
45. Eliade, *Yoga*, pp. 201, 206, 220.
46. *A Vision of the Last Judgment*, p. 87.
47. Frosch, *Awakening of Albion*, pp. 97, 149.
48. Eliade, *Yoga*, pp. 200–226.
49. Frazer, *Golden Bough*, abridged ed., p. 494.
50. Hughes, "Earth-numb," *BBC Radio 3*, p. 15.
51. Sagar, "Fourfold Vision in Hughes," in *Achievement*, p. 301.
52. Jung, *Psychology and Alchemy*, pp. 345–72.
53. Hughes, "Orghast: Talking without Words," *Vogue*, December 1971, p. 97.
54. Stuart Curran, "Blake and the Gnostic Hyle: A Double Negative," *Blake Studies*, 4 (Spring 1972), 117–33.
55. Hughes, "The Environmental Revolution," p. 81.

56. Jung, *Mysterium*, p. 414.
57. See note 3 above.
58. Hughes, letter to this writer, dated 21 December 1980.

10. Sanctus Sanctus (River)

1. Hughes, "Introduction," in Keith Sagar, *The Reef*, n.p.g.
2. Hughes, *River* (New York: Harper and Row, 1984), p. 22. Unless otherwise noted, all subsequent citations from the poems derive from this American edition. The Peter Keen photographs appear only in the 1983 Faber and Faber edition, which has different pagination. The lines within the poems and the sequence of the poems are identical, with two important exceptions: the sequence of the first three poems in the Faber and Faber edition is "The Morning Before Christmas," "Japanese River Tales," and "Flesh of Light," whereas in the Harper and Row it is "Flesh of Light," "Japanese River Tales," and "The Morning Before Christmas"; "Gulkana" in the Faber edition is expanded to "The Gulkana" in the Harper, with the addition of about forty-two new lines and other minor revisions.
3. Hughes, letter to this writer, dated 7 June 1985.
4. Hughes, "The Rock," in Read, ed., *Writers on Themselves*, p. 91.
5. Li Po, *The Works of Li Po*, trans. Shigeyoshi Obata, pp. 70, 82, 86.
6. Campbell, *Masks: Oriental*, p. 336.
7. Zimmer, *Myths and Symbols*, pp. 110–13.
8. See chapter 8 of this text and note 22 to chapter 8.
9. In Watson, *Complete Works of Chuang Tzu*, pp. 142, 122–23.
10. Ibid., p. 157.
11. Chang, *Creativity and Taoism*, pp. 203–207.
12. See Frye, *Fearful Symmetry*, pp. 135–41, 251; Paley, *Energy and Imagination*, pp. 79–81, 92, 168–69.
13. Erdman, *Poetry and Prose of William Blake*, p. 882.
14. Jung, *Psychology and Alchemy*, pp. 132–34, 299–300, 437.
15. Anne Ross, *Pagan Celtic Britain*, pp. 104–26.
16. See Blake, "Annotations to Berkeley's *Siris*," in Erdman, *Poetry and Prose of William Blake*, pp. 652–54. See also the discussion in Frosch, *Awakening of Albion*, pp. 27–28, 67, 97, 102, 127, 142–43, 149, 151, 155.
17. Juliet Piggott, *Japanese Mythology*, pp. 69, 71.
18. Hartley Burr Alexander, *North American Mythology*, in *The Mythology of All Races*, ed. Louis Herbert Gray, X, 255.
19. Daniel G. Hoffman, *The Poetry of Stephen Crane*, p. 90.
20. Information concerning the mating behavior of the damselfly and the dragonfly that appears in this and the subsequent two paragraphs derives from two sources: Philip S. Corbet, *A Biology of Dragonflies*, chapters 1 and 7; and N. W. Moore, "Notes on the Oviposition Behaviour of the Dragonfly *Sympetrum Striolatum* Charpentier," *Behaviour*, 4 (1952), 101–3. Damselflies (suborder Zygoptera) and dragonflies (suborder Anisoptera) comprise the order Odonata. Their mating and ovipositing behavior is so similar that throughout his text Corbet simply uses the word "dragonfly" when discussing species of either suborder.

21. Graves, *White Goddess*, pp. 58, 169, 126.

22. Hughes, *What Is the Truth?*, p. 121.

23. Boas, *Tsimshian Mythology*, pp. 76–79, 668–70.

24. Proinsias MacCana, *Celtic Mythology*, p. 110; Ross, *Pagan Celtic Britain*, p. 351.

25. *The Mabinogion*, trans. Gwyn Jones and Thomas Jones, pp. 125–26.

26. Blake, letter to Trusler, 23 August 1799, in Erdman, *Poetry and Prose of William Blake*, p. 677.

27. John Middleton Murry, *William Blake*, p. 13.

28. Blake, "THERE is NO Natural Religion," in Erdman, *Poetry and Prose of William Blake*, p. 2.

29. Blake, *A Vision of the Last Judgment*, in ibid., p. 545.

30. Zeami Motokiyo, *On the Art of the Nō Drama: The Major Treatises of Zeami*, ed. and trans. J. Thomas Rimer and Yamazaki Masakazu, pp. xxix–xlv.

31. Campbell, *Masks: Primitive*, pp. 291–95.

32. N. J. Girardot, *Myth and Meaning in Early Taoism*, pp. 61, 68–69, 73, 79–80, 84, 94–98.

33. In Erdman, *Poetry and Prose of William Blake*, p. 555.

BIBLIOGRAPHY

For a comprehensive listing of the publications of Ted Hughes, including reviews and BBC radio scripts, consult the periodic updatings of the Sagar and Tabor bibliography cited below.

Alexander, Hartley Burr. *North American Mythology.* In *The Mythology of All Races.* Gen. ed. Louis Herbert Gray. Boston: Marshall Jones, 1916.

Alvarez, Alfred. "Black Bird." Rev. of *Crow. Observer*, 11 October 1970, p. 33.

————. "D. H. Lawrence: The Single State of Man." In his *The Shaping Spirit: Studies in Modern English and American Poetry.* 1958; rpt. London: Chatto and Windus, 1961, pp. 140–61.

Andreae, Johann Christian. *The Hermetick Romance: Or the Chymical Wedding of Christian Rosencreutz.* Trans. E. Foxcroft. London: A. Sowle, 1690.

Appleyard, J. A. *Coleridge's Philosophy of Literature: The Development of a Concept of Poetry, 1791–1819.* Cambridge: Harvard Univ. Press, 1965.

Attar, Farid ud-Din. *The Conference of the Birds.* Trans. C. S. Nott. Boulder, Colorado: Shambala, 1971.

Auerbach, Eric. *Mimesis: The Representation of Reality in Western Literature.* Trans. Willard Trask. 1953; rpt. Garden City: Doubleday, 1957.

Baker, James Volant. *The Sacred River: Coleridge's Theory of the Imagination.* 1957; rpt. New York: Greenwood Press, 1969.

Balakian, Anna. *Literary Origins of Surrealism: A New Mysticism in French Poetry.* 2nd ed. New York: New York Univ. Press, 1966.

————. *Surrealism: The Road to the Absolute.* 2nd ed. New York: E. P. Dutton, 1970.

Barrie, J. M. *Peter Pan.* London: Hodder and Stoughton, 1911.

Barth, J. Robert. *The Symbolic Imagination: Coleridge and the Romantic Tradition.* Princeton: Princeton Univ. Press, 1977.

Bedient, Calvin. "New Confessions." Rev. of *Cave Birds, Remains of Elmet*, et al. *Sewanee Review*, 88 (Summer 1980), 474–88.

————. "On Ted Hughes." *Critical Quarterly*, 14, ii (Summer 1972), 103–21.

Bergonzi, Bernard. *The Situation of the Novel.* London: Macmillan, 1970.

Blake, William. *The Poetry and Prose of William Blake.* Ed. David V. Erdman. Rev. ed. Garden City: Doubleday, 1968.

Blofeld, John. *Taoism: The Road to Immortality.* Boulder, Colorado: Shambala, 1978.

Boas, Franz. *Tsimshian Mythology.* Washington, D.C.: Government Printing Office, 1916.

Bogan, Louise. "Verse." Rev. of *Wodwo*, et al. *New Yorker*, 30 March 1968, pp. 133–38.

Bolt, Sydney. "Ted Hughes: Laureate of Leucotomy." *Delta*, 42 (February 1968), 4–11.

Bowra, C. M. *Primitive Song.* New York: World Publishing, 1962.

Breton, André. *Manifestos of Surrealism.* Trans. Richard Seaver and Helen R. Lane. Ann Arbor: Univ. of Michigan Press, 1969.

Brooks, Cleanth. *The Well Wrought Urn: Studies in the Structure of Poetry.* New York: Harcourt, Brace, and World, 1947.

Browne, Sir Thomas. *Sir Thomas Browne's Works*. Ed. Simon Wilkin. London: William Pickering, 1835. Vol. V.

Brownjohn, Alan. "The Brutal Tone." Rev. of *The Hawk in the Rain*, et al. *Listen*, 2 (Spring 1958), 20–23.

————. "Heads, Tongues & Spirits." Rev. of *Cave Birds*, et al. *Encounter*, 51 (November 1978), 63–66.

————. "On Survival." Rev. of *Crow*. *New Statesman*, 16 October 1970, pp. 490–91.

————, et al., eds. *New Poems, 1970–71: A P.E.N. Anthology of Contemporary Poetry*. London: Hutchinson, 1971.

Budge, E. A. Wallis, ed. and trans. *The Book of the Dead: An English Translation of the Chapters, Hymns, Etc., of the Theban Recension*. 2nd ed. New York: E. P. Dutton, 1928.

————. *Osiris: The Egyptian Religion of Resurrection*. Rev. ed. New York: University Books, 1961.

Burton, Sir Richard F., trans. *The Book of the Thousand Nights and a Night*. London: Burton Club, 1885. Vol. V.

Burtt, E. A., ed. *The Teachings of the Compassionate Buddha*. New York: New American Library, 1955.

Bush, Douglas. *English Literature in the Earlier Seventeenth Century: 1600–1660*. 2nd ed. Oxford: Clarendon Press, 1962.

Butscher, Edward. *Sylvia Plath: Method and Madness*. New York: Pocket Books, 1977.

Campbell, Joseph. *The Hero with a Thousand Faces*. 2nd ed. 1968; rpt. Princeton: Princeton Univ. Press, 1973.

————. *The Masks of God: Creative Mythology*. New York: Viking, 1968.

————. *The Masks of God: Occidental Mythology*. New York: Viking, 1964.

————. *The Masks of God: Oriental Mythology*. New York: Viking, 1962.

————. *The Masks of God: Primitive Mythology*. New York: Viking, 1960.

Carr, W. I. Untitled review of *The Hawk in the Rain*. *Delta*, 14 (Spring 1958), 25–27.

Carruth, Hayden. "Here Today: A Poetry Chronicle." Rev. of *Crow*, et al. *Hudson Review*, 24 (Summer 1971), 320–36.

Chang, Chung-yuan. *Creativity and Taoism: A Study of Chinese Philosophy, Art, and Poetry*. 1963; rpt. New York: Harper and Row, 1970.

Chuang Tzu. *The Complete Works of Chuang Tzu*. Trans. Burton Watson. New York: Columbia Univ. Press, 1968.

Clark, Kenneth. *Civilization: A Personal View*. New York: Harper and Row, 1969.

Clausen, Christopher. *The Place of Poetry: Two Centuries of an Art in Crisis*. Lexington: Univ. of Kentucky Press, 1981.

Coleridge, Samuel Taylor. *Biographia Literaria*. 2 vols. 1817; rpt. Menston, Yorkshire: Scolar Press, 1971.

Conquest, Robert. "Intercontinental Missiles." Rev. of *The Hawk in the Rain*, et al. *Spectator*, 11 October 1957, p. 488.

————, ed. *New Lines*. London: Macmillan, 1956.

Cooley, Peter. "New Beasts: New Blessings." Rev. of *Crow*, et al. *Shenandoah*, 23 (Winter 1972), 88–93.

Corbet, Philip S. *A Biology of Dragonflies*. 1962; rpt. Faringdon, England: E. W. Classey, 1983.

Curran, Stuart. "Blake and the Gnostic Hyle: A Double Negative." *Blake Studies*, 4 (Spring 1972), 117–33.

Davie, Donald. "As deep as England." Rev. of *Wodwo*, by Ted Hughes. *Guardian*, 25 May 1967, p. 14.

————. *The Poet in the Imaginary Museum: Essays of Two Decades*. Ed. Barry Alpert. Manchester: Carcanet Press, 1977.

Dijkstra, Bram. *The Hieroglyphics of a New Speech: Cubism, Stieglitz, and the Early Poetry of William Carlos Williams*. Princeton: Princeton Univ. Press, 1969.

Eggeling, Julius, ed. and trans. *Satapatha-Brahmana: According to the Text of the Madhyandina School*. Vol. XLIV of *The Sacred Books of the East*. Gen. ed. Max Muller. Oxford: Clarendon Press, 1882, pp. 71–72.

Einstein, Albert. *Einstein on Peace*. Ed. Otto Nathan and Heintz Norden. New York: Schocken, 1960.

————. *Relativity: The Special and the General Theory*. Trans. Robert W. Lawson. 15th ed. 1952; rpt. New York: Bonanza Books, 1961.

Eliade, Mircea. *Myth and Reality*. Trans. Willard R. Trask. New York: Harper and Row, 1963.

————. *The Myth of the Eternal Return*. Trans. Willard R. Trask. New York: Pantheon, 1954.

————. *Myths, Dreams and Mysteries: The Encounter between Contemporary Faiths and Archaic Realities*. Trans. Philip Mairet. New York: Harper and Brothers, 1960.

————. *Shamanism: Archaic Techniques of Ecstasy*. Trans. Willard R. Trask. Princeton: Princeton Univ. Press, 1964.

————. *Yoga: Immortality and Freedom*. Trans. Willard R. Trask. 2nd ed. Princeton: Princeton Univ. Press, 1969.

Eliot, T. S. "The Metaphysical Poets." In his *Selected Essays*. 2nd ed. New York: Harcourt, Brace, and World, 1960, pp. 241–50.

Ellmann, Richard. *Yeats: The Man and the Masks*. New York: Macmillan, 1948.

Evans-Wentz, W. Y. *The Fairy-Faith in Celtic Countries*. 1911; rpt. New York: University Books, 1966.

————, ed. *The Tibetan Book of the Dead*. Trans. Lama Kazi Dawa-Samdup. 3rd ed. 1957; rpt. London: Oxford Univ. Press, 1974.

Faas, Ekbert. "Ted Hughes and Crow." *London Magazine*, 10 (January 1971), 5–20.

————. *Ted Hughes: The Unaccommodated Universe*. Santa Barbara: Black Sparrow, 1980 (Faas I).

Ferns, John. "Over the Same Ground." Rev. of *Wodwo*. *Far Point*, 1 (Fall–Winter 1968), 66–70.

Fine, Reuben. *The Development of Freud's Thought: From the Beginnings (1886–1900) through Id Psychology (1900–1914) to Ego Psychology (1914–1939)*. New York: Jason Aronson, 1973.

Fortune, Dion. *The Mystical Qabalah*. 1935; rpt. London: Williams and Norgate, 1941.

Frank, Joseph. "Spatial Form in Modern Literature." In his *The Widening Gyre*. Bloomington: Indiana Univ. Press, 1963, pp. 3–62.

Frazer, G. S. "Books." Rev. of *Crow*, et al. *Partisan Review*, 38 (Winter 1971–1972), 469–78.

Frazer, Sir James G. *The Golden Bough: A Study in Magic and Religion*. Abridged ed. 1922; rpt. New York: Macmillan, 1951.

————. *The Golden Bough: A Study in Magic and Religion*. London: Macmillan, 1911. Vol. II.

Freud, Sigmund. *Inhibitions, Symptoms, and Anxiety*. Trans. Alex Strachey. Ed. and rev. James Strachey. London: Hogarth Press, 1961.

————. *New Introductory Lectures on Psycho-Analysis*. Trans. W. J. H. Sprott. 1933; rpt. London: Hogarth Press, 1962.

————. *The Standard Edition of the Complete Psychological Works of Sigmund Freud*. Ed. and trans. James Strachey. 23 vols. London: Hogarth Press, 1952–1966.

Frey-Rohn, Liliane. *From Freud to Jung: A Comparative Study of the Psychology of the Unconscious*. Trans. F. E. Engreen and E. K. Engreen. New York: G. P. Putnam's Sons, 1974.

Frosch, Thomas R. *The Awakening of Albion: The Renovation of the Body in the Poetry of William Blake*. Ithaca: Cornell Univ. Press, 1974.

Frye, Northrop. *Fearful Symmetry: A Study of William Blake*. 1947; rpt. Princeton: Princeton Univ. Press, 1969.

Gayton, Anne H., and Stanley S. Newman. *Yokuts and Western Mono Myths*. Berkeley: Univ. of California Press, 1940.

Gifford, Terry, and Neil Roberts. *Ted Hughes: A Critical Study*. London: Faber and Faber, 1981.

Girardot, N. J. *Myth and Meaning in Early Taoism: The Theme of Chaos ("hun-tun")*. Berkeley: Univ. of California Press, 1983.

Gleckner, Robert. "Blake and the Senses." *Studies in Romanticism*, 5 (Autumn 1965), 1–15.

Graves, Robert. *The White Goddess: A Historical Grammar of Poetic Myth*. 2nd ed. New York: Farrar, Straus, and Giroux, 1966.

Greenberg, Martin. *The Terror of Art: Kafka and Modern Literature*. New York: Basic Books, 1968.

Greenway, John. *Literature among the Primitives: An Anthology of Myths, Tales, Songs, Riddles, and Proverbs of Aboriginal Peoples around the World*. Hatboro, Pennsylvania: Folklore Associates, 1964.

————. *The Primitive Reader*. Hatboro, Pennsylvania: Folklore Associates, 1965.

Hamilton, Ian. "Ted Hughes: *Crow*." In his *A Poetry Chronicle: Essays and Reviews*. London: Faber and Faber, 1973, pp. 165–70.

Harrison, Jane. *Prolegomena to the Study of Greek Religion*. 3rd ed. 1908; rpt. Cambridge: Cambridge Univ. Press, 1922.

————. *Themis: A Study of the Social Origins of Greek Religion*. 2nd ed. Cambridge: Cambridge Univ. Press, 1927.

Harrison, Tony. "Crow Magnon." Rev. of *Crow*. *London Magazine*, 11 (January 1971), 86–88.

Hecht, Anthony. "Writers' Rights and Readers' Rights." Rev. of *Wodwo*, et al. *Hudson Review*, 21 (Spring 1968), 207–17.

Hirschberg, Stuart. *Myth in the Poetry of Ted Hughes: A Guide to the Poems*. Dublin: Wolfhound Press, 1981.

Hoffman, Daniel G. *The Poetry of Stephen Crane*. New York: Columbia Univ. Press, 1957.

Holbrook, David. "The Cult of Hughes and Gunn." *Poetry Review*, 54 (Summer 1963), 167–83.

————. "Ted Hughes's *Crow* and the Longing for Non-Being." In *The Black Rainbow*. Ed. Peter Abbs. London: Heinemann, 1975, pp. 32–54.

Holmes, John. "A Poet Seeks the Limits of His World." Rev. of *Lupercal*. *Christian Science Monitor*, 25 August 1960, p. 8.

Holmes, Richard. "Ted Hughes: A Brutish Metamorphosis." Rev. of *Crow*. *London Times*, 17 December 1970, p. 15.

Horder, John. "Desk Poet." *Guardian*, 23 March 1965, p. 9.

Hughes, Ted. "A Fable." *Times Literary Supplement*, 9 September 1960, p. 70.

————. "After Lorca." *Poetry*, 103 (December 1963), 154–55.

————. "Asgard for Addicts." Rev. of *Myth and Religion of the North*, by E. O. G. Turville-Petre. *Listener*, 19 March 1964, pp. 484–85.

————. *Cave Birds: An Alchemical Cave Drama*. London: Faber and Faber; New York: Viking, 1978.

————. *Cave Birds*. BBC Radio 3. Prod. George Macbeth. Recorded 26 May 1975.

————. *Cave Birds*. Ilkley, Yorkshire: Scolar Press, 1975.

————. "Creatures." *BBC Home Service*. Prod. Owen Leeming. Recorded 5 May 1960.

————. "The Crime of Fools Exposed." Rev. of *The Collected Poems of Wilfred Owen*, ed. C. Day Lewis. *New York Times Book Review*, 12 April 1964, pp. 12, 18.

————. *Crow: From the Life and Songs of the Crow*. London: Faber and Faber, 1970; 2nd ed., 1972; New York: Harper and Row, 1971.

————. *A Crow Hymn*. Farnham, Surrey: Sceptre Press, 1970.

————. *Crow Wakes*. Exeter, Devonshire: Rougemont Press, 1971.

————. "Dylan Thomas's Letters." Rev. of *The Selected Letters of Dylan Thomas*, ed. Constantine Fitzgibbon. *New Statesman*, 25 November 1966, p. 733.

————. "Earth-numb." *BBC Radio 3*. Prod. Fraser Steel. Recorded 6 February 1980.

————. *Eat Crow*. London: Rainbow Press, 1971.

————. "Elmet." *BBC Radio 3*. Prod. Fraser Steel. Recorded 3 May 1980.

————. "The Environmental Revolution." Rev. of *The Environmental Revolution*, by Max Nicholson. *Your Environment*, 1 (Summer 1970), 81–83.

————. *A Few Crows*. Exeter, Devonshire: Rougemont Press, 1970.

————. *Five Autumn Songs for Children's Voices*. Bow, Devonshire: Richard Gilbertson, 1968.

————. *Gaudete*. London: Faber and Faber; New York: Harper and Row, 1977.

————. *The Hawk in the Rain*. London: Faber and Faber; New York: Harper and Row, 1957.

————. Intro. to *The Reef*, by Keith Sagar. Bradford, Yorkshire: Mallett, 1980, n. pag.

————. Letters to the author. 14 June 1981; 7 June 1985; 10 August 1985; 14 September 1985.

————. *Lupercal*. London: Faber and Faber; New York: Harper and Row, 1960.

————. "Modern Poetry." *BBC Talks for Sixth Forms*. Prod. Tom Butcher. Recorded 24 May 1963.

————. "Moortown." *BBC Radio 3*. Prod. Fraser Steel. Recorded 6 February 1980.

————. *Moortown*. London: Faber and Faber, 1979; New York: Harper and Row, 1980.

————. "Myth and Education." *Children's Literature in Education*, 1 (1970), 55–70 (Myth I).

————. "Myth and Education." In *Writers, Critics and Children*, ed. Geoff Fox et al. New York: Agathon, 1976, pp. 77–94 (Myth II).

————. "Now Read On." *BBC Radio 4*. Recorded 17 December 1970.

————. "On Writing for Radio." Unscripted interview with Anthony Thwaite. *BBC Third Programme*. Recorded 16 January 1963.

————. "Orghast: Talking without Words." *Vogue*, December 1971, 95–97.

————. *Orpheus*. Chicago: Dramatic Publishing, 1973.

————. *Orts*. London: Rainbow Press, 1978.

————. "O White Elite Lotus." *Critical Quarterly*, 4 (Winter 1964), 319.

————. *Poetry in the Making*. London: Faber and Faber, 1967. Published in America as *Poetry Is*. Garden City: Doubleday, 1970.

————. "Poetry Now." *BBC Radio 3*. Recorded 24 June 1970; rpt. in part in *Listener*, 30 July 1970, p. 149.

————. "The Poetry of Keith Douglas." *Listener*, 21 June 1962, pp. 1069–70.

————. *Prometheus on His Crag*. London: Rainbow Press, 1973.

————. "Quitting." Rev. of *Vagrancy*, by Philip O'Connor. *New Statesman*, 6 September 1963, pp. 293–94.

————. *Recklings*. London: Turret Books, 1966.

————. *Remains of Elmet: A Pennine Sequence*. London: Faber and Faber; New York: Harper and Row, 1979.

————. *River*. London: Faber and Faber, 1983; New York: Harper and Row, 1984.

————. "The Rock." In *Writers on Themselves*. Ed. Herbert Read. London: Cox and Wyman, 1964.

————. *Season Songs*. London: Faber and Faber, 1976; New York: Viking, 1975.

————. "Secret Ecstasies." Rev. of *Shamanism*, by Mircea Eliade, and *The Sufis*, by Idries Shah. *Listener*, 29 October 1964, pp. 677–78.

————. "The Space-Egg Was Sailing." In *New Poems 1970–71: A P.E.N. Anthology of Contemporary Poetry*. Ed. Alan Brownjohn, et al. London: Hutchinson, 1971, pp. 49–50.

————. "Superstitions." Rev. of *Astrology*, by Aldus, and *Ghost and Divining-rod*, by T. C. Lethbridge. *New Statesman*, 2 October 1964, p. 500.

————. "Ted Hughes Writes." *Poetry Book Society Bulletin*, 15 (September 1957), 1.

————. "Three Legends." *Journal of Creative Behavior*, 1 (July 1967), 18–20.

————. *'The Tiger's Bones' and Other Plays for Children*. New York: Viking, 1974.

————. "Tricksters and Tarbabies." Rev. of *Literature among the Primitives*, and *The Primitive Reader*, by John Greenway. *New York Review of Books*, 9 December 1965, pp. 33–35.

————. *Under the North Star*. New York: Viking, 1981.

————. Untitled rev. of *Men Who March Away: Poems of the First World War*, ed. I. M. Parsons. *Listener*, 5 August 1965, p. 208.

————. Untitled rev. of *Primitive Song*, by C. M. Bowra. *Listener*, 3 May 1962, p. 781.

————. "Vasco Popa." *Tri-Quarterly*, 9 (Spring 1967), 201–5.

————. *What Is the Truth?: A Farmyard Fable for the Young*. London: Faber and Faber; New York: Harper and Row, 1984.

————, ed. *With Fairest Flowers While Summer Lasts: Poems from Shakespeare*. Garden City: Doubleday, 1971.

————. *Wodwo*. London: Faber and Faber; New York: Harper and Row, 1967.

————, Ruth Fainlight, and Alan Sillitoe. *Poems: Ruth Fainlight, Ted Hughes, Alan Sillitoe.* London: Rainbow Press, 1971.

————, and R. S. Thomas. *Ted Hughes and R. S. Thomas read and discuss selections of their own poems. The Critical Forum.* Battle, Sussex: Norwich Tapes, 1978.

Hume, Robert E., ed. and trans. *The Thirteen Principal Upanishads.* 2nd ed. 1931; rpt. New York: Oxford Univ. Press, 1971.

Jacobi, Jolande. *The Way of Individuation.* Trans. R. F. C. Hull. New York: Harcourt, Brace, and World, 1967.

James, G. Ingli. "The Animal Poems of Ted Hughes: A Devaluation." *Southern Review,* 2, iii (1967), 193–203.

Janouch, Gustav. *Conversations with Kafka.* Trans. Goronwy Rees. New York: Praeger, 1953.

Jones, Alun. Untitled rev. of *Lupercal,* et al. *Critical Quarterly,* 2 (Summer 1960), 184–85.

Jones, Gwyn, and Thomas Jones, trans. *The Mabinogion.* London: J. M. Dent, 1974.

Jung, Carl Gustav. *Aion: Researches into the Phenomenology of the Self.* Trans. R. F. C. Hull. Ed. Sir Herbert Read, et al. Bollingen Series XX, Vol. IX, Part II. New York: Pantheon, 1959.

————. *Alchemical Studies.* Trans. R. F. C. Hull. Ed. Sir Herbert Read, et. al. Bollingen Series XX, Vol. XIII. Princeton: Princeton Univ. Press, 1967.

————. *Archetypes and the Collective Unconscious.* Trans. R. F. C. Hull. Ed. Sir Herbert Read, et al. Bollingen Series XX, Vol. IX, Part I. New York: Pantheon, 1959.

————. *Civilization in Transition.* Trans. R. F. C. Hull. Ed. Sir Herbert Read, et al. Bollingen Series XX, Vol. X. New York: Pantheon, 1964.

————. *Memories, Dreams, Reflections.* Trans. Richard and Clara Winston. Ed. Aniela Jaffe. New York: Pantheon, 1961.

————. *Mysterium Coniunctionis: An Inquiry into the Separation and Synthesis of Psychic Opposites in Alchemy.* Trans. R. F. C. Hull. Ed. Sir Herbert Read, et al. Bollingen Series XX, Vol. XIV. New York: Pantheon, 1963.

————. *The Practice of Psychotherapy: Essays on the Psychology of the Transference and Other Subjects.* Trans. R. F. C. Hull. Ed. Sir Herbert Read. Bollingen Series XX, Vol. XVI. 2nd ed. New York: Pantheon, 1954.

————. *Psychological Types.* Trans. H. G. Baynes, rev. R. F. C. Hull. Ed. Sir Herbert Read, et al. Bollingen Series XX, Vol. VI. Princeton: Princeton Univ. Press, 1971.

————. *Psychology and Alchemy.* Trans. R. F. C. Hull. Ed. Sir Herbert Read, et al. Bollingen Series XX, Vol. XII. Princeton: Princeton Univ. Press, 1968.

————. *The Structure and Dynamics of the Psyche.* Trans. R. F. C. Hull. Ed. Sir Herbert Read, et al. Bollingen Series XX, Vol. VIII. New York: Pantheon, 1960.

————. *Symbols of Transformation: An Analysis of the Prelude to a Case of Schizophrenia.* Trans. R. F. C. Hull. Ed. Sir Herbert Read, et al. Bollingen Series XX, Vol. V. 2nd ed. Princeton: Princeton Univ. Press, 1967.

Kahn, Charles H. *The Art and Thought of Heraclitus: An Edition of the Fragments with Translation and Commentary.* Cambridge: Cambridge Univ. Press, 1979.

Kerényi, Karl. "Wolf und Zeige am Lupercalienfest." In his *Niobe: Neue Studien über antike Religion und Humanität.* Zurich: Rein-Verlag, 1949, pp. 136–47.

Kessler, Jascha. "The Inner World Where Poets Wander." Rev. of *Crow,* et al. *Saturday Review,* 2 October 1971, pp. 39, 50–51.

Kirk, G. S. *The Nature of Greek Myths*. Baltimore: Penguin, 1974.

Klinkowitz, Jerome. "Vonnegut in America." In *Vonnegut in America: An Introduction to the Life and Work of Kurt Vonnegut*. Ed. Klinkowitz and Donald L. Lawler. New York: Dell, 1977, pp. 7–36.

Knight, Gareth. *A Practical Guide to Qabalistic Symbolism*. 2 vols. New York: Samuel Weiser, 1978.

Korzybski, Alfred. *Science and Sanity: An Introduction to Non-Aristotelian Systems and General Semantics*. 4th ed. Lakeville, Connecticut: International Non-Aristotelian Publishing, 1958.

———. *Time-Binding: The General Theory*. Lakeville, Connecticut: Institute of General Semantics, 1949.

Kroll, Judith. *Chapter in a Mythology: The Poetry of Sylvia Plath*. New York: Harper and Row, 1976.

Kunitz, Stanley. "The New Books." Rev. of *Lupercal*, et al. *Harper's*, 221 (September 1960), 97–104.

Lal, P., ed. and trans. *The Dhammapada*. New York: Farrar, Straus, and Giroux, 1967.

Le Guin, Ursula. Tape recorded interview with Charlotte Reed. 1973. PTC/813.54/L52zl.

Lévi-Strauss, Claude. *The Raw and the Cooked: Introduction to a Science of Mythology: I*. Trans. John and Doreen Weightman. New York: Harper and Row, 1969.

———. *The Savage Mind*. Trans. anon. Chicago: Univ. of Chicago Press, 1966.

———. *Structural Anthropology*. Trans. Claire Jacobson and B. G. Schoepf. New York: Basic Books, 1963.

Lewis, Peter Elfred. "The New Pedantry and 'Hawk Roosting.'" *Stand*, 8, 1 (1966), 58–65.

Li Po. *The Works of Li Po, the Chinese Poet*. Trans. Shigeyoshi Obata. 1935; rpt. New York: Paragon, 1965.

Lodge, David. *Working with Structuralism: Essays and Reviews on Nineteenth- and Twentieth-Century Literature*. London: Routledge and Kegan Paul, 1981.

Lorenz, Konrad. *On Aggression*. Trans. Marjorie Kerr Wilson. New York: Harcourt, Brace, and World, 1966.

Lowell, Robert. "On 'Skunk Hour.'" In *The Contemporary Poet as Artist and Critic*. Ed. Anthony Ostroff. Boston: Little, Brown, 1964, pp. 107–10.

MacCana, Proinsias. *Celtic Mythology*. New York: Hamlyn, 1970.

May, Derwent. "Bird Words." Rev. of *Crow*. *Listener*, 29 October 1970, p. 603.

Merton, Thomas. *Mystics and Zen Masters*. New York: Delta, 1967.

Michels, Agnes K. "The Topography and Interpretation of the Lupercalia." *Transactions of the American Philological Society*, 84 (1953), 35–59.

Moorehead, Alan. *Gallipoli*. London: Hamesh Hamilton, 1956.

Motokiyo, Zeami. *On the Art of the Nō Drama: The Major Treatises of Zeami*. Ed. and trans. J. Thomas Rimer and Yamazaki Masakazu. Princeton: Princeton Univ. Press, 1984.

Muir, Edwin. "Kinds of Poetry." Rev. of *The Hawk in the Rain*, et al. *New Statesman*, 28 September 1957, pp. 391–92.

Muller, Max. *The Mythology of All Races*. Ed. Louis Herbert Gray. Boston: Marshall Jones, 1918.

Murry, John Middleton. *William Blake*. New York: McGraw-Hill, 1964.

Myers, E. Lucas. "The Tranquilized Fifties." Rev. of *Lupercal*, et al. *Sewanee Review*, 70 (Spring 1962), 212–20.

Newton, J. M. "Mr. Hughes's Poetry." *Delta*, 25 (Winter 1961), 6–12.

———. "Ted Hughes's Metaphysical Poems." *Cambridge Quarterly*, 2 (Autumn 1967), 395–402.

Nietzsche, Friedrich. *The Birth of Tragedy and The Case of Wagner*. Trans. Walter Kaufman. New York: Vintage, 1967.

Nye, Robert. "Poetry." Rev. of *Cave Birds*. *London Times*, 7 September 1978, p. 14.

O'Flaherty, Wendy Doniger, ed. and trans. *Hindu Myths: A Sourcebook Translated from the Sanskrit*. New York: Penguin, 1975.

Olson, Charles. *Human Universe and Other Essays*. Ed. Donald Allen. New York: Grove, 1967.

Osborne, John. *Look Back in Anger*. 1957; rpt. New York: Bantam, 1971.

Paley, Morton D. *Energy and Imagination: A Study of the Development of Blake's Thought*. Oxford: Clarendon Press, 1970.

Parkinson, Thomas. *W. B. Yeats: The Later Poetry*. Berkeley: Univ. of California Press, 1966.

Patanjali. *The Authentic Yoga*. Trans. P. Y. Deshpande. London: Rider, 1978.

Perloff, Marjorie. "Poetry Chronicle." Rev. of *Crow*, et al. *Contemporary Literature*, 14 (Winter 1973), 97–131.

Piggott, Juliet. *Japanese Mythology*. Rev. ed. New York: Peter Bedrick, 1983.

Pilinszky, János. *Selected Poems*. Trans. Ted Hughes and János Csokits. New York: Persea, 1977.

Plaks, Andrew H. *Archetype and Allegory in the Dream of the Red Chamber*. Princeton: Princeton Univ. Press, 1976.

Plath, Sylvia. *The Journals of Sylvia Plath*. Ed. Ted Hughes and Frances McCullough. New York: Ballantine, 1983.

———. *Letters Home: Correspondence 1950–1963*. Ed. Aurelia Schober Plath. New York: Harper and Row, 1975.

———. "The Magic Mirror: A Study of the Double in Two of Dostoevsky's Novels." Smith College Undergraduate Honors Thesis, 1955.

Pound, Ezra. *The ABC of Reading*. New York: New Directions, 1960.

———. *Guide to Kulchur*. New York: New Directions, 1952.

———. *Literary Essays*. Ed. T. S. Eliot. New York: New Directions, 1954.

Press, John. *Rule and Energy: Trends in British Poetry since the Second World War*. London: Oxford Univ. Press, 1963.

Radin, Paul. *The Trickster: A Study in American Indian Mythology*. 1956; rpt. New York: Greenwood Press, 1969.

Ramanujan, A. K., ed. and trans. *Speaking of Śiva*. New York: Penguin, 1973.

Rank, Otto. *The Double: A Psychoanalytic Study*. Ed. and trans. Harry Tucker, Jr. Chapel Hill: Univ. of North Carolina Press, 1971.

Ransom, John Crowe. *The New Criticism*. Norfolk, Connecticut: New Directions, 1941.

———. *Poems and Essays*. New York: Vintage, 1955.

———. *The World's Body*. Baton Rouge: Louisiana State Univ. Press, 1938.

Rice, Cyprian. *The Persian Sufis*. London: George Allen and Unwin, 1964.

Richards, Ivor Armstrong. *Coleridge on Imagination*. 2nd ed. London: Routledge and Kegan Paul, 1950.

Rose, H. J. *Ancient Roman Religion*. London: Cheltenham Press, 1948.

Rosenthal, M. L. *The Modern Poets: A Critical Introduction*. New York: Oxford Univ. Press, 1960.

Ross, Anne. *Pagan Celtic Britain*. New York: Columbia Univ. Press, 1967.

Ryder, Arthur W., trans. *The Panchatantra*. Chicago: Univ. of Chicago Press, 1925.

Sacker, Hugh. *An Introduction to Wolfram's 'Parzival'*. Cambridge: Cambridge Univ. Press, 1963.

Sagar, Keith. *The Art of Ted Hughes*. 2nd ed. London: Cambridge Univ. Press, 1978.

————, ed. *The Achievement of Ted Hughes*. Athens: Univ. of Georgia Press; Manchester: Manchester Univ. Press, 1983.

————, and Stephen Tabor. *Ted Hughes, A Bibliography: 1946–1980*. London: Mansell, 1983.

Scholem, Gershom. *Kabbalah*. New York: Quadrangle, 1974.

Sergeant, Howard. "Poetry Review." Rev. of *Crow*, et al. *English*, 20 (Summer 1971), 66–77.

Shah, Idries. *The Sufis*. Garden City: Doubleday, 1964.

Sharkey, John. *Celtic Mysteries*. London: Thames and Hudson, 1975.

Smith, A. C. H. *Orghast at Persepolis*. London: Eyre Methuen, 1972.

Sohl, Robert, and Audrey Carr, eds. *The Gospel According to Zen*. New York: New American Library, 1970.

Sokel, Walter H. *The Writer in Extremis: Expressionism in Twentieth Century German Literature*. 1959; rpt. Stanford: Stanford Univ. Press, 1968.

Spector, Sheila. "Kabbalistic Sources—Blake's and His Critics'." *Blake: An Illustrated Quarterly*, 17 (Winter 1983–1984), 84–99.

Steiner, George. *Language and Silence: Essays on Language, Literature, and the Inhuman*. New York: Atheneum, 1970.

Stewart, John L. *The Burden of Time: The Fugitives and Agrarians*. Princeton: Princeton Univ. Press, 1965.

Stoppard, Tom. "'Orghast.'" *London Times Literary Supplement*, 1 October 1971, p. 1174.

Stryk, Lucien, ed. *World of the Buddha: A Reader*. Garden City: Doubleday, 1968.

Suzuki, Daisetz T. *Essays in Zen Buddhism, First Series*. Ed. Christmas Humphreys. 1949; rpt. New York: Grove Press, 1961.

————. *Essays in Zen Buddhism, Second Series*. Ed. Christmas Humphreys. 1950; rpt. London: Rider, 1958.

————. *The Essence of Zen Buddhism*. London: Buddhist Society, 1947.

————. *The Essentials of Zen Buddhism*. Ed. Bernard Phillips. New York: E. P. Dutton, 1962.

————. *Living by Zen*. London: Rider, 1950.

————. *Manual of Zen Buddhism*. Kyoto: Eastern Buddhist Society, 1935.

————. *Mysticism: Christian and Buddhist*. New York: Harper and Brothers, 1957.

————. "The Oriental Way of Thinking." *Japan Quarterly*, 11 (1955), 51–58.

————. *Zen and Japanese Culture*. 1938; rpt. New York: Pantheon, 1959.

————. "Zen and the Modern World." *Japan Quarterly*, 5, 4 (October–December 1958), 452–61.

————, Erich Fromm, and Richard De Martino. *Zen Buddhism and Psychoanalysis.* New York: Harper and Row, 1960.

Swanton, John R. *Tlingit Myths and Texts.* Washington, D.C.: Government Printing Office, 1909.

Symons, Julian. "Grigson: A Long Look Back." Rev. of *Cave Birds,* et al. *London Sunday Times,* 26 November 1978, p. 40.

Sze, Mai-Mai. *The Tao of Painting: A Study of the Ritual Disposition of Chinese Painting.* 2nd ed. Princeton: Princeton Univ. Press, 1963.

Tao-chi. *Returning Home: Tao-Chi's Album of Landscapes and Flowers.* Ed. and trans. Wen Fong. New York: Braziller, 1976.

Tate, Allen. "Tension in Poetry." In his *Essays of Four Decades.* Chicago: Swallow Press, 1968, pp. 56–71.

Thompson, Stith. *Motif-Index of Folk-Literature: A Classification of Narrative Elements in Folk-Tales, Ballads, Myths, Fables, Medieval Romances, Exempla, Fabliaux, Jest-books, and Local Legends.* Rev. ed. Bloomington: Indiana Univ. Press, 1965. Vol. II.

Thurley, Geoffrey. *An Ironic Harvest: English Poetry in the Twentieth Century.* London: William Clowes and Sons, 1974.

Toffler, Alvin. *Future Shock.* New York: Random House, 1970.

Turville-Petre, E. O. G. *Myth and Religion of the North: The Religion of Ancient Scandanavia.* London: Weidenfeld and Nicholson, 1964.

Vaillant, George C. *Aztecs of Mexico: Origin, Rise, and Fall of the Aztec Nation.* Rev. Suzannah B. Vaillant. Garden City: Doubleday, 1962.

Waley, Arthur, ed. and trans. *The Way and Its Power: A Study of the "Tao Te Ching" and Its Place in Chinese Thought.* New York: Grove Press, 1958.

Warren, Robert Penn. "John Crowe Ransom: A Study in Irony." In *John Crowe Ransom: Critical Essays and a Bibliography.* Ed. Thomas Daniel Young. Baton Rouge: Louisiana State Univ. Press, 1968, pp. 24–40.

Welch, Holmes. *Taoism: The Parting of the Way.* Rev. ed. Boston: Beacon Press, 1965.

Wellek, René, and Austin Warren. *Theory of Literature.* Rev. ed. New York: Harcourt, Brace, and World, 1956.

Wilhelm, Richard, ed. *The "I Ching" or Book of Changes.* Trans. Cary F. Baynes. 2nd ed. 1961; rpt. New York: Pantheon, 1962.

Wilkins, W. J. *Hindu Mythology, Vedic and Puranic.* 2nd ed. 1900; rpt. London: Curzon, 1973.

Williams, Miller. *The Poetry of John Crowe Ransom.* New Brunswick: Rutgers Univ. Press, 1972.

Wimsatt, William K., Jr., and Cleanth Brooks. *Literary Criticism: A Short History.* New York: Vintage, 1957.

Wollheim, Richard. *Sigmund Freud.* New York: Viking, 1971.

Wood, Ernest. *Yoga.* Rev. ed. 1962; rpt. Baltimore: Penguin, 1972.

Yeats, William Butler. *Essays and Introductions.* New York: Macmillan, 1961.

Young, Thomas Daniel. "Ransom's Critical Theories: Structure and Texture." *Mississippi Quarterly,* 30 (Winter 1976–1977), 71–85.

Zimmer, Heinrich. *Myths and Symbols in Indian Art and Civilization.* Ed. Joseph Campbell. New York: Pantheon, 1946.

INDEX

"Accused, The," 208, 212, 214, 222, 226
Achilles, 310
Acintyā, 118
"Acrobats," 13–14, 55, 75
"Acteon," 274
Adam, 22, 24–25, 94, 132, 182, 257–59, 262, 267, 272, 275, 278–86
"Adam," 280–81, 283
Adam and the Sacred Nine, 257
"Adam and the Sacred Nine" (*Moortown*), 25, 258–59, 262, 272–73, 279–86
Adam Kadmon, 25, 258–59, 262, 275, 279, 283, 285–86, 336
Adonis, 127, 137
"Advocate, The," 208
Aeschylus, 23, 269
"After Lorca," 89
"After Moonless Midnight," 289, 298, 300, 302, 306–308, 310
"After the first fright," 208, 225
"After there was nothing there was a woman," 208, 229, 231
Aggression. *See* Enantiodromia; Thanatos; Violence
Agoluz, 23, 186
Ainus, 90, 103–104
Albedo, 215, 218, 220
Albion, 153, 259, 262, 269–73, 275–76, 278, 281, 283, 286, 314, 336
Alchemy, 8–9, 12, 15, 21, 202, 206–207, 209, 214–21, 233, 258, 260, 283–84, 294–95. *See also* Albedo; *Aqua permanens*; *Caput corvi*; *Coagulatio*; *Destillatio*; *Lapis*; *Mortificatio*; *Mundificatio*; *Nigredo*; *Prima materia*; *Putrefactio*; *Rubedo*; *Sponsus* and *sponsu*
Allison, Susan, 196
Alvarez, Alfred, xvi, 2
Ambiguity, 14–15, 43
Amitabha, 118
Ananta, 119

"Ancient Briton Lay Under His Rock, The," 243–44
"Ancient Heroes and the Bomber Pilot, The," 53
"And Owl," 283
"And the Falcon came," 280, 282
"And the Phoenix has come," 23, 285
Andreae, Johann Christian, 216, 333
Anfortas, 169, 182
"Angel, The," 253–54
Angels, 55, 119, 237–38, 253–54
Angries, 35, 49
Anima, 106, 127, 142, 167, 169, 210, 219–20, 223–24, 226–29, 231–32
Anthesterion, 63
Antimodern, 17
Anubhāva, 194
Apollinaire, Guillaume, 88
Apple, 132, 159, 186, 192, 194
"Apple Tragedy," 132, 159
Aqua permanens, 218
Aragon, Louis, 88
Archetypes, 11, 170, 173, 188, 210, 318. *See also* Anima; Shadow
"As I came, I saw a wood," 208, 229
Ashbery, John, 17
Asmitā, 203–204
Assia. *See* Wevil, Assia Guttmann
"At the top of my soul" (#4), 192, 228
Atlas, 142
Ātman, 5, 100–103, 107, 110, 112, 117, 120–21, 123, 125, 127, 137, 197, 257
Attar, Farid ud-Din, 212, 215–16, 219, 229–30, 232–33, 305
Attis, 171
Auden, Wystan Hugh, 1, 33, 53, 72–73
Auerbach, Eric, 21–22, 255
"August Evening," 291, 303–304
"August Salmon, An," 308
Aztecs, 213, 217, 225, 333

Baboon, 187–88, 192, 218. *See also* Thoth
Bach, Johann Sebastian, 20
"Ballad from a Fairy Tale," 253–54
"Bang—a burning, A" (#41), 197, 201
"Baptist, The," 208, 217–18, 222
Bardo Thödol, xv, 6–7, 19, 23, 89–90, 92, 108–110, 116, 121, 125, 149, 151, 154–55, 160, 217, 219
Barrie, J. M., 245–46
Bashō, 111–12
Baskin, Leonard, xv, 144, 161, 186, 207, 209–11, 222, 235, 258
"Battle of Osfrontalis, The," 132–33, 143, 160
BBC radio scripts, xv, 55–58, 61–62, 86, 106, 157, 207, 212, 214, 217–19, 221–23, 225–26, 228–29, 246–47, 255, 258, 262, 268, 276, 284, 321
"Bear, The," 102–104
Bedient, Calvin, 18, 232
Beethoven, Ludwig von, 59–60, 119, 175
Beetle, 192, 277
Beltane fires, 76, 103
Bergonzi, Bernard, 79
Berkeley, George, 228
Beulah, 261–63, 268, 280, 295, 297–98, 300–301, 306. *See also* Blake, William
Bhagavad Gita, 198
Bhakti, 194, 204
Bible, 60, 98, 115–16, 120, 123, 125–26, 198, 220, 252, 254, 274, 285
"Big Animal of Rock, The," 237, 239, 249
"Billet-Doux," 50
"Birth of Rainbow," 263
Bismillah, 305–306
"Black Beast, The," 130, 134–35, 150
Black Douglas, 47
Blackness, 125, 129–30, 133–35, 137, 143, 148–51, 154, 156, 159–60, 212
Blake, William, xv, 3, 6, 12, 23–25, 85, 121, 127, 135, 149–51, 153, 161, 166, 197, 201–202, 211, 228–29, 232, 257–62, 269–81, 283–86, 288–89,

294–95, 297, 301–302, 306, 308–309, 311, 313–14. Works: *Europe*, 260, 272; *Four Zoas*, 24, 211, 258–61, 270, 274, 280, 295; *Jerusalem*, 24, 121, 135, 153, 211, 258–61, 271–74, 277, 281, 283, 314; *Marriage of Heaven and Hell*, 270, 283; *Milton*, 201–202, 285; *Urizen*, 260, 270, 275; *Vision of the Last Judgment*, 270, 277, 314. *See also* Beulah; Eden; Enion; Generation; Los; Luvah; Orc; Tharmas; Ulro; Urizen; Urthona
Bodhisattva, 7
Boehme, Jacob, 12, 202
Book of the Dead, Egyptian. See Egyptian Book of the Dead
Book of the Dead, Tibetan. See Bardo Thödol
"Boom," 92
Boundary lines, 262, 266, 272, 276
"Bowled Over," 87, 93
Bowra, C. M., 90, 147
Bradshaw, Graham, 214, 221
Bran, 303
Breton, André, 87–88
"Bride and groom lie hidden for three days," 13, 19, 142, 156–57, 167, 208, 230–31, 233
"Bridestones," 13, 251
British Broadcasting Company. *See* BBC radio scripts
Brontës, 234, 249
Brook, Peter, xv, 23, 120, 212
Brooks, Cleanth, 12, 14, 42–43, 48
Browne, Thomas, 64, 78–79, 92
Browning, Robert, 225, 227
Brownjohn, Alan, xvi, 40, 232
Buddha, 6, 108, 110, 118, 151, 155, 277–78
Buddhism, 99, 108, 112–13, 118, 123, 125, 151–52, 155, 157–59, 165, 227, 250, 271, 277–78, 280, 283, 286. *See also Bardo Thödol*; *Nirvana*; Zen
"Bull Moses, The," 69
Bulls, 69, 80, 171–72, 194
Bush, Douglas, 78
"Buzz in the window," 278

Cabbala, 19, 25, 103, 197, 258–59, 280, 284–86
"Cadenza," 96
"Calves harshly parted from their mamas" (#40), 197, 201
Campbell, Joseph, 5, 11, 16, 61, 91–93, 101, 220, 291
"Canal's Drowning Black, The," 243
Caput corvi, 216
Caritas, 142, 169, 225
Carr, W. I., 32
Castor, 74
"Casualty, The," 49
"Cat and Mouse," 72, 74
Cats, 72–75
Cave Birds, xvi, 10, 12, 15, 21, 142, 156–57, 167, 205–33, 235, 256–58, 278, 282, 284–85, 305, 332. ABC poem groups: 207–208, 213–14, 220, 223–24, 232, 235, 256, 332
Cernunnos, 181
Cerridwen, 167, 169–70, 189, 196, 198–200
Chamberlain, B. H., 90
Chang, Chung-yuan, 25
Ch'ang tao, 252
Ch'i, 239
Chikkai Bardo, 108, 116
"Childbirth," 43–44, 48
"Childish Prank, A," 129, 133, 143
Ching chiai, 250–51
Chirico, Georgio de, 187, 196
Chönyid Bardo, 108
Chou Wen-chung, xiv, xv, 6, 108
Christ, 8, 77, 186, 212, 218, 220, 258, 306, 314; as Mercurius, 214, 216, 258
Christianity. See Hughes and religion; Protestantism; Roman Catholicism
Chuang Tzu, 237–38, 248, 252, 292, 294, 335
"Churches topple" (#27), 194, 197–99
Chymical Wedding of Christian Rosencreutz, The. See Andreae, Johann Christian
"Citrine Glimpse, A," 259, 272
Clausen, Christopher, 205–206, 224, 232

"Cleopatra to the Asp," 80
Clytemnestra, 74
Coagulatio, 215
"Cock-Crows," 253
"Coffin, spurred by its screws, The" (#25), 194, 197–98
Coleridge, Samuel Taylor, 24–25, 37, 42, 52–53, 58, 91, 166, 203, 232, 256, 261, 273, 280, 288, 292, 302. See also Imagination: primary, secondary
"Coming down through Somerset," 262, 267–68
"Complaint," 41, 49, 51
Condwiramurs, 182
Conference of the Birds. See Attar, Farid ud-Din
"Conjuring in Heaven," 124, 154
Conquest, Robert, 31
Conrad, Joseph, 161
"Conversion of the Reverend Skinner, The," 49
"Cormorant, A," 294, 296
Cows, 114
"Crag Jack's Apostasy," 65, 67, 79
Crane, Stephen, 287, 301, 303
"Creation of Fishes," 299, 306
Crow, xiv, 10, 12, 15, 18–22, 26, 90, 92, 120–21, 122–62, 165–66, 168, 183, 193, 210, 230–31, 248, 277, 326–27
Crow (Cave Birds), 217, 232; (Moortown), 284–85
"Crow Alights," 149, 154, 183
"Crow and Mama," 124, 129–30, 133, 149
"Crow and Stone," 124, 134, 140, 150–51, 159–60
"Crow and the Birds," 22
"Crow and the Sea," 130, 159, 161
"Crow Blacker Than Ever," 129, 133, 143, 159
"Crow came to Adam, The," 284–85
"Crow Communes," 129, 133, 143, 155
"Crow Compromises," 161
"Crow Fails," 161
"Crow Frowns," 152
"Crow Goes Hunting," 133, 150, 160

"Crow Hears Fate Knock on the Door,"
123, 143, 150
"Crow Hill," 64, 74–75
"Crow Improvises," 124, 133, 135, 140
"Crow on the Beach," 140, 143, 151
"Crow Paints Himself into a Chinese
Mural," 160
"Crow Sickened," 134–35, 150, 159
"Crow the Just," 155–56
"Crow Tries the Media," 141, 158
"Crow Tyrannosaurus," 133, 140, 143,
150
"Crowego," 133, 148, 150, 160
"Crow's Account of St. George," 7, 124,
139–40, 150
"Crow's Account of the Battle," 7, 124,
138–39
"Crow's Battle Fury," 143, 150, 159
"Crow's Courtship," 130–31
"Crow's Elephant Totem Song," 155
"Crow's Fall," 134, 143
"Crow's First Lesson," 128–29, 138
"Crow's Last Stand," 151, 159
"Crow's Nerve Fails," 143, 159
"Crow's Playmates," 153
"Crow's Song About God," 131–32, 135
"Crow's Song of Himself," 124, 134, 140
"Crow's Theology," 143
"Crow's Undersong," 141–42, 158, 231
"Crow's Vanity," 155
Csokits, János, 191
Cubism, 14
Culhwch and Olwyn, 307
"Curlews Lift," 237, 246
Curran, Stuart, 284

Dadaism, 87–88
Dancer, 79, 194, 202–203, 305–306,
311, 332
Dante, 226, 291–92
"Dark Women," 103
Dasimayya, 195
Davie, Donald, 10, 16–17, 31
"Dead man lies, marching here and
there, The" (#42), 194, 197, 201
"Deaf School," 274–75
"Decay of Vanity, The," 50

"Deceptions," 255
"Dee," 298, 306
"Dehorning," 265
Descartes, René, 229, 274
Destillatio, 215
Devi, 194
Dhammapada, 155
Dharma-Kāya of Clear Light, 108–109,
116, 160
Diana, 274
Diogenes, 98
Dionysus, 77, 176, 178, 187, 194, 199
"Disaster, A," 132, 143–44, 150, 160
"Doctor extracted, A" (#24), 196
Donne, John, 18, 34, 41
Doppelgänger. See Double
Double, 181–82, 188, 210, 309. See also
Lumb's Double
Douglas, Keith, 93
Dove (Cave Birds), 216; (Gaudete),
179–80; (Moortown), 283–84
"Dove came, The," 283–84
"Dove-Breeder, The," 36–37, 50–51, 65
Dragonfly, 302–303, 338
"Dream of Horses, A," 68
Dreams, 11–12, 16, 65–67, 70–71, 73,
75–76, 92, 95–98, 166–68, 170–73,
175–88, 192; Lumb's Double's cattle-
yard slurry dream, 180, 184–85,
187–88, 192; Lumb's Double's fishing
dream, 182–83
Dunworth, 176

Eagle, 67, 206–207, 213–14, 217,
219–23, 228–33, 282; Aztec Eagle
Knights, 213; Solar eagle, 206–207,
213–14, 217, 219–23, 228–33, 282
Earth, 23, 66, 76–77, 184, 186, 203,
214, 237, 247, 253, 258, 270, 281,
294, 304. See also Mud
"Earth-numb," 278–79; (section of
Moortown), 257–59, 262, 268, 270,
272–79
Eat Crow, 86, 144, 209
Eden, 25, 132, 275
Eden (Blakean Edenic vision), 260,
261–62, 275, 278–79, 281, 283,

285, 289, 301, 306. *See also* Blake, William

"Eel, An," 305, 311

"Egghead," 19, 40–41, 48–49, 69

Ego, 5–8, 19, 25, 49, 94, 96, 99–100, 102–104, 107–108, 110, 125, 127–28, 130–34, 136, 143, 150–51, 155, 158–59, 178, 180, 215–16, 225, 228, 236, 249, 278, 295–96, 300, 307, 313

Egyptian Book of the Dead, 210, 217–18

"Eighty and Still Fishing for Salmon," 311

Einstein, Albert, 20–21, 27, 277

Eliade, Mircea, 10, 16, 61, 65, 70, 73, 89–91, 145, 190, 203–204, 229, 244, 292, 309

Eliot, T. S., 1, 10, 12–13, 17, 33–34, 293, 306

Elmet. See Remains of Elmet

"Elmet," 255

Eluard, Paul, 88

Enantiodromia, 11–12, 124–25, 136–37, 140, 145, 149, 158–59, 168, 178, 225, 235–36, 241, 328

Enion, 270

Enki, 129

Erdman, David, 295, 319

Eros, 12, 26, 28, 36, 39–40, 62, 65, 72–78, 91, 93, 104, 115, 137, 140, 167–68, 170, 173, 181–83, 188, 198, 216–17, 277, 300

Eschenbach, Wolfram von, 7, 182. *See also* Parzival

"Esther's Tomcat," 72–73

Estridge, 168, 173–75, 178, 180

Eurydice, 167

Evans, 175–77

Evans-Wentz, W. Y., 172, 190, 313

Eve, 132

"Every day the world gets simply" (#43), 197, 200–201

"Everyman's Odyssey," 79

"Examination at the Womb Door," 149

"Executioner, The," 208, 212, 226, 285

Eye, 22, 48, 50, 52, 69, 103, 113, 125, 134, 138–39, 149–51, 154, 156, 160,

166, 168, 183, 213, 221, 223, 229, 236, 254, 260–61, 270–71, 273–74, 280, 283–84, 305, 307–310

Faas, Ekbert, 3, 4, 8, 22, 71, 101, 125, 145, 187, 194

"Fable, A," 92

"Fair Choice," 41, 49

"Fairy Flood," 295

Falcon, 195, 209, 213, 280

"Fallgrief's Girl-Friends," 41

"Famous Poet," 40–41, 226

Faná, 131, 215, 232–33

Fantasy, 123–24, 151, 153

Faulkner, William, 268

Feathers, 39, 217, 220, 222, 253

"February," 64–66, 80, 119

"February 17th," 266

Feirfiz, 182

Felicity, 177–78, 180–85

Fern, 199, 226–27

"Fern," 227

"Finale," 207–208, 213, 233

Fire, 25, 43, 48, 71, 75–77, 79–80, 99, 100, 112, 144, 151, 180–81, 203, 212, 219–20, 260–61, 265, 269–71, 276–78, 280–82, 284–85, 291, 295, 303

"Fire-Eater," 75–77, 79–80

"First, Mills," 241–42

"First, the doubtful charts of skin," 208, 222, 227

Fish, 55–57, 59–60, 71, 107, 182, 275–76, 296, 302, 304–305. *See also* Salmon

Fisher King, 216

"Flanders," 93

"Flayed crow in the hall of judgment, A," 208, 222

"Flesh of Light," 291, 294–95

Folklore, xiv, 3, 11, 19, 21, 58, 85, 87, 89–90, 101, 122–24, 134, 140, 144–48, 156, 159–60, 172, 253–54, 296–97, 299, 306–307. *See also* Swan maiden; Trickster

"For Billy Holt," 241

Form, 14–15, 254. *See also* Modernism; New Criticism; *Paideuma*; Quest

"Formal Auctioneer, The," 267
"Four March Watercolours," 296, 298, 304, 306–307
"Four Tales Told by an Idiot," 259, 272
"Fourth of July," 66, 92
"Fox Hunt," 266
"Fragment of an Ancient Tablet," 131, 140, 159
Frank, Joseph, 16
Frazer, Sir James, 65, 76, 107, 202, 226–27
Freud, Sigmund, 6, 43, 73, 88, 94–95, 97, 132, 180, 327. *See also* Ego; Eros; Id; Instinct; Libido; Phylogenetic inheritance; Primal horde; Repression; Superego; Thanatos; Violence
Frosch, Thomas, 259–61, 281
Frye, Northrop, 259, 261
"Full Moon and Little Frieda," 86, 110, 113–14

Gallipoli, 16, 64, 76, 79, 81, 92–94
Ganeśa, 61, 117
Garten, 168, 176, 178, 181, 183
Garten, Mrs., 185
"Gatekeeper, The," 208, 216–17, 220
Gaudete, 2, 3, 6–7, 10, 12–13, 15, 18, 21–22, 53, 90, 120–21, 135, 156, 165–204, 210, 215, 220, 231–33, 246, 256–57, 278, 281, 284, 293, 301, 303, 309, 331
Gawain, 114, 185
Generation, 261–62, 270, 272, 275–78, 280. *See also* Blake, William
"Ghost Crabs," 19, 95–96
Gifford, Terry, 3, 145, 322
"Glare out of just crumpled grass" (#45), 197, 201, 204
Gleckner, Robert, 272
"Glimpse," 158, 160, 193
"Gnat-Psalm," 110–13
Gnosticism, 284
"Go Fishing," 13, 289, 293–94, 300
God (*Crow*), 124, 126–32, 137–38, 141, 160–61; (*What Is the Truth?*), 306
Godwin, Fay, xv, 234–36, 242, 246
"Gog," 6, 21, 92, 114–17

"Good Life, The," 68–69, 78
"Grass-blade is not without, The" (#26), 196, 198
Graves, Robert, 31, 93, 170–71, 197, 220
"Green mother, A," 208, 218
"Green Wolf, The," 87, 102–103
Greenberg, Martin, 179
Greenway, John, 144, 146–47
"Griefs for Dead Soldiers," 54
"Guide, The," 208, 218–19, 231
"Gulkana, The," 289, 295, 309–310

Hades, 176, 187
"Hag, The," 40–41
Hagen, Major, 168, 172, 175, 179, 184, 189
Hagen, Mrs. Pauline, 175, 179, 185
Hamilton, Ian, 18
"Hands," 267
"Happy Calf," 263
"Hardcastle Crags," 236, 238, 241, 247
Harrison, Jane, 63, 72
"Harvesting, The," 104, 301
"Having first given away pleasure" (#31), 196, 199
Hawk in the Rain, The, xiv, 4, 6, 12–13, 15, 18, 22, 25, 31–54, 56, 65, 67–68, 73, 75, 91–92, 226, 281
"Hawk in the Rain, The," 22, 41, 49–50, 56, 59
"Hawk Roosting," 57–58, 69, 71–72, 79, 305
"Hay," 255
"Hearing your moan echo, I chill. I shiver" (#36), 197, 200
Helen, 74
"Heptonstall," 119
"Heptonstall Cemetery," 13, 23, 253
"Heptonstall Old Church," 242
"Her Husband," 95
Heraclitus, 11–12, 112, 124–25, 136–37, 149, 151, 176, 181, 187–88; *Fragments*, 12, 181, 187–88. *See also* Enantiodromia
Hercules, 23, 167, 170–71, 186, 197, 210, 220, 303

"Here Is the Cathedral," 275
Hermes, 130–31
Hero, 11, 54, 91, 120, 146, 148, 160, 162, 198, 209–10, 214, 216, 218–21, 224, 226, 229, 230
Hesiod, 129
Hieros gamos, 202
"High Sea-Light," 249, 252
"Hill-Stone Was Content," 239, 249
Hinduism, 100, 119, 191, 194–95, 257. See also *Ātman*; Devi; Ganeśa; *Rig-Veda*; Śiva; Upanishads; Viṣṇu
Hirschberg, Stuart, xiv, 4, 145, 214
"His legs ran about," 208, 230–31
"Historian," 64, 79–80
History, 10, 16–17, 22, 51, 61–62, 64–67, 75, 80, 93–94, 98, 119, 125–29, 137, 178–79, 235, 240
Hoffman, Daniel G., 301
Holbrook, David, 18
Holdfast, 23
Holmes, John, 60
Holroyd, Mrs., 172–73, 180, 186
Holy Ghost, 216
Homer, 36, 310
Horace, 19, 205
Horder, John, 61, 63
"Horrible Religious Error, A," 129, 132, 134, 150
Horses, 53, 68, 104–105, 193
"Horses, The," 53
Horus, 197, 213
Hough, Graham, 32
"Howling of Wolves, The," 119
Hubris, 181, 183–84
Hughes, Mrs. Carol, 262
Hughes, Mrs. Edith Farrar, 45, 228, 234–36, 253–54
Hughes, Nicholas, 292, 309
Hughes, Ted: and author, xvii, 251, 285; childhood, 234–35, 243–45, 253, 312; education, xiv, xv, 6, 61, 317; marriage to Sylvia Plath, 13, 33, 43, 86–87, 117, 323; and Oriental culture, 4–10, 19–20, 22, 25, 27–28, 88, 92, 97–98, 105, 107–21, 127–28, 148–49, 151–62, 165, 189, 193–

94, 197, 202–203, 215, 233, 277–78, 286, 289; and religion, 27, 121–22, 157, 165, 192, 205, 225, 247, 249, 275 (*see also* Protestantism; Roman Catholicism); as visionary, xv, 4, 7, 22–23, 25, 52, 60, 169, 197, 201–204, 220, 229–33, 236, 250–59, 262, 268–73, 276, 278–86, 290, 292–93, 295, 301–302, 304–305, 307–308, 311–15; and Western culture, 5–10, 14–15, 19–20, 22–24, 27–28, 34–35, 37, 41, 46, 48, 54, 85, 92–94, 99, 107, 114, 116, 119–20, 122–24, 134, 145, 148, 151–52, 154, 165–66, 169, 186, 188, 192–93, 197, 201–204, 207, 215, 233, 247, 257, 277, 286, 289, 294. *See also* Alchemy; Ambiguity; *Bardo Thödol*; BBC radio scripts; Buddhism; Dreams; Folklore; History; Imagination; Irony; Landscape; Language; Metaphor; Mimesis; Modernism; Movement; Myth; Nature; New Criticism; Paradox; Primitive cultures; Protestantism; Quest; Realism; Reality; Roman Catholicism; Satire; Science; Shaman; Sufism; Surrealism; Theriomorphism; Time; Trickster; Two-way journey; *Vacanas*; Violence; World War I; World War II; Yoga; Zen
Hui-nêng, 155
Hun, 239, 253
"Huntsmen, on top of their swaying horse-towers, The" (#17), 193

"I heard a screech, sudden—" (#10), 192
"I know well" (#28), 196
"I said goodbye to earth" (#20), 196–97
"I skin the skin" (#38), 196, 201
"I watched a wise beetle" (#6), 192
Id, 31, 132, 180
Imagination, xv, 12, 19, 24–25, 32–33, 37, 40, 52–53, 57–60, 65, 68, 81, 87–88, 99, 121–22, 125–27, 140–43, 148–51, 154, 156–58, 160–62, 165–66, 168–69, 173, 177, 183–87,

Imagination (*continued*)
189, 197, 200–203, 206, 214–15,
228–32, 236, 239, 244–46, 251–52,
254, 256–57, 260–63, 265–73,
277–88, 294–95, 297–99, 301–
305, 308–10, 314; Coleridge's primary imagination, 24–25 (defined),
53, 166, 169, 189, 203, 228–32, 256,
263, 280, 302; Coleridge's secondary
imagination, 24 (defined), 37, 53,
166, 256, 280. *See also* Eden (Blakean
Edenic vision)
Imagism, 12, 34
"In a world where all is temporary"
(#7), 192, 247, 284
"In April," 249–50
"In Laughter," 124
"In the Dark Violin of the Valley," 293,
303–304
"In these fading moments I wanted to
say," 206, 208, 227, 231
"Incompatibilities," 15, 41, 49, 50
Industrial Revolution, 10, 19–20, 150,
235, 239, 241, 243, 247, 253–54
Instinct, 5, 6, 10, 12, 34, 75, 80, 92, 99,
104, 106, 109, 124–25, 131, 136,
148–50, 155–56, 168–69, 173, 175,
178–79, 181–82, 187–88, 190, 247,
274, 294
"Interrogator, The," 208, 210–12, 231
"Invitation to the Dance," 41, 53
Iron Man, The, 18–19, 26
Irony, 6, 14–15, 35, 38–40, 43, 45–49,
56, 69, 152, 155, 157, 159, 224, 227,
296–97, 313
Īshwara pranidhāna, 100, 118
Isis, 71–72, 188, 194, 210, 224, 229
Ither, 182–83

"Jaguar, The," 40, 48
Janet (*Gaudete*), 174, 180; (Ransom's
"Janet Waking"), 39
Jangama, 194–95
"Japanese River Tales," 297
Jennifer, 173–75, 180
Johnson, Dr. Samuel, 222
Jones, Alun, 60

Joyce, James, 17, 21
"Judge, The," 208, 211, 278, 305
Jung, Carl Gustav, 7–14, 16, 24, 26,
67–68, 75, 101, 106, 108, 117, 127,
131, 136–37, 145–46, 154, 157,
166–68, 170–71, 173, 177–78, 180,
188, 204, 206–207, 209–10, 212,
214–16, 220, 222, 228, 232, 258,
279–80, 284–86, 289. *See also*
Anima; Archetypes; Quest; Shadow;
Unconscious

Kafka, Franz, 3, 89–90, 119, 173,
179–80, 182, 209, 211
Kahn, Charles, 187, 330
Kant, Immanuel, 34
Karma, 93, 108–109, 114–15, 155, 326
"Karma," 93, 114–15
Keats, John, 53, 289
Keen, Peter, xv, 288
Kerényi, Karl, 63, 145–46
Kierkegaard, Søren, 1
"Kill, A," 149
"King of Carrion," 158–59, 161
"Kingfisher, The," 304–305
"Knight, The" (British *Wodwo*), 115–16,
216; (*Cave Birds*), 167, 208, 214–16,
224
"Knock at the Door, A," 275–76
Kōan, 116–17, 152
"Kreutzer Sonata," 119
Krogon, 23, 166
Kundalini serpent, 277
Kunitz, Stanley, 60

Lancashire Fusiliers, 76, 235
Landscape, xiv, 4, 15, 21–22, 24, 38,
91, 96, 104, 110, 112, 117, 119–20,
122, 124, 166, 197, 227, 235–56,
262, 279, 282, 286
Language, 12, 71, 97, 123, 126, 132–33,
160, 188–204, 227, 248, 261, 270–
71, 275, 294
Lao Tzu, 216, 237, 248–49, 252, 292–
93, 335
Lapis, 9, 134, 215, 218, 258
Larkin, Philip, 17, 27, 31, 36–37, 68

"Last Act," 295, 302, 312
"Last Load," 263–64
"Last Night" (*Moortown*), 264, 266; (*River*), 303
"Law in the Country of the Cats," 75
Lawrence, D. H., xvi
Le Guin, Ursula, 124
Levers, 239–40, 244
Lévi-Strauss, Claude, 10, 26, 61, 91, 101, 147, 179
Li Po, 290
Libido, 38, 67–68, 72, 74–75, 79, 92, 95, 104, 116, 170, 173, 177–78, 181, 186, 188, 204, 210, 260, 279
"Life Is Trying to Be Life," 273
Light (*Bardo Thödol*), 108–109, 116, 160; (Cabbala), 197, 202, 259, 280; (*Cave Birds*), 213; (*Gaudete*), 197, 202; (*Lupercal*), 73; (*Moortown*), 263, 272–73, 280–81; (*Remains of Elmet*), 243, 252–54; (*River*), 288, 291–92, 294, 300, 309, 311, 314; (Taoism), 23, 25, 252–54, 280, 291; (*Wodwo*), 98–99, 116
"Light Falls Through Itself," 253
Lightning, 117, 202–203
Lilies, 179–80
"Lineage," 149–54
Lion, 194
Lioness, 198
"Little Red Twin," 263
Locke, John, 134, 211, 228, 260
Lodge, David, 17–18
"Logos," 92–96
"Long Screams," 237
"Long Tunnel Ceiling, The," 238
"Looking for her form" (#32), 196–99
Lorca, Federico García, 89
Lorenz, Konrad, 26, 139
Los, 24–25, 121, 197, 201–202, 260–61, 265, 269–70, 277–78, 280, 282–83, 294, 314
Love, 7, 19, 36, 50–51, 65, 74, 77, 93, 116, 142, 156–57, 159, 170, 176, 179, 196, 212, 226, 230, 231, 310, 313–14
"Lovepet, The," 156, 158–59, 230

"Lovesong," 19, 142, 156, 158–59, 230
"Low Water," 291
Lowell, Robert, 33, 56
"Lucky Folly, A," 161
Lumb, Reverend Nicholas, 21, 166–69, 172, 175, 178–80, 186, 188–204
"Lumb Chimneys," 237, 247
Lumb's Double, 15–16, 20–22, 121, 167–68, 172–90, 203–204, 309–310
Lumen naturae, 202
Lupercal, xiv, 4, 6, 12–13, 15, 18, 25, 55–81, 92, 119, 186, 279, 301, 305
"Lupercalia," 63–64, 69, 80–81, 92, 94
Lupercalia ritual, 26, 63–65, 68, 75, 80–81, 92
Luvah, 259

"Macaw and Little Miss," 39, 41, 49–50
"Magical Dangers," 13, 124, 133, 135, 140–41, 150, 160
Mallarmé, Stéphane, 87
Mallory, Sir Thomas, 185
"Man hangs on, A" (#33), 199–200
"Man Seeking Experience Enquires His Way of a Drop of Water, A," 32
Mana, 72
Manicheanism, 284
"March Calf, A," 255
"March Morning Unlike Others," 263
Marduk, 198
"Martyrdom of Bishop Farrar, The," 44–45, 92
Mary, 77, 125, 137, 212, 231, 314. *See also* Tudor, Mary
Maud, 175, 177–78, 180–81, 184, 186
Māyā, 116
"Mayday on Holderness," 64, 75–76, 79, 81, 92
McCrae, John, 94
"Meeting," 46–47
Mercurius, 214, 216–17, 220, 258, 295, 311
"Merry Mink, The," 295, 299
Merton, Thomas, 110
Metaphor, xv, 12–19, 31–54, 68, 96
Michels, A. K., 63–64

"Milesian Encounter on the Sligachan,"
291, 296–97, 300, 306, 309
"Mill Ruins," 240–41
Milton, John, 3, 24. *See also* Blake,
William: *Milton*
Mimesis, xiv, 14, 16–17, 21, 36–37,
120, 123, 168, 275, 299
Modernism, xiv, xvi, 10, 16–18, 21–22,
25, 28, 45–46, 120, 122–23, 125–
26, 136, 144, 149–50, 162, 165, 173,
204–206, 214, 219, 222, 253–55,
258, 275, 288
"Modest Proposal, A," 5, 13, 41, 50–52
"Monument, A," 22, 258, 267, 284
Moon, 73, 113–14, 119, 202, 220, 299
Moore, Geoffrey, 33
Moore, Marianne, 58
"Moors," 239
Moortown, xiv, 3, 4, 11, 15, 22–24, 160,
167, 257–86, 301
"Moortown" (section of *Moortown*), 258,
262–69, 281
Moortown Elegies, 257
"Morning Before Christmas, The," 298,
300, 306
Morrigu, 198
Mortificatio, 215
Motokiyo, Zeami, 311
"Motorbike, A," 276
"Mount Zion," 243, 247
"Mountains," 110, 113
Movement, The, xiii, xiv, 17, 31–32,
36–37, 68
Mud, 22, 41, 98, 104, 106–107, 183–
84, 187, 189, 203, 246, 258, 267,
280, 294, 300, 303, 313
Muir, Edwin, 37
Mundificatio, 215
Munen, 118
Murry, John Middleton, 308
Music, 177–79, 192, 306, 309–10. *See
also* Beethoven, Ludwig von
"Music, that eats people" (#12), 192
Myers, E. Lucas, 33, 60
Myth, xiv, 3, 4, 15–16, 18, 22–23, 26–
27, 41, 46, 85, 87, 91, 93, 97, 101,
122–27, 129, 136, 142, 144–45,
149–51, 156, 162, 166, 169–70, 179,
198, 203, 206, 247, 258, 275, 284,
286, 296–97, 299, 307. *See also*
Primitive cultures
"Myth and Education" (Myth I), 8, 19,
125–26, 129, 142–43, 157, 160, 177;
(Myth II), 8, 52–53, 165, 205

Nandi, 194
Nature, 12, 15–16, 20, 24–25, 28, 38,
43–44, 46, 66, 70–71, 79–80, 87,
93–94, 99, 110, 112, 114–15, 122–
25, 127, 129–30, 132–33, 136–37,
139, 141–42, 145, 147–52, 154,
157–58, 160–61, 167, 170, 178, 193,
207, 212, 225–29, 231–33, 237–38,
241–42, 244–47, 249, 252–56,
259–65, 267–68, 270, 272, 275,
284–85, 288–89, 294, 296–98,
300–302, 304, 306, 311–13
"Nefertiti," 276
New Criticism, xiv, xv, xvi, 4, 12–17,
33–58, 63, 75, 81, 85, 92, 166, 224,
254, 280
"New Moon in January," 114, 119
"New Year," 298, 300, 306
Newton, Isaac, 143, 150, 244, 260, 274
"Nicholas Ferrer," 66–67, 78
Nicholson, Max, 122, 125–26, 129,
135–36
Nietzsche, Friedrich, 226
"Night arrival of seatrout," 278
"Night wind, muscled with rain, The"
(#22), 196–98
Nigredo, 215, 217, 220
Ninhursag, 129
Nirvana, 108, 110, 116, 219, 277
Nōh drama, 311
"Notes for a Little Play," 140
Nothing, 102, 113, 118, 125, 152–54,
161, 197, 252–53
"November," 79
"Now You Have to Push," 267
Nut, 198
Nye, Robert, 232

"O White Elite Lotus," 228
"October Dawn," 53
"October Salmon," 311–13
Odin, 185, 311
Odysseus, 227
Oedipus, 120, 130
"Oedipus Crow," 130
"Of Cats," 72–73
"Old Age Gets Up," 273
Old-Woman-Underneath, 142
Olson, Charles, 13, 56
"Only a little sleep, a little slumber," 208, 229
"Open To Huge Light," 25, 252
"Ophelia," 298
Orc, 259–60, 294–95
Orchard, Jack, 262
"Orf," 262, 267–68
Orghast, xv, 23, 28, 166–67, 179, 186, 210, 269, 284
Orpheus, 120, 166–67
Orts, 257
"Orts," 278
Osborne, John, 49
Osiris, 188, 194, 197–98, 215, 217–18, 224, 229
"Otter, An," 61–62
Otters, 61–62, 161–62, 190
"Out," 6, 21, 86, 93–94
Owen, Wilfred, 74–75, 93
"Owl flower, The," 208, 222
"Owl's Song," 151–52

Paideuma, xvi, 18, 28, 123, 162, 165, 168, 204, 255, 288
Paley, Morton, 260–61
Panchatantra, 7
Pandora, 269–70
Paracelsus, Philippus Aureolus, 202, 260
Paradox, 17, 43–45, 48–49, 56, 223–24, 293
Parkinson, Thomas, 59
"Parlour-Piece," 41, 43, 50
Parsons, I. M., 94
Parzival, 7, 169, 182–83, 224
Patanjali, 105, 204

Patroclos, 310
Peacock, 271, 277, 283
"Perfect Forms, The," 6, 79–80, 92, 186
Persephone, 106
"Phaetons," 41
Phoenix, 220, 230, 258, 262, 285–86
"Photostomias," 276–77, 279, 283
Phylogenetic inheritance, 95, 324
"Pibroch," 119
"Pike," 56–57, 59–60, 69, 71, 279
Pilinszky, János, 191–92, 195
"Plaintiff, The," 208, 212, 222
Plath, Sylvia, 4, 13, 33, 43, 56, 86–87, 117, 119, 144, 187–88, 196, 210, 216, 228, 236, 253–54, 323
Plato, 209, 226
Plotinus, 12, 284
Poetry in the Making, 2, 56–57
Poetry Is, 2, 56–57
Pollux, 74
"Poor Birds," 282
Popa, Vasco, 3, 86–87
"Postcard from Torquay," 276
Postmodernism, 17
Pound, Ezra, 2, 13, 17–18, 27, 60, 123, 206
Prabhu, Allama, 195, 198
Prajñā, 155
Prajñācakṣu, 103
Pramanath, 23
Prima materia, 215–16, 218, 229, 258
Primal horde, 44, 95, 324
Primitive cultures, 15, 17, 26–27, 61, 63–70, 72–73, 76–77, 89–91, 93, 101, 103–104, 113, 122, 125, 129, 134, 137, 142, 144–48, 151, 161, 170–71, 178, 180–81, 190–204, 209, 217, 220–21, 225, 228, 232, 236, 238–39, 244, 253–54, 278–79, 283, 296–97, 299, 307, 313
"Primrose petal's edge, A" (#18), 193
Prometheus, 7, 23, 269–73
Prometheus on His Crag, 13, 166–67, 257, 269–72
"Prometheus on His Crag" (section of Moortown), 258–59, 269–73, 279

Protestantism, 6, 19–20, 35, 45, 66–67, 119, 122, 124–27, 135–37, 139, 141, 145, 151, 153, 157, 235–36, 239–41, 244
Proteus, 128
Proust, Marcel, 21, 234
"Public Bar TV," 92
Puruṣa, 204
Putrefactio, 215, 217
Pynchon, Thomas, 17

Quest, 5, 7, 10–12, 14–15, 91, 116, 120, 127, 132, 188, 227, 232–33, 295, 314

Ra, 197
Radin, Paul, 11, 61, 90, 136, 144–48
"Rain," 263
"Rain comes again, The" (#13), 192–93
"Rain Horse, The," 104–105
Ramanujan, A. K., 194–98. *See also* Vacanas
Ransom, John Crowe, xiv, xvi, 12–13, 33–54, 58
Raven, 134, 147, 160, 214, 217, 232, 307
"Ravens," 265
Realism, xiv, 16–17, 22, 31–32, 37, 88, 120, 123–24, 166, 168, 175, 256, 275, 299
Reality (defined), 5, 7, 9, 15, 23, 24, 35, 38, 48, 125–26, 166, 169, 186, 191, 197, 201, 203, 215, 233, 236, 252, 256–57, 280, 284–85, 287, 292, 309
Recklings, 86, 93
Reiser, Anton, 20
"Relic," 75, 77–78
Religion. *See* Hughes, Ted: and religion; Protestantism; Roman Catholicism
Remains of Elmet, xiv, 3, 4, 7, 10–11, 15, 23, 25, 160, 166, 231, 234–57, 274, 281, 288–90, 294, 301
"Remain of Elmet," 240
Repression, 5, 6, 10, 12, 27, 39, 46, 50, 66, 74, 111, 116, 124–25, 127, 131, 136–37, 140, 156, 168, 170, 177–78, 181

"Rescue, The," 87, 96
"Retired Colonel, The," 65, 67, 78
"Reveille," 118
Reverdy, Pierre, 88
"Rhododendrons," 240, 247, 255
Rice, Cyprian, 232–33
Richards, I. A., 37
"Riddle, A," 208, 218, 222–26, 231
Rig-Veda, 200
Rinzai, 112
Ripley, 22, 106–107, 226
"Risen, The," 207–209, 213, 233
River, 15, 156, 160, 288–315
River, xiv, 4, 7, 11, 15, 23, 160, 166, 231, 256, 281, 286, 287–315
"River," 290–91
"River Barrow," 289–90, 293, 300, 306
"Riverwatcher," 305–306
"Roarers in a Ring," 53
Robbins, Gavin, 197
Roberts, Neil, 3, 145, 322
"Robin Song," 151
"Rock, The," 234, 246–47
"Roe Deer," 262, 267–69
Roman Catholicism, 63, 77–80, 92–93, 107, 116, 125, 142, 152, 181–83, 185–86, 207, 209, 212–14, 218, 220–21, 225, 242, 249, 314
"Root, Stem, Leaf," 102
Rosarium Philosophorum, 220
Rose, H. J., 63
Rosencreutz, Christian, 216, 218, 333
Rosenroth, Christian Knorr von, 286
Rosenthal, M. L., 3, 10
Rubedo, 215–16

Sādhana, 197, 283
Sagar, Keith, xvii, 2–4, 25–26, 33, 145, 187, 214, 220, 258–59, 277, 284, 301–302
Said, Edward, 27
Salmon, 279, 288–89, 292, 295–96, 298, 300, 306–15
"Salmon Eggs," 289, 291–94, 310, 313–15
"Salmon-taking Times," 288, 299–300, 306

Samādhi, 5, 101–102, 110, 291, 300
Śānti, 110
Sartre, Jean-Paul, 21, 119, 161
Satire, 6, 15, 39–41, 90, 226, 275
Satori, 100, 102, 110, 112–14, 116–17, 189, 274
"Scapegoat, The," 208, 218
"Scapegoats and Rabies," 7, 19, 22, 93, 97–100, 102, 107, 131
Schelling, Friedrich, 24
Schopenhauer, Arthur, 161, 255
Science, 10, 19–21, 27, 33, 42, 46, 92, 119, 121–27, 129, 135, 138, 141, 143, 145, 151, 153, 157, 165, 168, 226, 235–36, 239–41, 247, 260, 274
Scout Rock, 234, 246–47
"Scream, The," 208, 224–26
"Sea grieves all night long, The" (#35), 197, 200
Season Songs, xiv, 255–56
"Second Glance at a Jaguar," 19, 95
"Secretary," 40–41, 48
Self (Blakean), 270, 272, 282–83; (Jungian), 11, 13–14; (Oriental/Buddhist), 8, 19, 27, 99–101, 105, 107, 110, 114, 117, 119, 151; (shamanic/alchemic), 210, 217, 220, 230, 232–33; (Taoist), 236; (Western), 107, 125, 130–31, 268, 270, 274
Seneca, 23, 120
"September," 19, 51
"September Salmon," 294, 310–11
Serpents. *See* Snakes
Set, 194
"Seven Dungeon Songs," 259, 273, 279, 282
"Seven Sorrows, The," 255
Shadow, 11–12, 46, 117, 131, 136, 145, 157, 167, 173, 186, 188, 210, 215
Shah, Idries, 130–31
Shakespeare, William, 3, 34, 41, 51, 78, 125, 127, 137, 160, 172, 182, 218, 222, 272
Shaman, 4, 7, 15–16, 26, 70–71, 89–92, 106, 120, 122, 196, 198, 201, 203, 207, 214, 217, 220–21, 278
"She Has Come to Pass," 267

"She rides the earth" (#16), 193–94, 196
"She seemed so considerate," 208, 226, 231
"Sheep" (*Moortown*), 267; (*Season Songs*), 255
"Sheep Went On Being Dead, The," 240–41
Shelley, Percy Bysshe, 119
Shên Yün, 252
Shura, 120, 157
Sidpa Bardo, 108–109, 114, 125, 148–49, 151, 155, 160, 219
Simultaneity, 16, 52, 125, 148, 151–52, 165, 176, 179–82, 287, 310
Śiva, 61, 100, 117, 191, 194–95, 203–204
"Six Young Men," 46–48
"Skylark came, The," 280–82
"Skylarks," 13, 110–12
Smayle, 181
Snakes, 25, 77, 80, 118–19, 132, 150, 161, 258–59, 262, 277, 286, 288, 294–95, 302
"Snow," 86–87, 105–106, 323
Socrates, 212, 226, 277
Sogis, 23, 166, 186
Solar eagle. *See* Eagle
"Sole of a foot, The," 285–86
"Soliloquy of a Misanthrope," 41
"Solstice Song," 255
"Something was happening," 208, 221, 228–29, 232
"Sometimes it comes, a gloomy flap of lightning" (#30), 197–98
"Song," 19, 51, 53
"Song, The," 279
"Song for a Phallus," 160
"Song of a Rat," 86, 116–18
"Song of Longsight," 273–74
Sono-mama, 111–13
"Space-Egg Was Sailing, The," 140
"Speech out of shadow," 278
Spirit, 5, 23, 52, 67–68, 90, 101, 118, 128–29, 132, 134, 136, 165, 167, 172, 174, 180–81, 183, 186, 194–95, 214–16, 218, 220, 230, 232, 236,

Spirit (*continued*)
238–39, 242, 245–46, 248–50, 258,
263, 269, 280, 282–85, 287–89,
291–95, 300–15
Spitteler, Carl, 9
Sponsus and *Sponsa*, 215–16, 220,
229–30, 232
"Spring Nature Notes," 255–56
Square, 239, 252
"Stations," 96–97, 102
Steiner, George, 189–90, 198
Stewart, John L., 46
Stone, 134, 150–51, 159, 239–40,
248–50, 253–54. *See also Lapis*
"Strangers," 291, 300
"Struggle," 263, 266
"Stump Pool in April," 294, 300
Suffering, xiv, 7, 23, 77, 87, 97, 112,
114, 166–67, 169, 172, 181, 185,
193–97, 200, 204, 206–207, 210,
223–24, 227, 229, 231–32, 247–48,
257, 269, 271, 301, 313
Sufism, 19, 130–32, 135, 137, 150–51,
215, 233. *See also* Attar, Farid ud-Din;
Fanā
"Sugar Loaf," 96, 109, 113
"Suitor, The," 104
"Summoner, The," 208, 210, 225
Sun, 67, 71, 76, 79–80, 89, 111–13,
134, 185, 196–97, 202, 212–13,
216–17, 219–20, 222, 230, 232–34,
243, 261, 263, 269–70, 273, 281–
83, 291, 294, 299, 304, 311, 314–15
"Sun, like a cold kiss in the street, The"
(#29), 197
"Sunday," 104, 116–17
"Sunstruck," 242
Śūnyatā, 99–100, 102, 110, 115, 125,
152–54, 158, 189, 197, 286, 329
Superego, 88, 132, 180
"Surprise," 263
Surrealism, xiv, 3–4, 15–16, 22, 70, 76,
81, 85–88, 92, 95–96, 98, 103–104,
107, 109, 120, 122–23, 133, 139,
141, 158–60, 166–67, 169, 173,
175–77, 182, 186–88, 192–94, 209–

10, 227, 231–32, 247, 255–57, 273,
310
Sutcliffe, John, 235
Suzuki, D. T., 10, 110–11, 113, 153. *See
also* Zen
"Swallow—rebuilding—, The" (#21),
194, 196–97, 220
Swan maiden, 253–54, 297, 335–36
Swanton, John, 146–47
"Swift comes the swift, The," 282
"Swifts," 255
Symons, Julian, 232

Tabor, Stephen, 3, 25–26
T'ai hu stones, 249
Táin Bó Cúalnge, 198
Tantric Buddhism, 280, 283
Tantric Yoga, 169, 194, 197, 202,
277–78
Tao, 238, 246, 248–49, 251–52, 256,
288, 292–93, 301, 313–14
Tao-chi, 250–51
Taoism, xv, 7, 19, 25, 233, 236–38,
246–57, 280, 284, 289, 291, 300,
313–14, 335
Tate, Allen, 12, 33–35
Tefnut, 196, 198
Tennyson, Alfred, Lord, 112
Thanatos, 6, 26, 28, 43–44, 62, 64–65,
74–80, 87, 91–95, 107, 116, 120,
165, 324
Tharmas, 85, 260, 270
"That Girl," 275
"That Moment," 140, 143
"That Morning," 292, 308–309
"Theology," 118–19
"There Came Days To The Hills," 241
Theriomorphism, 61, 63, 65–72, 75,
80, 103, 117, 194, 213, 249–50, 289,
294, 301, 321
"Things Present," 64, 79
"This is the maneater's skull" (#14), 193
"Thistles," 95
Thomas, Dylan, 1, 31, 33, 41, 85, 88,
101
Thor, 185

Thoth, 187–88, 190
"Thought-Fox, The," 37–38
"Thrushes," 69–71
Thurley, Geoffrey, 256
Thwaite, Anthony, 106
Tiamat, 198
Tibetan Book of the Dead. See Bardo Thödol
"Tick Tock Tick Tock," 244–46, 253, 289
T'ien, 239, 253
Tiger, 277
"Tiger Psalm," 277
Time, 7, 13–14, 16–17, 38, 41–42, 51, 54, 74, 78, 80, 85, 93–94, 98, 104, 112, 114–15, 151, 181, 184, 187, 245–46, 249, 261, 268, 283, 308. *See also* Simultaneity
Tlingit, 134, 142, 147
"To Paint a Water Lily," 55–56
Toffler, Alvin, 26–27
"Top Withens," 239, 249, 255
"Torridge," 303
"Tractor," 262, 267–68
"Trance Of Light, The," 252
"Tree," 248, 294
"Tree, A," 248, 294
Trees: alder, 303; apple, 186; ash, 185; beech, 185; Cabbalistic Tree of Life, 25, 103, 202, 259; Cosmic Tree of primitives, 77; Golden Bough, 202–203; hemlock, 303; oak, 166, 169–72, 185, 193, 197, 201–203, 303; Odin's, 311; sycamore, 199; Yggdrasil, 185
Trevrizent, 182
Trickster, 4, 11, 15, 122, 124–25, 134, 136, 144–48, 150, 157, 159–60, 162, 168, 182–83, 299, 307
"Truth Kills Everybody," 124, 128, 133, 140, 148–49, 159–60
"Trying to be a leaf" (#9), 192, 201–202
Tudor, Mary, 44–45
"Two," 244
"Two Eskimo Songs," 161

"Two Legends," 149–54
"Two Phases," 50
"Two Wise Generals," 40, 46–47
"Two-way journey, 5–6, 8–10, 22, 38, 166, 169, 186, 191, 194, 197, 201, 203–204, 215, 233, 236, 278
Tz'ŭ, 238, 253, 288, 301

Ulro, 260–62, 268, 270–74, 276–77, 280. *See also* Blake, William
Unconscious, 11, 34, 67–68, 77, 81, 170, 179, 182, 188, 207, 210, 215, 220, 224–25, 227–28, 230, 236, 247, 252
"Under the Hill of Centurions," 292, 299–300
"Under The World's Wild Rims," 243
"Unknown Soldier," 93
"Unknown Wren, The," 282–83, 285
Upanishads, 19, 100–101, 110, 112, 117, 121, 127, 137, 140, 202. *See also* *Ātman*; Hinduism
Urizen, 211, 260, 277, 280–81
"Urn Burial," 64, 78–79
Urthona, 260

Vacanas, 19, 191, 194–98, 232
Valley Spirit, 236–37, 254
"Vampire," 41
"Vegetarian, A," 93, 108–109
Venus, 127, 137, 216, 303
Verlaine, Paul, 87
"View of a Pig," 56
"Vintage of River Is Unending, The," 291
Violence, xiii, xiv, 6, 12, 16–18, 21, 26, 28, 40, 43–44, 47, 65–66, 68, 70–71, 74–80, 87, 91–95, 122–38, 140, 142, 145, 148–49, 151, 159, 168, 198, 240–41, 319, 320–21, 322, 328–29, 334. *See also* Enantiodromia; Thanatos
"Viper fell from the sun, The" (#23), 196
Viśṇu, 61, 119, 197, 200
"Voyage, The," 75, 77
Vulture, 167, 269–71

Waley, Arthur, 238–39
"Walking bare," 208, 219, 227, 233
"Walls," 240, 242, 247
Walsall, 176
Walsall, Mrs., 177
Warren, Austin, 14–15, 254
Warren, Robert Penn, 35
"Warriors of the North, The," 119, 240
Water (in alchemy), 218; (as mutability), 311–13; (in Taoism), 248–49, 254, 314
"Waving goodbye, from your banked hospital bed" (#19), 192, 196
"Weasels We Smoked Out Of The Bank, The," 237
Wellek, René, 14–15, 154
Wells, 296, 306
Wesley, John, 235, 244
"West Dart," 291, 293–94
Westlake, 173–74
Westlake, Mrs., 175–76
Wevil, Assia Guttmann, 4, 120, 157, 160
What Is the Truth?, 306
"What steel was it the river poured" (#39), 197, 201
"When Men Got To The Summit," 239
"When the still-soft eyelid sank again" (#34), 196, 200
"Where The Mothers," 237
"While She Chews Sideways," 264–65
White Goddess, 93, 170, 172, 181, 185–86, 188–89, 192–94, 196–99, 203, 231, 278, 289, 294, 308, 312–13, 325
"Whiteness," 294–95, 298
Whitman, Walt, 158
"Widdop," 253
"Wild Duck, The," 280–81
"Wild Rock," 239
"Wilfred Owen's Photographs," 72, 74–75
Williams, Charles, 1
Williams, Miller, 38
Williams, William Carlos, 276
Wimsatt, William K., 14
"Wind Flashes the Grass, A," 88, 95–96, 109

Wings, 20–21, 96, 119, 201, 218–20, 232, 238, 252–54, 257, 278, 300, 335
"Wings," 20–21, 119
With Fairest Flowers While Summer Lasts, 125, 137
Wodwo, xiv, 6, 10–11, 15–18, 20–21, 25, 71, 76, 85–122, 127, 152, 160, 165–66, 301
"Wodwo," 110, 114, 120–21
Wolf mask, 64–69, 92, 119, 321
Wolves, 51–52, 64–69, 76, 92, 103, 119, 169, 272–73, 321
"Word That Space Breathes, The," 239, 253
World War I, 47, 74–76, 93–95, 119, 235, 240–41
World War II, 27, 93, 119, 191, 244
Worringer, Wilhelm, 16
Wound, The, 22, 87, 92, 106–107, 226
Wu wei, 216, 248–49
Wyrd, 92–93, 97, 119

Xipe, 217

Yang, 237, 247–49, 251–53, 274, 284, 335
Yeats, William Butler, 1–2, 5, 17, 58–60, 71–73, 77, 79, 91, 306
Yin, 236–37, 247–49, 251, 274, 284, 335
Yoga, 9, 19, 100–102, 105–106, 169, 194, 197, 202–204, 220, 256, 276–77, 291, 300. *See also* Patanjali; *Samādhi*; Tantric Yoga
Yoka, 115
"You Drive in a Circle," 117–18
"Your mother's bones wanted to speak, they could not," 208, 228
"Your tree—your oak" (#44), 194, 197, 201–203
Yuki-onna, 297

Zen, 19, 100, 102, 110–13, 115–17, 123, 125, 152, 155, 157, 159, 165, 202, 274. *See also Prajñā*; *Prajñācakṣu*; *Satori*; Suzuki, D. T.

Zeus, 77, 202
Zimmer, Heinrich, 61
Zoroastrianism, 284
Zosimos, 284